TEACHING TRANSLATION AND INTERPRETING 2

BENJAMINS TRANSLATION LIBARY

The Benjamins Translation Library aims to stimulate academic research and training in translation studies, lexicography and terminology. The Library provides a forum for a variety of approaches (which may sometimes be conflicting) in a historical, theoretical, applied and pedagogical context. The Library includes scholarly works, reference books and post-graduate text books and readers in the English language.

Volume 5

Cay Dollerup and Annette Lindegaard

Teaching Translation and Interpreting 2
Insights, Aims, Visions

TEACHING TRANSLATION
AND INTERPRETING 2
INSIGHTS, AIMS, VISIONS

Papers from the Second *Language International* Conference
Elsinore, Denmark 4 - 6 June 1993

Edited by

CAY DOLLERUP
ANNETTE LINDEGAARD
University of Copenhagen

JOHN BENJAMINS PUBLISHING COMPANY
AMSTERDAM/PHILADELPHIA

The paper used in this publication meets the minimum requirements of American National Standard for Information Sciences — Permanence of Paper for Printed Library Materials, ANSI Z39.48-1984.

Library of Congress Cataloging-in-Publication Data

Teaching translation and interpreting 2 : insights, aims, visions / [edited by] Cay Dollerup, Annette Lindegaard.
     p.   cm. -- (Benjamins translation library, ISSN 0929-7316 ; v. 5)
  Selection of papers presented at the 2nd Language International Conference which was held June 1993, Elsinore, Denmark.
  Includes bibliographical references and index.
  1. Translating and interpreting--Study and teaching--Congresses. I. Dollerup, Cay. II. Lindegaard, Annette. III. Language International Conference (2nd : 1993 : Helsingør, Denmark) IV. Title: Teaching translation and interpreting two. V. Series.
P306.5.T4   1994
418'.02'071--dc20   94-10141
ISBN 90 272 1601 0 (Eur.)/1-55619-682-2 (US) (alk. paper)   CIP

John Benjamins Publishing Co. · P.O. Box 75577 · 1070 AN Amsterdam · The Netherlands
John Benjamins North America · 821 Bethlehem Pike · Philadelphia, PA 19118 · USA

TABLE OF CONTENTS

INTERPRETING AND CLASS

SCREEN TRANSLATION

TOOLS

WORKS CITED

INDEX

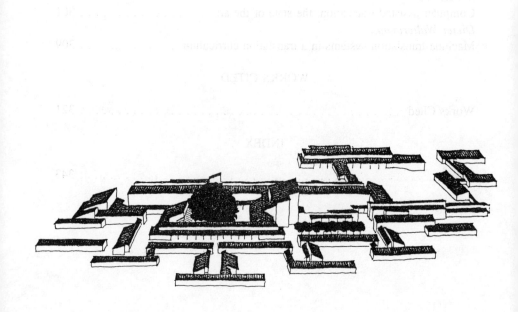

EDITORS' FOREWORD

SKHLOSS/FORST SKU

Jagtpavillonen

EDITORS' FOREWORD

The present volume comprises a selection of papers presented at the Second *Language International* Conference: 'Teaching Translation and Interpreting: Insights, Aims, Visions', which took place at Elsinore, Denmark, in June 1993. The volume is dedicated to the teaching of translation and interpreting as an activity which is discussed internationally. In editing the volume, we have chosen to start out from insights into multi- and plurilingual settings, then proceed to discussions of aims for practical work with students, and to end with visions of future developments within translation for the mass media and the impact of machine translation.

Multilingual settings, and the central role of translation, are discussed in the three first articles.

The first of these presents the interpreting services and the training programme at the European Commission. The interpreting services were established with the European Community - now better known as the European Union - and they have grown with it. The services at the Commission are now by far the largest of their kind in the world. Looking back at the development of the interpreting services, Christian Heynold deals with the Commission's experience and concludes with a discussion of problems in managing interpreting with a multitude of languages.

The next article takes us to another continent where several languages exist within one nation, but the perspective is different, for in multilingual Nigeria described by Evaristus O. Anyaehie, it is a foreign language, English, that serves as the official language throughout the nation. Against this background, Anyaehie outlines a translation programme preparing future professionals for dealing with many working languages among their users. In the last article in this section Niranjan Mohanty from yet another country with numerous languages, India, stresses that translation is in itself a symbiosis of cultures and argues that for a fusion to take place, translators must be cognizant of numerous societal parameters in both source and target languages if they are to bridge the cultural gaps.

The next contributions focus on linguistic barriers and how they may be overcome. Moses Nunyi Nintai from Cameroon deals with problems in translating Francophone African literature which mirroring African realities, and proposes a number of approaches for teaching students consciousness of the complexities of their task. Manouchehr Haghighi (Iran) argues that the Renaissance constitutes the major cultural divide between the West and other parts of the world and that an awareness of the impact of the Renaissance on European thinking is a prerequisite for successfully teaching translation from European languages. Meta Grosman (Slovenia) suggests that an understanding of the otherness of cultures is required by would-be translators if their perceptions of texts for translation are to be appropriate. Christiane Nord (Germany and Austria) discusses adaptation and translation from a functional point of view and argues that an all-out functional approach should be used for translation teaching. The point of departure for Heidrun Witte (Spain) is also functional, but her line of enquiry is the actual translational commission. She posits that translators must be taught to be above naive intercultural communication and that they must sometimes take upon them the job of enlightening clients. And finally, Gabrielle Becher (Spain) discusses the use of advertisements for introducing students to other cultures as well as teaching them factors to be taken into account in culture-oriented translation.

The subsequent articles deal with principles and specifics of translation teaching - and the quality of it. Andrew Chesterman (Finland) sets the scene by discussing translation processes - and translation learning - in terms of the philosopher Karl Popper's schema for the scientific method with its never-ending spiralling towards unattainable perfection. Chesterman is followed up by Sergio Viaggio (UN), who has translation tasks and approaches reflect on advances in translation theory. Daniel Gile (France) deals with the usefulness of the process-oriented approach in training programmes and points out that, among other things, it leads to a considerable reduction in student errors due to faulty analysis of texts. Jeanne Dancette (Canada) presents readers with preliminary findings from think-aloud protocols of student translations of a text concerned with economics, and concludes that although successful translation may well take place without a major conceptual framework, it does presuppose that the correct textual and extratextual linkages and inferences are made. Cay Dollerup (Denmark) discusses some procedures for systematic feedback to translation students which combine individual and collective assessments. María Julia Sainz (Uruguay) elaborates on this point from other angles, including references to student rights and explicit information to students about the underlying 'ideologies' and taxonomies. In his contribution, Arnt Lykke Jakobsen (Denmark) suggests that it may be more beneficial for translation teaching to focus on the end product, notably in terms of tasks which are, in his terminology, 'warm' (authentic), rather than on translation of texts outside a situational context. The section is closed by Alexis Nouss (Canada) who discusses two dominant theories of interpretation of texts, and concludes that the validity of an interpretation is ultimately dependent on the community's acceptance of it.

The volume then concentrates on the teaching of interpreting. Holding the view that a historical perspective will enhance the understanding of the profession both among trainees and full-fledged practictioners, Margareta Bowen (USA) deals with the history of interpreting. David Bowen (USA) discusses the merits and disadvantages of various trends of interpreting teaching, also touching on students and student backgrounds. Robin Setton (Republic of China) presents pedagogics from a non-Indoeuropean language perspective and deals with considerations underlying the progression in the interpreter programme in Taiwan. Referring to results and observations from her own classes, Bistra Alexieva (Bulgaria) discusses the pros and cons of teaching note-taking techniques in interpreting and concludes that this is useful when combined with analytic training. Using personal experience from professional work, Viera Makarová (Slovakia and United Kingdom) details how she teaches students to manage under poor working conditions. Nancy Schweda Nicholson (USA) describes the teaching of interpreting to trainees whose mother tongues are unknown to the teacher. And Leonor Zimman (United Kingdom) discusses a number of methods for making would-be community interpreters face the dilemma of intervention vs non-intervention in community interpreting situations. Sylvia Kalina (Germany) discusses the problems involved in tackling authentic interpreting material for the purpose of research, and hence for the improvement of teaching. And Franz Pöchhacker (Austria) attempts to establish criteria for assessing quality in simultaneous interpreting, touching upon a large number of parameters whose pertinence is evaluated.

Then follows a number of articles dealing with screen translation, a fairly new field in translatology. Irena Kovačič (Slovenia) argues that relevance theory provides an explanatory framework for reductions in subtitling, but stresses that mere familiarity with the theory itself will not make for perfect subtitling. Ian Roffe and David Thorne (United Kingdom) describe the societal and linguistic background for the subtitling programme at the University of Wales and present a series of transfer problems used for teaching purposes. In the next contribution Henrik Gottlieb (Denmark) discusses courses for subtitlers as well as the parameters which must be taken into account for an assessment of quality from a professional point of view. This section is rounded off by Yves Gambier (Finland) who deals with the larger context of audiovisual translation and suggests the establishment of an international course in language transfer in the media.

The last contributions focus on translation and tools. In the first article, M. K. C. Uwajeh (Nigeria) emphasises the usefulness of translational activity as a tool for linguistic insight into the workings of the source languages, and the potentials for teaching translation at the same time. Peter Baumgartner (Germany) describes the methods used in translation training at the Flensburg Polytechnic for ensuring the proper technical terminology, including, for instance, parallel texts and break-down into textual components.

The last two articles concentrate on machine translation. Robert Clark (United Kingdom) suggests that most prejudices against machine translation do not hold good. He stresses the importance of new technologies and discusses a number of available translation programmes in terms of their usefulness for the professional, arguing that today it is necessary for trainee translators to be familiarised with machine translation. The final word is left to Dieter Wältermann (USA), who describes the machine translation training programme at Carnegie Mellon University. He presents the course and its components and provides a detailed discussion of the integration of the Translator's WorkStation in the course.

All told, then, the volume reflects an ongoing debate about the role of teaching translation and interpreting at the end of the twentieth century.

This discussion is international. At first glance, it may therefore seem as if we are Eurocentric in choosing the European Union (EU) as the point of departure. But this is a deliberate choice, indeed a statement: There are good reasons for focusing on the EU in a book which reaches out to language professionals all over the globe:

We suggest that the formation of the EU has been the strongest single factor behind the present professionalisation and internationalisation of translation work, giving translation studies new vitality and creating the keen interest in teaching translation and interpreting, and - possibly as a ripple effect - also subtitling and other types of interlingual transfer evidenced in this and similar books.

The EU is admittedly controversial in politics and is often considered bureau-cratic. On the other hand, the decisions reached in democratic agreement among the EU's twelve member states affect the everyday life of more than 300 million people: the EU represents by far the most intimate multinational peacetime (and peaceful) cooperation in human history.

To language workers, the EU is important in professional contexts, for its size, for its emphasis on quality (however elusive) in language work, and for its pivotal role in forcing language professionals, such as interpreters and translators to discuss their work. These statements need some explanation for the uninitiated reader:

Operating with nine official languages, the EU has the most extensive language services of any major organisation in the world, and, serving the central needs for communication between the member states, they form the backbone of the cooperation.

This language-based polical cooperation has created a need for professionalism in language work. This need for professionals is eminently obvious to the decision-makers who use the language products every day at EU meetings and the EU institutions therefore employ thousands of language professionals. Their very number creates needs for new translators and improvement in quality. Their public visibility has become very high. Unlike the language workers outside institutionalised settings, these highly-paid professionals are also perforce obliged to discuss concrete translation work with in-house experts and delegates, that is with clients and users. In terms of organisation, they often work in teams and therefore discuss translational products with their colleagues and departmental 'revisors': translation and interpreting are no longer the exclusive provinces of gifted individuals in ivory towers with little or no societal input, working on a person-to-person basis for power-brokers, making up personal files of proper translations for specific clients, or polishing literary masterpieces.

In tangible financial and political ways, EU has set the scene for contemporary international discussions on translation. It has also, we suggest, a paradigmatic character for future international cooperation in terms of the practice, management and training of language professionals, not only in Western Europe, but all over the world. The diffusion of that experience among teachers and researchers, general discussions of the situation in other parts of the world, and presentation of practical problems and theoretical considerations of central concern to teaching will further interlingual and cross-cultural cooperation.

Cay Dollerup   and   *Annette Lindegaard*

ACKNOWLEDGEMENTS

The organisers of the conference wish to thank The Danish Research Council for the Humanities for support tendered towards the plenaries.

We also wish to record our gratitude to the 'International Office' (The Danish Ministry for Education) and to 'The Danish Democracy Fund' (The Danish Foreign Ministry) for grants to scholars who could not otherwise have attended the conference.

We are grateful to the Department of English (University of Copenhagen) for financial help for the final work on the present book.

Many people helped us edit it. It is unfair to single out any, but nevertheless we wish to express our deepest thanks to Mr Henrik Gottlieb for casting an ever vigilant eye on our efforts, to Ms Marion Fewell, to Dr Viggo Hjørnager Pedersen, and to Mr Robert Storace.

The pictures from Denmark which grace this volume are reproduced with the kind permission of *Mr Poul Andersen* and *Politikens Forlag*.

LANGUAGE AND CULTURE
IN COOPERATION

HELSINGIÖRS HAVN
seet fra den nordre Side.

INTERPRETING AT THE EUROPEAN COMMISSION

Christian Heynold, European Commission

I represent an international organisation which uses, so to speak, the product of teaching and training of interpreting, that is, fully fledged conference interpreters, and my article deals with interpreting, oral communication, at the European Commission. Translation is written communication, and is handled by an altogether different Directorate General at the Commission.

The three elements of the subtitle of this volume, "Insights, Aims and Visions", serve as signposts for my discussion.

History

First, then, some insights: our Service is the largest conference and interpreting service in the world - it is a Joint Service, so it caters for several EC institutions not just the Council of Ministers and the Commission, and renders its services at meetings globally, not only in countries in the European Union.

Our service has grown from a small group of interpreters back in the 1950's, to some 400 permanent staff now. It started with the Coal and Steel Community where the President and founding father of the European Community - now better known as the European Union - Frenchman Jean Monnet, worked with a German Vice President, Franz Etzel. They had no common language. So right from the start, there was a *genuine need* for interpreting.

In 1958, the first President of the Commission, W. Hallstein asked Mrs. van Hoof-Haferkamp to set up an interpreting service with 11 interpreters.

At that time, we had 6 member states and four languages: French, German, Dutch and Italian. The Treaties establishing the European Economic Communities and EURATOM were drawn up in those four languages in texts which were equally binding. At the very beginning in 1958, the Council of Ministers adopted a regulation (regulation N°1) stating that all four languages should be official *and* working languages.

In 1973, Denmark, the United Kingdom and Ireland joined the Union, adding Danish and English, so that there were now 6 working languages.

In 1981 Greece gained entry, and then there were seven. The newest members, Spain and Portugal brought the number up to the present nine working languages for the 12 member countries in 1986.

It requires 27 interpreters with a total of 72 language combinations to cover nine active and passive languages at a meeting.

We organise some 50 meetings a day now inside and outside Brussels, but not all, I hasten to add, with 9 languages and 27 interpreters.

Languages and organisation

So far the number of languages has tended to increase with new member states. Since this ties up with democracy and the freedom to express oneself in one's own language, outsiders easily get the impression that this process can go on indefintely. This, however, is not the case. Rather we must find out how we can combine democracy (defined as the right of expression) with efficiency in terms of the smooth running of international meetings.

Referring to the subtitle again - one of our aims is to be efficient and pragmatic. We want to provide the high-quality interpreting which is our hallmark, not just to provide interpreters for the sake of it.

In this context, it is worth seeing how another international organisation has tackled the language problem. With 180 member states, the UN manages fine with 6 languages. It dealt with the language problem quite early. In the 1970's, when it passed from 5 to 6 languages, it commissioned a report. This paper, the King report "on the implications of additional languages in the UN", states:

> Such an addition, because of the non availability of staff handling all the language combinations involved, could be achieved only at the expense of quality (e.g. as a result of the general use of the relay method of interpretation ...) and the inspectors venture to doubt whether member states would willingly accept any general lowering of standards. (p. 44, §144)

The UN, of course, is different from the European Union, for, unlike the Union, the UN is not passing binding laws. Directly or indirectly, European Union laws, regulations and directives affect all citizens in the member states and must therefore necessarily be *translated* into all nine languages.

Here, however, we are concerned with *interpreting*. It goes without saying that civil servants and experts who prepare directives and regulations must understand and be understood in their meetings. This means that if, say, a Greek delegate does not master any other language, there will be interpreting into Greek. If the delegate can follow the discussion in another language but but does not master it actively, his needs are covered as follows: there is no interpreting into Greek, but interpreting from Greek into one or of the more generally understood languages such as English, French and German. We call this an asymmetric interpreting system.

This example is a key to our work: we cover *genuine needs* for most meetings, especially at the Commission.

It is different in the Council of Ministers, where the 12 member states are always represented. At the ministerial level we always have to provide interpreting from all the nine into all nine languages since all participants demand the right to speak and to understand discussions in their own, officially recognised language. Even there, the situation is more relaxed at times. Ministers want to have more direct contact, for instance at lunch and dinner, so those who can, switch to other languages. On these occasions there are no complaints about loss of rights and identity. Problems are often solved at informal gatherings, where protocol is waived and Ministers are placed according to language abilities with a minimum of interpreters around. In fact, we do have dining rooms equipped with booths in Brussels and Luxembourg. Even when they are used, the number of languages involved is reduced, for nine booths around the table are not conducive to a relaxed and informal atmosphere! Helmut Schmidt and Valery Giscard d'Estaing enjoyed a special relationship, not least because they communicated easily in English and they always sat together. Conversely there must always be an interpreter present when Helmut Kohl and John Major meet.

All told, most nationalities generally prefer direct contact, no matter how good the interpreters. Interpreting should be used only when *needed*. If it can be avoided, it should be avoided. This is a matter of common sense: a poor interpreter is worse than no interpreter, for the simple reason that poor interpreters may make people believe that their rendition is adequate. Interpreters must be excellent in order to fulfill their difficult task. It is also important that interpreters are motivated - just like all other professionals - and feel that they are needed. It is demoralising to sit in a booth, redundant, because delegates asked for interpreting as a matter of principle but do not use the product.

Other considerations

There is also a financial side to it. As President Delors put it, "We pay a high price for Europe." Interpreting is expensive and should therefore be used properly. The cost of operating the interpreting of one meeting from and into all nine language is about 15,000 ECU a day.

So, all told, there are several reasons why the Union must look ahead and ask if it can go on adding more languages.

This is a political question, and I am no politician but an official who must follow political instructions. Our service reports directly to President Delors. All we can do is draw attention to cost and feasibility if we continue to expand the services.

In this context, it is pertinent to point out that it has always been a problem to find qualified candidates for the profession. In terms of human resources, we are also faced with a shortage. I mentioned that we had around 400 interpreters on the permanent staff. Yet we must take in free-lancers all the time, for on the average we have about 750 interpreters working in 50 meetings, which means that some 45% of the interpreters employed at any given time are free-lancers.

The in-house training programme: the 'stage'
Background and impact

Good interpreters do not grow on the trees. We discovered this about 25 years ago at the eve of the first enlargement of the EC. No university could offer us, for example, qualified interpreters with Danish, so we decided to set up our own postgraduate programme.

This is a six-month in-house training course, a 'stage' in our terminology. The trainees are university graduates in any university discipline with a solid linguistic background, the ability to absorb and analyse an argument and a talent for communication. By now 50% of our staff have been trained by us. However, we are not a school. We started our training scheme out of necessity, and we are not bound by any treaty to continue to do so forever.

Thanks to this programme we have accumulated a certain know-how over the years, and we are ready to offer our experience to others, inside and outside the European Union.

Thus, we have not only trained interpreters for the EC-languages but also - in the framework of cooperation agreements - for the Republic of China, Hong Kong, Turkey, and for Central and Eastern Europe within the TEMPUS programme. We are passing on our know-how and experience to the Czech Republic, Poland, Hungary, Albania and recently also Vietnam.

Let us take the Czech example: so far 6 teacher interpreters have come to our service for study visits of 1 to 3 months to sit-in on training sessions and tests in order to observe our methods. This will enable them to set up postgraduate interpreting courses at home. The main point is that our programme should have a ripple effect.

Selection for the 'stage'

Our programme starts with a selection or, as we call it, an 'aptitude test'. We are in contact with university career advisers all over Europe to find suitable candidates. Interested parties apply - we have processed more than 30,000 applications in the last 30 years, held over 450 aptitude tests, and eventually recruited a total of 400 of the applicants.

The selection procedure is highly competitive and rightly so.

First, candidates must have the right qualifications, and less than 20 per cent of the applicants foot that bill. We are looking for a quick mind, a talent for communication and for the ability to speak fluently and naturally in the mother tongue. In addition to the mother tongue, successful applicants must have a solid knowledge of at least 3 more European Union languages. That may sound cynical - but with only 6 months training time, we must be demanding on language knowledge.

At the aptitude test, the panel is made up of senior interpreter trainers. The candidates are convened in groups of about ten. We give them short, uncomplicated speeches with a line of reasoning or with logical series of points which can be memorised easily without taking notes. Candidates must then render these speeches into their mother tongue. Of course, alert candidates will note advice and criticism directed both at themselves and at the others. On the basis of a few hours including general questions, the panel will have a fairly good idea of who has the knack for the profession. It is inevitable that even more will fall by the wayside in the course of the training because they find it too demanding and too stressful. But the job *is* stressful and some cannot cope.

Contents

The training programme, then, lasts only six months. Admittedly, that is a very short time for learning the skills. Yet we believe, and the facts bear us out, that six months are enough for candidates with the aptitude, the background knowledge, the flair and the will.

The course itself has three parts.

Roughly speaking the students are organised in working groups, each of them headed by an experienced in-house interpreter trainer who supervises the group and does classes about twice a week. In addition, one day is set aside for a session where all trainees work with a large panel of experienced interpreters.

The first part coincides with the first month and consists of "memory exercises", that is, listening, concentration and analysis in order that the trainees learn to follow a logical argument, see the speech in blocks, as I describe it, and reconstitute it by retaining the essentials of the argument in consecutive renditions. Although some students are uneasy about it, they must not take notes, for it is necessary to make them grasp and retain ideas, not words. When they get the point of a lecture, they can then give a natural account of it in their own words.

After the first month we introduce note-taking and with it a new set of headaches, namely a loss of the listening ability students have acquired, and all too much attention to scribbling and deciphering of notes. We do not teach a particular note-taking system. We prefer to give guidelines and let trainees develop individual systems. As experienced interpreters we can guide, advise and correct but the rest is up to the individual.

At the end of the second month, the first eliminatory test is held.

We then return to the basic guiding principles: listening, analysis and delivery as we introduce simultaneous interpreting. After another two months of training in simultaneous and (continued) consecutive interpreting, comes another eliminatory test. And, at the end of the course, after 6 months, is the final recruitment test. At this point, trainees must perform well enough for us to say: "I can work with this colleague at a meeting."

Given our aim of functioning efficiently, you will appreciate that the learning process has barely begun. New interpreters will learn from senior colleagues every day. It is rather like passing a driving test in the country and then learning to manage in rush hour traffic in a capital city.

Comments

The interpreters trained this way have to work for us for at least two years -that is what we ask in return for the training. They are free to become civil servants in our service if they pass an "open competition" ('concours'); or they may go on to other jobs after the two-year term: Somebody with a wide academic background has better chances of profiting from professional mobility than somebody familiar with only one field.

Our 'stage' is based in Brussels where we have a large corps of experienced staff interpreters.

The unique nature of the Brussels course is that the training is provided on the spot by the future employer and that trainees are taught in their future working environment. They sit in on meetings during the last 2 months of the course to practice in dummy booths (disconnected booths) in the presence of their trainers.

Within the EU, we have also run our course or part of it in member states. For example, we have had 'stages' in the European University Institute in Florence, Italy, where we provided the interpreter-trainers and the students benefited from the multilingual environment with students and staff at the Institute as speakers. The results were mutually beneficial, for while the trainees got authentic lectures for excercises, the speakers learned how to deliver speeches for interpreting, which was important since many would later participate in multilingual meetings.

There have also been "stages" in Lisbon, Portugal, and at the Diplomatic School in Madrid, Spain.

In short: we are open to and welcome anyone who wishes to see how we train interpreters and compare our experience with their own.

Visions of the future

What about the visions of tomorrow's world as far as Europe's languages are concerned.

concerned.

I already outlined some problems facing us and the realities we must cope with. And although there is little that can be said with certainty, there are still some indications as to what the future may bring.

These indications include

1) the conclusions of the European Council in Lisbon of June 1992. It says specifically: "To ensure effective communication in meetings, pragmatic solutions will have to be found by each of the institutions."

2) the fact that so far negotiations with states applying for membership are conducted in English. And

3) the fact that any solution must take into account financial implications. Let me exemplify by using the Scandinavian languages. If Norway and Sweden become members of the Community on a par with Denmark, there is no doubt that Norwegian and Swedish will become *official* languages and that all legal documents must be *translated* into these languages. But in interpreting the situation is different: many Scandinavians do understand one anothers' languages and may well prefer to have *one* Scandinavian working language in interpreting. I refer to the interview with the Swedish Prime Minister Carl Bildt (*Børsen* 28 May 1993). He is in favour of just one Scandinavian working language in the EC. In the "Nordic Council" the Scandinavians work together very efficiently without interpreters. And the Danish linguist Allan Karker prophesies that the common Scandinavian linguistic heritage will come out strengthened in European Community cooperation (1993: 75). A pan-Scandinavian booth would be a relatively cheap solution for the Commission.

However this may be, the moment of truth will come, probably at the next intergovernmental conference scheduled for 1996. It will comprise a review of the European Institutions, and   discuss European opening to Central and Eastern Europe, including the management of a Community of 15, 20 or 25 members.

For our service a Community with 15 languages is a 'nightmare scenario'. This would imply 210 language combinations as opposed to the present 72; this requires at least 45 interpreters in 15 booths at each meeting. No matter how competent the interpreters are, this would involve a multiplication of relay-interpreting, where interpreters must interpret the renditions of interpreter colleagues instead of the original because they do not understand the source language. This will pose a quality problem, and, as you recall, quality is one of our prime concerns. It also involves managerial problems, not to mention the architectural one of fitting so many booths into a conference room.

Facing this scenario we must stop playing the ostrich burying its head in the sand hoping that the problem will go away. It will not. It will take courage, political will, and political agreement to reach a pragmatic solution. Tentative solutions are, for instance, the introduction of

1. one single or a limited number of working languages, or,

2. a central relay language, that is, a system where all speeches were rendered only into one language, for instance English, and then interpreted into all the other official languages.

With the introduction of the latter system, English could play the same pivotal role as Russian did in the former Soviet Union where all speeches in executive bodies could be delivered in the delegates' own languages, to be interpreted directly into Russian, and from there interpreted into all the other Soviet working languages.

Alternatively, an artificial man-made language like Esperanto could be introduced, or even - why not - we might return to Latin or Greek. It sounds far-fetched, perhaps, but anything is possible.

The problem is there, and the central challenge is to combine democracy with efficiency.

LANGUAGE STATUS AND TRANSLATION STUDIES:
A NIGERIAN PERSPECTIVE

Evaristus O. Anyaehie, Abia State University, Uturu, Nigeria

Nigerian language policy

The core of the Nigerian language policy has not changed since independence in 1960. English has continued to be the first official language. Hausa, Igbo and Yoruba, dominant languages of the former northern, eastern and western regions of Nigeria, have continued to be federal official languages. Today, with the creation of 30 local states, these languages, spoken by about 50 million Nigerians, are still used for federal official and media broadcasts. The rest of the 250 languages, spoken by the other half of the population, have state or local government status depending on the number of languages in the state or local government area and their relative demographic importance.

This language policy has its corollary in the federal education policy which stipulates that pupils at the elementary and secondary schools learn one of the three major vernacular languages that is not their mother tongue. This policy is based on the theory that mother tongue education, particularly at the early stages of the child's development, guarantees better conceptualisation of phenomena and ensures a more solid base for nurturing the technological culture needed for national development. But where the child's mother tongue does not have a privileged state or local government status, this policy fails to attain its primary objective and the child may be constrained to speak English and as many as three indigenous languages.

The language grading system in Nigerian translation schools, manifestly based on generally accepted psychological and environmental theories of language acquisition and learning, does not quite reflect this national policy. Educated Nigerian English, distinct from the many forms of pidgin or 'broken' English, has understandably continued to assume the status of 'A' language (L_1). The first foreign language is considered as 'B' language (L_2). The mother tongue is classed 'C' (L_3) without any distinction.

In this article, we will take a cursory look at the shaping of the Nigerian language policy since independence, the resulting shifts in status of the languages spoken in Nigeria and their impact on translation practice and studies. We will also review the A-B-C language grading system within the psychological and environmental theoretical framework on which it seems to be based and assess its

application to the individual Nigerian's bilingual experience. From these observations and reflections, we will attempt to make proposals for the planning of
translation studies in a multilingual culture.

Language status and national policy interpretations

In the spirit of the budding Organisation of African Unity, the 1962 Addis-
Ababa conference of African ministers of education considered it desirable to
make every African speak English and French fluently and thus enhance the development of one large African family without language barriers and, presumably, without the intervention of translators and interpreters (UNESCO 1962). So,
energetic efforts were made in Nigeria to step up the teaching of French. Since
every Nigerian was expected to speak French and since the vernacular languages
had little or no social status, professional translation involving European as well
as local languages was not taken seriously.

But, by 1976, when another generation of African ministers of education met
in Lagos to the beat of the Festival of African Culture, the heat of the intra-African English-French bilingualism had almost gone (Damida 1977). The new focus
was on "democratisation", "cultural identity" and "development". In Nigeria, new
educational provisions were made to promote the teaching of vernacular languages in primary and secondary schools. Universities created or upgraded privileged linguistics and vernacular language departments that soon churned out local
language graduates. Vernacular language experts under the umbrella of the Linguistics Association of Nigeria coined vernacular metalanguage so as to avoid the
use of English for teaching indigenous languages. There was a corresponding up-
surge in the production of vernacular language reading texts, plays and films.
This shift in status of vernacular and foreign languages created the first real need
for an elite group of professionals who would facilitate trans-national communication in English and French.

This need was eloquently expressed in the 1982 Dumbleton report on Language
services in West Africa (Dumbleton 1982) which focused on translation and conference interpreting services in English and French for the Economic Community
of West African States. Inaugurated in 1975, this community now has an esti-
mated 200 million inhabitants living in 16 sovereign nations. The Dumbleton report stressed the need for training and upgrading of language professionals to
serve some 60 officially recognised international or intergovernmental organisations including member states. There were for instance only 40 interpreters in
the sub-region. Many of the international organisations located in the sub-region
also had their translations done elsewhere.

Two pertinent remarks in Dumbleton's immensely realistic report deserve mention. The first is an observation that "students entering translation schools at the pre-university level do not have sufficient knowledge of their foreign language or even of their mother tongue or vehicular language" (Dumbleton 1982: 11). The second is a recommendation that translators and interpreters be trained at the postgraduate level "to work into their first language from two foreign languages" (Dumbleton 1982: 12). The paradox in these two remarks is that a proposal primarily concerned with improving transnational communication in English and French should recommend the use of vernacular working languages in translation studies programmes. Dumbleton's views reflected awareness of the prevailing situation in Africa's multilingual cultures. They could also be explained from the perspective of the individual bilingual experience, using the theoretical framework on which the A-B-C grading system seems to be based.

Language status and individual bilingual experience

Piaget's claim that language acquisition in the monolingual child is tied to sequenced cognitive development (Inhelder and Piaget 1966) is generally accepted. Also accepted are Chomsky's (1965) and Lenneberg's (1971) claims that beyond some age limit (between 11 and 14 years) no language can be learned in the same sequenced and dialectic manner characteristic of first language acquisition. These two claims largely constitute the ontological basis for the unquestioned distinction made between "acquiring" a first language and "learning" subsequent languages.

Being the result of an acquisition process, the educated native speaker's language competence has generally been adopted as the model of 'perfect' mastery of a language towards which the second language learner should strive. One weighty argument advanced for this attitude is that language acquisition is marked by an "emotional attachment" to the various cognitive developmental stages. It is with the acquired language that one would most spontaneously "think", "feel" and even "dream". This language would be the most likely to be used when one is highly stressed or is obliged to mobilise all cognitive capacities for full perception and interpretation of phenomena. One such instance could be the interpreting of highly condensed discourse for which Seleskovitch (1981: 41) recommends the mother tongue as 'A' language into which interpreting should be done. Dumbleton's report seems to adopt this view.

Theoretically, based on the above and on the assumption that monolingual and bilingual developments relate to the mind in the same manner, a Nigerian who begins learning English as a second language at about the same time as the mother tongue would probably apply his sequenced cognitive capacities equally to the mastery of the two languages. Provided that the languages have similar exposures to family, school, work and other environments, the educated Nigerian would develop the same emotional attachment to the two languages and could pass for a perfect bilingual as defined both by Ervin and Osgood (1954) and Lambert (1958). If this purely hypothetical scenario could be used to explain the 'A' grading of educated Nigerian English, it should equally be used to categorise as 'A' an acquired vernacular language used in about the same contexts as English.

Past the threshold age bracket suggested by Chomsky and Lenneberg, environmental exposure would seem to determine the mastery of any other language to a level functionally equivalent to 'acquired' language competence. This would explain the attribution of the etiquette 'A' to the "preferred" language of an adult immigrant whose mother tongue is generally less solicited in a foreign land and could therefore go for a 'B' status. This environmental consideration does not explain the 'B' grading of the second European language - French - placed before any of the Nigerian vernacular mother tongues all classed 'C'.

The above language development scenarios reveal a non consistent weighing of psychological and environmental parameters in the A-B-C grading of the Nigerian translator's working languages. With the vernacular languages acquiring more social and technical status, their frequency of use has increased, particularly among speakers of the three majority languages which enjoy the status of sole official vernacular language in many monolingual states. Chief executives in the public and private sectors often seize the first relaxed opportunity to discuss in the mother tongue with equally educated colleagues, switching to English and other languages when they have to express notions that are not yet localised in the mother tongue. This observation is probably not scientifically based enough to sustain the claim that, in situations where the same notion is localised in English and the mother tongue, the latter would provide a faster and more effective medium for its mental processing.

A lesson for the planning of translation studies

For years to come, and for many reasons, it is not likely that any vernacular language will replace English as the first official tongue of Nigeria. The national language policy has continued to be discrete on the issue of vernacular languages. Material resources for developing these languages are limited. Research efforts are inadequately sponsored and co-ordinated. Inter-lingual status rivalry could be escalated with a return to civilian democratic government. But, with their growing use for official, business, technical and various social communications, those vernacular languages that enjoy unchallenged official status in many monolingual states may eventually claim the dominant role in the educated Nigerian's language configuration, thus giving English a 'B' or 'C' status.

This development need not compromise the effective use of English for intra-Nigerian and international communication and for translation purposes. If adequately "acquired" or "learnt", a 'B' or 'C' English could be more effectively used than an officially guaranteed 'A' English that is communicatively deficient. This English will naturally continue to assume a more complex Nigerian aspect as each of the resurrecting vernacular languages leaves marks on its sounds, lexis and even syntax. Its all-time adequacy for international translation and interpreting services may therefore not be taken for granted in translation schools which should offer highly weighted courses aimed at exposing the translator or interpreter trainee to other dialects of English world-wide.

In this regard, French, seen as a foreign language, is more likely to maintain its foreign and 'international' features among the few Nigerians who speak it, particularly if it is not learnt at the Nigerian borders from those who are doing with French what the non educated Nigerian is doing with English. But this French may have to be a 'C', 'D' or even 'E' language since, going by the provisions of the Nigerian language policy, the study of French at the university may well begin after the acquisition of two or more vernacular languages and English. With this understanding, a Nigerian minority language speaker could still be a good English-French interpreter, despite the many vernacular languages he speaks very well.

With the above observations on dynamic language policy provisions and changing social and functional status of languages in contact, what seems to be needed is a more realistic planning of translation studies in Nigeria. Ihenacho's (1991) call for the promotion of a translation culture among Nigerians even at the primary and secondary schools suggests a long term solution to the problems of translation studies in a multilingual Nigeria. According to him, the Nigerian child could be trained to appreciate the structures of the languages he has been destined to speak with real life context in view. A child so prepared would move more easily from tongue to tongue, scaling the hurdles of vernacular languages separating him from English, French and other foreign languages. It is this same culture that would enable the translator-trainee to move more freely from one dialect of English or French to the other in response to a given communication situation.

The Language Centre of Abia State University, in Nigeria, has integrated this vision in its translation studies programme. Alongside English and French, the indigenous mother tongues: Hausa, Igbo and Yoruba are working languages for the 24-month postgraduate professional MA degree in Translation Studies with options in Translation, Conference Interpreting and Terminology.

The training of vernacular language professionals responds to the increasing need for translators and interpreters to serve over seventy per cent of Nigerians who, unable to communicate effectively in English, are often denied their minimum language rights. In this regard, the Language Centre seeks to enlighten the Nigerian private sector and such government departments as the judiciary, the media houses, the agricultural extension and health services on the need for competent vernacular language translators and interpreters.

The above training scheme has stimulated a number of research projects in comparative linguistics; language teaching methodology; harmonisation of vernacular language alphabets, orthographies and metalanguage; terminology. Research findings by translator trainees and teachers are expected to add to what we know about the translation process and could be mobilised for propagating the translation culture so vital in a multilingual nation. Broadly conceived, these research findings could be of interest to other researchers within and outside Nigeria since what may be regarded as "peculiarities" of African language situations could be pointers to our limits in understanding the universal phenomena of human language.

TRANSLATION: A SYMBIOSIS OF CULTURES

Niranjan Mohanty, Berhampur University, India

Introduction

This article suggests that translation, in essence, is not only a bi-lingual activity, but, at the same time, a bi-cultural activity. It further tries to show that through his act of translation, the translator generates a symbiosis between the source culture and the target culture.

The article limits itself to literary translation, and, for convenience and ease, I have restricted my examples to the translation of Oriya and Bengali into English, which is the second language for most Indians.

Translation, culture and language

It is hard to do justice to all translation scholars who have pointed out the cultural dimension in translation work, but from an Indian point of view, it is reasonable to mention particularly 'Translation across cultures', a special issue edited by Gideon Toury of the *Indian Journal of Applied Linguistics*. In this issue, printed as a separate volume in 1989, the cultural dimension is discussed by the editor,[1] Mary Snell-Hornby[2] and Vladimir Ivir.[3] Translation studies have expanded their scope and dimension so as to include culture studies. Devoting my article to such a perspective of culture, I propose to view translation as a process that consciously and quasi-consciously constitutes a meeting point where cultures are mutually enriched. Of course, this is not the same as propounding the view that the source culture is fully absorbed into the target culture. Yet I believe that the degrees of untranslatability can be minimized by a determination to bring the source culture to the target culture through translational practices.

Like religion, language defines one's identity and measures the immensity of a society or community or country. In multiple ways it enshrines the deposits of a particular culture whence the language draws its sustenance. The co-ordinates of a culture are revealed and reflected through language. Apart from being a vehicle of communication, language is thus a transmitter and repository of cultural signifiers. It is an identity intensifier involving the social, cultural, and religious issues with which a nation remains eminently preoccupied. Edward Sapir claims that "language is a guide to social reality." (1956: 69) The Soviet semiotician Juri Lotman views language as a "modelling system" and literature and art as a "secondary modelling system":

No language can exist unless it is steeped in the context of culture; and no culture can exist which does not have a center, the structure of natural language. (Lotman and Uspensky 1978: 212)

D.P.Pattanayak, an eminent Indian linguist observes:

Language is both an expression of culture as well as a vehicle for cultural transmission. It is both cause and an index of social and cultural change. (Pattanayak 1981: 155)

The languages of India

India is a multi-lingual, multi-cultural subcontinent. The enormity of its linguistic and cultural diversity is baffling not only to Westerners but also to Indians themselves. This diversity calls for forging a link between one language and another, between the sub-culture of one region and that of another. Indian people have been familiar with a three-tier system of language learning and acquisition comprising (a) the regional language or the mother tongue, (b) the national language, Hindi, and (c) the official language or the acquired language, English. In spite of such diversities in terms of language, translation and translation studies have remained marginalised phenomena without necessary professional orientation.

According to a 1991 census there are 1,652 mother tongues in India. All 26 states have their regional or state languages. Fourteen languages are used in mass communication, higher education and administration. In such a complicated linguistic context, translation should have assumed a dominant role. Unfortunately translation has not achieved such prominence.

People of India are all more or less acquainted with the national language, Hindi. Hindi is the language of Northern India. In Southern India most people dislike and at times detest Hindi. So Hindi has not been a palatable language in the South. People prefer English to Hindi. The people in the South still believe that Hindi as a national language has been imposed on them. Yet, for the sake of national integrity and unity, the people of the South have become less vociferous in their complaint. Hindi is the language in which television programmes are transmitted, All India Radio news is broadcast, movies are circulated throughout the country, and the national political leaders deliver their speeches to the public. Thus the role of television, the All India Radio, and films, in making the national language familiar, is deep-seated. In multiple ways people are exposed to Hindi, and accordingly even a villager in Orissa, whose mother-tongue is Oriya, does not feel that it is urgent to translate Hindi into Oriya. But when it comes to the transmission of regional films, translation of the dialogues becomes essential. It is interesting to observe that the subtitles are not in Hindi - the national language, - but in English.

Therefore, translation from one regional language into another is less frequent than the translation from one regional language into English. The need for translation is scarcely felt by the common man. R.N. Srivastava observes:

> It is worth emphasizing that, in spite of an intricate system of multilingualism, speakers of the Indian speech community do not feel any serious difficulty in speech interaction. This is because there is a continuous chain from the most illiterate variety of local village dialect to the highly specialized role of English as an associated language, with the reciprocal intelligibility between the hierarchically ordered adjacent areas. (Srivastava 69)

But on the other hand, for an educated man working from a literary perspective rather than a oral perspective, translation becomes a necessity. The Indian Academy of Letters (Sahitya Akademi) honours Indian writers and poets in English with awards every year. National Book Trust of India plays a significant role in publishing books in English translation from the regional languages. Thus English or Indian English has become a veritable part of this subcontinent's cultural heritage. Therefore English has a meaningful translational activity in India.

M.P.Rege, the editor of *New Quest*, rightly maintains in an editorial:

> English continues to be the dominant language in central administration, courts of law, industry and commerce, technology, medicine, universities, research institutes, that is in all areas in which the rising generation will have to make their careers. This situation has to be deplored as unnatural, but, perhaps it would be unfair to blame those who, rather than make a determined effort to end it, help to continue it by acquiescing, for it is a situation we have all inherited as colonial legacy. Without in any way underestimating the inherent capabilities of Indian languages, one has to recognise that, as things are at present, English is the only available linguistic medium for continuing activities which require a certain level of conceptual sophistication, clear and precise formulations of statements and policies and speedy and successful intercommunication between participants. (1990: 67)

Although it is a second language, English plays a dominant role. When translated into English, a regional language text reaches a larger audience in India. It also has the opportunity of reaching out to all the English-speaking countries of the world. However, if the same text were translated into another regional language, the symbiosis of the source sub-culture with the target sub-culture would take place at a faster rate than that of its translation into English.

Let us consider here L_1 to be the source language or the mother tongue of an Indian. Let L_2 be all other regional languages, and L_3 be Hindi and L_4 be English. From the point of view of learning $L_2 = L_3 = L_4$ for an Indian. For an Indian whose mother tongue is L_1, L_2 and L_3 remain as alien as L_4, although L_2 and L_3 are of Indian origin. From the school level, and for that matter even from the familial level, one is more exposed to L_4 or English than one is exposed to L_2 or L_3. Therefore, translating a text from L_1 into L_2 or L_3 creates a very delicate and intricate problem.

Translation from L_1 into L_2 or L_3 poses a considerable difficulty in the sense that it is very difficult to find people who are *really* competent in L_1 and L_2 and L_3, so as to seriously pursue translational practices (say, for example, from Oriya to Bengali or Hindi). Even if a text is transated from Oriya into Bengali, the scope of its readership becomes extremely limited. So for a larger audience or readership, the text in Oriya has to be translated into all other regional languages. What makes the situation complicated is that in the absence of translators capable of direct translation, one must resort to using an English version of the Oriya text for, for instance, Bengali and Hindi translations. With such translational practices the translated text in L_2 or L_3 is doubly divorced from the source language text. This process of translation poses a danger in the sense that nuances of the original text might escape the translator. So the authenticity of the translation in L_2 or L_3 would naturally depend on the authenticity of the translation into L_4, namely English. But then the problem that arises is how to measure and examine the authenticity of the translated text (either L_2 or L_3 or L_4). Under these circumstances, I am compelled to believe that the authenticity of a particular text in translation is likely to be severely and heavily distorted. In the Indian context, I would, therefore, suggest that the translation should be done from L_1 into L_2 or L_3 rather than of L_1 through L_4 or L_2 to L_3.

The role of translation
The next significant aspect that I would like to emphasise is the role of the translator. There is no doubt at all that the translator takes great pains to create a new text for the target culture. The translator becomes an agent for effecting a symbiosis of the source culture and target culture at the linguistic level. The overall symbiosis of cultures would take place on the metalinguistic level and would depend on the nature of accessibility of the source culture into the folds of the target culture. This process is further rendered possible by what Walter Benjamin calls the translator's willingness to "defamiliarise" the source language. Benjamin argues that

> Good translation does not seek to dispel the foreignness of languages but on the contrary allows its native language to be affected, expanded and defamiliarized by the foreign tongue. Therefore, the translator engages in the task of transforming the totality of his native language by liberating it from the servitude of sense and sending it adrift to pursue its own course according to the laws of fidelity in the freedom of linguistic flux. (Benjamin 1968: 80)

Thus, on the one hand, the translator expands the scope of the source language by setting it 'adrift in the freedom of linguistic flux': on the other, he defamiliarises the same language in the context of the target culture. I would like to add a very important point here. I believe that it is not the scope of the target language that is expanded but the scope of the deposits of source culture from which the translation originated that is enlarged. In other words, in translation two activities happen simultaneously: one of defamiliarisation of the source language and one of familiarisation of the source culture into the target culture. If the values, attitudes and relationships which constitute the source culture are reflected thouroughly in the source language, and if the translation is executed with excellence and perfection, I am sure that the initial symbiosis of two cultures at the linguistic level would lead to the same process in the societal level. In order to make my point clear I cite here two examples. In the course of my translation into English of prayer songs and poems of Salabega, a 17th century Oriya devotional poet, I was sure that Salabega, whose fame as a poet never spread beyond Orissa, would now be known outside his native language and that the Orissan sub-culture could at least be made available to other non-Oriya States in India and to America and Europe. Salabega, the son of a Brahmin widow and of Muslim Lalbeg, the *subahdar* of Bengal Bihar, Orissa, was wounded in the battlefield. The wound did not heal despite royal treatment. He sought advice from his Hindu mother, who advised him to surrender himself totally at the feet of the Lord Krishna. As the son of a Muslim, he was initially reluctant, but, because of the intensity of pain, he had no other choice. On the nineth day of his prayer he dreamt that Lord Krishna sat beside him and gave him *bibhuti* (sacred powder). Salabega used the *bibhuti* on his wound. The Lord disappeared. Early in the morning, when he woke up, he discovered that he had recovered. He ran up to his mother to narrate the miracle of the dream. From that moment he became a staunch devotee of Lord Krishna. In the course of time he came to Puri to see Lord Jagannātha in the famous temple. After seeing Lord Jagannātha he was convinced that there was no difference between Lord Krishna and Lord Jagannātha. He spent the rest of his lifetime composing poems in praise of Lord Jagannātha. Salabega's poetry celebrates the greatness of Lord Krishna and Lord Jagannātha as the saviours of mankind. He humanised the divine incarnations. Salabega's poetry celebrates the myths and miracles which were associated with these two lords and unconsciously registered the profundity of Oriya people's faith in these deities. This miraculous but invisible bondage of an individual to his culture and religion can indeed be depicted in English. Lord Krishna's immortal love affair with his aunt Radha has been described with such impassioned intensity that this can be felt even in English. Thus, I believe that the English rendering of Salabega's Oriya poems would not only acquaint the reader with Orissa's history but also introduce one to the cultural co-ordinates of Orissa. The idealised form of man-woman or lover-ladylove relationship has been captured through the eternal love affair between Radha and Krishna. What Salabega does in his poetry in order to immortalise them is simply to bring these lovers to the human level and try to infuse into them all that is essentially human. This relationship does not abnegate the body for the consummation of love, yet the body has been transcended through love. This relationship, however paradoxical it might appear, constitutes the co-ordinates of Indian culture in terms of man-woman relationship.

In the following poem Salabega deals with the superiority of the spirit over matter, soul and body. He believed that, at the utterance of Lord's name, the mortals could hope to achieve redemption.

Knowing all,
and listening to everything,
you never become wise
you never seem to have learnt anything.

Close your eyes only once,
and the whole world sinks,
withering away from you.
Yet you do wail for others,
weep showers for others in vain.

Your kith and kin
only render you a smiling company
to your wealth and prosperity.
When you sleep beyond the seasons
it is only Govinda who leads your way
to the sea of silence.

The golden parrot sits and quietly sings
in the earthen cage of your body.
When the bond of relationships withers away,
it flees, leaving the cage bare
on the harsh earth.

Bare is the river's mouth.
Why do you build embankments
on shallow nothingness?
Why do you shed tears in vain
in front of your son
when you are certain
of your exit?

Whatever you embraced as yours
whatever you fenced as your own
is nothing more than an open field.
Surely, you would leave behind all you had,
all you had won, all you did preserve,
even the weeds of years
clutching and clinging to your body.

Somehow the day passes
with the concoction of joy and sorrows,
and the night in resting and sleeping.
Never could you pray, never did you utter
the names of the Lord.[4]

This poem perceptibly depicts the essence of Hindu philosophy - a crucial part of Indian culture. So I suggest that in the English rendering the symbiosis of Indian and English cultures has taken place. The poem in English translation becomes accessible to an English culture that has enshrined within itself the futility of materialistic progress against spirituality.

Every language has its natural cadence and rhythm. It is difficult to translate this cadence and rhythm. Yet I believe in translation a new cadence is created that partly defamiliarises the cadence of the source language and partly creates a new cadence in the target language. The translator, therefore, has to develop his love for these cadences. Or, as Donald Hall phrases it:

> One's own common speech, one's culture, one's society, one's common life, one's uncommon psyche add their own waters.... Cadence translates only rarely and partially, good translations attend to image and overall structure in cadences managed in the language translated into. (*The Weather for Poetry* 65-66)

The Oriya cadence cannot be re-created in any other language. But in translation a new cadence is created in the target language. The reader's experience is deeply associated with this cadence. In other words, part of the cadence becomes familiarised with part of the target language. Thus through cadence, symbiosis also takes place at the linguistic level.

William Radice, translator of Tagore's poems, for whom Bengali was either L_2 or L_3, termed translation a 'marriage'.

> In a way, translation is like a marriage. Two people - the original poet and the translator - bring their two natures together to create a joint enterprise that is subtly different from their individual... Well we know in life marriage can never be quite perfect, but most of us believe it is still worth attempting. (Radice 1986: 34)

I am convinced that translation not only initiates the process of absorption of two minds, but also renders possible the marriage of two cultures, where the source culture is bound to become infused into the target culture. Yet there are difficulties in effecting symbiosis of cultures at the linguistic level. In Oriya language, *mana,* includes both mind and will, heart and soul. But in translating it into English I must choose either 'mind' or 'will' or 'desire'. In the case of the devotional poets of Orissa, *mana* referred more to the heart and less to the mind. In translating the word into English what one is likely to miss is the *dhvani* - the essence of poetry, according to classical Sanskrit poetics. Similarly the Oriya word *abhiman* and the Bengali word *maan* pose problems for translators. No English equivalents are available. The meaning of these words includes many e-motions and feelings. It is a mixture of mild anger and wild love: a concoction of subtle anger and violent sense of possessiveness. Vexation, anger, unhappiness and disgust may constitute a psychic state. But the word *abhiman* is not the expression of psyche alone - it exposes the condition of a heart that has been slighted or wounded. When such words occur, translators have to invent an illuminating situation or to provide footnotes and detailed expository explanations of the words cited. For example, I faced considerable difficulty in translating "Rim Jhim Rim Jhim Barasa ratire" into English. If I translate the phrase as "In a night of rain" or "It is night and the rains drip, drop, drip, drop", I feel I miss the intended effect or what Walter Benjamin calls the "intento" of the original:

> The language of a translation must give voice to the 'intento' of the original not as reproduction but as harmony, as a supplement to the language in which it expresses itself, as its own kind of *intento*. (Benjamin 1968: 79-80)

The target language should not only serve as the transmitter of information. It should serve as the repository of *dhvani*.

The *dhvani* in classical Sanskrit poetics corresponds with the total effect emanating from the harmonious orchestration of form and meaning. In other words, *dhvani* represents the sophisticated relationship that exists between form and meaning in the poem. K. Krishnamoorthy sums up the concept represented by *dhvani*:

> *Dhvani* or the soul of poetry is the suggested overflow of the poet's thoughts and feelings in all their pulsating intensity and discovered by the reader at the other end. Poetry thus transcends the confines of time and space and becomes an abiding treasure for humanity. *Dhvani*, whatever its form - since its forms are indeed infinitely rich - enriches poetic expression and becomes the only viable norm for all aesthetic value-judgment... Logically speaking, *Dhvani* is what comes to be grasped by the sensitive reader after the stated beauties have slid away from the margin of his attention. It begins where the obvious meanings end as it were. (Krishnamoorthy 1985: 121-22)

The classical Sanskrit grammarians headed by Bhartrhari made it clear that *dhvani* was the equivalent of *sabdabrahman* or logos in the philosophy of Sanskrit grammar. It is the first cause. It retains its all-comprehensive and metalinguistic significance. Anandavardhan of Kashmir writing his *Dhvanyaloka* or 'The light of *dhvani*' in the 9th century A.D., asserted that *dhvani*, when structurally analysed, was all-comprehensive and pervasive of all micro-element in poetry. Thus *dhvani* included word and meaning, sound and sense, name and form, and, in absolute metalinguistic terms, God and his glory. My primary intention in digressing from the symbiotic nature of translational process is simply to examine whether translation can transplant the *dhvani* of the source language in the target language. I earnestly believe that such a transplantation is possible provided that the translator treats translation not as an exercise but as a mediation in which not only two languages but also two cultures support each other. Only when such a transplantation becomes possible, one realizes that translation effects the symbiosis of culture deposits more positively and profitably. Recently I translated a Bengali poem entitled "Maa" or "Mother" by one of my poet-friends, Debi Roy. Let us see if the *dhvani* of the poem in the source language is reflected in the translation.

THE BENGALI VERSION

Maa -
Koler opár khola *Rāmāyán*. Udash chokhē bhāri chasma.

Maa -
Chokh ekbar Ramāyánēr pātāy, aar ekbār
oi doore, talmálo-payer damal-natni,
                                     khola gèt, na berié jaē!

Maa -
badoti - bēsh bado, giechhē bideshē, chithi o'
asheni mashadhikkāl!

Maa -
Karta giechhen swargē...ekatha keno udē asē?
Chokhē ki bali? Dristio jhāpsā, samnèr jākichhu
sab aspástá, dhoan, - ēr bhitar natni doudē ēsē
bookē jhampae...

Maa -
chokher jàl gadiē padē Rāmāyánēr halood pātāy!⁵

                                              (*Desh* 17 October 1992)

ENGLISH RENDERING

Mother:
The *Ramayan* lies open on her lap;
her eyes, beneath the glass, grave.

Mother:
her eyes flutter once on the pages of *Ramayan*
and then on the unruly grand-daughter,
dragging her faltering steps to the gate,
                                     open yonder.

Mother:
the eldest son has gone abroad;
more than a month lapsed,
but no letters!

Mother:
her man has already left for the heavenly abode...
why does this thought fly back?
Dust in the eyes?
Her vision dim; all is opaque, smoke-like...
And in the meanwhile, the grand-daughter
comes leaping to her chest
and begins to dance.

Mother:
her tears trickle down to the yellow pages of the *Ramayan*!

I have attempted to retain both the structural unity of the original poem and its spirit. The poem reveals a familial experience. Mother's loneliness has been laid bare. But the reference to *Ramayan*, the great Indian epic, serves as the co-ordinate of culture. Even without a footnote on the *Ramayan*, the translated poem is capable of evoking the plight of the lonely mother in the absence of her husband. This loneliness is partially relieved by the presence of the granddaughter. Torn between the memories of her husband and the present company of the grand-daughter, her eyes no longer hold back her tears. The images in the poem are sharp, well-defined and to the point in evoking the mother's emotion. I believe I have managed to retain the *dhvani* of the original. In order to clarify the significance of the *Ramayan*, a footnote can be added. *Ramayan* is an epic that depicts the victory of good over evil. At the same time it shows the intimacy, the relationship between Rama, the hero and Sita, the heroine. Rama accepted banishment for fourteen years just as he was about to become the king of Ayodhya. Sita merrily accompanied Rama to the forest. This togetherness was temporary, for Ravana, the evil incarnate in order to avenge the insult of his sister Surpanakha, stole away Sita from her cottage. Rama grew lonely. Yet he and his brother Laxman could defeat Ravana, the king of Lanka, and could rescue Sita. The Rama-Sita relationship is an ideal: both have experienced loneliness.

Ramayan is a religious book and hence old men and women read it to redeem themselves from the pangs of loneliness and to achieve salvation. This faith is peculiarly Indian. Thus, the incorporation of *Ramayan* into the poem makes Deby Roi's poem significant. I am sure that a footnote would make a reader in the target language and target culture fully aware of the significance of the *Ramayan* as a cultural coordinate of the source culture. I am hopeful that a symbiosis of cultures could come full circle by this method of translation.

Teaching translation

Keeping in mind the significance of translation as an instrument effecting symbiosis of cultures, I have conceived a model of teaching. Translators or trainee translators would take a 'bridging course' in which the teaching of the cultures involved is central, and more than the mere teaching of language. The purpose of such a course would be to enable the translator to identify the areas of translatability of the source language into the target language. He would try to discover the areas into which he can construct a bridge, not only between two languages but also between two cultures. The languages, the language structure, the grammar and the phonetics in both must be taught. The translator must have acccess to the language history and literary history of both languages. Access to dialects, and familiarity with registers of both languages would enable the translator to handle any language situation. The translator should be trained to identify the characteristics of each culture, especially those that stand out in relation to the 'contrastive culture', the culture-specific features which we might term the 'intensifiers of cultures', in addition to the peculiarities of the language situation. A bridging course along these lines could to be introduced in three phases. In the first phase the translators would be trained to acquire competence of source and target language. In the second phase they would be taught to acquire knowledge of the cultural intensifiers, so as to enable them to identify the points of convergence and divergence. In the third phase the translators should learn to identify culture intensifiers. These three phases are summarised as follows:

Phase I

Acquisition/Teaching of linguistic and cultural competence in

Source Language + Source Culture
Target Language + Target Culture

Phase II

Identification of cultural identifiers by contrastive analysis between

Source Language + Target Language
Target Language + Target Culture

Phase III

Exemplification of culture intensifiers

a) National linguistic peculiarities:
Is the culture monolingual, bilingual, multilingual?
Is there a dominant second language? What does this imply for language and culture?

b) What are the media for teaching in schools and higher education, in terms of language, in terms of teaching methods, norms, and so on?

c) School:
What types of school are there ?
And what is the relationship between students and teachers?

d) Nature of the Family:
Is it patriarchal or matriarchal? is it based on concepts of extended families or on a nucleus family?
    What are the gender and generation relationships:
    Father - mother
    Father - son
    Father - daughter
    Mother - son
    Mother - daughter
    Grandparents - grand children
    Father/mother-in-law/ - son/daughter in-law

f) What is the literacy rate? How does this affect language, language policy, and culture?

g) Religion: minority or dominant?

h) Sources of national and private (family) income:
agriculture, industry, civil service, etc.

i) Type of government

j) History: colonised, coloniser, independent

h) Literature: history of literature, and the nature of popular and dominant genres.

i) Myths: traditional, vs. created

In my discussion I have illustrated how factors of this type must be taken into account in translation work. It is true that I have not referred to all such factors, but this would have been a Herculean task. I hope I have illustrated that any of these points may be relevant to specific translations. Therefore, I sincerely believe that teaching these three phases would be of benefit to translational practice. This way of teaching would not only make the translators acquire the competence of source language and target language, but would also enable them to have a comprehensive knowledge of both cultures so as to accelerate the process of symbiosis of cultures. I am hopeful that, in the years to come, re-searchers and theoreticians would make attempts to invent new teaching methods so that translation will become a scientific activity with a sound professional orientation. Even after so many theories, so many new methods of teaching trans-lation, I am sceptical about the harmony between the theory and practice of trans-lation, unless theoretical thinking is integrated in teaching.

Notes

1. Gideon Toury. 1989. Integrating the cultural Dimension in Translation Studies: an Introduction. In: Toury, Gideon (ed). 1989. *Translation across Cultures*. 1-8.
2. Mary Snell-Hornby. 1989. Translation as Cross-cultural Event. In: Toury, Gideon (ed). 1989. *Translation across Cultures*. 91-105.
3. Vladimir Ivir. 1989. Procedures and Strategies for the Translation of Cultures. In: Toury, Gideon (ed). 1989. *Translation across Cultures*. 35-46.
4. Salabega. *White Whispers*. Unpublished manuscript. Translated from Oriya by Niranjan Mohanty. 24-25.
5. Debi Roy. 1992. Maa. *Desh*, October 17.

CULTURAL BARRIERS - TACKLING THE DIFFERENCES

TRANSLATING AFRICAN LITERATURE
FROM FRENCH INTO ENGLISH

Moses Nunyi Nintai, Cameroon

This article discusses factors which should, in my opinion, be taken into account when translators are to be trained to work with two languages neither of which is their mother tongue. This is the case in many places in Africa, such as my own country, Cameroon, where French and English are the primary languages of published literature.[1] Translation of African literature between European languages, notably French and English, has been carried out since the middle of this century, but little has been done formally to train the translators who disseminate this fast growing literature to the rest of the world.

The current situation

Even today most written African literature is not published in the national languages, but in European languages of colonization (English, French, Portuguese, and Spanish). Nevertheless, only a few of these works have been translated between these European languages. Indeed, Ade Ojo estimates that translation "has not succeeded in affecting up to five per cent of African works" in European languages.[2] Few Africans are interested in or do literary translation; the vast majority of trained African translators work for government services, international organizations, and private companies. Most of the translations of African literary works from French into English have been done by university scholars and critics (specialized in African literature) who also engage in literary translation as a sideline.[3]

Most literary translations are published (and often requested) by European and American companies, and only a few in Africa.[4] Publication is dominated by prose fiction; this may reflect the taste and preferences of readers, but it is clearly also due to the fact that most African literature is prose fiction. Publishers are cautious about drama and poetry which are less popular. Consequently, poems by one or several poets are usually selected and translated for anthologies.[5]

The interests, ideology and cultural values of the large readership in Europe and North America continue to play a decisive role in the selection of African literary works translated. Moreover, publishers are often guided by market forces, publishing only translations they feel would satisfy their target audience and be economically profitable.

Objectives of training

The vast majority of literary translators have not received any formal training. Since there seem to be fundamental problems about such training, many institutions have been reluctant to introduce such courses, but in view of the shortage of qualified African literary translators, certain institutions are, nevertheless, attempting to provide relevant training.[6] The definition of the objectives, nature and pedagogics of such training is, however, problematic.

Many practising translators question the possibility of and need for teaching translation or imparting the competence and skills that would enable a person to translate texts, especially literary texts. Arguments range from insistence that the ability to translate is a gift (and so cannot be formalized and transmitted), that the translation process is too complex to be reduced to a mechanical operation (hence the failure of machine translation), to the assertion that translation skills can be acquired and improved only through practice and experience. Even if one admits that literary translation requires a certain "creative gift", there are grounds to posit that training could enable those who are not gifted to acquire and improve the necessary skills. That is why, I believe, there are several schools of translators today.

In my view, a training course in the translation of African literature should aim at imparting the required knowledge and skills, laying particular emphasis on the features distinguishing Europhone African literature from the corresponding European ones.[7] Translating African literature from French into English would thus require competence in the two languages involved, ability to analyze and transfer source text message, and an adequate knowledge of African literature. The following is my vision of such a course.

Contents of training

Literary translator training should comprise theoretical as well as practical courses. In African literature, besides focusing on fundamental problems common to literary translation from French into English, students would need to be introduced to research and studies carried out on the translation of sub-Saharan literature between English and French by scholars such as Ade Ojo, Brenda Packman, Charles Nama and Timothy Asobele. Practical translation exercises and analysis of existing translations should offer students the opportunity to translate sample texts and see how others have solved certain translation problems.

Theoretical insights could enable students to become aware of their task, available translation options, and of factors involved in decisions and choices. Thus rather than formulating translation rules and principles, theoretical courses could focus on describing and explaining the implications of the distinctive features of

Francophone African literature for translation. For example, students must realize that French is often used in sub-Saharan literature to express the world view and an extralinguistic reality peculiar to those parts of Africa, and that the resulting "double language" requires that the translator be also familiar with the African language which influenced the French in question. Furthermore, students must take into account not only the two cultures of the source text (French and African), but also the target text cultures (English, African, and non-African reader's, as the case may be). In order to convey the content, students should be taught how to analyze texts within their African historical, political, social, and cultural contexts. In some works, information about the authors and their position within the literary tradition may further enhance comprehension; for instance, information about the author, Camara Laye, will shed much light on *L'enfant noir* in which some events can be adequately interpreted only in the light of Laye's youth in Guinea.[8] In references to African culture and environment, students should examine how to render the names of local objects, dishes, dress, drinks, etc. Other questions to be discussed include: How can the translator convey the two cultural dimensions of the source text? How can African-based proverbs, imagery, dialogue, and other rhetorical devices be rendered? How can one render language switches between French and "français petit nègre"? How can a translation be made accessible to a heterogeneous audience of Africans and non-Africans? Will the uninformed reader need more information in order to understand and appreciate the translation? If so, how can such information be provided? (Within the text, in footnotes, in a glossary or in an introduction?) In trying to answer these questions, the following comment by Ade Ojo deserves consideration:

> Not only is [the translator] to be faced with the African version of the European language that he is to translate from but he has to do a very thorough study of the socio-cultural backgrounds against which the [source text] is written and where the [target text] will be read. The translated version of the [source text] must therefore have a tinge of Africanness; it must also possess the style of the original text and express very appropriately the mind of the writer. (1986: 296)

The practical exercises should be organized so that they complement the theoretical courses. This implies that selected texts aim at illustrating aspects discussed in theory and enable students to explain the translation decisions they eventually make, or comment on existing translations. For example, discussions could focus on how different translators have coped with similar problems, and the impact of the various choices: while translators generally maintain culture-bound terms and expressions, there are instances where words for local dishes, dress, drinks, etc. are mistranslated either because of inadequate analysis of the source text or because of unfamiliarity with the extralinguistic context as we find in John Reed's rendition of "bâton de manioc" (from Ferdinand Oyono. *Une vie de boy*,

p. 7) as "cassava sticks" (*Houseboy*, p. 3), and in Peter Green's translation of "noix de cola" (from Mongo Beti's *Mission terminée*, p. 59) by "chewing gum" (*Mission to Kala*, p. 64), respectively.[9] This exercise could also be extended to the translation of culture-bound proverbs and other oral literary devices, the ways in which translation choices suggest the target readership, and other aspects. Existing translations can serve to show translator creativity in literary translation. Students should, of course, be encouraged to read Anglophone African literary works by prominent writers such as Chinua Achebe, Ngugi wa Thiong'o, and Wole Soyinka; this will expose students to creative writing that would be useful if the "Africanness" of the source text needs to be reflected in translation.

Furthermore, samples from untranslated works can be examined and translated, either in class or as homework; students' choices could be discussed, proposing other options and determining which of them should be adopted in the exercise and why.

Students could also be introduced to the profession of literary translator, for instance, by having prominent translators and publishers of Francophone African literary works talk to students about their difficulties in the field and how they cope with them. Admittedly, in pedagogical environments, students are often likely to make every effort to account for the literary qualities of the source text and respect the original author's lexical and syntactic choices. However, in the real world, the literary translator will have to deal with the publisher and the target audience. Students need to be aware of the role and influence of the publisher in the final translation of a literary text; they need to know that the publisher will often influence the overall translation strategy, and even "edit" or "tailor" translations to the taste and expectations of the target readers and for other commercial reasons.

Moreover, students must also be acquainted with some of the potential functions that the translated African literary text will have to fulfil: for instance, making an African work in French available to Anglophone readers; conveying the cultural setting and values in the work; producing a fluent or transparent translation that will make enjoyable reading for a given audience; highlighting the literary qualities of a particular work. These functions are different from those of the classroom; and students who eventually become professional translators should be made aware of them and how they can best be achieved.

Conclusion

The above views are not intended as rules or the only way of teaching the translation of Francophone African literature into English; they represent only my conception of how to teach literary translation. Teaching methods and perspectives necessarily depend on, and are best adapted to, the specific circumstances and needs of teachers and students; teachers will select methods and approaches to suit their goals and preferences. Obviously, teachers will sometimes rely on their intuition and competence to solve certain problems.

Despite the danger of training too many literary translators for a market often marked by very low demand, relevant courses could be introduced in universities in Africa for students interested in the profession on even a part-time basis; in fact, most of those trained will, in all likelihood, come to work with publishing houses or on a free-lance basis alongside other main jobs. Nevertheless, the importance of consultation and cooperation among teachers cannot be overemphasized. Consequently, seminars and conferences to discuss pedagogical problems and exchange experiences would go a long way towards promoting the teaching of literary translation. Teachers must be encouraged to participate in research projects, and exchange programmes between schools and universities will expose students to different approaches and experiences. I am convinced that with the introduction of appropriate courses, especially in African universities, and better teaching techniques, interest in the translation of African literature would be greatly enhanced.

Notes

1. Cameroon is officially bilingual (French and English). The French-speaking provinces of the country account for about 80% of the population. Since much of the written literature is expressed in French, translators could contribute to the development of Cameroonian literature by making Francophone literary works available to Anglophone readers in Cameroon and other countries through translation.
2. The Role of the Translator of African Written Literature in Inter-cultural Consciousness and Relationships. *Meta* 31 (1986), 298.
3. These translators include Africans (Modupé Bodé-Thomas, Simon Mpondo, Olga Simpson, etc.) and non-Africans (Clive Wake, Dorothy Blair, John Reed, James Kirkup, Richard Bjornson, etc.). Although Africans are becoming increasingly involved in the translation of African literature, the field is still dominated by non-Africans, especially Britons and Americans.
4. These companies include Heinemann (African Writers Series), Longman, and Macmillan in Britain; Présence Africaine, Hatier, Peuples Noirs, P.J. Oswald, and Gallimard in France; Three Continents Press in the United States. In Africa, translations have been published by New Horn Press in Nigeria, Les Nouvelles Editions Africaines in Senegal, and regional offices of Heinemann in Ibadan (for West Africa), Nairobi (for East Africa), and Gaborone in Botswana (for Central and Southern Africa).
5. For instance, Clive Wake has compiled *French African Verse with English Translation* (1972) and Melvin Dixon has translated a collection of Senghor's poems under the title *Léopold Sédar Senghor: The Collected Poetry* (1991).
6. Such is the case, for instance, at the Advanced School of Translators and Interpreters (ASTI), University of Buea, Cameroon, where students are encouraged to translate excerpts from African literary works, especially between English and French, in partial fulfilment of the requirements of the postgraduate diploma in translation.
7. These features have been examined, in relation to English and French, in my article "African Literature in European Languages: Major features and Implications for Translation", in

Proceedings of the 13th FIT World Congress. London: ITI. 1993. I, 564-572.
8. The discussion refers to Camara Laye. *L'enfant noir*. 1953. Paris: Plon; translated by James
Kirkup & Jones Gottlieb. *The African Child*. 1959. London: Collins.
9. The novels are Mongo Beti. 1957. *Mission terminée*. Paris: Buchet/Chastel; translated as
Mission to Kala by Peter Green. 1958. London: Muller. And Ferdinand Oyono. 1956. *Une vie de
boy*. Paris: Julliard; translated by John Reed. 1966. *Houseboy*. London: Heinemann.

SUPRA-LINGUAL ASPECTS OF LITERARY TRANSLATION

Manouchehr Haghighi, Allameh Tabataba-ii University, Iran

This article deals with culture-bound problems in literary translation. My angle will be Persian and the focus will be on English and Farsi. When I, after having taught translation of political and scientific texts, turned to teaching literary translation I suddenly encountered a whole new set of problems. I quickly realized that it required more than a mastery of the two languages to make a felicitous translation. The main problems in translating English literary texts into Persian and vice versa, are the cultural, social and moral barriers which separate the European and Iranian cultures. Therefore I tried explaining to my students the cultural differences between Europe and Iran, but found that this was very difficult. In my opinion, European values, norms, attitudes and perceptions are rooted many centuries back, specifically in the Renaissance, and today these are blended into the texture of Western society and taken for granted. But as my students had a non-European background, these multifarious supra-lingual elements very often led them to complete lack of understanding or a distorted view of the ideas expressed in European literature. Some of the students' responses indicated that they regarded these ideas as something of another world or even another planet light-years away from Earth.

One of the things I discovered was that the closer we got to modern times, the more insurmountable seemed the cultural and social barriers. For instance, the students had less trouble translating Chaucer's *The Canterbury Tales* than rendering Shakespeare and Marlowe into Farsi. I assumed this was due to the fact that the latter two were influenced by the humanistic ideas of the Renaissance. They saw man as a unique individual whose conditions (his relationship to society, nature and God) should be reflected and discussed in their works. And though language certainly adds to the beauty of their works, it is not the main issue of their texts. For example, when we worked on Hamlet's monologue "To be or not to be..." I had to make a choice: either I would teach the students how to make a literal translation of the text without analyzing the cause of Hamlet's grievance in the light of humanism and the social and cultural norms of Shakespeare's time or I would go into extensive discussions on Shakespeare's time, humanism, the Renaissance concept of the ideal man and so on. I first opted for the literal translations, but soon discovered that these could not convey the message - not only were they unfair to the writers, but they also gave me moral qualms. The burden on my conscience was so heavy that I sometimes feared that the offended ghosts of the writers would one day come to haunt me. Moreover, students' responses often prompted me into discussions, as when they asked "why doesn't Hamlet kill his uncle as soon as possible?" or when they thought that when Hamlet talks about "to be or not to be" he is merely reflecting on life and death. So I was forced to abandon the idea of teaching students how to make a purely literal translation. And then came all the barriers, conceptual ambiguities and misunderstandings that usually hinder a meaningful translation and the gap between the students and the authors seemed so wide that they would never be able to meet.

When we had finished working with Shakespeare and Marlowe, I assumed we would have less problems when we were going to try our hand at translating 20th century poets. I had erroneously thought that since the language of the modern poets is superficially simpler and since they are, after all, our contemporaries, it would be easier to understand their works and thus to translate them. But bitter facts soon dawned upon me: the ideas and concepts behind the deceptively simpler language were even more complicated than those of the Renaissance poets. New dimensions had been added to them and the gap between these poets and my students was wider than ever.

To clarify my point I will mention the difficulties my students had translating T.S. Eliot and Samuel Beckett. Eliot's *The Waste Land* was conceptually enigmatic to them, mainly because they could not grasp his theme of 'spiritual emptiness'. Nor could they understand the loneliness and the useless waiting of the characters in *Waiting for Godot*. They could not understand that by letting the characters exchange so few words, Beckett wanted to demonstrate that man has nothing more to say. And I cannot not blame my students, for their lack of understanding is due to culture-bound factors which tie up closely with the Iranian versus the Western world. They have not got the Europeans' experience of the First and the Second World Wars. They have not experienced the diminishing role of religion to the same extent that the Europeans have; they have been less influenced by materialistically-oriented economic, political and social theories than people in the Western World; they have not felt the pressures of mass society and conformism! These and similar developments have shaped the frame of mind of Western man and has influenced his literature. No wonder Iranian students cannot grasp the concepts in modern Western literature. They have been brought up in a traditional society where a fixed and never-changing view on man, nature, society and God has been inculcated incessantly. A society which, for different reasons, has not been through a process similar to that of the

European Renaissance. This difference in cultural and historical backgrounds has brought about mental differences, too. The task is then to reconcile the two contrasting cultures and their fundamentally different conceptual frameworks when translating from one language into the other.

In my opinion the two cultures and two mentalities can never be fully reconciled. We may be able to come to some sort of reconciliation by providing students and translators with background information, but this will never be sufficient to make up for hundreds of years of cultural and social differences, arising from various periods of development such as the Renaissance, the Enlightenment, the French Revolution, the industrialization of Europe, etc. These developments have not only changed the material and physical life of man, but have also transformed his perception of the world. Undoubtedly, in this process of faster and faster transformation, poets and writers (who are usually seen as the antennae of society) have been even more susceptible to the changes than the ordinary man, and have therefore been more easily and profoundly influenced by them. Thus the gap between Western and Oriental societies has widened. While people in the West were occupied with scientific and technological advancement, people in the Orient were still preoccupied with their traditions. They live in different worlds.

These cultural differences have also led to linguistic differences. For example, the word 'loneliness' in a play like Beckett's *Waiting for Godot* has a metaphysical connotation and refers to man's universal loneliness, his being left in a void without any supreme power to turn to. To most of my students it simply means being alone in the sense of not being in the company of other people. A number of new concepts have entered the Western languages mainly in the wake of the profound changes affecting Western civilization in the 19th and 20th centuries: growing materialism, the declining role of Christianity, the findings of psychologists and sociologists and the increasing pressures of mass society. They include concepts such as 'alienation', 'self-alienation', 'anguish', 'disillusionment' and 'spiritual emptiness'. We do have Farsi equivalents, but these are purely literal and not conceptual. They can replace the English words, but they do not communicate the ideas. To the Iranian mentality words covering metaphysical experiences seem odd. Not that the Iranians do not have metaphysical experiences, but they describe them differently and see them from another perspective.

In conclusion, I would like to stress that translators must have background information about the writers whose works they are translating and about the ideas they are discussing. This information may not be of great help to the translators, but they are better off with it than if they are left completely in the dark. In my opinion, some literary works are almost untranslatable (at least into Persian) because they are so heavily charged with concepts that are unfamiliar both to the translator and the reader. But in spite of all barriers and misinterpretations, I think that we should go on translating literature, because this is one of the best means of bringing about reconciliation between cultures. And although this takes time we should not give up hope.

CROSS-CULTURAL AWARENESS: FOCUSING ON OTHERNESS

Meta Grosman, University of Ljubljana, Ljubljana, Slovenia

It is not difference that makes for divisiveness; rather it is the lack of appreciation for diversity that interferes with successful cross-cultural communication.

von Raffler-Engel

Introduction

This article discusses cross-cultural awareness as an awareness of the otherness and differentness of others, or rather, of foreign cultures in all their complexity. This presupposes a capacity for noticing, and, consequently, for understanding and tolerating the otherness of foreign cultures and their literary products. If cross-cultural awareness is cultivated, it can prevent the automatic tendency to perceive the other and the different in terms of the known and the familiar, whereby foreign texts are divested of their very otherness. With literature's special capacity for drawing us into other worlds, literary translation offers the unique possibility of re-creating imaginatively an alien society with its different problems and solutions. Cross-cultural awareness promotes open-mindedness beyond one's own cultural border, contributing to a better understanding between people. Conceived in this way, it seems a prerequisite for all successful communication in a world rapidly turning into a multicultural village. Cross-cultural awareness is particularly important to those involved in the promotion of foreign literature, whether literary translators, critics and editors of literature in translation, teachers and students of foreign literatures, or those reading merely for pleasure.

Cross-cultural awareness thus constitutes an indispensable body of knowledge about the possibilities and relevance of differences between cultures and literatures which must be integrated into the training of students of translation. The aim of this article is to point out the need for a better understanding of cross-cultural reading, and to show how existent literary translations can contribute to heightened cross-cultural awareness in order to reduce undue assimilation in literary translation.

If we want to develop the ability to perceive and appreciate the otherness of foreign literary texts in a cross-cultural context, we must first have some understanding of how and why we tend to assimilate when we read. In its basic, initial stage, cross-cultural assimilation is but a form of the usual reader assimilation of the text, resulting from an effort to make sense, to force the text into acceptability. The readers' appropriation of the meaning of the text according to their needs or desires and according to their culture-specific critical assumptions and predispositions, has come to be regarded as an inevitable consequence of the process of active meaning-production.

The translator as reader

The significance of the translator's own reading of the source text, as first described and analysed by Beaugrande in 1978, is by now well established. Both the statement that translators are readers who translate their reading experience to other readers (Oittinen 1992), and the analysis of the process of translating in terms of scenes and frames (Vermeer and Witte 1990), emphasise the fact that no translator can claim impersonal access to the textual meaning, nor is it possible to translate in a social vacuum. Contrary to other individual readings, the translator's own reading will not remain private but will become that meaning of the source text which will be passed on as its translation to the readers in the target culture. The translation thus simultaneously closes off the source text and opens new possibilities for its interpretation. This fact compels the translator to a particularly attentive reading which presupposes a capacity to reflect on one's own interpretation and its culture bound particularities. In such reflections the translator can be assisted considerably by a knowledge of the process of cross-cultural reading, which should, accordingly, be taught in courses on literary translation.

Studies of cross-cultural reading

Some tendencies in cross-cultural reader responses were demonstrated as early as 1932 by Bartlett, who clearly showed how readers assimilated unfamiliar information in culturally alien texts to their own culture at all the levels of reading. On the immediate textual level they omitted material which appeared irrelevant, or turned unfamiliar textual items into more familiar counterparts. On the level of story construction, they persistently rationalised the whole story and its details and virtually divested it of all puzzling elements in order to render it more acceptable, comfortable and straightforward. To make it fit their own ideas of how stories should be, and so produce what seemed to them a more coherent whole, they attributed special importance to certain incidents and reordered all other incidents around them.

Since Bartlett, several scholars have examined reading in a cross-cultural context. Kintsch and Green (1978) studied the role of culture specific story-schemata in the comprehension of stories. Harris, Schoen and Hensley (1992) established experimentally the impact of cultural scripts and other associated cultural knowledge on story recall, whereas Kang (1992) described some effects of culture-specific background knowledge and subsequent reading inferences in the process of cross-cultural comprehension and interpretation. Halász (1991) demonstrated cross-cultural differences between the readings of American and Hungarian readers. In their study of the impact of text variables on personal resonance, László and Larsen (1991) have shown that cultural proximity of texts generates a large proportion of personally experienced, culturally rich, and vividly remembered events.

Cross-cultural differences are above all noticeable in the field of story construction that reveals a strong tendency to rewrite virtually the whole story in accordance with the reader's own culture-specific expectations (Vargo, forthcoming; Grosman, forthcoming). This tendency is especially strong in the final thematization at the post-reading stage, at which the reader tries to make sense of the whole.

In the latter field Krusche (1990) has provided an illuminating analysis of the cross-cultural variation in students' thematization of Kafka's *Das Urteil* depending on their different culture-bound concepts of human relations. His complex study reveals considerable consistency in the thematization of the text within nationally homogeneous groups of readers and great differences among readers of different nationalities. Each group of readers - European, Algerian, Indian, Japanese and Chinese - formed its own thematization of this complex text in accordance with their various concepts of family structure, of the role of the father, his authority, and similar elements.

New interdisciplinarily conceived projects which involve readers from several and rather diverse cultures promise to bring a more complex and comprehensive picture of similarities and differences in the response to literature in a cross-cultural context (Dollerup, Reventlow and Rosenberg Hansen 1993).

Case studies

Assimilation and shifts occurring in the immediate encounter between the reader and the text are more difficult to trace simply because they are harder to recognise and impossible to recall at the post-reading level. However, it is in the immediate processing of the text that contrastive studies of original and translation can help to reveal shifts and loss of meaning in a cross-cultural context, and can accordingly be used in order to sensitise the students of translation to such loss and its consequences. These naturally vary a great deal since they depend on the quality of the text, the particular relationship between the source and target culture, and the individual translator. When choosing the translations to make the students of translation aware of the pitfalls of cross-cultural reading, all these factors have to be taken into account.

Some texts presuppose a well-defined knowledge of culturally specific pheno-mena, such as a specific social structure, on the part of the reader or rather the translator. In case translators do not possess the knowledge of such an underlying social structure, or are unaware of its fundamental differentness and the import-ance of such differentness for the appreciation of the text, they are likely, without realizing it, to assimilate the text to the familiar social structure of their own different culture and thus lose the otherness of the original, reducing its inter-pretative potential.

We can observe this process at work in the Slovene translation of Jane Austen's *Pride and Prejudice*, in which we find several examples of unnecessary assimilation, invisible to readers acquainted with the translation only.[1]

The original is firmly based on *gentlemanliness*, which transpires through the deeds and linguistic behaviour of all the characters and thus defines them, whereas the Slovene translation offers an inconsistent rendering of the social structure by muddled translations of polite address, titles and references to gentle-manly behaviour.

Taking for granted the reader's knowledge of the position of the gentry and the underlying concept of gentlemanliness, Austen uses the word 'gentleman' and its derivatives carefully and consistently in *Pride and Prejudice*. Unaware of the im-portance of these words and the underlying concept, the translator does not render them with the same consistency. The Slovene translation sometimes re-tains 'gentlemanlike' and 'gentleman' - the use of this loanword is permissible according to Slovene dictionaries - whereas on other occasions, without any special detectable reason, it renders these words by "gospod" and its derivative "gosposki". Being the usual translation for 'Mr' preceding the family name, "gospod" also refers to all male characters presented by surname and therefore fails to provide an adequate textual clue for the reader's construction of the social status of the characters involved. On the contrary, in some references, as for in-stance in Elizabeth's description of herself as 'a gentleman's daughter' (Austen: 366), though trying to explicate the text by adding "rod" [= 'origin'] to "gos-poski", the translation only makes a Slovene reader wonder about Elizabeth's standing. In this way the intrinsic social satire is often lost while the text acquires some of the characteristics of a trivial romance.

Careful examination of examples of such assimilation and the losses of meaning they occasion, can help students to see the differences between the translation and the original, and teach them the necessity of an attentive and open reading in cross-cultural contexts.

Examples of various forms of assimilation of character, due to the translator's inattention to particular character features, are also quite frequent in translations which are closer to our time and world than *Pride and Prejudice*. Apparently minor changes in the description of characters can mediate distorted presentations of them. This is illustrated by, for instance, the Italian translation of David Lodge's novel *Small World* (1985), entitled *Il professore va al congresso* (1990).[2] Professor Zapp's comment on the changed circumstances of academic life, in particular the disappearance of library work thanks to the introduction of photocopying, which induces him to "work mostly at home or on planes", ends with a matter-of-fact statement: "I seldom go into the university except to teach my courses" (p. 44) in the English original. This statement seems to be in perfect accord with the entire paragraph, its ironical overtone, and with Zapp's personality. Conversely, the Italian translation of this sentence: "Io vado all'università raramente, e soltanto per tenere i miei corsi" (p. 62) ascribes to Zapp a commonplace attitude of certain Italian professors, which is not in keeping with American notions of responsible professorship and not at all in accord with the Zapp image of the original. The German translation "An der Universität bin ich eigentlich nur zu meinen Seminaren" (p. 52) comes much closer to the original. The Italian translation cannot uphold the respectability of university professorship for Italian readers, who take this profession much less seriously than other nationalities. Obviously sharing the Italian attitude, the translator renders university titles inconsistently, also because 'il professore' is used more often and has a rather broad meaning in Italian.

Texts in which the reader's perception and ideas of the characters depend to a large extent on the characters' direct speech can present special cases of untranslatability. Thus, for instance, all the attempts to translate Mark Twain's *Huckleberry Finn*, with its four distinct culture-specific dialects, are bound to fail in trying to present Huck and Jim in the same way as in the original. Every attempt to render Jim's words, the most direct and revealing repository of his unassertive, loving, irrational, passionate, and reliable humanity, is of necessity inadequate, because no other language has an equivalent sociolect or can even distantly imitate Black-American English. Thus all translations have to find substitutes, often inadequate variants of slang, which fall short of mediating Jim's original dialect. Translations of *Huckleberry Finn* have never attained the popularity of the original because it is impossible to recreate the central characters through their speech.

The Slovene translation, for instance, renders the entire text in standard Slovene, thus reducing this novel to a mere adventure story, intended for children aged 12 to 14. Though the differences between the original and the translation seem quite obvious at first sight - and a back translation is a shock to everybody who has read the original - it is far from easy to analyse the profound differentness of the original. The analysis must move beyond a contrastive scrutiny and this calls for cultural studies and for analysis of all the culture-specific features lost in translation.

Discussion

The reader's ignorance of the specific socio-cultural context of foreign literary texts and of their textual repertoire usually leads to misperception and assimilation of the different and unknown instead of an enriching awareness of the unfamiliar and incomprehensible. That is why it is easier to uncover assimilation at work in a translation than to notice one's own tendency to assimilate the unfamiliar textual elements, for the simple reason that assimilation is part and parcel of the reading process. Contrastive analysis, however, provides an efficient tool for illuminating the lost otherness of texts, especially in cases where assimilation is unnecessary. The process of illuminating the differences between source and target culture is of paramount importance in enabling students of translation to form a more complete notion of the text, since the differences can be analysed only after they have been made visible. Once the differentness of the text has been identified as such, it can be related to and compared with the student's own culture. The comparison with one's own culture also leads to seeing the differentness of the other culture and so opens the ways of learning about it, or rather perceiving its presence in a foreign text.

Illuminating the different also promotes a more complex appreciation of a text in which students can simultaneously view it from two perspectives, namely their own perspective as well as that of the other and the different. The two perspectives can have a dialogical relationship and yet remain separate, thus combining the effort to enrich the reading and to enhance the awareness of the otherness of the other without losing one's own perspective. Without illuminating, the culture-specific differences may remain unavailable for inspection and thus subject to suppression by assimilation or misperception. Illuminated differences are easier to inspect and to manage adequately.

By making students aware of subtle translational shifts which are invisible from the usual post-reading perspective, contrastive analysis of the original and the translation can help students of translation to make finer cross-cultural distinctions. Having discovered the differentness and having learnt to tolerate it, they will not be disturbed by it. They also come to know the precarious nature of their own reality and their reader expectations. By virtue of this thorough understanding of the foreign text they are in a better position to decide more competently what to retain, what to adapt, and how to handle the foreign and unknown in relation to their own culture. Cross-cultural awareness acquired in this way can enable the students to view each translation - including their own - as a context-bound reading, reflecting the peculiarities of its time and culture.

Notes

1. Austen, Jane. 1968. *Prevzetnost in pristranost*. Translated by Majda Stanovnik. Ljubljana: Cankarjeva založba.
2. The references are to David Lodge. 1985a. *Small World*. Harmondsworth: Penguin. The Italian translation is: David Lodge. 1990. *Il professore va al congresso*. Milano: Bompiani. And the German translation is: David Lodge. 1985b. *Schnitzeljagd*. Munich: Paul List Verlag.
I would like to thank Professor Tjaša Miklič for calling my attention to the translations of David Lodge's novels.

Østerlars Kirke

TRANSLATION
AS A PROCESS OF LINGUISTIC AND CULTURAL ADAPTATION

Christiane Nord
University of Heidelberg, Germany, and University of Vienna, Austria

Introduction

In this article, I would like to elaborate on the relationship between translation and adaptation from a functional point of view in order to show that a strict delimitation of translation proper as against adaptation does not lead us anywhere neither in the practice nor in the teaching of professional translation (including the translation of literary texts). Since professionality is what we are (or should be) training our students for, this new perspective is bound to have consequences for the training methods used at the academic institutions for teaching translation and interpreting.

To illustrate my approach, I have chosen brief examples, particularly book titles, which can be considered as paradigmatic texts, exhibiting 'in a nutshell' all the functional aspects which are distributed over many pages in other texts or text types (Nord 1993). Therefore, they are particularly apt for classroom discussions on functional translation problems.

Equivalence and adaptation

The concept of 'translation proper' hinges on equivalence, and equivalence was introduced into translation studies parting from the standpoint of linguistics in the early sixties by Nida (1964) and Catford (1965) in the English-speaking area, and adopted, later on, as 'Äquivalenz' by Kade (1968) in the former GDR and Wilss (1977) and Koller (1979) in the Federal Republic. As Mary Snell-Hornby has made clear (Snell-Hornby 1988: 15), *equivalence* is not 'equivalent' to *Äquivalenz* (nor to *équivalence* or *equivalencia*, for that matter); therefore I shall focus on the German-speaking authors and base the following considerations on the concept of equivalence in the German sense.

Purely linguistic equivalence between elements of the language system, which was the main concern of the "stylistique comparée" in the late fifties (see Vinay and Darbelnet 1958, for example), very soon proved inadequate as a criterion for the translation of more complex structures, such as texts. Thus, pragmatic aspects were included in the model. In order to be 'equivalent' to the source text, a target text then has to fulfil various requirements with respect to each level of textuality, which I resume as follows:

a) As far as *pragmatics* are concerned, an equivalent target text has to have the same function or communicative effect as the source text, being addressed to the 'same' group of recipients.

b) With respect to the *linguistic* dimension, an equivalent target text has to imitate or 'mirror' the stylistic features of the source text.

c) As regards the *semantic* dimension, an equivalent target text has to convey the same 'meaning' or 'message' as the source text.

In his recent book on translation skills, Wilss (1992) wonders why precisely the defenders of the functional approach want to 'do away' with equivalence. In his view,

source text and target text can only be related to each other by *some form or other* of a microtextual and macrotextual equivalence relationship, which is given even in those cases where a text is not actually translated but - e.g. in the sphere of literature - "transplanted" (Wilss 1992: 197. My translation and italics).

Maybe it is just this "some form or other" that has made functionalists look for an alternative concept. Koller (1993) is even less explicit. He presents the following example (without stating context or source):

A. Finland *Finnland*   *Finlande*
   Kartor *Cartes*   *Karten*   *Maps*
   Karta över Finland och Helsingfors
   Map of Finland and Helsinki
   Karte über Finnland und Helsinki
   Carte de Finlande et d'Helsinki

B. Det finns i Finland.
   Finland - naturally.
   Finnland - das Erlebnis.
   Finlande - naturellement vôtre.

Koller claims that the fundamental difference between the versions in A and B is "evident". In A, he says, there is a "translational (that is, equivalence) relationship" between the Swedish originals and the English, German and French versions, whereas in B, the English, German and French versions are "rather independent text productions" which do not have much in common with the original (Koller 1993: 54. My translation).

I do not think that this is evident at all. In A, I detect a formal linguistic equivalence between Swedish *över* and German *über* (which, by the way, is not acceptable in connection with *Karte*) and between *Karta, Map, Carte* and *Karte* (where in connection with the name of a town *Stadtplan* or *plan* would have been correct in the German and the French version, respectively).

In B, the anaphoric pronoun *det* indicates that the sentence is part of a text and/ or a combination of text and photographs and that it is probably referring to the natural beauty of the Finnish countryside. The repetition of the syllable *fin(n)* produces a particular metrical effect which makes the phrase sound like a slogan. The 'equivalent' translations, that is, the corresponding formulations in the target language system (*This is what you find in Finnland, Das gibt es in Finnland* or *Cela se trouve en Finlande*) would definitely not achieve such an effect. Therefore, the translators tried to find another solution: The English and the French versions 'play' on the ambiguity of *natural* and *naturel*, whereas the German version uses a rhythmical device which suggests an identification of *Finnland* and *ein Erlebnis* ("a unique experience"). From a functional point of view, these versions are 'translations' all right: instead of the linguistic form, they 'translate' the (intended) function of the slogan, adapting the form to the conventions of the respective target culture in order to make sure that the target recipients will be able to recognize the functional markers of the text type.

As it seems, this kind of adaptation is not accepted in Koller's equivalence model although it actually leads to a functionally equivalent target text which would perfectly conform to Nida's postulate of "dynamic equivalence" (1964). Thus, Koller even gives up the progress achieved by the adoption of pragma-linguistic aspects in translation theory. He allows "text-producing" procedures (instead of text-'re'producing procedures) only ad hoc and in special cases, where they are limited to a particular text element and intended "to transmit implicit source text values or to increase text comprehensibility for the target text readership" (Koller 1993: 53. My translation). It is interesting to note that these procedures are usually more readily accepted in non-literary than in literary translations where a 'faithful' rendering of the formal or surface characteristics of the source text is preferred.

The problem is that these conditions do not cover the wide range of adjustments which may become necessary in any translation process, nor do they account for those cases where implicit source text values should remain implicit or where comprehensibility is not the aim of the translation at all. There are texts, for example, where it is precisely the lack of (general) comprehensibility which determines text function, as in hermetic poetry or in certain legal texts. Moreover, this restricted view on adaptation as something incompatible with translation leads to 'untranslatability' in quite a number of cases.

Let us look at an example again:

Alan Bates: Fair Stood the Wind from France.
Peter Howell: Wuthering Depths.

These titles contain intertextual allusions to a line from Shakespeare's drama *Henry V* and to the title of Emily Brontë's novel *Wuthering Heights*. Intertextuality in its various functions can only 'work' within a cultural or literary system (see Nord 1993: 200). Even when the works in question have been translated into a target language or belong to the so-called "world literature", an allusion to a translated text would never be able to produce the 'same' communicative effect as a quotation from a work that belongs to the literary canon of the readers' own culture. Therefore, these titles - as well as most plays on words - are "untranslatable" within the framework of a strict equivalence model.

Functionality and adaptation

A functional approach would solve these (and other) problems both in terms of theory and translator training. Looking at the two titles mentioned above, we will ask what kind of function the intertextual allusion is intended to achieve. Is it meant to inform the readers about the contents or the stylistic features of the book? (These would be referential functions.) Is it intended to appeal to the readers' aesthetic sensitivity, attract them to buy (and read) the book and/or guide their interpretation of the text? (These would be three different varieties of the appellative function.) At any rate, the two titles are designed to distinguish the books from any other existing ones. (This is the distinctive function which is common to book titles and proper names.) After finding out the (intended or possible) functions of the source title, the translator would have to decide which of these functions, and in what hierarchical order, could or should be aimed at by the formulation of the target title. And this hierarchy of (intended) target functions sets the guidelines for the translation process.

In the light of these considerations, the translation of Aldous Huxley's *Brave New World* (another Shakespeare quotation) by *Le meilleur des mondes* (a quotation from Voltaire) is no 'better' or 'more equivalent' than the translation of Marcel Proust's *À la recherche du temps perdu* (which is no quotation) by *Remembrance of Things Past* (Shakespeare again) simply because it gives a target-literature quotation for a source-literature quotation. Any translation criticism would have to take into account that perhaps the poetic function of the Proust title is more easily achieved in the target culture by alluding to a poetic text than by merely reproducing the semantic content or the syntactic structure of the original. And these considerations can easily be applied to any other problems arising in the translation of other text types which are of more frequent use in translator training.

In this vein, the framework of a functional approach would therefore allow any transfer procedure which leads to a functional target text, that is, cultural adaptation, paraphrase, expansion, reduction, modulation, transposition, substitution, loanword, calque, literal translation or even omission (see also Hermans 1991: 166). It is the aim of the translation, the skopos as Vermeer (1978) terms it (see also Reiss and Vermeer 1984) or the "application or use the translation is intended to have in the context of the target situation" (Roberts 1992: 7) which determines the transfer methods used in the translation process. It is interesting, by the way, that this idea has been taken up by Hewson and Martin (1991), although the authors never refer to any of the German skopos theoreticians. The skopos rule is a very general rule which does not account for specific conventions prevalent in a particular culture community. It might even be paraphrased as "The end justifies the means", and this would indeed mean that the translator is free to choose any translation skopos for a particular source text. The principle of loyalty, which I have introduced into the functional approach (Nord 1991 and 1992), sets limits to the variety of possible translation skopoi, obliging the translator to consider the author's communicative intention(s) and the readers' expectations towards a text marked as a 'translation'. As a principle, loyalty is not specified in the general model; what it really means for the translator in a particular translation task is specified by the culture-specific translational conventions prevailing in the culture-communities involved. Translational conventions which ask for 'literal translation' have to be taken into account as seriously as translational conventions which allow an adaptation of some or all text dimensions to target-culture standards.

'Taking into account' does not mean, however, that the translator has to follow the conventions in any possible case; conventions can be counteracted or even changed. But the translator cannot just 'override' the expectations of his or her partners in the cooperative activities implied in any intercultural text transfer.

Source-text functions and target-text functions
Parting from a functional analysis, the translator tries to find out the function(s) which can or would be achieved in the source-culture situation by the source text as a whole and/or by any separable in-texts (such as examples, metaphors and similes, quotations, plays on words, etc.), comparing them to the function(s) required for the target text. If there is any possibility of achieving the same function(s) by the target text in its (prospective) target-culture situation, the translator would be free to decide on the transfer procedures which may become necessary, and adaptation is one of them. Let us take a book title as an example again:

Simone de Beauvoir: Une mort très douce
German translation: Ein sanfter Tod;
English translation: A Very Easy Death.

Beside the phatic, the metatextual and the distinctive functions which are common to all titles (see Nord 1993), this book title seems to be intended to achieve an emotive function by the elements *très douce*, which is reinforced by the soft dark sound produced by the phrase. The German translation is apt to achieve this function precisely by avoiding both the translation of *douce* by its literal equivalent *süß* (which has connotations of liveliness and happiness) and the reproduction of the adverb *très* by its systematic equivalent *sehr*, which would indeed lead to a sharp, hissing sound: **Ein sehr sanfter Tod* or even **Ein sehr süßer Tod.*

The English version, however, substitutes the emotional function of *douce* by the evaluative function of *easy*. Whether a death is easy or not can be judged from outside, from the doctor's point of view, whereas *douce* describes the feelings of the dying person. Thus, the English title sounds very matter-of-fact (which is in part also due to the nominality of the phrase) and would probably not achieve the same emotive function as the original. Another adjective and an adjustment or adaptation of the syntax structure might have led to a functionally more adequate title like, for example, **Dying softly/gently* or perhaps **Dying is sweet.* This would also be in line with formal conventions: An empirical analysis of approximately 1600 German and 1800 English book titles has shown that both verb patterns and sentence patterns are much more frequent in English fiction (1,5% and 6,5%, respectively) than in German fiction (0,5% and 3,5%) or French fiction (0,3% and 4,8%) (Nord 1993: 60).

But text functions need not necessarily be the same for the source and the target text. For French readers, the Beauvoir title does not contain any explicit or implicit reference to the fact that the book is a fictional text; for them, this information is implied by the author's name, who is known as a writer of fiction. For English readers, this may not be as evident. Therefore, it might be wise to use a sentence pattern and not a verb pattern, because in English book titles, verb patterns are more frequent in non-fiction (4,4%, for example: *Living with Alzheimer's Disease*) than in fiction (1,5%) (Nord 1993: 60).

As we see, there is a shift of functions in the target title in this case. That is, the information about the genre which in the source culture is given by the author's name is shifted to the title in the target-language formulation.

But there may also be cases where the target text has to achieve a function which is not vital for the source text (or vice versa). Again, we can take titles as a case in point. If the author is a famous writer in the source culture, but not known (as yet) in the target culture, the original title does not need to achieve an appellative function, whereas the translated title would have to attract the prospective readers' attention. This may be a motive for the references to an 'exotic' setting (very popular as an appellative feature in German fiction: 5%) introduced in the German translations of the following titles of two novels by the Cuban author Alejo Carpentier.

Alejo Carpentier: Los pasos perdidos [literal translation: Lost Steps]; German version: *Die Flucht nach Manoa*;
Alejo Carpentier: El acoso (literal translation: The Siege); German version: *Finale auf Kuba* (see Nord 1993: 240).

I will not discuss here whether the suggested versions have been the best or the only way to achieve an appellative function in the target titles; what I would like to stress, however, is the fact that adaptations often are the only way to ensure that a translation 'works' in the target-culture situation it is produced for.

The functional approach in translation teaching

Choosing the functional approach for translation practice will have considerable impact on translation teaching or translator training.

a) The linguistic features of any text are determined by the situation the text is used in. In 'normal' intralingual communication, we know the situation in which and for which we produce an utterance or a text. In the traditional translation class, however, teachers often ask the students to translate the source text 'as such', that is, without specifying the situation or purpose the translation is needed for. Therefore, trainee translators commit grammatical mistakes even in their own native language, which they never would have made in spontaneous intralingual communication.

Experience shows that when the prospective communicative situation is clearly defined, linguistic errors are committed less frequently. Therefore, a commission or assignment which defines the intended function or functions of the target text can be expected to reduce the number of linguistic errors or faults in students' translations.

b) By contrasting the target situation (especially with regard to the prospective recipients and the intended text function or functions) described in the translation assignment with the functional analysis of the source text in its own communicative situation, translation problems can be detected in advance (Nord 1992). This procedure makes it easier for the trainee translator to develop translation strategies for the solution of a particular translation problem which are designed for the translation of the whole text and not for individual units such as words or phrases.

c) Translation strategies should follow a 'top-down' procedure:

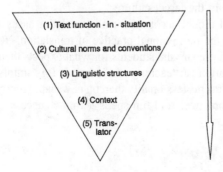

(1) Text function - in - situation
(2) Cultural norms and conventions
(3) Linguistic structures
(4) Context
(5) Trans-
    lator

This means: in a first step, a particular translation problem (for instance, a play on words) is analysed with regard to its function in the text and in the target situation (1). The analysis leads to a decision whether the translation has to be adapted to target-culture norms and conventions or whether it should reproduce source-culture conventions used in the source text (2). This decision sets limits to the range of linguistic means to be used (3), from which the translator chooses the one which fits into the specific context, such as text-type, register, style, etc. (4). If there is still a choice between various means, the translator may decide according to individual stylistic preferences (5).

The degree of difficulty of a translation task can then be judged according to the form of the triangle. The lesser the constraints set by situation or convention, the larger will be the margin for individual preference decisions. In this case, it will be less easy to find plausible and intersubjective reasons for their functionality and consistency, which makes the task more difficult for the trainee.

d) The functional approach is consistent: unlike the equivalence model, it does not suggest different norms for literary and non-literary translation. Therefore, it can be applied to the translation of every kind of text and between every pair of languages and cultures. Thus, it is more appropriate as a framework for methodological principles and strategies and would make translator training more rational and even more 'economical' as well as more independent of language and culture specific peculiarities.

e) The functional approach is an 'inclusive' model: Unlike the equivalence model, which considers certain forms of intercultural text transfer as 'non-translations', the functional approach includes all forms as long as they are functional and based on the loyalty principle. Thus, even the production of (a particular form of) equivalence in the target text can be one possible translation skopos, which might form the last step in a teaching progression leading from easier to more difficult tasks. In the initiating phases of teaching, however, it would be wise to start by translating strongly conventionalized texts with clear functions, such as instructions or tourist brochures, for which existing models and parallel texts can be found in the target culture.

f) The functional model accounts for all translation tasks a translator will be confronted with in the professional practice of translation. 'Realistic' translation assignments, which prepare the students for what expects them in 'real life', provide a good motivation for teaching and learning. It is simply more fun to work on texts which ask for professionality than on newspaper reports which are hardly ever translated in practice. And fun spells learning success.

Concluding remark

In conclusion, I would like to say that my own experience in using the functional approach in translator training shows that the trainees commit less grammatical and pragmatic mistakes, they learn a lot about cultures and conventions, and they seem to have quite a bit of fun doing all this!

TRANSLATION AS A MEANS
FOR A BETTER UNDERSTANDING BETWEEN CULTURES?

Heidrun Witte, Universidad de Las Palmas de Gran Canaria, Spain

Theoretical bases

Modern functional translation theory has defined translation and interpreting as complex communicative action, the main aim of which is to establish communication between members of different cultures in accordance with a previously determined communicative target purpose or *Skopos*, as Vermeer termed it (Vermeer 1983; also Reiss and Vermeer 1984).

Culture is understood as the sum total of a social community's behaviour patterns, including the 'rules' of behaviour and its (material and immaterial) 'results' (Göhring 1978 and 1980).

Functional translation theory also distinguishes between *paraculture* (that is, the culture of a society as a whole), *diaculture* (namely subgroups within a social community), and *idioculture* (which is individual). The definition of culture refers to a dynamic concept, so that the delimitation of any cultural unit depends in each case on the perspective of the observer/interactant (group of observers/interactants) and his/their respective purpose of analysis (see Vermeer 1992a).

In accordance with the functional approach, in the following the translator (throughout this paper "translator" will refer to both translators and interpreters) is considered an expert in cross-cultural communication and his *bicultural competence* regarded as a basic prerequisite for his work.

To enable students to develop an adequate bicultural competence, translation training must emphasise the different *roles* involved in the translation process. This implies the necessity of stressing the ignorance most clients will have of the foreign culture and their unawareness of the problems of intercultural communication in general.

The most comprehensive functional approaches in translation theory have so far been developed by Hans J. Vermeer (1983) and Justa Holz-Mänttäri (1984).

The following discusses some of the basic arguments of their approaches, that is "Scopos Theory" (*Skopostheorie*) and "Theory of Translational Action" (*Theorie vom Translatorischen Handeln*), respectively, with regard to pedagogical implications.

The concept of communication

Before discussing some of the problems arising from intercultural communication, we will examine the concept of communication as such.

Social psychology, communication studies and discourse analysis have demonstrated that any communicative act necessarily involves various 'levels', on which 'communicative messages' are 'exchanged' (Gumperz 1982; see also Poyatos 1983).

Methodologically speaking, there are three different levels in communication (Witte 1992a):

(1)   the *object level*, which refers to the 'contents' of what is being communicated;

(2)   the *communicative level*, which refers to the intention/purpose behind the communicative act; and

(3)   the *personal/interaction level* by which we refer to the idea the interactants gain of each other and to the relationship that evolves between them in the course of the interaction. (This level is usually termed "metacommunicative". See, for example, Kendon 1981; 1982.)

When people communicate, they tend to be conscious of levels 1 and 2: you want to tell somebody something and - if prompted - you will usually be able to explain why and for what purpose.

As far as level 3 is concerned, however, people are usually not aware that they are constantly communicating to each other a certain 'image' of themselves and of their interpretation of the interaction situation (including their interpretation of the interaction partner).

EXAMPLE:

In "Western" business negotiations interactants tend to concentrate either on the subject matter at hand or on the result to be achieved, such as the signing of a contract. They do not, however, seem to be equally concerned with one another at the personal level, nor to be conscious of how their behaviour is interpreted by the other party. Nevertheless, in the end, each party will actually have acquired a (usually subconscious) idea of the other which may range from sympathy to a feeling of "what a strange guy" (see e.g. Reuter, Schröder and Tiittula 1989).

Naive intercultural communication

In intercultural communication the problem becomes more complex: culture shock theory has taught us that people who do not have previous 'knowledge of' the foreign culture they deal with in specific intercultural situations, tend to *project* their own cultural frame of reference onto the foreign culture. That is, they interpret and evaluate foreign behaviour in accordance with their own cultural rules of conduct, and act according to the behaviour patterns of their own culture (e.g. Furnham and Bochner 1986; see also Poyatos 1983).

This 'projecting' attitude constitutes an inevitable, indeed necessary process in cognition in general: we would not be able to assimilate new experiences if we perceived them as completely new. We have to be able to relate them ('to compare' them) to categories we already know (Detweiler 1980; see also Lakoff 1987).

In turn, these categories are learned in a process of socialization, through which individuals gain active and passive knowledge of the behaviour conventions ("rules of conduct") operative in their respective social communities.

Once individuals have gone through this socialization process, they will find it extremely difficult to 'free' themselves of the result: they will always 'see the world' through the 'filter' of their own culture.

This is no plea for cultural relativism (understood as determinism) but merely a reference to sociology's well-documented claim that the decisive influence exerted on the individual by primary socialization cannot be repeated with any comparable force in secondary socialization(s) (Berger and Luckmann 1989).

It is thus inevitable that we get to know other cultures 'on the basis of' our own (primary) culture: in intercultural contact, people will necessarily 'compare' foreign cultural phenomena to their own cultural background (see Müller 1980; and 1986).

However, the more one learns about another culture the less one will turn to one's own culture for comparison. Instead, one will become increasingly more able to use the foreign culture itself as a frame of reference, that is, perceive and interpret it in terms of itself, although (methodologically speaking) one's own culture will always remain the 'deepest' level of comparison (Witte 1987).

Therefore, the idea people form about a foreign culture will usually not correspond to the image the culture would claim for itself. Nevertheless, such an idea generally does exist in people's minds and will necessarily influence their behaviour in concrete cross-cultural situations.

To sum up: in intercultural communication, the everday 'neglect' of the interaction level, as described above, becomes aggravated in that it is precisely on this level where most *unconscious culture-specific projection* takes place.

The translator's bicultural competence
The translator thus deals with (at least) two persons from different cultures who have preconceived ideas about each other, ideas which, in general, are not 'adequate' in so far as they do not correspond to the respective foreign culture's 'self-image'.

Therefore, the translator's *bicultural competence* cannot merely consist of a competence in the cultures he works with but must also comprise what we have elsewhere called a "competence between them" (Witte 1987): The translator must be able to judge/estimate (from his perspective) the clients' 'knowledge' (or 'lack of knowledge') of one another's culture and to anticipate the impact this knowledge may have on behaviour patterns in the concrete cross-cultural situation.

It is only by interrelating the two cultures that the translator is in a position to compensate for the clients' 'inappropriate' preconceptions and projections as well as the 'inadequate' active behaviour patterns they may lead to.

We have already discussed how communication necessarily involves the "interaction" level. It follows that any professional concept of communication will have to include not only the contents and intention of the message but also the participants in the communicative situation. This means that the translator must operate with a much 'broader' concept of communication than the 'restricted' everyday notion held by his clients. If we claim that translation and interpreting are to establish intercultural communication *professionally*, then translational action must be based on *professional concepts* (Holz-Mänttäri 1984 and 1986).

Towards better understanding between cultures

"To achieve a better understanding between cultures" translators must, then, take into account all three levels of communication and pay more attention to the interaction level than it has received so far, in order to avoid culture-specific projection as far as possible. In other words, they should strive to *transmit an image of the source culture to the target receptors that corresponds to the image the source culture would claim for itself.* (The "image a culture claims for itself", however, can be distinguished further as (1) its self-image; (2) the image of itself with regard to other cultures, that is, the image it believes/wants to evoke in another culture.)

The practical realization of any such attempt would first of all presuppose that the client saw the relevance of the interaction level for satisfactory cross-cultural communication. But since the client is not an expert in intercultural communication, he is usually not aware of its problems. Judged from the translator's professional perspective, the client's purpose/scopos is normally rather 'restricted' (Vermeer 1989).

In order to achieve successful cross-cultural communication as defined from a professional viewpoint, *the translator may therefore consider it necessary to make the client modify his original purpose.*

There are, of course, practical difficulties in any such attempt in our society here and now. As has been pointed out by Hönig (1992), the translation market is still much more willing to accept bad translations than self-confident translators. Nevertheless, professional performance requires professional concepts.

Social recognition and appreciation of the translator's work cannot be achieved unless the translator himself recognizes and insists upon his social responsibility (Vermeer 1990; Robinson 1991).

So far, our discussion has been focused mainly on face-to-face interaction.

As far as written translation is concerned, the aim to transmit an image of the source culture as close as possible to its self-image can certainly not be achieved successfully by the still predominant translation strategy for literary texts.

The vast majority of literary texts today are translated according to what Christiane Nord (1991) calls "exoticizing" translation strategies.

These "exoticizing" translations certainly meet an existing demand. However, the way they are usually done does not transmit anything like the self-image of the source cultures, but rather fosters existing stereotypes and prejudices among the target public.

Since there is a culture-specific interrelation between behavioural phenomena and the values attributed to them within a society, perceiving and interpreting behaviour also implies evaluating it. The mental image we form of a social phenomenon, is thus necessarily composed of denotative and connotative elements (see Vermeer and Witte 1990; also Vermeer 1992b).

However, literary translation still favours linguistic surface structures, without bearing in mind the value attributed to certain source-cultural behaviour patterns in the target culture.

EXAMPLE:
In German translations of Spanish novels one frequently comes across Spanish housewives having their morning chats in bars, workers drinking three glasses of wine at eleven in the morning and little children running about in the streets long after midnight.
In Germany a bar is a rather obscure place where you go to drink, possibly even get drunk; a German wine glass is three times the size of a Spanish one; German parents send their small children to bed at seven or eight in the evening.
A German receptor without previous experience of Spanish culture will therefore be greatly surprised (to say the least) by such phenomena and may well question Spanish domestic order, working morals or educational responsibility. (See Stackelberg and Kroeber 1986 for a similar argument; also Poyatos 1983.)

"Exoticization" does not necessarily lead to negative effects in the target culture. And "exoticization" may also be a legitimate translation scopos (that is, an intentionally pursued strategy).

However, translation procedures which transfer behavioral phenomena from the source to the target culture by merely reproducing linguistic surface structures generally 'bring about' exoticizing effects more or less unconsciously (and, accordingly, should not be termed "strategies").

Such translations generally fail to anticipate the ground on which the target text will fall, that is, they 'forget' about the target receptor and his culture-specific background. This is why, in our view, such translations do not serve to develop an "understanding" between cultures. They cannot be described as representing responsible translational action either.

Teaching

In terms of pedagogical considerations there are two main points about the problem of intercultural communication:

Firstly, students have to become aware of the potential difficulties of intercultural communication.

Elsewhere (Witte 199ba), we have therefore insisted upon the necessity of establishing the subject "intercultural communication" as a special topic in translation training. Here, students should be introduced to the ways in which socialization and communication work within one culture, in order to learn, in a second step, to see the difficulties likely to turn up in cross-cultural contact because of existing behaviour differences.

Secondly, students have to be made aware of their clients' 'unawareness' of the problems of intercultural communication and of their usually inadequate cross-cultural knowledge.

Once students have learned something about their working cultures and have developed a certain cross-cultural knowledge, they tend to take at least some degree of cross-cultural sensitivity for granted in everyone. They usually find it hard to imagine that the majority of their future clients will have no special training in problems of intercultural communication and will therefore simply be incapable of distancing themselves from their own cultural background.

In addition to an insufficient capacity to adopt the perspective of a 'naive' receptor, students sometimes seem to confuse the concept of "taking into account the target receptor" with the application of concrete translation strategies like "simplifying the target text" or "adapting it to the target culture".

It is essential that students are made to understand that *bearing in mind the target situation does not in itself entail a specific translation strategy*, but first of all it means anticipating the possible effects different translation alternatives may have upon the target receptor.

However, our stress on the relevance of culture differences must not lead to a static idea of culture specificity with the students and should therefore be backed up with discussion of the relativity of 'detecting' culture-specific traits. Although the translator may acquire a relatively high degree of "biculturality", he will, like everybody else, never be able to loosen himself completely from his primary culture. To a certain degree, he will therefore always perceive foreign cultures from his own 'culture-bound' perspective.

No attempt 'to reach' foreign cultures can be more than an approximation.

Students must be taught to regard this 'never-ending' endeavour of approaching foreign cultures not as a vain attempt but as an integral part of their future profession. Only then will they recognize the potential inherent in translation as a means to achieve a better understanding between cultures.

ADVERTISEMENTS IN TRANSLATION TRAINING

Gabriele Becher, Universidad de Las Palmas de Gran Canaria, Spain

Introduction

In this article, we shall discuss some results of a recently initiated project that investigates not only the use of newspaper and magazine advertisements in translation training, but also the communication and translation strategies behind them. Our objective is to analyse advertisements of different cultures in class and to demonstrate the enormous importance cross-cultural knowledge has for the translator. We intend to sensitize students to the fact that advertisements may include specific aspects of a source culture, which must be taken into consideration when translating for a target culture.

General objectives

The general objectives are that students
1. become acquainted with other cultures through advertisements, and
2. learn about translation-orientated text analysis and text production
To reach these objectives, we have subdivided our material into 3 categories:
A. Advertisements involving the "home" culture as self portrayal or "inner eye vision". (German and Spanish examples)
B. Advertisements involving "a different/foreign" culture seen through the "spectator's eye".
    a) Advertisements in Spanish of a German product in Spain
    b) Advertisements in German of a Spanish product in Germany
C. Advertisements of the same product in both languages and cultures, with the same layout.

The material

The analysis of different advertisement material includes:
1. a linguistic and functional text analysis (following Nord's Model for Translation-Oriented Text Analysis (1991));
2. an analysis of non-verbal means;
3. an analysis of the interrelationship between illustration, text, product and cultural frame;
4. a cross-cultural analysis of verbal and non-verbal means and communication strategies; and

5. an analysis of underlying translation strategies.

Advertising and translation

Commercial advertising is a form of *propaganda*, in so far as "propaganda" is defined as any attempt to influence the development or change of attitudes of an audience (McDavid and Harari 1967: 371).

Advertisements are normally produced to sell or to announce something, mostly by persuasive arguments, so that they influence attitudes and/or behaviour. When somebody reads, listens to or watches advertising information, this communication is communicated to the receptor. Therefore, advertising forms part of human communication, by means of multimedial systems. Commercial advertising is used in the mass-media, for instance, TV, films, radio, newspapers or magazines. Advertisements are thus received via visual, aural or written channels.

Receiving information involves decoding and conversion into already existing information patterns.

In focusing on newspaper and magazine advertisements, we deal with verbal written information and non-verbal illustrations and their interrelationship.

Analysing texts automatically involves language; and *language* is "a system of social conventions specifying relationships between certain symbols (either verbal ones or graphic ones) and certain ideas or concepts. As such, language is a *cultural product* that influences the structure and organization of the individual's thought. ... The greatest social significance of language is that it permits the communication of ideas and experiences from one individual to another" (McDavid and Harari 1967: 171).

This social, or rather *"cultural"* component of language and of any communicative process, is most important for a discussion of advertising: advertising as a means of communication is at the same time an instrument for transmitting culture.

Following the text typology by Katharina Reiss (1983), advertisements can be described as operative text types. Their main communicative function is to *appeal*, trying to change the reader's opinion or behaviour, provoking impulses, reactions and actions, producing a persuasive effect through language and illustrations.

Newmark argues that the *vocative* function of language is used in advertisements "in the sense of *calling upon* the readership to act, think or feel, in fact to *"react"* in the way intended by the text" (1988: 41).

If the primary communicative function of advertising is to appeal, the persuasive effect of language attempts to influence attitudes or behaviour, and if language is considered a cultural product, then advertising may be said to reflect in some way or other the cultural background of a community. And different communities with different cultural backgrounds need different stimuli to provoke the same reaction-response.

Consequently, if the sender has any special intention as to *how* the addressee should receive and decode the information, the transmitter of the information must take into account the social conventions of the addressee's community in order to be successful.

When we speak of "different communities", we do not refer only to different language communities: all over the world we can observe regional differences of habits, customs or social behaviour, even within the same society. For example one needs different advertising strategies and campaigns to promote the drinking of tea in the north of Germany than one does in the south, independent of the language.

Of course, it is even more important to take into account cross-cultural behaviour differences between communities with different language systems.

Recent translation theory has repeatedly emphasized the importance of cross-cultural knowledge for the translator. Translation has to take into account verbal and non-verbal communication strategies. As mediators between cultures, translators are considered representatives of different cultures, not only because of their linguistic abilities, but also because of their knowledge of culture-specific behaviour patterns in general.

Teachers often describe the difficulties they have in making students aware of culture-specificity and its relevance for translation: to teach what we call "life and civilization" is quite difficult and even more so if we think about which concrete aspects we have to take into consideration in translation training.

Introducing cross-cultural analysis of advertisements as a pedagogical instrument in preparatory translation classes seems to be a method of drawing the students' attention - through inductive procedure - to cross-cultural behaviour differences and communication difficulties potentially resulting from them: if we introduce advertisements from two different language communities through comparative studies, students must become aware of the importance of cross-cultural knowledge.

Analyses of different types of advertisements
In the following discussion we present only one example of each type.

Advertisements involving the 'home' culture as self portrayal:
Example 1: DEUTSCHER WEIN - EINZIG UNTER DEN WEINEN
We introduce an advertisement in German about German wines. It looks like

this:

We ask the students to analyse the advertisement and comment on it as follows:

a) What do you notice about the illustration? (information value, associations,etc.)

b) Analyse the text (function, slogan, external form, syntax, rhythm, etc.)

c) Analyse the relation between text, photograph and illustration.

We follow Baraduc's theory (1972: 105-115) that text and illustrations belong to two different systems. The function of the illustrations/photographs is the representation of reality, and the function of the text is the structuring of that reality. We therefore first emphasize that both photograph and illustration in the advertisement presents us with something 'typically' German: namely German architecture, mostly in the central and southern parts of Germany, as well as German commercial life in the Middle Ages, represented by the small drawing.

In the analysis of the verbal part of this advertisement we identify the

following communication strategies:
a) the use of superlatives in the slogan,
b) the almost poetical syntax
c) the folk song titles describing the typical autumn atmosphere in Germany, and
d) the German customs of keeping wines in stock against the long, cold winter evenings.

In the interrelationship of text and the illustration/photographs, we recognize a clear double appellative function: the rational, informative aspect is expressed in the text and the emotive aspect is expressed through the illustration/photograph.

This advertisement is thus an example of a self portrayal of German culture, or "inner eye vision".

In more general terms, the didactic advertisement, which is pedagogical in its own right, illustrates a distancing effect: the same advertisement acquires greater informative value instead of keeping its appellative function.

When we use examples of this type in translation training, we cover two areas: firstly, we introduce knowledge about a country and culture, and secondly, we train students in translation-oriented text analysis and in advertising strategies in general.

Examples of this type are also useful in translation training because students become aware of the culture-specific aspects in advertisements.

*Advertisements involving **a different/foreign** culture*
The second step is to introduce students to information about cultures in advertisements through "the spectator's eye vision", by looking at advertisements for German products in Spain and for Spanish products in Germany.

a) First we look at *German products and how they are introduced in Spain.*

In addition to numerous advertisements which use stereotypes, such as "German quality" (ZEISS, WMF-cutlery), or "qualified German engineering" (OPEL), there are other examples which indirectly reflect German culture.

In Example 2: MEICA. LA TENTACIÓN DE LUTERO [Luther's temptation] (next page), the Spanish addressee is taken back to the 15th century and the world of Martin Luther in order to be introduced to several types of German sausage. The text plays with words from Luther's life and refers to his character. In the practical lessons with our students here we insist on an exhaustive text analysis in order to make them aware of any detail so that they are forced to look critically at the culture-specific aspects expressed in this advertisement.

b) Secondly, we analyse *Spanish products and how they are advertised in Germany,* by introducing a series of examples, like the one on the opposite page.

Example 3: CARLOS PRIMERO. LA NOCHE - LA VIDA

It is primarily the picture which calls the addressee's attention to the advertisement: it shows a bottle of brandy and a photograph of young Mediterranean people enjoying themselves in the evening. In the text of this German advertisement, we recognise Spanish words "la noche - la vida", and then there is a stereotyped description of Spanish nights - throbbing, full of life and warmth.

Thus, examples of this type also transmit cultural aspects of a community to the students, but as seen from abroad, from a spectator's perspective. They often include the stereotyped views cultures have of one another.

Advertisements of the same product in both languages and cultures
Our pedagogical objectives in the previous examples have been to demonstrate the existence of direct or indirect cultural information in advertisements and to sensitize our students to these phenomena.

The subsequent examples of the same advertisements in different languages focus on the analysis of strategies for text production. Later on, the knowledge of text production strategies in advertising and the ability to analyse such strategies may become relevant for the elaboration of translation strategies.

As mentioned, mediators of operative texts must take into account the function of the target text. This means that it has to be adapted in terms of its appeal to the mentality and to the general socio-cultural conditions of the addressee in the target culture.

Our objective in using advertisements in preparatory translation training is therefore to make students aware of the necessity to take into account the socio-cultural background of the target culture. Students have to learn that cross-cultural transmission of operative texts implies adaptation to the socio-cultural background of the target culture, including, possibly, the production of a new text in the target language.

In order to reach this objective, we introduce several advertisements in both languages. In pedagogical progression they are compared with regard to the relevant verbal and non-verbal elements.

Example 4: BOSCH: EIGENTLICH WOLLTE ER NUR EIN SCHAUKEL-PFERDCHEN BAUEN/ TODO EMPEZÓ POR UN BALANCIN

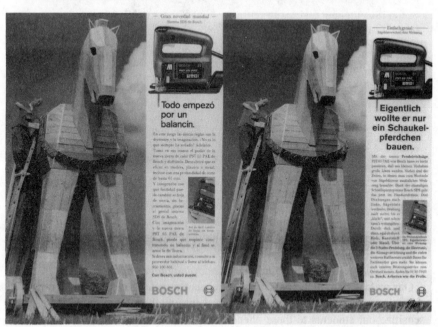

We present our students with the original German source text. We first analyse the pragmatic situation factors, that is to say:
- text function (operative text, advertisement, persuasive strategies)
- addressee (the average German citizen)
- intention of the transmitter (BOSCH's aim is to sell the product)
- relationship between text and illustration (the illustration takes up half the advertisement space, and text and illustration are connected in a way that would make either incomprehensible if presented in isolation).

Among the culture-specific aspects we emphasize the illustration which shows a bald German citizen engaged in a "Do-It-Yourself" job in the open air. In Germany this is quite normal; almost everybody does "Do-It-Yourself" jobs around the house and is proud of it. There is a well equipped toolbox, a drill and saw in every household.

The text insists on two very important aspects for the German addressee: the technical innovations and the possibility of working like a professional (since the German is an amateur).

The average Spanish customers have a totally different attitude and background: they are not accustomed to doing jobs around the house, since they normally buy finished products.

In the Spanish text the message is focused on "do it yourself", in order to convince the addressees that this activity produces fun and creativity. The function of the advertisement is not to enter into technical details - therefore we find fewer than in the original version - but to motivate the Spanish addressees to carry out handiwork and convince them that the easiest way is to do it with Bosch.

By presenting our students with the version translated for the Spanish customer, and by making the same analysis, we call their attention to the importance of culture-specific aspects in translation of advertisements.

The examples of this third type help students develop an idea about how to adapt advertisements to target cultures. They find out about detailed cross-cultural translation strategies by means of comparison and can then apply their theoretical knowledge in practice using advertisements.

Concluding remarks

In our discussion of various types of advertisements we have shown that ads directly or indirectly communicate culture-specific aspects and that this must be taken into account whenever we deal with advertising for different target cultures.

We have tried to demonstrate that by virtue of this special communicative and culture-specific character, advertisements may serve as an excellent instrument for discussing the transmission of culture and, at the same time, constitute an important pedagogical instrument in preparatory translation training.

TRANSLATION AND CLASS

STEEN GADEN
I
HELSINGØR

KARL POPPER IN THE TRANSLATION CLASS

Andrew Chesterman, University of Helsinki, Finland

One of the problems in translation teaching is how to build a mass of individual insights into a coherent whole. I have found the philosophy of Karl Popper to be a real inspiration in this respect. It has provided me with a rich conceptual framework which is theoretically satisfying and also eminently practical. This article introduces some of the central aspects of this framework.

First, though, a couple of words of introduction. Karl Popper was born in Vienna in 1902. He studied music, and also worked as an apprentice to a cabinet-maker for a time, before moving into mathematics and philosophy. He was critical of the logical positivism of the Vienna Circle, opposed both fascism and Marxism, and became an enthusiastic Social Democrat. After a period teaching philosophy in New Zealand, he emigrated to England in 1946, and was Professor of Logic and Scientific Method at the London School of Economics for many years. His major work has been in the philosophy of science, but his most recent publications have been more concerned with cognition and the workings of the mind. I shall be focussing mainly on some of the ideas in his *Objective Knowledge. An Evolutionary Approach* (1972).

Problem-solving

Through much of Popper's work there runs a simple thread: the idea that knowledge advances by means of problem-solving. In particular, the objective knowledge of science does not start with data, or with theoretical axioms, but with problems. Popper's view of the scientific method is illustrated in a schema which he uses again and again in slightly different forms, applied to many areas of life, from evolution to politics. The schema is:

$$P1 \longrightarrow TT \rightarrow EE \rightarrow P2$$

P1 represents an initial problem, which may be of any kind whatsoever. TT stands for Tentative Theory: this means the first hypothesis, the first attempt to solve the problem. Given the fallibility of human nature, this tentative solution is unlikely to be right, or even the best possible. In Popper's view it is immaterial how you might arrive at this TT - imagination, guesswork, chance, rational deduction, whatever. For scientific knowledge, the crucial stage is not the nature of this first hypothesis but how it is tested: EE stands for Error Elimination. This refers to the process whereby the TT is tested and refined. At this stage it is the responsibility of the scientist to submit his Tentative Theory to the most rigorous testing possible. Since no theory is ever more than a hypothesis, no theory can ever be proved true, but theories can be shown to be false or inadequate. A theory that cannot be falsified may or may not be a good theory, but according to Popper it cannot be an empirical one. Further, the goal of empirical science is not 'truth' (because absolute truth can never be known) but rather maximal verisimilitude, or truthlikeness. The result of the EE process is not, therefore, 'the right answer' or 'a perfect theory', but in fact a new problem, P2. P2 might be a refined or reformulated version of P1, a consequence of P1, a lack of fit between TT and the data, something at a more general level that perhaps subsumes P1, or whatever. P2 in turn is then subjected to testing etc., and so the process goes on. Knowledge is never final.

In translation studies, P1 has taken many forms. At the most general level, P1 can be simply "what is translation/translating?" Many traditional answers to this question have been metaphorical: translating is giving a performance of an original; reproducing an original; betraying an original, and so on. Such answers may bring us insight, but they are not empirical in Popper's terms, since they cannot be falsified.

Other questions that function as P1 have been: what is the best way to translate? what is equivalence? how can we program a machine to translate? what counts as a translation, in a given culture at a given time? what goes on in the translator's head? how can metaphors be translated? And many more. The progress of translation studies can thus be seen as a vast network of intertwined TTs that have been set up to answer a huge number of P1s, plus the EE that takes place within the community of translators and scholars assessing the TTs, plus the subsequent P2s. In teaching translation studies, or theoretical aspects of translation generally, it is obviously vital to specify the P1 to which a particular TT or EE attempt is related; for apparent disagreements between theoretical views often turn out to be because these views are linked to different initial problems.

Translation as theory

Perhaps more relevant to the practical translation class is the way that a translation can itself be seen as a Tentative Theory. After all, the initial problem faced by a translator is: how shall I translate this text (or: this sentence/ this word/ this idea ...)? At multiple levels, all translations are proposed solutions to such a P1, tentative theories. Different translators, different times, usually come up with different solutions. There is nothing "final" about a translation, insofar as a translation is merely a theory like any other theory. And just as it makes no sense (in Popper's terms) to claim 'perfection' for a scientific theory, so there is no reason why a translation (*qua* theory) should be 'perfect'. This point of view suggests that much of the traditional argument about equivalence has been nothing but a confusion of red herrings.

Note that, in Popper's view, it does not matter *how* a particular translation (= theory) is arrived at. This argument would run counter to the claim (e.g. by Wilss and some others) that the evaluation of a translation must take into account the translation process. On the contrary: in the view I am propagating, the interest is not in how to get to a TT but in what happens when we have already got one. (At this point it is mnemonically convenient to point out that TT may denote not only Tentative Theory but also Target Text, or at least Tentative Target Text.) What matters is the Error Elimination stage.

An approach along these lines is in fact advocated by Gile (e.g. 1992b, and in the present volume (pp. 107-113)). In his model, for any element of the source text, the translator first develops a hypothesis of what it means and how it might be translated, and then tests this for plausibility and target language acceptability. Testing involves a wide range of procedures, from documentary research, compatibility with background knowledge of the world, assumptions about background knowledge of the readers, and so on. Any errors or shortcomings are eliminated, and alternatives proposed, until the translator is satisfied.

Criticism and corroboration of a translation

The TT can thus represent, initially, the first draft of a translation. In Popper's schema it then undergoes the process of Error Elimination, criticism, revision. In the advance of objective knowledge in general, it is this stage that distinguishes the scientific method from other methods; by analogy, it is this stage that shows up the difference between amateur or trainee translators and professionals. For professionals, this is a crucial and time-consuming stage. Draft versions are checked against other possibilities, against other parallel texts, against reference books, against other people's opinions, and so on. Account is taken of sociolinguistic factors, target language norms, readership response, readability requirements, etc. etc. The more one knows about how a translation can be assessed, the more rigorous this Error Elimination process becomes. Hence, by the way, the usefulness of purely theoretical knowledge for professional translators: it makes for more demanding hypothesis-testing, suggests more pertinent questions to be asked of the TT.

Notice two things here. First, in order to criticize a translation (a draft) it is not sufficient simply to say what you think is wrong with it; Error Elimination includes the necessity of replacing an inadequate item with one that you think is better. Criticism thus includes the suggestion of improved versions, which themselves are then subject to the same critical process. And alternative versions themselves must be justified, defended, corroborated.

Which leads to my second point here: corroboration. Popper uses this as a technical term in his view of scientific methodology. To the extent that a Tentative Theory has been exposed to rigorous Error Elimination, and has survived this testing process, to that extent the theory is said to be corroborated. That is, it is not "proved true" or anything of that sort; but it is shown to be a pretty strong theory, a well corroborated theory. The more rigorous the testing that a theory survives, the higher is its degree of corroboration. In other words, the more feedback you can get about your translation, and the more feedback it survives, the better it will be shown to be, in the sense that it will be well corroborated.

An obvious application of this idea is in the use of pair work or group work in class, or exercises involving the repeated revision of a translation (one's own or someone else's). A class might continue revising a translation until a version is arrived at that is within the acceptability range of all members of the group - and then this version could still be submitted to a parallel group. Like theories, a translation is never 'finished'.

Translational competence

This view of the translation process has obvious implications for the way we see translational competence. Here I would like to draw on a definition proposed by Pym (1992: 175, referring to his own earlier work). Pym also argues that translators "theorise", and in fact that the ability to theorise is an integral part of translational competence. His formulation is extremely Popperian, and it may be paraphrased as follows.

Translational competence comprises two abilities. (1) The ability to generate a series of possible target texts for a given source text (where I think we can read 'text' as anything from an individual item or feature to a complete text). (2) The ability to select from this series, "quickly and with justified (ethical) confidence," the particular version most suited to a given readership.

In other words, a translator must be first able to produce a range of Tentative Theories, and the more the better, since the wider the range, the more likely the possibility of ultimately selecting an optimal version. Secondly, a translator must be able to criticize these TTs, to carry out an exhaustive Error Elimination process; this requires not only knowledge of the readership, target text function, desired relation with the source text, etc., but also knowledge about how to self-criticize; how to select relevant criteria to weigh different possibilities against one another; how to take into account general translational principles prevailing in the relevant cultures at the time; and so forth. In Pym's words, such a definition of translational competence "recognises that there is a mode of implicit theorisation within translational practice, since the generation of alternative TTs [target texts] depends on a series of at least intuitively applied hypotheses" (1992: 175).

It is precisely at this point that theory joins hands with practice: in fact, there can be no practice without theory. And there can be no better justification for the need to encourage trainee translators to become aware of and familiar with purely theoretical ideas. To quote Pym again:

> Unsung theory ... may thus be seen as the constant shadow of what translators do every day; it is what improves as student translators advance in their specific craft; it is the mostly unappreciated form of the confidence slowly accrued through the making of countless practical decisions; it is what most competent translators know without knowing that they know it (1992: 175-6).

World 3 and plastic control

One of Popper's most influential concepts is that of World 3. This is a notion that he first developed as part of an epistemological argument dealing with subjective and objective knowledge, but the concept has since seemed to take on an independent life of its own, and not just in Popper's own work.

Popper distinguishes between three worlds. World 1 is the world of physical objects or physical states, what we normally call the objective world. World 2 is the world of states of consciousness, mental states, feelings and the like - traditionally, the subjective world. World 3 is the world of what Popper calls "the objective contents of thought" (1972: 106). World 3 is the site of scientific knowledge, the contents of libraries, scientific ideas, theories, ideas, arguments, problems.

World 3 entities are distinct from World 1 ones. A book (as a World 1 entity) may be destroyed - even all copies of it - but its ideas may survive. Of particular interest here, however, is the way World 3 interacts with the other worlds. World 3 entities are, in the first place, products of World 2, that is, of human minds. But (like the concept of World 3 itself) once these entities have entered World 3 they can exist there independently of World 2. Ideas pass from people to people in conferences, for instance. But now comes the crux: World 3 entities can subsequently affect both World 2 and World 1. A new idea you come across may affect the way you think yourself, your own World 2; it may even affect the way you act on your environment, on World 1.

The nature of this effect of World 3 is not deterministic: Popper is no determinist. Yet he also argues against the extreme indeterminist postulate of absolute freedom. His key concept here is "plastic control". This is understood as a kind of flexible control plus feedback. Popper explains the idea thus (1972: 240-1):

> the control of ourselves and of our actions by our theories and purposes is a *plastic* control. We are not *forced* to submit ourselves to the control of our theories, for we can discuss them critically, and we can reject them freely if we think they fall short of our regulative standards. So the control is far from one-sided. Not only do our theories control us, but we can control our theories (and even our standards): there is a kind of *feed-back* here. And if we submit to our theories, then we do so freely, after deliberation; that is, after the critical discussion of alternatives, and after freely choosing between the competing theories, in the light of that critical discussion. (Italics original)

With respect to translation, and the teaching of translation, I think the implication is clear. "Theories" here are ideas about translation: the whole collection of principles, norms, arguments, commonly agreed rules-of-thumb and the like that constitute the set of expectancies about translation within a given culture at a given time. All these exist in World 3. To the extent that we accept these World 3 entities, they do indeed exert a plastic control over our translatorial action. But before we can accept them, before we can even weigh them up criti-cally, we have to be aware of them. Hence, of course, the importance of teaching such things overtly.

Hence, too, the usefulness of volumes like this one, which may even churn up new World 3 entities. Thus we help to create our own future.

Linguistic ethics

Much has been written recently on translatorial ethics (see e.g. Robinson 1991; Pym 1992). While Popper does not discuss the ethics of the translator as such, his general views on ethics seem to me most applicable here.

Popper's view is based on a kind of upside-down utilitarianism. He criticizes the Benthamite assumption that what matters is the greatest happiness of the greatest number: why is it moral to increase the happiness of someone who is doing all right anyway? More urgent than the maximization of happiness is the minimization of suffering.

Note how here too Popper's schema is appropriate: minimizing pain is, as it were, a form of Error Elimination. We do not start from some kind of ideal state of bliss, any more than we start from some kind of absolute truth. True, such ideals may function as regulative guiding lights, exerting their plastic control from World 3; we may have our visions of Paradise lost. But we live in the real world, where we can only grope tentatively forward by trial and error, eliminating errors where we can along the path to truthlikeness, and eliminating suffering where we can along the path to a just society.

For translators, I suggest that the first application of such ethics is in the conception of the translation process not as something straining for an ideal, but rather as one of minimizing error, what we might think of as "communicative suffering". That is, the translator's task is to minimize misunderstanding. It is this, not some mythical equivalence, that is the fundamental motivation for the way a translator approaches the source and target texts, for any adjustments, revisions and the like that may be necessary. I take this to be the bottom line of everything the translator does.

The corollary to this linguistic ethics is manifest in Popper's stress on clarity, which for him is perhaps the most important standard of language.

Bootstraps

Popper also uses his schema to illustrate his understanding of the Darwinian theory of evolution, which he links to a theory of the functions of language. Like animal languages, human languages have functions of self-expression and signalling, but unlike the former they also have higher functions, in particular those of description and argumentation. The language of these higher functions is primarily exosomatic, in that descriptions and arguments are World 3 entities, and it is this property that allows the development of rational criticism and hence of reason and humanity as such. The rational criticism inherent in the proposing of Tentative Theories and the process of Error Elimination becomes the tool by which mankind evolves. Popper thus claims that his schema "gives a rational description of evolutionary emergence, and of our *self-transcendence by means of selection and rational criticism*" (1972: 121. Italics original).

The schema is thus a model for education and personal growth, too, for one's personal research and development programme, as it were. Translators learn from their own previous translations, their own previous errors; they can learn from exposure to new translations, from ideas about translation and its theory. They can become better translators. In Popper's terms, they do this first by interacting with others, by soliciting feedback etc., in critical communicative dialogue. But secondly, they do this *themselves,* through their own inner self-criticism: note Popper's *self-transcendence.*

In this way "we lift ourselves by our bootstraps" (1972: 121). Or, to quote one of my own bootstraps (Chesterman 1993: 78): "we translate ourselves."

THEORY AND PROFESSIONAL DEVELOPMENT: OR ADMONISHING TRANSLATORS TO BE GOOD

Sergio Viaggio, United Nations

This article has been prompted by the following assertion in Anthony Pym's otherwise formidably insightful *Translation and Text Transfer*: "Happily, general translational practice has quite probably changed far less than theory" (1992a: 190). I beg profoundly to disagree: If translational practice had not lagged so far behind theory, most translations would be much better, and fewer readers would have so much trouble with their electronic gadgets. The aim of his and most works on translatology ought to be, precisely, to influence the way translators translate, and not, as in descriptive approaches, merely take stock of it. A lot has been justly said about the deplorable chasm between translatology and translators; that should be a reason for us to try and meet practitioners at their working tables or, better, before they get to them: at the university, where the theoretical rationale (a redundancy if there ever was one) of the practical *do's* and *dont's* is to be learned.

Of course, much profit is to be derived from observing good translators and studying good translations. But how do we determine who and which they are, and what makes them so? Unless we postulate a provisional concept of what a translation should be, there is no way we can determine how close to or how far from it any particular effort falls. If, on the other hand, we do set such criteria, we can then elicit general or specific principles, rules, methods, strategies that prove systematically successful, or at least more successful than others. Once thus elicited, they become inevitably those standards a translation should follow- even if for the nonce, until superseded by new, more advanced ones; exactly as is the case in any other discipline.

It is, I think, clear that the moment a theoretician comes up with a definition of what a translation is, he is also, up to a point at least, defining what it is not, and the degree of conformity to what it is acts automatically as a quality quantifier. Unless we agree with scholars such as Gideon Toury, for whom a translation is whatever a given culture considers it to be[1] (and even then, we can safely state that in our culture the best translation of an owner's manual is the more intelligible one), prescriptivism is inescapable. If there is no right, or at least better way of translating, then we are all wasting time, breath and money: there is nothing but language to teach.

What nearly all translators, from the best to the worst, seem to have in common is precisely a lack of any coherent, systematised, weighted conceptual framework behind their practice. Observing them allows to glean more *dont's* than *do's*. As Albert states:

> Each translator (whose task is to *create* equivalence) will have an individualised equivalence-concept... [His situation] is often the most uncomfortable: Even if he knew all the possible equivalence-types which may come up while translating a specific source-language text, he is, as an expert, fully aware of the fact that he will not be able to create total equivalence between the two texts: his 'freedom' only means that he has a choice as to which equivalence-types to reject and which to keep. (Albert 1993: 13)

A translator, he adds,

> always needs some kind of global conception (idea, strategy, philosophy) when translating *any* text. There is some kind of philosophy in *all* acts of translating, even if the translator himself is not aware of it or tries to deny it: the latter is often the case, for in my opinion it is more often than not **the lack of awareness of such a philosophy which makes poor translations really bad** (Albert 1993: 13. His italics, my bold type).

However, he laments further on, "no theory of translation will tell the translator which features are, or should be, more significant than others in a specific text; there is no higher forum to which he can turn concerning the adequacy of his decisions" (Albert 1993: 13).

Perhaps not so much in literary translation, but as far as pragmatic texts are concerned, the situation with theory, to my mind, is not half as bad, as I shall endeavour to show. To begin with, and if he knows his translatology, the translator is not that much more at the mercy of his personal intuition, competence *and* luck than a physician faced with any specific case. Collective knowledge and professional lore bring the qualified practitioner of any discipline safely further and further into his realm. If translatology has been born at all, it is because translation, in its broadest sense, has itself changed drastically over the last forty years or so: It has ceased to be a mainly literary side activity of knowledgeable or incompetent *dilettanti* to become a full-fledged, mainly technical profession. The bulk of translations being now production-related, an overwhelming social need has arisen for the specialist at translating. The sheer fact that we can now make a living not just translating, but talking and writing about translation or teaching it is yet a further proof of our amateur craft's coming of age into a profession, that is the conscious, socially conditioned and recognised practice of a discipline. It is no coincidence that, in general, translatology is most developed where translations are better; translations, on their part, happen to be better where they are better paid, and better paid where they are more readily recognised as essential aids to economic production, the work of necessarily highly qualified practitioners. So much so, that the translator of literarily inane but politically relevant or production- or trade-related texts stands to make much more money than the heirs of Dryden and Gerard de Nerval.

That being said, the gap between collective professional lore and the lagging or pioneering individual physician is probably minute compared with the extremes we witness in our field, where stragglers are so rife and far behind, and pioneers so few and far ahead - again, a typical phenomenon at the inception of any discipline or science. The bulk of our practitioners do not approach their task scientifically; they do not even see translation as communication; many an interpreter, for instance, is not even aware of the difference between written and spontaneous oral speech. It is a shame, of course, but quite inevitable: We are at a stage where scientific thought is beginning to creep into our ranks, where individual ideas and insights have only started becoming a systematic body of knowledge, where we actually read and criticise each other. We owe it to the profession and to the rest of our colleagues to be prescriptive, to tell them that adequacy takes precedence over equivalence, and textual equivalence over local correspondence; that there is no point in setting out to translate without a clear concept of our own and the original's *skopoi*.

For instance, we understand now that there are as many possible valid translations of a given text as there are different uses for the target-language versions. Nida's dynamic equivalence, Newmark's semantic vs. communicative approaches, Seleskovitch's interpretive theory, Reiss and Vermeer's *skopos* theory, and Gutt's application of relevance theory are but more and more refined ways of conceptualising this crucial epistemological leap. All of them have been dialectical stages in the evolution of the concept of what translation should accomplish and the ways to attain it; and all of them have given, if not birth, at least a theoretical foundation to - precisely - different ways of translating. Any serious and qualified translator who has followed this evolution cannot have failed to refine his practice as well. But, as I have pointed out, this progress is still far from permeating general translational practice worldwide: most translators go on without even realising that the texts they are called upon to translate are functionally different; thus an ad, a prescription, a notice, a contract, even a poem get the same literal once-over.

Most of my professional life I have lived in New York, where everything seems to be translated into Spanish. I can aver that the overwhelming majority of the pragmatic translations of any kind I have encountered have ranged from bad to gruesome, not only linguistically, but, above all, conceptually: they are the product of an incompetently carried out *misconceived assessment* of what a translation is or, rather, should be. I know but very few of those translators; yet most of those I do know - some of whom are very good linguists - have somehow or other abandoned or failed at other professions and decided to put their non-specialised linguistic knowledge to remunerative use:[2] their craft has improved haphazardly - if at all - with time. Spanish translations at the UN, for instance, have gotten at best marginally better over the last four decades, while there seems to be no coherent approach among the six language sections as to how to translate any single document (the French section, mindful of their watchful readership, will tend to be *cibliste* and go communicative, while the Spanish, fearfully *sourcière*, usually goes semantic, for example).[3]

Now, advances in translatology, the refinement and specification of the concept of translation itself, its progressive delimitation from neighbouring phenomena such as adaptation have been the result of a deeper understanding of language, discourse, and communication. The descriptive part of translatology, I submit, is mainly in the hands of linguistics, stylistics, poetics, discourse analysis, communication theory, cognitive psychology, neurophysiology, and what not - in short, of all those disciplines that describe for us what communication, and more specifically lingual, and still more specifically mediated interlingual communication is and how it works. On the basis of such evolving description, it is our collective task, insofar as we can, to conceptualise translation and to find, rate and make explicit the means to achieve it.

The time will certainly come when Nida, Seleskovitch, Vermeer, Gutt, and Pym will be names analogous to those of Archimedes, Faraday, and Newton, their theories partially borne out, partially refuted, surely superseded by theories based on a more thorough and deeper knowledge of the world and the mind. Up to a point, it is beginning to happen: *skopos* and relevance have placed dynamic equivalence in a new, more proper context; pretty much as relativity did to universal gravitation. Both have themselves been criticised already: *skopos* by Pym and Gutt, relevance by Tirkkonen-Condit (1992). The main difference between translatology and the more established disciplines is that, exactly as with the beginning of all other sciences, metaphysics and speculation have not as yet taken their rightful place behind scientific observation and experimentation; but that too is very much happening already, particularly with respect to simultaneous interpreting.

Translation has often been described as intelligent reading followed by competent writing; true, but not enough. If it were, any intelligent reader and competent writer who knew his languages could translate professionally. Despite interested and disinterested assertions to the contrary, it is not normally the case, and even when it is, it is not altogether satisfactory. I have known several excellent writers who know their passive languages to the hilt, and whose translations of UN development projects leave a lot to be desired: their linguistic instinct prevents them from excessive awkwardness or outright mistakes, but they never seem really to grasp what translation is all about: their version of a camcorder owner's manual would undoubtedly be better than most, but still too dependent on an original which is, for all practical purposes, irrelevant. The boldness to let go of the original, to deverbalise, to assess the *skopoi* of source- and target-text requires something additional between intelligent reading and competent writing. Translatology is there to provide it.

Let us hypothesise how a translator might have refined his practice as a response to the development of theory: Take as an example precisely the owner's manual of a camcorder to be translated from English into Spanish for the Latin American and Spanish markets. The intuitive, uninitiated translator (one of our beginner students, for instance) would try and produce a literal translation. All he knows is English and Spanish; he has no tools other than his bilingual dictionary. A phrase such as "Press on the lid until it clicks into place"[4] will give him a real headache. At the threshold of translatology proper, our translator can already safely extrapolate Vinay and Dalbernet's (1957) insight into the basic difference in the way French and English go about making sense: English operates on the plane of reality, French (and Spanish) - on that of understanding. Our translator can then understand that, at the sheer linguistic level, a radically different approach is required for rewriting. It is the sudden irruption of sound, of reality, that gives him his pain; but if he chooses to switch to the level of understanding, he could safely write "*oprima la tapa hasta que calce*" ["push the lid until it fits into position"]. He can already think in terms of the linguistic/ stylistic acceptability of the target text. Translation theory has already begun helping our translator map his way between the kind of language equivalences. His translation has become idiomatic. But that is still not quite enough for a successful target-language owner's manual. He must go on reading.

Next, Nida will lead him to think in terms not only of linguistic idiomaticity, but that of cultural acceptability as well. The original goes "Keep an image of your favorite batter in his moment of glory." Our translator has now stopped to ponder the fact that, while baseball is extremely popular in Central America and Cuba, the national game elsewhere in the Spanish-speaking world is football. So he does not hesitate to add a football centre-forward; except that in football it is not so much the player but the goal that matters, so he writes on "*Conserve una imagen de su bateador favorito en su momento de gloria o de ese formidable gol de medio campo*"[5] ["Keep an image of your favourite batter in his moment of glory or of that astonishing goal from mid-field"]. Our colleague has realised two crucial points: one is that he may adapt, even rewrite; the other is that he *must*. He has had his first insight into the true science of translation: translation works not on languages but on texts; texts are not language specimens but communicative intentions linguistically consigned; and in this kind of pragmatic text, target culture acceptability is of the essence. He may share my and many others' doubts about whether the Bible really lends itself to the same approach as a camcorder manual, but he will feel sure a camcorder manual does.

Our hypothetical translator will next have the opportunity of reading Seleskovitch and Lederer. Aware of the distinction between meaning and sense, he starts thinking like the user he is translating for. Sense, as grasped by the reader, is the extra-linguistic product of the connection the reader establishes in his mind between the linguistic meaning of the utterance and what he knows about the world. So shared knowledge of the world between addresser and addressee is crucial for an utterance to be understood by the latter as intended by the former. Our translator sees that the fundamental thing is not so much that the text be idiomatic and culturally acceptable, but that it help its reader use the device. He tries to place himself in the reader' shoes. This allows him to detect better ways of having the sense carried across to a Spanish speaker. He feels free to be more explicit than the original or, more crucially, *less* so. He has also learnt that communication works on the basis of the principle of synecdoche, so he strives to make sense as plainly as possible with no unnecessary repetitions or moronic instructions such as "In order to replace the cassette, open the lid marked cassette on the left side of your HARAKIRI 6000 Super eight hand-held compact enhanced image recorder. After opening the lid, replace the cassette, then close the lid once again (see figure 2 below on this page)." He knowingly and boldly writes "*Para cambiar la cassete, abrir la tapa (figura 2)*" [To replace the cassette open the lid (figure 2)]. He will also have made an additional conscious effort to go beyond searching for the right electronics terminology, and to try to understand how the gadget *works*, so as to make sure his Spanish explanation is accurate - not just linguistically, culturally and commercially, but also practically.

If our translator has access to Russian translatologists such as Schweitzer (1973), he begins to look upon his task not so much as a search for linguistic and other kinds of equivalence, but as the quest for adequacy. Adequacy with respect to the ends pursued, rather than equivalence of the means employed; a point he will be able to round up next in his literature, when he chances upon Reiss and Vermeer, Neubert and Lvovskaja. He now asks himself why the text was written, why it is going to be translated, and for whom. Conscious of the relevant factors to be looked at in the situation, he can be sure that the originator of the translation wants basically one thing: to sell camcorders. Within that global *skopos*, the owner's manual is meant to complement the product. Pleasantly presented, idiomatic, clear and concise instructions are as important as an attractive packaging and a futuristic design. Our ideal colleague will now do away with the baseball batter altogether, mindful that 99% of the camcorders will be sold in Mexico, Venezuela, Colombia, Peru, Argentina and Spain, rather than in Cuba or Panama. The disadvantage of leaving out, as it were, a few owners is more than outweighed by the concision, coherence and familiarity of a monocultural text.

Further in his reading, our translator encounters Gutt's adaptation of relevance theory (1990 and 1991). He sees now the crucial difference between *interpretive* and *descriptive* use. He will have finally corroborated a nagging suspicion that entered his mind the very day he was advised against translating literally: to wit, that the original, in this specific case, is for all practical purposes immaterial. The English manual is but a model, a format, a sequence of text and images whose only constants are, precisely, the images. So his real job is not to come up with a translation as he initially conceived it, as a source-language dependent target-language text - albeit a linguistically, culturally and practically adapted one. Now he realises that his version must be first of all faithful a) to the originator's and the users' economic *skopoi*, and b) to electronic extra-linguistic reality. Gutt will tell him that what he is supposed to produce is not a translation at all, but a parallel text. The original has systematically referred to an "engine." In the last page there is a glossary, where it is explained that "throughout this manual, the term *engine* refers to the camcorder." Our hypothetical colleague stops racking his brain to find a plausible equivalent for "engine," writes "*cámara*" throughout and does away with the imbecilic terminological gimmick, together with the glossary entry. He takes Gutt's point that "the receptor language texts are intended to achieve relevance in their own right, not in virtue of their interpretive resemblance with some source language original" (1991: 57). In principle, then, no formal conformity between source and target text need be expected, function reigns supreme, and practical acceptability in the target culture carries the day.

Pym's analysis of translation as a reaction to transfer (1992a, 1992b) would shed even newer light on the essence of the problem, helping our colleague better understand his task, nay his responsibility as a translator. Before asking why the text is to be translated, a new question springs now up in his mind: Why has this text been transferred to a position where it is going to be translated? He already knows why he blithely well-nigh disregards the original when translating a camcorder owner's manual: the original is hopelessly irrelevant. Nevertheless, our colleague's last effort reproduced at the beginning a dense page blackened with minute writing, where the reader is warned, among other things, that the device's warranty is issued as mandated by article 4.2 of statute 4321(b) of the Laws of the Commonwealth of Massachusetts, but that the provisions of such statute apply only partially in Virginia, are void in Colorado, and become somewhat illegal in Delaware. Does it do any harm if, disregarding his financial reflexes, he follows his translatorial instinct and omits this purely and simply? On the contrary, answers Pym: the status of the reader of the text transferred through time and/or space, whether to be translated or not, can be *participative, observational*, or *excluded*. In the case of the camcorder owner's manual, the "translation" (as, by the way, its original) is meant for participative readers only. All references to source-country institutions, commercial practices, and dealers automatically turn anybody not residing in the US into mere observers, and must be eliminated.

The, say, Colombian reader - unbeknownst to him, and to the originator of the translation, but not any more to our translator - is but going to be confused, misled or simply put off whenever he is excluded from participation. It is *his* device, he bought it and paid good money for it, he does not give a hoot if a special tax applies in Ohio, or if the warranty is not valid in California. He wants a manual that will tell him clearly and concisely how to use his gadget. For him, there is only one manual: his, in Spanish; whether or not it happens to be a translation or an adaptation from another language is absolutely immaterial. He has already bought the device. Not only does he not need to be reminded at every turn that it is a "HARAKIRI 6000 Super eight hand-held compact enhanced image recorder" that he must learn to handle, but - in Spanish at least - this kind of onomastic overkill is irritating and intrusive. (The initiator should also have had it in mind, of course: He has already sold the camcorder. All he really wants now is that his client should be happy and use his toy adeptly. He is not interested in the least in having to abide by his warranty.)

Thus, our translator would have seen himself constantly develop as one leaving most of his colleagues farther and farther behind. He would have dared increase his fees (his translations have become, after all, shorter and shorter). And if he is not yet a translator but a student leaving the university to try and make it as a professional, he would find out in no time that many, perhaps most, of the originals he will be called upon to translate will be pragmatic texts such as this manual. And when confronted with his first real-life translation, he will be already better armed than most veteran self-made colleagues.

In both cases he will be totally aware that the original has, for all practical purposes, no author - only originators and intermediaries. It will be his duty as a true specialist at translating to talk them into accepting his expert view of textual reality and securing from them maximum formal leeway. His chances of succeeding will basically depend on the fact that, besides providing a communicatively competent text (the idiomatic and accurate product of a correctly assessed *skopos*, whereby descriptive use prevails over interpretive use in order to ensure the reader's participative status), he can verbalise the rationale for it, that is explain the *theory* behind it - more or less the way a physician explains to a patient why she should take the prescribed pill and not the one recommended by her aunt. Only when a translator has secured (earned, that is) his client's trust and respect as a specialist at mediated interlingual communication can his professional relationship with him be akin to that between the lawyer, the physician or the architect and theirs. Our translator will realise that, given the indispensable linguistic ability, it is his knowledge of the specifics of translation as a discipline that will give him the edge over equally talented intuitive practitioners.

If only the rest of his competent colleagues had become aware of this, if only they strove collectively to have it understood and accepted by the initiators, if only they dared rewrite and adapt whenever it is called for, if only they did not lag so far behind theory, how much more translators would be recognised as full-fledged professionals ... and how much more money we would all be making!

Notes
1. For a deeper elaboration of the point, see Viaggio (1992a).
2. The French dichotomy is Ladmiral's (1990), the English one Newmark's (1981; 1988).
3. As quoted by Pym (1992b: 187-188), and Gutt (1991: 6-7).
4. All the following examples have been extracted from actual texts.
5. If our translator is, besides, a competent stylist, he will also change the second *su* to *un*.

THE PROCESS-ORIENTED APPROACH IN TRANSLATION TRAINING

Daniel Gile, INALCO & CEEI (ISIT), France

Product-oriented vs. process-oriented training approaches

Traditional translation training is based on translation assignments which are corrected in class, with teachers criticizing or approving the students' choices and presenting their own solutions. Although the method is operational, it is less than optimal on two points:

- It focuses on the product rather than on the processes, which means that inferences for the correct processes are to a large extent made by the students themselves, with little possibility of control by the teachers. This is one reason why many authors (such as Delisle 1981; Komissarov 1985; Gentile 1991; Larose 1992; Shlesinger 1992a) have advocated the use of theory in training. It is, however, difficult to integrate theory into practice in a product-oriented approach, the more so since many practitioners, including teachers, strongly oppose theory (as noted by for instance Gémar 1983; Komissarov 1985; Pöchhacker 1992a; Sager 1992; Viaggio 1992c).

- Very often, students reject the teacher's criticism and solutions because of diverging linguistic norms and because they feel attacked. This slows down the learning process.

If teachers focus on the process, they can be less critical of the product and, to a large extent, avoid such problems.

On the other hand, a process-oriented approach also has potential limitations:

- Because its focus is on the process, it may not be a powerful tool for product fine-tuning.

- In order to be able to operate on the processes, teachers need to learn or develop explicit process rules, and they are sometimes reluctant to do so.

- In order to use the rules efficiently, teachers need to be able to convince the students that they are correct. This again requires theoretical preparation. It is very difficult to come up with explicit rules that are simple enough to learn (in a practical, professional course, theory should not take up too much time and energy), and yet cover all the difficulties students may encounter.

Process-oriented training has been advocated by several teachers in recent years (Martins 1992) and is becoming increasingly popular with translation teachers, as will also appear from several articles in this volume. It has been practiced in several forms, including a series of exercises developed by Delisle (1980). This paper introduces the process-oriented training methodology developed at the Department of Japanese and Korean Studies of the Institut National des Langues et Civilisations Orientales (INALCO) in Paris. It has also been used in other contexts, including workshops for experienced translators.

A process-oriented translation training system

The basic philosophy of the system can be summed up as follows:
- During the process-oriented part of the course, trainees are considered as students of translation methods rather than as producers of finished products. Throughout this period, their target language texts essentially serve as a looking glass revealing their methods, insofar as their problems are generally symptoms of methodological weaknesses. Problems which can be attributed to linguistic deficiencies are not dealt with during the process-oriented phase of the course.
- Teachers take a normative attitude as far as the processes are concerned. As regards the product, they put questions to the students whenever possible rather than criticise them ("Why this choice?" "Did you consider alternatives?" "If so, what made you choose this solution?" "Are you satisfied with this solution as far as logic/clarity/language is concerned?").
- Processes are supported by theoretical models which explain and integrate them. The most important one is the sequential model of translation, discussed below (See also Gile 1992b).
- Problem diagnosis can be done partly by analyzing the product and partly by putting questions to the students as explained above. Written problem reports by the students are a very useful tool for diagnosis: When handing in translation assignments, students are also required to report in writing the problems they encountered while doing the translation - difficulties in understanding a particular sentence, in reformulating an idea, in finding the meaning of a source language term, in finding a good target language equivalent, etc.

The sequential model of translation and error analysis

The model is shown on the opposite page. It was developed for pedagogical purposes. It is not intended to be a full or accurate description of the translation process, but as a framework beginners can use in order to optimize their production and avoid the most common errors.

The model consists of a 'comprehension phase' and a 'reformulation phase'. Translation starts with a 'translation unit' (which is not to be understood in a strictly scientific sense, but as an intuitive entity consisting of a word or small group of words that translators deal with at the micro-textual level - in our experience the intuitive nature of the definition has not caused problems for trainees). It is read. Its meaning is inferred from the text as a meaning hypothesis. This hypothesis is then checked for plausibility on the basis of the translator's existing linguistic and extra-linguistic knowledge. If the first meaning hypothesis is deemed plausible, the translator can move to the reformulation phase. If not,

Figure 1. *The sequential model of translation.*

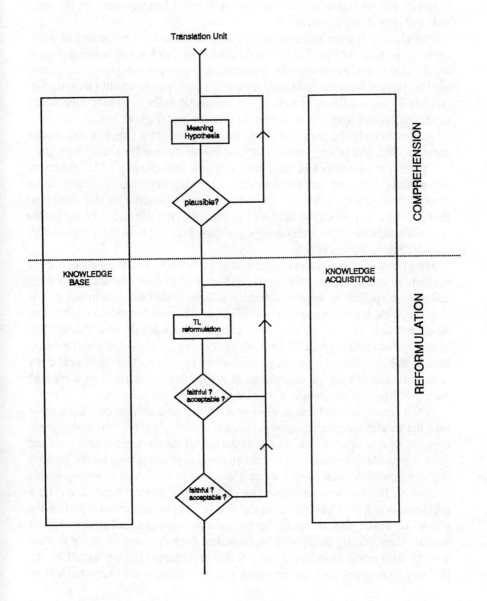

110 Teaching Translation and Interpreting 2

the translator must find another hypothesis and check its plausibility, etc.

In the reformulation phase, the translator formulates a first target language text for the translation unit. He then tests it for fidelity and for linguistic acceptability. If results are not satisfactory, he writes a new target language text for the same unit and tests it again, and so on.

Periodically, fidelity and acceptability tests are conducted for groups of translation units, as good results at the single translation unit level do not ensure good results at the text level: sentence segments, full sentences and even paragraphs may be skipped between individual translation units just as repetitions and other stylistic incompatibilities as well as terminological drifts (a lack of consistency in terminological usage) may emerge in a larger text segment.

At every step of the process, existing linguistic and extra-linguistic knowledge must be used, and whenever necessary, additional knowledge must be sought.

One of the advantages of the model is that it conveniently labels necessary components of correct translation work ('comprehension phase', 'reformulation phase', 'comprehension loop', 'reformulation loop', 'plausibility test', etc), and thus provides an easy way of indicating to students, both linguistically and graphically, the location of the methodological weaknesses that have led to most errors and infelicities (Gile 1992a).

For instance, a grammatical error most often indicates that the student did not perform an acceptability test properly. Bad spelling in one occurrence of a word and correct spelling in another definitely indicates that the problem lies in this test. When the student's translation is illogical, it is probably due to the fact that he did not do a 'plausibility test' in the 'comprehension phase', or a 'fidelity test' in the 'reformulation phase'. Terminological errors can almost always be traced back to an ill-conducted 'knowledge acquisition' operation. Terminological drifts (a lack of consistency in terminological usage) can be ascribed to a missing 'acceptability test' on groups of translation units.

When finding a problematic word or statement in a translation, the teacher asks the student whether this solution sounds logical, plausible, linguistically acceptable, and consistent with the rest of the text. If the student thinks it does and gives a plausible explanation, the teacher can accept the answer on the grounds that the procedure was correct, even if the student's solution is wrong by his standards. The teacher can also make a mental (or written) note of recurrent problems which will have to be dealt with in the product-oriented part of the course. However, students usually answer spontaneously that the segments are not logical, linguistically acceptable or consistent with the rest of the text, thus making their own diagnosis of their faulty procedures. Having identified the problem themselves, they are presumably more willing to take remedial action.

Implementation and results

We started introducing the process-oriented approach in our scientific and technical Japanese-into-French translation classes at INALCO about 10 years ago. For that purpose we developed a set of basic concepts and models (Gile 1990a; 1992b). Over this period we have made the following observations:

1. Psychologically, the process-oriented approach seems to generate less stress than the product-oriented approach.

2. Students are interested in the models and rules that are presented to them, and tend to accept them.

3. There are difficulties with problem-reporting, which the students tend to forget during the first few assignments because it is new to them. However, once they become accustomed to the idea, problem-reporting becomes a very efficient tool. Not only does it help the teacher with error diagnosis, but it also requires that the students carry out a methodological analysis and reflect upon fundamental questions, which makes them more receptive to instruction on issues such as: "To what extent is it admissible to deviate from the text?", "What is the reliability of background documents if their terminology is variable?", "How should one deal with source text segments which seem illogical even after much analysis?"

We consider problem-reporting a strong component of the process-oriented approach.

4. There is a fast and considerable reduction in the number of errors due to faulty analysis of the source text and there were remarkably few logical contradictions in the students' texts.

In our view, this is the most positive result of the process-oriented approach.

5. However, as far as difficult decisions are concerned, the process-oriented approach seems to be of little help to the students.

This is probably due to the fact that rules presented to the students are too general to be used for specific decisions where intuition and experience play an important role. We do have a number of models, rules and methods for areas which are not covered by the sequential model, but, inevitably, there are some problems which they do not address adequately.

6. The process-oriented approach does not seem to improve the students' implementation of additional knowledge acquisition.

The problem apparently lies in motivation. Although they know that additional information is needed, students do not perform the necessary operation thoroughly enough, probably because of the time and effort required.

7. The process-oriented approach is moderately efficient with respect to the linguistic quality of the output.

There are three reasons for this:

a. In the process-oriented approach, the teacher only questions the students' norms, without the rectification which is found in a product-oriented approach.

b. For lack of sufficiently strong motivation, even when they are aware that the linguistic quality of their target text leaves something to be desired, students tend to go through the 'reformulation loop' (writing a target language version of the translation unit, then testing it, then correcting it, testing it again, etc.) a few times and then stop, even if the result is not satisfactory.

c. Testing for acceptability does not necessarily prevent a text from being unacceptable. Distinct text writing tactics need to be taught for this purpose.

The process-oriented approach described here therefore only helps students do away with *some* of the linguistic weaknesses of their initial output.

Conclusion

The process-oriented approach has been very popular with students. It was especially appreciated by self-taught practising translators who attended the course or workshop after several years of professional experience. It does seem rather powerful as a methodological guiding approach in that it strongly and rapidly reduces product deficiencies attributable to incorrect translation methodology. However, it is definitely not a sufficient teaching tool for students whose motivation is weak and for those whose linguistic norms in the target language are poor, insofar as it does not teach how to write. Similarly, it does not provide solutions for specific, difficult cases. We therefore feel that the approach is very useful in the first part of a course, but that product-oriented teaching must follow.

We strongly recommend the process-oriented approach in two specific cases:

1. Courses for experienced translators, who want to improve their methods rather than acquire basic expertise, which they already have. Such translators are also particularly sensitive to product criticism. Therefore, a process-oriented approach is more appropriate for them than a product-oriented approach.

2. Courses involving source or target languages that the teacher does not know. This occurs in various international cooperation programmes. In such cases, the teacher is not in a position to inspect the product as such, but may provide useful guidance through process-oriented methods.

COMPREHENSION IN THE TRANSLATION PROCESS: AN ANALYSIS OF THINK-ALOUD PROTOCOLS

Jeanne Dancette, Université de Montréal, Canada

To understand a text is to actualize links that may or must be established between given elements in the textual structure and other elements pertaining to intertextual and extratextual information. It is to build a meaningful and coherent representation of the text. Such a representation does not operate at the semantic level only but more at the "level at which linguistic and non-linguistic information are mutually compatible" (Jackendoff 1985: 95), that is at the conceptual level.

Paradoxically, translation - which is a linguistic operation concerned with semantics as well as syntax and morphology in their relation to semantics and to the rules of well-formedness of both the source and target texts - cannot occur successfully without this meaningful and coherent conceptual construction.

This broad assumption, however, needs to be qualified:

a) Successful translation *can* occur to a certain extent without an elaborate conceptual construction, that is with a limited understanding. This could correspond to what Cunningham (1985: 235) calls "literal comprehension" as opposed to "inferential comprehension" and "creative response", which he sees as higher levels of comprehension. In the few occasional instances of isomorphy between languages, literal translation and even sometimes mere transcoding are possible. In such cases, literal comprehension is enough.

b) Conceptual construction as a cognitive process does not guarantee successful translation, for the main reason that the conceptual links made by the translator may be wrong, albeit coherent.

We are concerned here with the notion of referring. If reference is defined as a "relationship between expressions in a language and things in the real world that these expressions refer to" (Jackendoff 1985: 29), then we are dealing with the interaction between linguistic performance (decoding linguistic structures, identifying their grammatical class and meaning) and cognitive conceptualization (relating the meaning of these structures to a "text-world model", to use de

Beaugrande's terminology (1980: 77). I will show that in the event of a comprehension difficulty, a reader (translator) must be looking at the right paradigm in order to succeed. In other terms, his decoding of a given structure is dependent on his expectation (however rudimentary) of a hypothetical tentative text-world representation.

The experiment

To illustrate this, I will present some preliminary results of an empirical study using videotaped think-aloud protocols with a group of five translation students.

The students who volunteered for the study were chosen on a random basis; two had two or three years professional experience, the others had hardly any experience at all; they were given five segments of text from news magazines; they received the entire article but were told to translate only one or two sentences in each article. The simulated pragmatic situation was that a French editor wanted to publish the translation of the article. He noticed that a segment had been omitted and asked the student to translate the missing passage.

The students were given four dictionaries: the *Webster's New Collegiate Dictionary*, the English-French *Robert-Collins*, the *Petit Robert* and the *Sylvain*, an English-French dictionary of accountancy and related sciences. These dictionaries are the usual tools of translators in their normal work and were considered to be sufficient for the task.

After a short briefing on the think-aloud method, the students were asked to verbalize their thinking; they were recorded and video-taped. After the translation, they were given a questionnaire, the purpose of which was to establish more precisely whether they knew the meaning of a few key words or concepts used in the text. No time limit was set; they performed their task in one and a half to two and a half hours.

All the texts presented problems that we assessed as average for professional translators, but rather difficult for students of translation. I will present parts of the protocols dealing with one such text.

A LEADING INDICATOR THAT'S LEADING IN THE RIGHT DIRECTION
Is business activity starting to stir? Chief Economist Irwin L. Kellner of Chemical Bank notes that the Commodity Research Bureau's spot industrial-price index recently hit its highest level in over a year and is more than 10% above its early February low. *Although a lead strike in Peru helped push the index higher, Kellner notes that 10 of its 13* **components** *have posted* **gains** *since February.* "At the very least, the rise in the index suggests that the economy is still expanding," says Kellner, "and it may just be the first sign of an acceleration in economic growth. (*Business Week* October 5, 1992)

The students had to translate the passage in italics; the words in bold ("leads", "components", "gains") indicate where errors were made:

Lead: Three students missed the unit altogether, which at first sight is surprising considering that they had dictionaries; a fourth student translated by "production" (grève de production) after a twisted, fallacious reasoning discussed below.

Components was mistranslated by "facteurs" in one case and by "usines" ['factories'] in another.

Gains (in *posted gains*). Two students translated this word by "profits" or "bénéfices", thus shifting from the semantic field authorized by the text to another unauthorized one. The student who chose "usines" for *components* chose "bénéfices" for *gains*, which is at least coherent.

The passage also contained notional difficulties, that is difficulties depending on 'encyclopedia-type' knowledge in a given field, namely economics.

LEAD STRIKE.- If one knows that spot prices mainly concern raw materials, then it can be inferred that *lead* [led] belongs to the class of commodities or raw materials, and does not refer to *lead* [li:d] as is mischievously suggested by the title. Graph 1 identifies this link as an implication; it occurs at the pragmatic level.

Graph 1

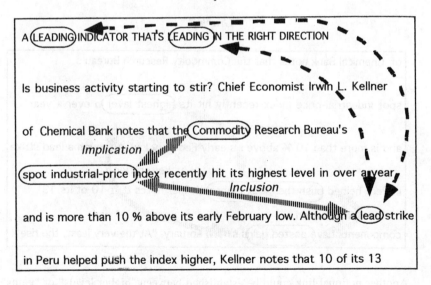

INDEX refers linguistically to "spot industrial price index" and to "components", since an 'index' by definition involves averaging components. Graph 2 indicates a co-referential link occuring at the linguistic level.

Graph 2

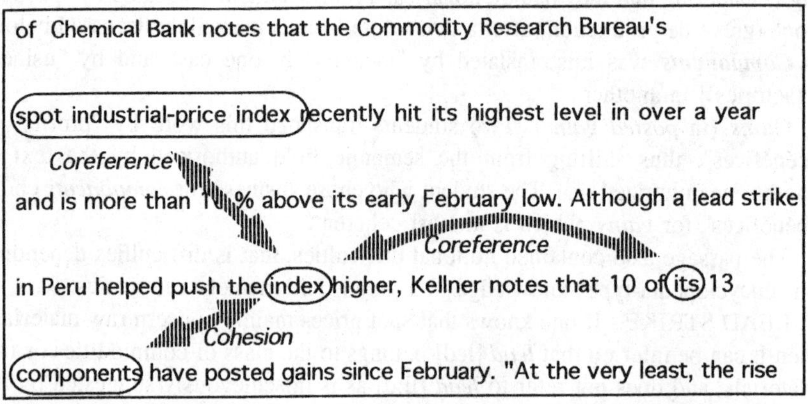

of Chemical Bank notes that the Commodity Research Bureau's

spot industrial-price index recently hit its highest level in over a year

Coreference

and is more than 10 % above its early February low. Although a lead strike

Coreference

in Peru helped push the index higher, Kellner notes that 10 of its 13

Cohesion

components have posted gains since February. "At the very least, the rise

GAINS in the phrase "posted gains" is the repetition of the topic; as shown in Graph 3, it relates to "highest level" and "push the index higher". I term this link 'thematic reiteration'.

Graph 3

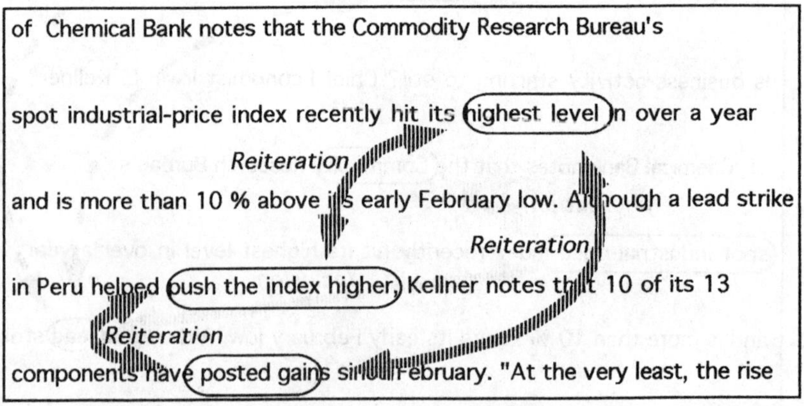

of Chemical Bank notes that the Commodity Research Bureau's

spot industrial-price index recently hit its highest level in over a year

Reiteration

and is more than 10 % above its early February low. Although a lead strike

Reiteration

in Peru helped push the index higher, Kellner notes that 10 of its 13

Reiteration

components have posted gains since February. "At the very least, the rise

Another notional link could be established between "higher levels" or "gains" in the "industrial price index" and the "expanding economy". However, this link was not crucial for the translation.

Let us now turn to the students' approach to these lexical and notional difficulties. The analysis of their protocols and the answers to the questionnaire made it possible to trace lexical errors back to conceptual or notional shortcomings.

Translator A: translation and protocol

Bien qu'une grève au Pérou ait fait monter l'index encore plus haut, Kellner fait remarquer que 10 de ses 13 composantes ont affiché une progression certaine depuis février.

Bien qu'une partie de la progression de l'index soit due à

Bien que la progression de l'index soit en partie explicable par une grève que le Pérou a recemment connue, Kellner fait remarquer souligne que dix des treize composantes de cet index ont affiché une progression certaine depuis février.

Except for the rendering of *lead* and *index*, this translation is good both for its lexical and phraseological precision and for its rhetorical structure. This student is the only one who paid attention to the internal argumentation signalled by *although*, as can be demonstrated by the progression from a literal translation: *bien qu'une grève au Pérou...* [**crossed out**] to a more elaborate one: *bien que la progression de l'index soit due* [**crossed out**] *soit en partie* [**added**] *explicable par une grève...*

I submit that with the omission of *lead*, it was impossible for the student in question to build the conceptual connectivity of the passage; lacking a complete and correct conceptual representation of the text, he could not "catch on" to *lead*. The protocol ran as follows:

1   [**Reads**] OK, alors lire le texte ... aussi je vais lire ce qui est avant, le petit paragraphe,
2   histoire de comprendre; ... alors c'est l'index des prix industriels... [**Reads**] OK, although a
3   [li:d] strike in Peru ... helped push the index higher ... 10 of its 13 components ...
4   components de quoi? de l'index! [**Reads**] ... posted gains since February ... hum, [li:d] strike
5   ou [led]? ... [**Takes** *Webster*] ... bon, y a rien, y a pas [li:d] strike dans le dictionnaire, on
6   va regarder le bilingue ... [**Takes** *Collins*] ... [li:d] strike ... [**Reads**] ... strike, strike, à strike
7   y a rien ... [li:d] ou [led]? non, rien à strike ... on va le traduire littéralement parce que ...
8   grève au Pérou ... a fait monter l'index encore plus haut ... Kellner note que ... fait
9   remarquer que ... nous a ... non, fait remarquer que 10 de ses 13 composantes ... de l'index
10   ... ont affiché une progression certaine, nette, depuis février ... Ça veut dire quelque chose
11   ça? [**Reads**] non! l'index, c'est l'index de quoi, en fait? des prix ... qui est monté ... ah, OK!
12   qui est monté par rapport au minimum qu'on avait connu en février ... une grève au Pérou
13   a fait monter l'index encore plus haut ... OK ... bien qu'une partie de la progression de
14   l'index soit due explicable ... bien qu'on puisse expliquer ... bien que la progression de
15   l'index soit en partie explicable par une grève ... [li:d] strike ... par une grève ... y a quelque
16   chose là-dedans ... [**Takes** *Sylvain*] pff, y a rien du tout dans ce truc-là! [li:d] strike ... ça
17   veut dire du plomb quand même! [li:d] strike ou [led] strike?

It is easily seen that in line 2 the student situates the theme *industrial price index* leaving out *spot*. In lines 10-11 he notices that it does not make sense. So he re-calls *price* index (line 11) and is temporarily satisfied with his self-explanation, then he goes on translating and returns to *lead strike* (lines 16-17) and right until the end he knows that he missed out something important. He spent 7 minutes out of 15 on *lead*.

There is one link he did not make: the link with COMMODITY or SPOT PRICE (see Graph 1), which was necessary to understand that *lead* is included as a specific of the generic *commodity* and, as such, *lead* is a component of the spot industrial price index. We can see (line 13) that he knows the meaning of *lead*, but rejects this reference. From his questionnaire, it turned out that he knew what an 'index' is in economics and also that *lead* is an important export article in Peru. Moreover, he was well-versed in economics (as an MBA) and was an experienced translator. Why did he fail?

Wrong paradigm

Misled by the title of the article, he was looking for an adjective modifying *strike*, such as *general strike* or *wildcat strike*. I believe he was looking into the wrong paradigm, because he could not use his thematic knowledge to the best; he had no clear notion of *commodity* (he thought of consumer goods instead of raw materials) and he did not know the meaning of *spot* (which he admitted afterwards). So, we have an illustration of the impossibility of deciphering the meaning of a text segment properly: our translator's syntactic decoding (modifier vs. complement) is hampered by the shortcomings of his text-world representation; he had the wrong expectation about the grammatical slot of the word he is looking for. His semantic representation of the text was too rudimentary to allow him to accept the correct connection when he made it in line 13 ["*lead*, it cannot be *plomb*"].

Translator B: translation and protocol

Bien qu'une grève de production au Pérou ait contribué à augmenter l'indice, Kellner constate que 10 des 13 constituants ont inscrit des gains depuis le mois de février.

This protocol shows a different pattern - a very sketchy text-world representation - and illustrates how a good linguistic intuition can abort because of a poor use of dictionaries.

1   [**Reads**] Although a lead [li:d] strike in Peru helped push the index higher, Kellner notes
2   that 10 of its 13 components have posted gains since February. Eh! que c'est compliqué!
3   lead [li:d] strike in ... des grèves de ... [**Takes** *Sylvain*] index, l'indice, c'est ça index, indice
4   ... indice c'est ça; a lead [li:d] strike: lead, délai. OK, une grève de production, bien que des
5   grèves de production aient aidé à hausser l'indice aient contribué à faire augmenter ... à
6   augmenter l'indice, Kellner constate que [**Reads**] components ... have posted gains ...
7   [**Takes** *Collins*] posted gains ... mmm ... que ses composants, que ses constituants [**Takes**
8   *Sylvain*] component [**Takes** *Collins*] component: composant, constituant ... ça veut dire que
9   10 de ses 13 ... [**Takes** *Collins*] post ... ont inscrit des gains ... Kellner constate que 10 des
10 13 constituants ... qu'est-ce que je vais dire pour posted gains ... [**Takes** *Collins*] j'ai

11   l'impression de perdre la mémoire ... inscrire des gains ... inscrit des gains depuis février,
12   le mois de février.

Coming across *lead strike* (line 3), the student says: "strike in -, grève de -" (as in *grève des postes, du charbon*). She expects to find the sector affected by the strike. So far so good. She identifies the locus of the gap properly. She just needs to look up in the dictionary under *lead* as a substantive. But she opens the dictionary of accounting and accidentally finds *lead time* with the translation equivalence *délai de production*. So she analyses as follows: The dictionary says *lead time* equals *délai de production*, and I know that *time* means "délai", then *lead* [li:d] means "production"; so I can infer that *lead strike* means "grève de production".

She was satisfied with this and felt no need to make more elaborate conceptual links since the phrase *grève de production* fits. (It took her 12 seconds for that decision; and she performed the task in five minutes and 30 seconds) Because she translated the words, she believed that she understood it, which is not the case. Her protocol shows that she established conceptual connections neither with *spot industrial price index,* nor with *commodity.* Her entire reasoning occurred within the scope of the segment to translate, and for that task, which was her only concern, she relied heavily on dictionaries which she opened 7 times, looking up *index, lead, gains, post, component.* Before commenting on that attitude, I will present the third example and contrast the two.

Translator C: translation and protocol

Bien qu'une grève dans le secteur du plomb au Pérou ait contribué à la hausse de l'indice, Kellner observe que 10 des 13 composants ont enregistré des profits depuis le mois de février.

1   [**Reads**] lead, qu'est-ce que c'est? ah! plomb ... posted gains, afficher; il y en a qui prennent
2   leurs désirs pour des réalités ... Bien qu'une grève dans le secteur du plomb ... c'est bien,
3   oui! au Pérou ait contribué ... aïe aïe aïe, de temps en temps j'ai des problêmes ... [**Takes**
4   *Collins*] qu'est-ce que je regarde? [Index] ah oui! c'est bien ce qui me semblait ... ait ...
5   pushed the index higher ... comment on dit ... ait contribué à la hausse de l'indice, Kellner
6   observe que 10 des 13 ... composants ... composantes ... have posted gains ... ont affiché?
7   non, ont enregistré des gains ... de quoi? qu'est-ce que c'est que cet index ... Commodity
8   Research ... the industrial-price index ... indice des prix industriels ont affiché des profits...
9   probablement dans le secteur de ... des profits depuis le mois de février ... next!

This student is the only one who found "plomb" right away for *lead*. She runs through the text (5 minutes in total) and translates with ease till she encounters the word *gains*. Here, in lines 7-8, she establishes a connected network between *index, commodity research bureau* and *industrial-price index*. However, as can be judged from her answer on the questionnaire asking for the definition of 'index', she only has a vague idea of how an index works. So she builds a new text-world representation, coherent but different from the text. Her reasoning seems to go as follows: if the industrial prices are higher, then corporations can make more profits; and she switches from the idea of larger profits for corporations to higher profits for the components. Her text-world representation is at the level of the enterprise, not at the level of the raw materials whose price index is an indicator of economic trends. So, she is in the wrong paradigm, in microeconomics rather than macroeconomics.

Cognitive mapping vs linguistic constructivism
The last student's reasoning provides an example of 'mapping': she maps the sentence onto a model of reality she is familiar with. Conversely the previous student constructed a semantic representation using the form of the linguistic input. So this is a case of cognitive mapping versus linguistic constructivism, as discussed in McGonicle (1986: 143-146).

Concluding remarks
I have used these three students to discuss how semantics intersects with conceptual representation; however, I remain perfectly aware that the validity of any experimental study is limited to the scope of the experiment. I am presenting preliminary results of a pilot experiment that will be further analyzed, expanded and replicated.

Also, when dealing with protocols, it is necessary to be aware of the fact that protocols, even when they are combined with questionnaires and interviews, are only a posteriori and clumsy and possibly false justifications for a performance. So experiments of this type cannot be used to verify hypotheses. They can however produce valuable data on what blocks and hampers the comprehension process, and thus may contribute to a theory of natural languages processing as well as improved teaching methods.

In that regard, translation that encompasses the multi-sentence contexts of discourse and verbal reasoning is particularly suitable for this kind of open-ended experimenting. It shows that text comprehension is more than the interpretation of isolated words and even sentences. Any study of discourse comprehension must account for processes whereby language calls forth appropriate knowledge, and processes whereby wording and grammatical construction alter this interpretation.

Note
1. We want to thank our research assistant Stephen Dupont for gathering the experimental data and the Social Science in the Humanities Research Council of Canada for funding this research.

SYSTEMATIC FEEDBACK IN TEACHING TRANSLATION

Cay Dollerup, University of Copenhagen, Denmark

Translation classes and foreign language teaching

This article presents some methods and ways for systematically tackling a problem in translation teaching which is usually disregarded in the genteel society of translation studies, namely the existence of a large interface, an overlapping area, between foreign language learning and translation. As noted by Gideon Toury "translation abounds in manifestations of interlanguage" (1979: 224). It is therefore no surprise that teachers are confronted with large numbers of foreign language errors in translation classes, notably in the beginning. If the existence of this overlapping is openly acknowledged, it follows that translation classes must strive to minimise this interface between foreign language teaching and translation, and to shorten it in order to focus on translation as such. It is true that the specific problems are not identical between all - or for that matter any two - language pairs, but the general problem is there.

The Danish background

The feedback system I am going to discuss has been developed for Danish university students of English in their first three years at university.

Students of English have chosen English of their own volition. Translation is, however, mandatory, which means that classes will include students who consider translation a waste of time as well as those who find it fun, and any of whom may later come to work professionally with translation. In terms of language proficiency, Danish undergraduates are good by international standards: they have been taught English in school for at least eight years, and in addition, Danish society is functionally bilingual in many respects thanks to a barrage of English language material on television, radio, in entertainment, foreign trade, and tourism.

Translation has always been an important part of foreign language study programmes in Denmark, for, in some measure or other, university graduates were always expected to be able to translate. Yet the role of 'translation' is not well-defined: formerly most graduates would become college ('gymnasium') teachers, and to this day much 'translation' at college level is synonymous with grammar drills, a practice copied from the teaching of the classical languages. On the other hand, university graduates would also become editors, authors, scholars and professional translators, and they, too, would have acquired their first schooling in translation at university. The content in translation classes was always practical work, but the ideology would differ according to the teacher's attitude. And today, with more emphasis on theoretical approaches to translation, there are enormous differences in teacher views on the objectives of translation classes.

The persistence of the grammar drill attitude can, in no small measure, be attributed to the fact that English and Danish are closely related Indo-European languages which have basic syntactical and grammatical points in common. They also share numerous words both from Indo-European origin (such as 'arm', 'house'/'hus') and from Danish introduced by Danish settlers in England in the 8th to the 11th centuries (e.g. 'live', 'sky', 'egg', 'they'). These linguistic facts affect translation as well as views on translation: in many cases an interlinear translation between Danish and English will make sense, although the actual wording may jar.

Translation classes must, in my opinion, first and foremost come to grips with typical 'interlanguage errors' in the Danish-English language opposition; this must be done to further the main objective, namely to emphasise translation as translation proper. Thanks to the proximity of the language pair, translation can be based on careful textual study and a high degree of linguistic approximation between source and target-language expressions. In translation classes for beginners, I include tasks that illustrate fundamental translation problems and which often lead to class discussion of major questions in translation studies. But, by and large, the class format does not allow for taking up all general problems in translation theory in a systematic way. This must be done in more advanced classes and in other ways.

Classes may comprise more than forty students. Classes as large as this are found nowhere else in the Danish educational system.

These sketchy comments serve to illustrate that my feedback is largely made up to ensure teacher survival, a modicum of individualised feedback and an open class discussion of points of communal interest. In some respect or other, all Danish teachers develop their own way of surviving.

Some views behind the feedback system
In various ways, the system I am about to describe is affected by my view that translation is a social activity, primarily as communication, but also in a larger social context.

Communication, translation, especially between closely related languages, must be a close semantic approximation to the source text, or, to put it in traditional terms: it must have a high degree of fidelity. This view involves a taxonomy of

translation as communication which covers the spectrum:
(a) an excellent translation,
(b) the minor inaccuracy where the original meaning is preserved in the target language,
(c) a distortion, but no more so than the meaning of the original can be grasped,
(d) an incomprehensible rendering. It may confuse, but will rarely lead astray,
(e) a self-contradictory rendering which is misunderstood,
(f) a rendering which reads fluently and makes perfect sense in the source language but distorts the meaning of the original. (Dollerup, 1982)

Most freshman students's translations are easily bracketed as (b) to (d)s, that is, as muddled and confused renditions, which are either understandable to the (imaginary) target audience (b-c), or at the very least by the teacher (d).

Type f is the gravest error which can be committed in translation. However, it is doubtful whether it can be stamped out. The best one can do is presumably to call attention to it in classroom settings and hope to make students better at avoiding it in professional work.

Even within these categories, there are variations in importance: a distortion involving only a word will usually (but not invariably) be less serious than the one affecting a sentence, and so on. Here, by way of illustration, are two examples of distortion (category f), from my classes:

EXAMPLE 1:
Source text: Da ægteparret fik tømt skabene *for* en masse ragelse, fandt de obligationer for 150.000.
Target text: When the married couple had emptied the cupboards *for* a lot of junk, they found bonds worth 150,000.

In this case the distortion is caused by a 'false friend' (*'for'*) in the rendition of the preposition: in Danish the couple emptied the cupboards *of* the junk. In English they were remunerated *with* the junk. On the other hand, the erroneous rendition only affects this one segment linguistically; in terms of content, the error is subordinate in the context where the most pertinent point, identical in the two languages, is that the couple acquired some valuable bonds.

In another example we get a speciously correct translation in Danish of the English original.

EXAMPLE 2:
Source text: Dublin's modern progenitors were "Black Tom" Wentworth, Earl of Stafford, a Yorkshireman, and James Butler, 2nd Earl of Ormond, an Anglo-Irish Protestant.
One Danish rendering goes: Det moderne Dublins fædre var Sorte Tom Wentworth, Jarlen af Stafford, en mand fra Yorkshire, og James Butler, Den anden Jarl af Ormond, samt en engelsk-irsk protestant.

This fluent rendering has, however, transformed *two* persons in English into *six* in Danish. As this is the only information we have about the founding fathers of modern Dublin, this distortion carries more weight than the previous one.

There is one further aspect which must be taken into account in an assessment of translations. In a strict sense, all errors in translation violate the trust of senders and addressees. The continuum outlined above takes into account the gravity and implications of these violations, but it disregards the social dimension, for the immediate social implications of translation errors are different.

I believe that in real life most errors in the bottom category (f) are not detected. Conversely, there are severe social reprisals for one particular subgroup of errors in the second type (b), namely minor distortions which are fully understandable. Errors in this category divide easily into two types: one type of errors is not obvious to most non-natives (and perhaps many natives), such as unidiomatic collocations and clumsy phrases, whereas the other subgroup, namely formal errors, are spotted by every person with even the most superficial knowledge of the target language. Misspellings and syntactical errors typically lead to the immediate loss of respect for the translator with both senders and addressees. These latter subgroups may, of course, sometimes be identical with interlanguage errors: with Danes, for instance, errors in concord in English are 'interlanguage errors' because Danish has no distinction between the verb forms of the third person singular and other persons.

Errors of this type belong to the social dimension of translation: they have little to do with textual proximity and semantic fidelity. Yet this societal parameter is so important that it, too, must be taken into account when student performance is assessed and it must be included in any feedback in translation teaching.

The physical framework

In my translation classes for beginners, students receive a booklet at the beginning of term. The booklet contains a series of instructions, general advice,[1] a page of the notations which will be used, that is signs, symbols and abbreviations used for correction, a copy of the feedback sheet, and all texts to be translated. All texts are authentic and unedited texts, selected because they present real-life translation problems. They are considerably more difficult than the texts given at the finals. Most of them have been used previously in classes. The first texts are very short, down to fifty words and they tend to be non-fiction. Gradually they become longer - up to seven hundred words - and as we advance there will be more literary texts. The average length is 300-350 words. Translation work goes both ways, from Danish into English and from English into Danish. The Danish-English directionality is dictated by the real-life fact that most English translations from Danish are made by Danes as Danish is not known by many foreigners. The translation into Danish is based on the implicit understanding that graduates must also master Danish.

The first major problem in class is that undergraduates will know 'translation' from the 'gymnasium' (which corresponds to Die Oberstufe, the lycée, the two first years at American Universities). It means that students have got the impression that translation is a kind of disguised grammar drill, and, accordingly, that the main point is to figure out where the teacher set the traps - one, two or three - depending on the length of the sentence. This implies that the rest of the translation of the source text - usually phrased in immaculate Danish - is to be a word-by-word rendering. For this reason the first texts I use in classes are very short to make students realise that this procedure does not work in real translation.

The feedback

The feedback is given in class and consists of three components, namely corrections in the translations which the students have handed in (shown on page 126); an oral discussion in class covering adequate as well as inadequate renditions (directed by a 'model', page 127); and a feedback form assessing strengths and weaknesses with each student (page 128).

The feedback in the translation

The first type of feedback is found in the student's own translation. It is returned individually to students at the beginning of the session, with the correction signs and symbols listed and explained in the booklet.

The point of departure is the student suggestions in the target language. This means that the primary yardstick is the general linguistic competence of individual students as evidenced in that particular translation; in other words, the stick is held higher with good students than with poor ones.

In the same vein, teacher solutions suggested retain as much of the students' phrasing as possible in order to allow for a translation adapted to each student's personality, rather than the best way out. Incidentally, I rarely suggest alternatives, or mention why a given solution is bad, unless the student's problem will not be discussed in the class session at all, because it falls outside any pattern which we have time to discuss.

Two student translations - shown on the next page - will serve to illustrate this correctional part of the feedback system, although they will not allow of a detailed discussion of the teacher responses.

With their corrected translations in hand, students gain a general idea of which solutions were brilliant, which were acceptable, and of any specific objetions on

Two student translations with correction marks

The most remarkable thing about the church of Vestervig
is the size. It appears enormous in the landscape. It is
the second largest Jut(landic) ashlar church. Only the
cathedral in Viborg is larger. As a result of a necessary
repair about 1920, it may appear glossy, but it is definit-
ly (is) one of the most important monuments of the Middle Ages.
It is well worth a visit. Everything is influenced by
tourist in cars : a fine parking ground is placed just
across the church.

The thing you notice the most about Vestervig Church is its size.
It looks hugely in the landscape and after Viborg Cathedral it
is in fact the largest church built out of ashlar altogether. It
may seem a bit finicky- a result of a by the way much needed
renovation from around 1920, but it definitely belongs with our
most important monuments from the Middle Ages and it is worth a
visit. They have planned everything for driving tourists as well-
a supercool parking lot right across from the church.

Excerpt of model translation

Danish source text: Det mest påfaldende
Adequate solutions: What is most remarkable
                          The most remarkable   *feature   about*
                                      striking
Inadequate solutions: · **no prop-word**

Danish: ved Vestervig Kirke er størrelsen.   Den syner kolossalt i
Adequate solutions: + *Colossal in the landscape, it is...*
   the Vestervig Church is   its sheer size.   It dominates
   the Church of Vestervig is   its size.   It stands out
   Vestervig Church is   the size of it.   enormous   the
                                                      It looks colossal   in
                                                                vast
Inadequate: **bulk**   **seems**
                                   dimensions   **appears**
                                                            -ly
                                              It looks huge   in the -

---

Danish: landskabet, og næst efter Viborg Domkirke er den faktisk
Adequate: *Next to the Viborg Cathedral it is, in fact, (by far)*
   scenery (?).   in fact,   second to
   landscape .   It is,   actually,   next to   the Viborg Cathedral,
Inadequate: countryside
   - surroundings

Danish: den største jyske kvaderstenskirke overhovedet. Den kan virke en
Adequate: the largest of all Jutish ashlar churches.   may seem
   the largest ashlar church in all Jutland.   It   seems
   the largest Jutland (?)   ashlar church.   Some will find it
          Jutish
Inadequate: **at all.   It may/can look**
                                   altogether.   It may come across
                     built of ashlar altogether.

Danish;   smule slikket - et resultat af en i øvrigt nødvendig istandsættelse...
          finicky   which is due to some urgent repair work
          smart   which is the outcome of a - necessary - restoration
       a bit trim   which is due to some urgent repair work
          shined up   which is the result (??) of a restoration, which was, incidentally,
          sleek
       licked which is a result of an otherwise much needed renovation

No marks =   **The feedback form**
No problem for you, OR
Not checked in this translation

-   **+**

1. TEXT
   omission .... |_|_|_|_|_|
   addition .... |_|_|_|_|_|
   insufficiently checked .... |_|_|_|_|_| (Tense. Numbers. Other)

2. SPELLING
   capital letters .... |_|_|_|_|_|
   words .... |_|_|_|_|_|
   compounds .... |_|_|_|_|_|
   split words .... |_|_|_|_|_|

3. PUNCTUATION
   relative clauses .... |_|_|_|_|_|
   object clauses .... |_|_|_|_|_|
   other .... |_|_|_|_|_| (Longish discourse. Adverbials. Other)

4. WORDS/ WORD KNOWLEDGE
   elementary .... |_|_|_|_|_|
   rare .... |_|_|_|_|_|
   idioms and phrases .... |_|_|_|_|_|
   constructs .... |_|_|_|_|_|
   plural vs singular forms .... |_|_|_|_|_|
   calques .... |_|_|_|_|_|
   false friends .... |_|_|_|_|_|
   contaminations .... |_|_|_|_|_|
   equivalents .... |_|_|_|_|_|
   irregular verbs .... |_|_|_|_|_|
   change of word class .... |_|_|_|_|_|
   gender .... |_|_|_|_|_|

5. SYNTAX/GRAMMAR
   concord (subject - verb) .... |_|_|_|_|_|
   concord (other) .... |_|_|_|_|_|
   genitive .... |_|_|_|_|_|
   article .... |_|_|_|_|_| (Indefinte. Definite. Form)
   preposition .... |_|_|_|_|_|
   adverb, form .... |_|_|_|_|_|
   adverb, position .... |_|_|_|_|_|
   prop-word .... |_|_|_|_|_|
   tense .... |_|_|_|_|_|
   modal verbs .... |_|_|_|_|_|
   parallelisms .... |_|_|_|_|_|
   relations .... |_|_|_|_|_| (Parataxis. Hypotaxis)

6. EXPRESSION
   collocations .... |_|_|_|_|_|
   calquing .... |_|_|_|_|_|
   construction of sentence .... |_|_|_|_|_|
   idiomatic usage .... |_|_|_|_|_|
   style .... |_|_|_|_|_|
   precision .... |_|_|_|_|_|
   word order .... |_|_|_|_|_|

7. OTHER COMMENTS

my part. Students soon grasp the differentiation in the system: it moves from a plus (+) for fine phrasing over a dot under words I object to, a wavy line for unquestionable mistakes, to a straight one under real howlers, namely the formal errors. Students therefore immediately know whether we are concerned with sophisticated points in syntax or something that should turn up once only in a university undergraduate career.

Students also soon catch on to the fact that we are operating with fine shades between the two extremes, namely the plus as opposed to the circular arrow signifying a 'distortion'. Since there are rarely indisputable 'teacher improvements', most signs only serve to alert the students to the fact that they must keep track of what is happening in class.

The oral analysis in class

The second component in the feedback is oral. It is a class discussion of solutions.

In translation, there are usually several equally valid or at least adequate renderings in terms of individual words, idioms, clauses and sentences. I consider it important that students are introduced to a multiplicity of valid solutions in translation work. For this purpose I make up the model shown on page 127, which covers the opening sentences of the exercise we saw in the previous illustration. The chart notes all student suggestions. In class all adequate - and (why not admit it?) brilliant - solutions which have surfaced in student translations (or mine) are presented first. Deviations between style and content in adequate target-language renditions are discussed. Attention then focuses on inadequate renderings. Like the correct suggestions, they are read out one by one, and students are asked to specify the inadequacy or distortion. This is done by demanding an explanation of what the infelicitous renderings mean. The erroneous renditions are discussed in class both for the benefit of those who did not write them and for those who did: everybody hears an explanation as to why the suggestions were not adequate, and, hopefully, a heightened awareness of language use.

There are a few points to be made clear: I never, ever, identify students who have committed a specific 'error', but it often happens that students give themselves away, for instance by laughing when they realise what is wrong; and it is rare for me discuss elementary howlers because they are corrected individually in the written translations. The approach makes for lively discussions where points in the translation may illuminate central principles and problems in translation, as well as confrontations between student views and mine, perhaps even corrections of the latter. And, thirdly, since I find it very depressing not to laugh at times, I will take in some tricky, or funny, errors made in previous classes.

The feedback form
The third component is the feedback form (shown on page 126). It is a systematic and individualised assessment so that all students receive an evaluation of their translations.

Comprising a total of 42 problem areas in interlingual transfers between Danish and English, loosely grouped as 'collation', 'spelling', 'syntax' and 'expression', the feedback form covers most errors generated in translations between Danish and English, and, in my opinion, they also move from formal errors and manifestations of interlanguage to points which are more pertinent for 'good' translation work. Each area is assessed on a five-scale differential which is filled out for each student translation: I have a look at each translation, and, then, taking into account the overall possibilities for committing errors of a given type, I indicate all problems revealed in the translation. If, for instance, I know that it is possible to commit five errors in concord, and I find two in one translation, this is marked in the middle category: a warning to the student that this may be an overall weakness. The feedback is thus individualised at this point. No two feedback forms are completed in the same way. Of course, no *single* translation exercise will generate all points, nor indeed will individual students make the errors to the same extent in every exercise. But when students compare these feedback forms after, say, ten translations, they can identify their own weak spots and do something about them.

My use of the evaluation sheet is not the same with beginners and advanced students: initially the top differentials which cover formal points are used fairly frequently, and it must also be stressed that I mark only errors. In the advanced classes, it is the strengths and the stylistic points at the bottom which are marked.

Doubtless, it has been noted that I have not discussed the use of computer spelling and grammar programmes in translation classes. I certainly accept their existence, and appreciate that they will change the translator's workplace. Yet in teaching, I believe we must operate on the premise that we are educating specialists who can also manage competently on their own without access to machine translation. In that context, it is a weakness that the existing systems are either cumbersome or too rigid in their approaches to allow for creativity in translation work: this, on the other hand, is appropriately lauded in my classes.

Discussion
The procedures presented here are not the be-all and the end-all of translation studies, for despite all the technicalities there is still subjectivity galore. I am not infallible, and I do not catch all student errors (In the first example given, for instance, there are a few slips: "tourists", "across *from*", and "beginning"). Stu-

dents will ask me why I have not corrected errors I discuss in class in their translations. Also, it may turn out that in the course of my correction work, I change my mind - true, in the recorded history of Dollerup classes, no more than one grade, but nevertheless enough to make students aware that protests may bring forth some public teacher contrition which can be used for individual self-repair and face-saving. Similarly, students occasionally catch me out in a solution which I have classified as wrong, and point out that it is correct, for instance, by interpretations overlooked, in dictionary entries I missed in my work, or simply by having a referendum in class on proper language usage. Or it may be that their and my language usages differ, or perhaps even that we are dealing with semantic shifts due to language change. In these cases my way out is to have a public vote.

As far as the evaluation sheets are concerned, students will turn up to ask probing questions about why I have not marked particular types of error which they have noted were discussed in class - where the only proper answer is a blush of shame. The model shown on page 128 is actually the eighth one. I occasionally find weak points about it - points that I have not included, or that the sheet covers irrelevant matter. But then the next batch of translations makes me change my mind again and stick to the version I use.

These are minor details: what matters most in translation classes is that students become aware of linguistic problems, formal as well as semantic ones, and use this knowledge in subsequent translation work. It is more useful to heighten the undergraduates' general linguistic sensibility than to correct one specific error, so if I overlook something or judge too harshly, it is all done in the pursuit of that honourable goal.

It is in the nature of things that all teaching must work, otherwise life as a teacher would be hell. As far as I can make out, the feedback discussed does work: my students appear to do away with the formal errors; they seem to fare slightly better at exams, and some of them remember classes years later. But of course this may be an illusion.

Finally, no two classes of students are the same: procedures, advice, and teacher performance may change - or may have to change - with new classes. So there is a subtle interplay between teacher personality, teacher feedback, student personality, teacher and student idiolects and sociolects, class size and general knowledge of the languages used and the translations done.

These differences are large even in a small country like Denmark. Therefore it would be presumptuous to suggest that the procedures presented in this article are applicable in classrooms other than mine. However, the bottom line is that by an identification of the most prominent errors in translations between specific language pairs, and by calling students' attention to them systematically, these errors can be eradicated, with blood, sweat and tears. Accordingly, some of the features and some of the ideas discussed here may inspire others operating with other language pairs to do something, either along the same lines or in radically different ways, to improve feedback in translation classes in different climes and under foreign skies.

Notes

1. Among the pieces of advice is a general exhortation to translate texts other than those used in the classroom and then to discuss these translations in study groups outside class (which usually means at somebody's home). This makes for peer-correction which I find a very effective means of doing away with elementary howlers.

STUDENT-CENTRED CORRECTIONS OF TRANSLATIONS

María Julia Sainz, Universidad de la República, Uruguay

Background information

At the University of the Republic of Uruguay in South America I teach translation from English into Spanish. The Translation Course is one of the courses taught at the University's School of Law. It is placed there because the degree awarded is that of Public or Certified Translator, that is, it allows graduates to translate and sign public documents, which in this way become official translations.

In 1885, the School of Law of the University of the Republic of Uruguay (the only state university in the country) was authorized to issue the degree of Public Translator as a way of regulating the work of translators. At the official level in Uruguay, translations done by Public Translators have become mandatory since the late XIX century for all documents either coming from other countries to be submitted to State organizations or for documents issued by Uruguayan organizations to be officially considered abroad, such as letters rogatory, powers of attorney, decrees, awards, affidavits, certificates, and financial, commercial, and technical documents in general.

Article 28 of Act No. 12.997 dated 28 November 1961 defines the Public Translator as "a University professional who has a liberal career and is a trustee of public faith whose activity is mainly intellectual".

After many changes in the course of this century, the School of Law has had a four-year course leading to the degree of Public Translator since 1976. It is the only institution in Uruguay where such a course can be taken. Like all the other courses at the University of the Republic of Uruguay, it is absolutely free of charge. Students are admitted irrespective of age, sex, race and colour.

To enter the course, candidates must have finished their secondary education (six years) in Uruguay and must sit for an entrance exam both in Spanish and in the language(s) to be taken. This exam ascertains whether candidates have a sufficiently adequate knowledge of those languages with which they intend to work. The specific objective of the School is not to teach languages but to train students to become high level specialists in a profession which uses languages as its main tool. To pass the entrance exam in English, candidates are required to have a level similar to that of the Cambridge Proficiency Exam. (See Sainz

1992: 69)

The language pairs offered by the School (English, French, Italian, Portuguese and German) are always in combination with Spanish, and students are required to work in both directions.

Courses run from March to October and the evaluation system consists of five tests in the course of the academic year. With a work load of around 15 hours per week, the subjects in the four years are:

First year:	Foreign Language I
	Spanish I
	Applied Linguistics
	Public Law
Second year:	Foreign Language II
	Spanish II
	Theory and Methodology of Translation
	Private Law I
Third year:	Foreign Language III
	Culture of the Foreign Language
	Professional Practice I
	Private Law II
	Private Law III
Fourth year:	Foreign Language IV
	Professional Practice II
	Foreign and Comparative Law
	Language Workshop.

Because it is a part-time programme, courses are scheduled in the late afternoon or early evening. In order to attend any given year, students must have passed all the subjects covered in the preceding one.

The University does not offer any courses in interpreting, but rules and regulations state that Public Translators may act as official interpreters in case of marriages (when one of the spouses does not understand Spanish), wills, judicial proceedings in which non-speakers of Spanish are involved, etc.

Evaluation system

I will start the discussion of my topic with a Socratic thought. Socrates said that ideas exist but are scattered: all we have to do is find them. The idea I would like to awake here is one of the topics I feel most concerned about, since it has to do with the type of evaluation system that we, as teachers, choose. I am not thinking of tests or end-of-year exams but of how these tests and exams as well as any passage we ask our students to translate can produce useful feedback for our courses at an on-going micro-evaluation level (as opposed to macro-evaluation, carried out by authorities at the national or international level).

In their book *Adult Learning Principles and Their Application to Programme Planning*, Brundage and MacKeracher (1980: 21-31) established some principles which make us see the need for a student-centred approach to learning which can be applied to our translation classes. These are some principles:

1. Adults learn best when they are involved in developing learning objectives for themselves which are congruent with their current and idealized self-concept.

2. The learner reacts to all experience as he perceives it, not as the teacher presents it.

3. Adults are more concerned with whether they are changing in the direction of their own idealized self-concept than whether they are meeting standards and objectives set for them by others.

4. Adults do not learn when over-stimulated or when experiencing extreme stress or anxiety.

5. Those adults who can process information through multiple channels and have learnt 'how to learn' are the most productive learners.

The term "student-centred" has been fashionable in language teaching for some time now. It can describe different ideas: a student-centred class; a student-centred course; a student-centred approach, etc. I am going to discuss a student-centred approach to correction of translations at our university in Uruguay.

Some students have never been asked to think about themselves as *students* nor to answer questions about their ways or strategies of learning, furthermore, some never thought they had any strategies of learning at all. They need to be made aware of all this and to derive benefit from their past experience in the learning process.

In Confucian terms "If you give a man a fish, you feed him for a day. If you teach him how to fish, you feed him for a lifetime." I designed the questionnaire in Illustration 1, on the next page, in order to sensitize my students to their own position regarding the translation course they had chosen. I suggest this questionnaire can pave the way to teach students how "to fish".

Teachers must make it clear that there are no right or wrong answers to these questions and that the students' answers are going to be used only as feedback and food for discussion later on. The purpose of the questions is also to give students a wider insight into their own learning process and make them aware of the rationale underlying class activities.

Some students find it difficult to give accurate answers (or at least the type of answers that can be useful for teachers). Therefore, teachers can help them to clarify their thoughts and avoid answers which are too generalised or vague.

Student-focus process

I designed a process which I called "student-focus process" to help both teachers and students become aware of the learning process involved in correcting translations. In other words, how to learn from mistakes.

Illustration 1

Student's name: ....

QUESTIONNAIRE

1.   WHAT DO YOU EXPECT FROM THIS TRANSLATION COURSE?

     ...   Learn more about language
     ...   Learn more about the culture/literature of the language
     ...   Keep in touch with a language I already know
     ...   Other. Specify ....

2.   WHAT DO YOU THINK MAKES A GOOD TRANSLATION STUDENT?

3.   WHAT DO YOU THINK IS THE BEST WAY TO LEARN TRANSLATION?

4.   WHAT TYPE OF ACTIVITIES WOULD YOU LIKE TO DO IN YOUR
     COURSE? WHY? For example:

FORMAL LEARNING	INFORMAL LEARNING
... grammar exercises	... reading in the SL and TL for voc., register, style, etc.
... doing translations at home	... comparing official translations
... pair-work translations	... watching a film / video + subtitles

5.   HOW DO YOU ORGANIZE YOUR LEARNING?   Material you use:
     (monolingual-bilingual dict.; grammar books; your own notes)

6.   HOW WILL YOU ORGANIZE YOUR TIME FOR THIS COURSE?

This process is not only about what our students want (and need) but about the kind of students *we* as teachers want (and need). It is not only about who our students are but about who *we* are and about what level of teaching they are entitled to as learners. By this I mean whether we teachers adopt a human rights based approach to translation teaching at the University when dealing with learners' rights. Following Francisco Gomes De Matos' "Checklist for Teachers" (1991: 256), this approach could also be called "student rights based". The list goes like this:

Do my students have the right to make translation errors?
What kinds of errors?
Are they told about the typology of the errors referred to?
How empathic can I be, when evaluating translation accuracy and appropriateness?"

The process I have in mind is shown in Illustration 2:

Illustration 2: The student-focus process

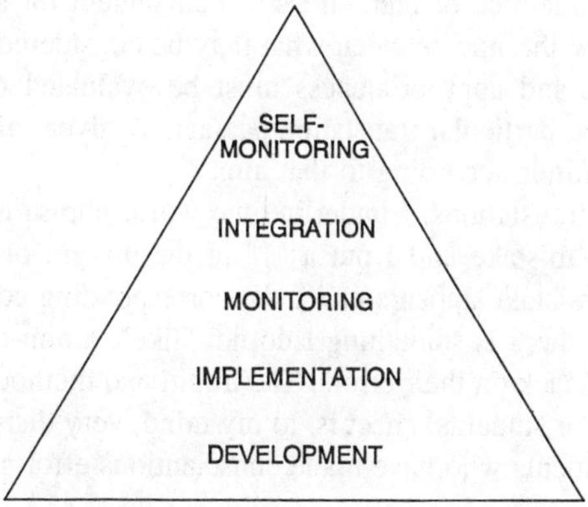

The process comprises various stages. On the bottom line of the pyramid we have the DEVELOPMENT stage intended to understand and anticipate students' needs in order to respond to those needs more efficiently.

How do we build understanding and how do we retrieve feedback? I can see how students performed at the entrance exam for the translation course, consisting of translations from and into Spanish plus a 'Use of English'. This helps me to build up knowledge about my students and anticipate what level my first year class has. Although, as I said before, the level required to pass the entrance exam in English is equivalent to the University of Cambridge Certificate of Proficiency, there are problems that appear in translations which are quite different from those where the language is used for other purposes (for instance composition, précis writing, grammar exercises).

As teachers, we should establish common ground from the very beginning. Students have the right to know the evaluation system we will be using to evaluate their translation work throughout the year and we should be consistent in its use. They have the right to know who is in charge of judging their work, who is fully responsible for it, and who they have to address in case of further questions. Let me give an example: I tell my students that the translations they are handing in will be corrected exclusively by me (not by my assistant or by the two of us) but only if this is really the case.

In order to make our correction clearer, it is practical to ask students to leave a margin on the left-hand side of the paper on which they write their translation and to skip every second line. This margin is divided into a column for Serious Mistakes (S) and one for Minor Mistakes (M).

What strategies can be devised for correction so that it becomes a way of learning instead of a source of fear, stress or punishment for students? It is not my aim here to draw the line between what may be considered serious or minor mistakes. Accuracy and appropriateness must be evaluated depending on the teacher's aim for that particular translation passage. A given mistake can be considered serious or minor according to that aim.

When correcting translations, I underline the word, phrase or sentence where I believe there is a mistake and I put a "1" in the margin of the line where a minor or a serious mistake appears under the corresponding column. This is my only way of saying there is something I do not "like", a non-aggressive way of giving students feedback on their errors. The traditional method of re-writing the correct version on the students' sheet is, to my mind, very disruptive, frustrating and stressful for students who have made conscientious efforts to carry out their assignments.

In the IMPLEMENTATION stage, students get the 'Correction Chart' shown on the opposite page. The chart is divided into four columns: Mistakes/Possible Correction/Source/Type of Mistake. Under 'Mistakes' students write the word, phrase or sentence which was underlined as incorrect in their translation. Under 'Possible Correction' they try to produce an "error-free" version. They may do so on their own since, quite often, by simply being made aware of their mistake, they can produce a correct version.

However, it may happen that they are unable to do so and may have to resort to their classmates. It is here that peer work and peer correction prove invaluable tools. Peers may provide students with answers which they consider correct. Unlike students in many other countries, Uruguayans tend to ask their peers for

Illustration 3: Correction Chart

Student's name:
Text File No.:
Date:

Mistakes	Possible Correction	Source	Type of mistake

an answer first, thus welcoming peer correction.

If no peer can help them, students may want to consult a reference source (that is a dictionary, a glossary, their own notes, etc.). If there is still no satisfactory answer, they may resort to their teachers.

The source of the answer for their correction is entered under the column 'Source' as: 'Myself'; 'Peer'; 'Dictionary'; 'Teacher'.

The column 'Type of mistake', filled in by the students, can become a good exercise to help students recognize what types of mistake they are making and consequently eliminate them.

While students are filling in the 'Correction Chart' teachers can walk around the class checking that students are filling in the chart and help them out if necessary. This allows for a very personal and individual contact with each student, an effort highly appreciated, especially if classes are somewhat large (15+). This is the stage I call MONITORING. Teachers can monitor the process in order to make adjustments as the course unfolds, on the basis of the information they retrieve from the 'Correction Charts'.

Once students have gone through all their corrections in this way, they have a clear picture of their main difficulties. Sometimes students do not know how to make progress in their work simply because they cannot identify their own weak points. If they find they have been able to correct most of their mistakes on their own (many attributed to 'Myself' in the 'Source' column), this may well show that they are not meticulous enough but they know how to do it well and that they should show more care in the future. If the word 'Peer' comes up too often, it may mean that they are performing below the average. If the word 'Teacher' outnumbers the rest, it may be that that particular text is beyond the students' level. This is a most important piece of feedback which teachers can take into account next time they give out a text to translate.

Once finished, the 'Correction Charts' are handed in to the teachers, together with the translation, so that they can be checked more closely after the class. Teachers can make any corrections that either escaped them in class or could not be done for lack of time. Then the charts are given back to the students to be filed.

This is followed by the INTEGRATION stage. Teachers can fill in their own chart of 'Types of Mistakes' for a particular translation piece. This chart may vary from one passage to another. It may, for instance, include the following list of types of mistakes:

Connectors	Prepositions
Grammar	Punctuation
Lexical items	Style, register
Misunderstanding	Syntax
Nouns (agreement)	Tenses
Omission	

In order to fill in this 'teacher's correction chart', teachers can ask the class for the maximum number of times each type of mistake appeared in the translated text. By analysing this chart the necessary remedial or reinforcement work can be integrated into class work. In this way, the feedback received from the students can be turned into effective measures for working on those mistakes immediately afterwards.

Teachers can also encourage self-assessment by their students since "an important supplement to teacher assessment, self-assessment provides one of the most effective means of developing both critical self-awareness of what it is to be a learner, and skills in learning how to learn" (Nunan 1984: 116).

In student-centred correction, learners must have the chance of monitoring their own work. SELF-MONITORING is a stage during which students can check their own progress in the course and, at the same time, become critical about their learning. By screening their performance in various translations during the course of the year, they can see for themselves where their difficulties lie.

At the bottom of the 'Correction Chart', students are asked to circle the figure, ranging from +3 to -3, which they think best matches their idea about their performance in that particular translation passage and to make any other comments. Students have the right to express what they think about their performance as well as to voice their opinion of their teachers' evaluation.

Conclusion

The charts and questionnaires were designed with translation students in mind. They are an attempt to try to dispel the element of fear or stress implicit in any written assignment. However, they are subject to constant revision and changes in order to be improved.

If we do not take our students and their rights into account, we run the risk of creating unaware and selfish professionals in the future, professionals who have never been given the chance of developing their own opinion about their work and who are unable to judge whether their work is accurate and appropriate simply because nobody ever made them think about it when they were studying at university. My contention is that we should build these "little cells" of awareness in our translation students.

Small changes can sometimes produce great effects. If we do not do things well in education, we see the repercussion in 10 to 20 years' time. In this light, I would like to reword what I said at the beginning about the kind of translation students we want and end on a question: "What type of translation *professionals* do we want?"

STARTING FROM THE (OTHER) END:
INTEGRATING TRANSLATION AND TEXT PRODUCTION

Arnt Lykke Jakobsen, Copenhagen Business School, Denmark

How I used to teach translation

I would like to begin by telling a true story from the not so distant past. It is the story of the way my colleagues and I taught translation at the Copenhagen Business School.

Let me mention some of the useful things we did, lest they be forgotten.

- We told students about the standard sources of information, not only printed and electronic dictionaries, but also encyclopedias, textbooks, manuals, etc.
- We also told them about sources of potentially relevant information beyond the standard sources.
- We told students that when working on a translation, they would probably find more relevant information in parallel target language texts than anywhere else.
- We told them that if they used bilingual dictionaries, they should always consult monolingual, target language dictionaries for verification.
- And we struggled to convey to them our own love of words and to communicate our own insatiable appetite for knowledge.

What we also did, however, was give students a source text *we* had found, instruct them to go home and translate it for next week - availing themselves of as many relevant sources of information as possible. After finishing and handing in their translations, usually students would have to wait another week before seeing their work again. In order not to waste valuable time, however, we asked them to do the next translation in the course of that week, while we were correcting the previous translation task. So, by the time we met again in class, our heads would be full of the errors students had made one and sometimes several weeks earlier (and forgotten all about), and their heads would be full of the problems in a text which would not be discussed until the following week.

Not the most harmonious meeting of minds, obviously. Small wonder that our students were not inspired and not motivated by the texts they were asked to translate and that the same errors kept returning with nightmarish persistence despite our intuitive or systematic efforts to get rid of them. The wonder is that we thought for so long this was the way to teach translation.

Diagnosis of false assumptions

Part of the explanation for our misconceptions about teaching translation is no doubt historical. The grammar translation tradition has been incredibly strong in many countries - and for centuries.[1] Though many teachers hesitate to accept it, the truth of the matter is, as has often been demonstrated, that the main emphasis in such correction work has always been on formal aspects, spelling and punctuation, and on grammar (de Beaugrande 1984: 6). In addition, the translation tasks were often so difficult that students would spend hours searching dictionaries for possible hints in a bewildering array of potential equivalents; equivalents of words they would probably never themselves have dreamed of using. So, what went by the name of translation was obviously first of all an attempt to teach the foreign language by focussing on grammar and vocabulary. If students learnt to translate in the end - and I think the method does not entirely rule out this possibility - we can still ask if there are not more effective ways.

Perhaps the least satisfactory element in the old method was the implied assumption that a translation departs from a source text only. It is a very persistent assumption that translation is a sequential process moving, metaphorically speaking, from left to right, from a source text through a translator to a target text. That translation is essentially an interpretative activity. That a translation is only a reproduction of another text. That a target text is not a text in its own right.[2]

This leads to the assumption that translation can be understood as the application of a combination of transfer rules and translation strategies to a source text, again without reference to the purpose, point, function or skopos of the target text. It also implies that it is possible to approximate the ideal translation of a given source text through a process of gradual optimisation of equivalence relations between the target and source texts.

But translation cannot be understood or explained in those terms. Target text production is never mere source text reproduction (Jakobsen 1993: 161). A target text which is the result of the application of transfer rules and translation strategies to a source text is bound to be a pseudotext. And if we assume that for each source text there is one, and only one ideal target text - the teacher's version - we make no provision for the creative variety and flexibility of target text production.

Translation begins with a target

For the above-mentioned reasons, the discussion as to whether translation starts with a source text or starts somewhere else may not be entirely trivial. I have come to the conclusion that for the purpose of teaching translation at the Copenhagen Business School it is preferable - for pedagogical reasons - to change the spatial metaphor and argue that translation begins with a need for a text. It starts with the target text, and with all the usual questions we ask ourselves when we sit down to write a text.

Translation is text production

If we ask what translation is like - in behavioural terms - surely the most obvious point of similarity is with writing texts. Translation is a type of text production.

I shall not attempt to say what ordinary text production is like, and I certainly do not wish to say that translation is ordinary text production. It is not difficult to think of features that make translation special. For instance, if we think of *inventio*[3] in classical rhetoric, the first phase of language production where a writer gets his ideas, we find important differences. And even more so in the second phase, the *dispositio*, where the author's ideas are organised. The pragmatic characteristics of translation are also different from those of ordinary text production. Hence the familiar questions about the extent to which it is the author/sender or the translator who communicates through the text. Here, one extreme position is to argue that the translator does not communicate at all, but merely provides a text which enables other people to communicate. The other extreme regards the translator as an author, not a mere producer of texts.

But again, for pedagogical reasons, I would suggest that we begin by emphasising the basic similarity between translation and text production: in each case the primary task is to produce a text.

On closer inspection, we also find that several of the apparent differences are not so fundamental after all. In the *inventio* phase, for instance, it may be true that text production results from a bright idea suddenly invading an author's mind, but it is also true that one may get bright ideas from reading other texts. In accordance with the ecological order of the day, textual material is constantly produced from recycled waste - with or without the word processor's cut-and-paste function.[4]

The fact that the *dispositio* seems to leave the translator little room for manoeuvring does not define translation either. Lots of text types have an obligatory sequence of elements. Conversely, in functional translation, a translator may be free to reorganise matters dramatically.

And as for pragmatics, the world is full of text production situations involving *cooperation* between several parties.[5] Letters may be dictated, or written from a brief oral instruction, or from somebody else's notes. This is a frequent form of cooperation between decision-makers and communicators, and the communicator often has to fill in new material.

Texts that result from cooperation are frequently written either in response to another text (a letter is often a reply to another letter), or on the basis of other textual material. The editor or copy-writer of a newspaper reads reports, faxes, and telexes from international news agencies before writing or rewriting an article.

It is also characteristic of text production in general that textual background material is often available in a form that makes it necessary to summarise here, to elaborate there, and to change the style of a third passage, etc. It is this interface between translation and non-translational text production, which makes it possible to integrate writing and translating.

Integrating translation and writing

Believing that writing comes before translating, we now begin by training writing skills at the Copenhagen Business School. Writing tasks are specified with respect to situation and purpose and based on a variety of textual material, including parallel texts. Some of the background material provided for a writing task may be in a foreign language. Thus, if students are learning to write texts in Danish, some of the background material may be in English (or another foreign language), but students are not invited to translate. The amount of background material in other languages may then be increased up to a point where it is difficult to tell whether students produce their texts with or without translation.

The progression I am describing here, still belongs mainly in the 'visions' sub-category in the present volume's triad of "insights, aims, visions". The course is still in the design phase. I am convinced, however, that placing translation within the whole spectrum of text production, and consistently exposing students to authentic parallel texts, will help them develop greater critical awareness of acceptability norms and textual models in the target language, both when they are translating into their native and into a foreign language. Also, by not demanding real translation until quite late in the course, we believe we have minimised the risk that translation tasks result in pseudo-text production.

Thus, by starting from the other end, by starting with a clear view of the target text, we improve translation.

Process orientation

We also need to address the other main problem in the nightmare version of teaching translation, however. This was the lack of motivation among students due to our use of uninteresting source texts which often seemed to have been chosen primarily to make sure that there would be a certain quantity of errors in student translations of them. This is something we hope to remedy by process orienting translation teaching, a pedagogical point which follows naturally from the emphasis on text production in the course.

Over the past few years, there has been a great deal of interest in process oriented composition in Denmark.[6] This approach, which is heavily indebted to American ideas about composition, is now moving into the Danish school system at all levels.[7]

In process oriented translation, students and teachers are active at the same time. Thus, tuition enters into the student's world while a source text is being interpreted, while potential equivalents are being considered, and while the target text is in the process of being created. Tuition comes in at a point when texts are still 'warm'.

'Warm' texts

A text is 'warm', first of all, if it is needed for *a genuine communicative purpose*. Therefore, specimen texts must be given low priority. However, this requirement is not at all easy to fulfil in class. At the Copenhagen Business School, we would like to teach students to write or translate a variety of administrative, legal, commercial, and technical texts, but it is difficult to create a situation in which students feel that such texts have a genuine communicative purpose. On the other hand, at our educational level, we cannot have students only writing letters to their fiancé(e)s, or applications to get into exchange programmes, and we feel that there are already enough student diaries in the world.

The challenge is clear. Writing tasks must be maximally relevant and interesting to students while involving all the language elements required by the curriculum. Charging students with giving in-house information (in a foreign language) to exchange students is an example. This provides a genuine communicative purpose, and it involves a fair degree of professional language although the range of text types may be limited. Another possibility is peer group review of texts. The prospect of having a text subjected to peer group review will often increase motivation considerably. Students know their fellow students, know how to deal with their verdicts, and so tend to respect this kind of feedback (Kock and Tandrup 1989: 16).

A text is also 'warm' if it is *still in the process of being made*. One main reason why students forgot all about their translations in the old system was the simple fact that we begin to forget a text the moment it is completed. Time is not the crucial factor here. What matters is whether or not a text is finished. If the text is still in the process of making, feedback received a week after production may still be felt to be highly relevant.

Many translation and text production problems do not have simple right-or-wrong solutions. Composition workshops allow teachers a better view of text production than the finished products, and traditional student errors are not the most interesting problems in such an environment. Here, translation and text production may be approached in a far more constructive manner. Teachers may now bring up ideas, suggest relevant tools, solve problems - and correct errors -while a text is still in the making, and students will immediately see and feel the difference. Teachers are no longer merely instructors and assessors, but partners in a relevant, interesting and collaborative writing task.

This brings in a third key element in what makes a 'warm' text. A text stays 'warm' and interesting as long as a student or a group of students are *responsible* for it. This is probably the crucial element, for it means that in the end we can only expect students to learn from working with texts they themselves find interesting.

Managing process orientation

It is obvious why some teachers have second thoughts about process oriented class work. They would like to be able to plan and prepare classes, to know when students are going to learn about orders and invoices, and they are not easily convinced that students will learn proper English if all their errors are not corrected. If we accept process orientation and if we accept that texts must be interesting to students, are we not losing control?

In my view, process oriented class work cannot help but develop a new learning style. Process orientation means accepting that relevance criteria have to be found in an open dialogue with students. It is never enough that a teacher finds a text interesting. In fact, the whole issue of how much theory, how much knowledge and how much skill a course should include is at stake here. Text linguistics, to take an example, will not be accepted by students merely because teachers recommend it. Unless teachers are able to make students feel - in writing, in translating - that it makes an important difference, they are not likely to get away with lecturing on the importance of cohesion. In accepting that relevance is negotiable we are indeed giving up control to some extent, but only because we are certain that the gains in motivation and learning are greater than the losses in authority and control.

Some of the practical problems should not be underestimated, however. The facilities may not be available. Thus, when our own school was built in the late 1980's, nobody took into account that students might actually work there. Most of their work was expected to be homework. Such problems can be very tangible, but the basic problem about process-orientation is that it affects the student-teacher relationship in ways which even some students dislike. It changes our own culture.

Conclusion: an example

Despite such problems, I take an optimistic view of all this. In a class I taught recently, we did a role play about a chemical plant in Brazil. At some point the student playing the role of managing director was required to make a written statement about the company's environmental policy. The student's first impulse was to write 'Sod the environment' - a spontaneous first attempt, which the student rejected after a moment's reflection since it did not harmonise with what she felt the manager ought to be writing.

The teacher's chance to work pedagogically in this new educational culture lies in this open space immediately after the emergence of a text production problem, when - as pointed out by Andrew Chesterman in this volume - a tentative theory has been rejected and its successor has not yet been fully shaped. This interval is felt to be critically important by the student, who is therefore highly motivated to accept help. Obviously, our job is to provide relevant help to the best of our ability and in a spirit of constructive cooperation. And without taking advantage of the situation, we can fill this empty space with surprising amounts of theory, grammar, stylistics, pragmatics -you name it.

It was only after several excursions into many of these areas and after looking at many written statements both in English and in Danish that we finally agreed that the student's fifteenth formulation of the passage in the manager's letter would do. It now went: 'Though we have invested heavily in treatment facilities for toxic waste, we cannot honestly claim that the environment is always out first priority.'

In the end, it was impossible to say to what extent elements of translation might have helped in shaping the statement, but here, finally, was an opening text for which the student and the teacher were both willing to take responsibility, and without thinking about it this student had also taken an important first step towards becoming a good translator.

Notes

1. Dollerup (1993: 146): "In Denmark 'translation' in foreign language teaching at the secondary level (lycée, college) is largely used for grammar drills in accordance with medieval practices".
2. This idea is inherent in the traditional conception of a translation as a 'version' (from Latin 'vertere') of an original — whether authorised, revised or otherwise.
3. *Inventio* is treated by Corbett under the heading 'Discovery of Arguments' (Corbett, 1971: 45-298). *Dispositio*, or the arrangement of arguments (or material), is dealt with on pp. 299-413.
4. The intuited similarity between paraphrase (or intralingual translation) and translation proper (in the sense of interlingual translation) has often been noted, perhaps most influentially in

Jakobson (1959). However, most translation theorists have been content to point out with Jumpelt (1961: 10) that they were only concerned with translation from one language into another.
5. Notably Holz-Mänttäri (1984).
6. For instance Andersen & Detlef & Raahauge (1991); Galberg Jacobsen & Skyum-Nielsen (1988); Kock & Tandrup (1989); Rønn-Poulsen & Brandt-Pedersen (1986).
7. See for instance de Beaugrande (1984); and Hillocks, Jr. (1986).

TRANSLATION ASSESSMENT: A CASE FOR A SPECTRAL MODEL

Hasnah Ibrahim, Universiti Utara Malaysia, Malaysia

Introduction

Different text types and different reasons for translating call for different strategies. Though long recognised,[1] this fact is not universally accepted: those who agree often reject the normative and the prescriptive, whilst those who do not, or who accept it grudgingly, may at best pay lip service to it; most linguistic-based writings on translation, for example, while purporting to be neither prescriptive nor normative end up, usually, by providing norms for producing the 'best' translation.[2]

The division of opinions has pedagogical implications - and hence there is a controversy on the teaching of translation (as discussed in Holmes 1988). Total rejection of norms and prescriptions is untenable; it would render impossible the work of teachers of translation, whose "major task" is "to impart norms to the students" (Holmes 1988: 109). But stylistic 'tyranny' ought also be avoided. So we must adopt a realistic approach to the teaching of translation. The acceptance of a variety of various acceptable translations does not imply that there are no 'wrong translations' or 'mistranslations'. Even a cursory survey of verse-translation in the Malayo-English tradition would show a difference between the "possible", the "potential" and the "preposterous" (Hofstadter 1980: 378),[3] and to minimise the occurrence of the last type, the pedagogic branch of Translation Studies must, when necessary, be 'prescriptive' and 'normative', and must be able to distinguish the "possible" from the "potential" and the two from the "preposterous". For teaching purposes, a means must therefore be found to differentiate not just the acceptable from the unacceptable, but also one product type from another. The assessment (that is, differentiation) of product types, implies that there are various strategies leading to different acceptable product types: there is a spectrum of possibilities. Students of translation in particular must be made fully aware of the existence of many product types, and not be exposed exclusively to prevailing norms. Otherwise they will not be sufficiently versatile and creative when new norms call for new translation strategies and translation products.

In the context of differentiation, the notion of a spectrum is not new to translation. Rose (1981) notes that translation types differ according to their position on the autonomy spectrum. Rose's schema is polarised, the two poles being 'source text autonomy' and 'target audience needs'. In this schema, a position on the spectrum indicates both the translator's relation to her/his material and her/his relation to her/his audience. The translator can operate within the extremes of 'reverence' to 'reference', and the translation product from 'presentation' to 'adaption'. The spectrum therefore places different product types between the two extremes in an ordered structure, perpetuating the historical dichotomy of 'literal' versus 'free'.

The present study extends the concept of the translation spectrum, and, by means of a field-study approach, attempts to identify and label the components of the spectrum which are known. By introducing a neutral nomenclature, and hence by avoiding the historical dichotomy, it hopes to introduce a measure of objectivity into the subjective operations of assessment, that is, evaluation and criticism, in theory as well as in classroom practice.

The translation spectrum

The fact that a text can be translated in several defensible ways,[4] means that the translation spectrum can be compared to the iridescent spectrum obtained from the *refraction* of white light. Like white light, the text can be completely represented only by itself; each version obtained in translation, like each colour of the spectrum, is only a partial picture of the original.[5]

The components of the spectrum must be labelled systematically,[6] in order to make for an unambiguous, objective discussion of the various modes of translation.[7] Earlier attempts to label them have not been successful, for they do not reflect the fact that there may be several acceptable translations of a text. Larson (1984: 11), for example, describes a continuum ranging from the "very literal", through the "literal", the "modified literal", the "inconsistent mixture", the "near idiomatic", the "idiomatic" (which is supposed to be the "translator's goal"), to the "unduly free". Newmark (1988: 45) proposes a spectrum in which the modes are labelled: "word-for-word" translation, "literal" translation, "faithful" translation, "semantic" translation, "adaptation", "free" translation, "idiomatic" translation and "communicative" translation. Such labels perpetuate the historical dichotomy, and because the terms are loaded, it is difficult to use them for discussions of translation products, whether theoretically, or for work in the classroom. Newmark's use of the terms "word-for-word", "literal" and "faithful" translations is, to cite one instance only, confusing to students, for most writers make no such distinction; "literal", or "word-for-word" translation is usually understood to be an attempt to be 'faithful' to the original.

A new nomenclature

The present article attempts to set up a new nomenclature which, I suggest, avoids the problems inherent in having conflicting definitions and uses. It will make for an increased awareness among students (and researchers) about processes and products in translation. It is developed in accordance with Peter Newmark's useful reminder that "any terms translation theory ... invents should be 'transparent', that is, self explanatory" (Newmark 1981: 36). Thus *each term representing the translation process will be prefixed "trans-"*. All suitable existing terms will be retained, but several new terms will have to be introduced,[8] since, like 'cooking', the term 'translation' has become a blanket term.[9] Graham (1985) reminds us that to sustain and so to continue discussions on translation, several conditions must be met, namely:

> At least some agreement about the use of basic terms in question must be reached. Words ... are to be used in ways that will permit rather than prevent further revision of our ideas about the objects and actions they designate. No immediate or even ultimate agreement about the real nature of such referents is required; what is needed is simply a willingness to consider various proposals as possibly true and perhaps more plausible than others advanced in the past. Those basic terms ought to be used indexically; almost like proper names, without bearing any meaning that would determine as necessary or a priori the truth of statements expressing a particular theory or individual belief on the matter under discussion. Conventional notions of ... translation tends to be self-defeating in that they imply their own infallibility and so deny or somehow preclude the collective search for agreement, despite differences, that characterises the inevitably historical pursuit of an essentially empirical subject. (Graham 1985: 23)

The terms I suggest here are derived empirically and describe pathways along which translation proceeds. The process in which the translator tries to preserve the tone and style of the original, for example, could be labelled *trans-emulation*. This is different from *trans-imitation*, where the translator makes a deliberate attempt to imitate the style of another author other than the one of the original, for example, if Thomas Hardy were translated into the style of Malaysia's Shahnon Ahmad, which would roughly correspond to translating Tolstoy into the style of Thomas Hardy.

Alexander Fraser Tytler (1791) uses the term 'transfusion' for the transference of sense from the original text. The term could be resuscitated in the form of *trans-fusion*, to denote a process whereby the transference of the sense of the original transcends all other activities.[10]

The translation of the classics for children, or of technical texts for lay readers, could be labelled *trans-elucidation*, which would be different from *trans-explication*, by which the original text is explained, but not necessarily simplified, in the translation. Both are to be distinguished from *trans-adaption*. This last process could describe the translation of, for example, economics texts for secondary school use, where, for the sake of relevance, illustrative cases are changed to suit the local economic scene.[11] This term, in turn, could be distinguished from *trans-manipulation*, where the changes made reflect an ulterior motive on the part of the translator.

Another term to consider is *trans-forming*. It is the least interesting type of change in the translation of poetry, namely, a shift from verse to prose. At a more general level the term describes the change from one genre to another, for instance, prose to verse or a novel into a play.

Trans-metamorphosis could be used to describe the more intricate changes that occur when one verse form is translated into another one. *Trans-creation* is where the translator exercises the poetic license of an artist, without trans-forming or trans-metamorphosing. A strictly literal (or 'word-for-word') translation, must also be included in the spectrum. In view of the mostly negative connotations of the phrase "literal translation", the terms *trans-mapping* and *trans-imaging* might perhaps be appropriate. If trans-mapping were reserved for the automatic and uncritical word-by-word translation, trans-imaging could be used to describe a desirable and successful trans-mapping, where there is perfect equivalence.

Trans-position is a translation in which locality is completely transposed. Early translations of European folktales into Malay were trans-positions: Cinderella became *Chendralela*, and the fairy godmother became *nenek kebayan*; Reynard the Fox became the much-hated villain *Sang Lamri*. In trans-position thus, the cultural nouns are completely transposed.

In the translation of plays, it may be necessary to make changes, to make the play come alive for the new audience. The term *trans-vivification* would be appropriate for this process. "The translation of a translation . . . of a translation" is a *trans-derivation*. A text could be said to have been trans-derived *n* number of times, to warn readers of changes.

What manner of operation then is translation, since it spans so many possibilities? I define translation to be a *heuristic, psycho-sociolinguistic process which transfers a text from a perceived cultural state, the From-State, to a projected cultural state, the To-State.* This definition accounts for the different modes by taking into consideration all the variables affecting the process. The psycho-sociological aspects, for example, are an indication that translators, as well as the environment of which they are a product, are part of the factors affecting the end-product. Recognition of the heuristic nature of the process introduces the 'why'-factor; trans-imitation is distinguished from parody only by the translator's intention. The type of text translated also dictates the translating strategy.[12] The term cultural state indicates the presence of the 'when'- and 'where'- factors. I prefer the terms 'From-State' and 'To-State' to 'source' and 'target' because the earlier terms are 'value-laden' (Bassnett-McGuire 1980). Besides, the use of English as an international lingua franca blurs the term 'target' in translation so that there is no target at all.

Conclusion

The above nomenclature could, I suggest provide a means for identification of different types of translated texts and for clarifying the nature of translation for students. Especially with students it can be argued that it is necessary to use neutral terms, so that they are not baffled with conflicting usage in their textbooks. At a more general level, it will have been noticed that the use of neutral terms has allowed the discussion of translation types to move away from the usual controversies, and in so doing, opens up for a clearer picture of the translation process. The terms themselves are dispensable, and could be replaced with more elegant substitutes, but the underlying concepts are sound.

The spectral model forces both students and teachers to be aware of the complexity of the translation process. This is important, as the failure to take this into account has doomed most linguistic theories to simplistic forms. This has serious implications in machine translation. A machine is only as good as the software fed into it; a simplistic notion of translation will result in inadequate software. By considering the more complex options revealed by a spectral model, it may be possible to develop a more sophisticated program.

Acceptance of the possibility of the various product types is important to the teaching of translation. Like art students, students of translation ought to be taught different styles and strategies, so as to be able to come up with the most appropriate translation for specific texts, at a particular time and place, for a particular purpose.

The trans-processes identified here will, however, be more helpful in macroscopic discussions of translated texts than for micro-level discussions. The reason is that at the macro-level, each trans-process is a complex of several basic processes. The micro-level strategies have been widely discussed in most writings,[13] but, because different authors use different terms, or the same terms with different connotations, it is difficult to discuss this aspect of translation. This points towards a need for a similar standardisation of terms for use at the micro-level as well.

Notes

1. Bodmer (in Lefevere 1977: 21) notes that there will be as many translations as there are intentions; Snell-Hornby (1988) notes that there is no *one* way of translating.
2. Bell (1991: xvi), whilst claiming to avoid giving "commandments for the creation of 'the perfect translation'", has listed methodological options available to the translator who wishes to be as 'faithful' as possible to the original.

3. Hofstadter (1980) labels pathways which are taken routinely in going from one state to another as *possible* pathways and names the pathways "which would be followed only if one is led through them by the hand" as *potential* pathways, which would be followed only if special external circumstances arise. In the translation of Homer into English, a verse translation would be one of several possibilities, such as the translation of Chapman, Dryden, Pope, R. Fitzgerald and Lattimore. A fictitious example of a 'potential' pathway would be a translation of the *Odyssey* into the style of prose of James Joyce's *Ulysses*.

4. A proverb, for example, can be translated in at least three ways, according to the reason for translating: namely by replacement with an equivalent proverb from the target culture (for a Nidaean dynamic effect in the translation of prose fiction), by retaining the original proverb (to introduce the foreign culture), or by just giving the meaning.

5. Savory (1957: 54) notes that most readers of translated works seem to be aware of this, consulting more than one translation whenever possible.

6. A study of the various terms used to describe translation types shows that even terms like 'word-for-word', 'sense-for-sense' mean different things to different people (see Ibrahim 1992: 174-177).

7. Newmark (1991: 57) illustrates what happens when the various modes are not differentiated; commenting on Chukovsky's writing (Chukovsky 1984), Newmark notes that, "On one page he says he wants 'precision' above everything else. The next three pages he is condemning 'precision' at every turn."

8. Considering the great (on-going) contribution Translation Studies make to the professional (technical) vocabulary of other fields, it is ironic that the field itself is devoid of an "accessible terminology" (Bassnett-McGuire 1980), that would allow a general discussion of the translation process.

9. See Ibrahim (1991 and 1992).

10. The term trans-fusion is different from the term 'transfusion' as used by Shelley, which implied preservation of both the sense and the style of the original, which is trans-emulation in the present nomenclature.

11. The Malayan experience would testify to the need for this mode. In the post-independence fervour of preparing text-books in the national language, an economics book used in Australian secondary schools was translated into Malay, without adaptation. It was then found to be unsuitable for use in Malayan secondary schools.

12. Snell-Hornby (1988) discusses this at length.

13. See, for example, Vinay and Darbelnet (1958, as quoted in van Slype et al. 1983), and Malone (1986).

TRANSLATION AND THE TWO MODELS OF INTERPRETATION

Alexis Nouss, Université de Montréal, Canada

There is an old joke about a rabbi and two villagers who complain about each other. The rabbi listens to the first one and concludes: "You're right." The man leaves happy. He listens to the second one and concludes: "You're right." And the second man leaves happy, also. The rabbi's wife comes into the room and tells her husband: "I heard everything. How could you tell the first and then the second man that they're both right? They cannot both be right." The rabbi stays silent for a moment, then says: "You're right, too."

All teachers of translation are familiar with this dilemma. We want to encourage our students' creativity and, at the same time, teach them the rules of acceptability, according to the norms of the target language, culture and society. True, each translator has his own version, and one is no better than the other, but there are limits. Or are there? Is any translation acceptable? What are the criteria of refusal? Should we arrive in class with our own 'perfect' version and persuade the students of its qualities or should we be open to any suggestion?

This is a concrete pedagogical issue but we may find answers by elevating the question up into a more general framework. True answers may be found in hermeneutics which I define as the study of the nature and the rules of interpretation, that is the study of the meaning of signs (as opposed to semiotics which is concerned with how signs carry meaning). Hermeneutics deals with the issue at hand: are there limits to translations (or interpretations in the hermeneutical perspective) of a given text? Here both hermeneutics and translation theory confront the main question raised by post-structuralism, deconstruction and now the ideology of political correctness: why do some interpretations (of history, of culture) prevail over others? Here we take part in a very modern debate about the uncertainty of all meanings. It is no surprise that the great thinkers of our century, from Freud to Heidegger and Derrida, have considered the problem of translation.

The theories of interpretation admit two currents, indeed two interpretations of interpretation, which Umberto Eco describes as follows: "On one side it is assumed that to interpret a text means to find out the meaning intended by its original author or - in any case - its objective nature or essence which, as such, is independent of our interpretation. On the other side it is assumed that texts can be interpreted in infinite ways."(1990: 24)

So the question we first asked becomes: does translation have to do with the first or the second model of interpretation? According to traditional ideology of translation theory, translation is on the side of the recollection of meaning, of truth to be unveiled and restored, of an original text whose essence is to be discovered according to the rules of the game. But one could argue equally well the opposite: translation entails the need for re-translations according to ever-changing linguistic, social, cultural and historical frameworks in which the meaning of texts can be reinterpreted.

In our quest let us remember that, not only do we have a patron saint, Saint Jerome, but we are lucky enough to also have a god: Hermes, the Greek god of artists, robbers - and translators. As the celestial messenger, it is obvious that Hermes is the god of translators: are they not all carrying a text from one language to another? Are they they not also stealing a message from its original context to deliver it to another? Hermes is not only a mythical figure. He gave his name to a spiritual movement in the Western world at the beginning of our era: Hermetism. Hermetism is usually studied as an esoteric trend and a rival to Christian spirituality in religious studies. But Umberto Eco sees it as a system of thought in the fields of semiotics and hermeneutics. Furthermore, Eco is the author of *A Theory of Semiotics* and *Semantics and the Philosophy of Language* as well as *The Name of the Rose* and *Foucault's Pendulum.* Both books deal with esoteric and occultist matters.

Eco's views on the semiotic contents of hermetism have to be placed within the context of his research, begun in the '70s, about the role of the reader in the creation of meaning and Peirce's idea of 'unlimited semiosis', that is the potential limitlessness of interpretation. In that work, Eco naturally encountered the ideas of the radically critical trend known as deconstruction (Jacques Derrida, Paul de Man and J. Hillis Miller, among others) and its claim that there is an infinity of possible readings of any text. Eco reacts against what he judges to be too extreme a position by establishing norms for acceptability of interpretations; for although any interpretation is possible, they are not all acceptable.

Eco's first argument against the infinity of interpretations is well known to translators and grounded on ethics. The interpreter and the translator have a moral duty not to exceed certain limits of interpretation. I introduce here the notion of morality because texts are not only dead marks on pages but play a role in society and culture. It is impossible to justify Jack the Ripper's acts through specific readings of the Scriptures, Eco says ironically (1992a: 24). I will add that numerous crimes and persecutions have been committed in Western history through faulty translations of the Scriptures. On a less tragic note, translations of Hegel, Freud and Heidegger have produced a range of philosophical schools of impressive diversity. *Ich* and *es* are not identical with *ego* and *id* and are not *le Moi* et *le Ça*. It is not only a question of words: these words, indeed concepts, are responsible for divergent German, English and French modern conceptions of the human psyche.

But Eco also wants to make his point by showing that the discussion is not new and that the attitude of deconstruction can be traced back to the antique Hermetic philosophy.

Since its Greek and Latin foundations, our world has been a world of reason, or more precisely, we see the world through the grid of rationalism. Reason implies norms, standards, limits, measures. For translators, reason means awareness of linguistic and cultural interactions and interferences: 'visiter quelqu'un' is not acceptable in French, and to translate 'a diner' in a Kerouac road novel to 'un bistrot' is a faulty transgression of both the American and the French social systems.

But the human mind is also fascinated by an opposite reality: transformations, metamorphoses, Heraclitus vs. Aristotle, the being of things vs. the constant becoming of things, space vs. time, and, for translators, two separate texts vs. one message, or the plurality of languages vs. the unicity of speech (to stress the more precise difference in French between 'langue' and 'langage'). Eco finds the expression of this concern in the system of thought known as 'Hermetism', which corresponds to the ethnic diversity of the Greek Empire at that time (2nd century before Christ), a mosaic of peoples and cultures close to our contemporary world which, then as now, calls for translation.

Hermetism believes that truth is not a delimited whole but consists of fragments and that there are many ways of expressing it, however contradictory these may be. Each book "contains a message that none of them will ever be able to reveal alone" (Eco, 1992a: 30). This position has been illustrated in translation theory by Walter Benjamin, with his famous metaphor of the original and its translation "as fragments of a greater language" (1977: 78). In accordance with this definition of truth, Hermetism believes that real knowledge does not lie on the surface but is secret, hidden: "Thus truth becomes identified with what is not said or what is said obscurely and must be understood beyond or beneath the surface of a text." (1992a: 30) How surprising to recognize in this strategy associated with Gnostic and Hermetic beliefs some elements of the translation method proposed by Eugen Nida, whose theory comes from his practice as a Christian translator of the Bible. In translation the boundaries between Faith and Heresy are not so clear.

Another consequence of the Hermetic definition of truth and meaning brings us back to our field. The hidden nature of true knowledge makes it also an alien knowledge, distant in time, like a forgotten knowledge, and in space, as if possessed by foreign cultures (Druids, Celtic priests or Eastern wise men, for example) and thus spoken in a foreign language. Whereas the unifying ideology of the Greek Empire called for the use of one language only, Hermetism, spreading through territories of the Greek Empire, called for translation as the only way to reach true knowledge. This may be the place to emphasize that Hermetism offers a specific interest to translation studies for a historical reason. Eco is not only concerned with a specific spiritual movement from the second century before Christ. He studies its diffusion as a recurrent pattern of thought in the history of Western ideas. His genealogical survey tells us that Hermetism celebrated a second victory over rationalism during the Renaissance, when, reworked by Neoplatonism and Christian Cabalism, "the Hermetic model went on to feed a large portion of modern culture, ranging from magic to science." (1992a: 34). Now to us this latter period is of tantamount importance since this was the epoch when translation came into existence as a specific activity, due to the formation of linguistic and national boundaries in Europe. If translation is a circulation of messages and a transfer of significations, it has a lot in common with the Hermetic idea of the universe as a field of unlimited semantic connections.

But the most essential feature of Hermetism for us appears in a semiotic perspective: its belief that interpretation is indefinite. This springs from the Hermetic conception of the world as "one big hall of mirrors, where any one individual object reflects and signifies all the others" (Eco 1992a: 31) A plant would refer to the human body, which in turn would refer to a celestial body, which in turn would refer to an angelic entity and so on. Meaning is constantly sliding in a universe created by a god in whom all contradictions are resolved or contained, as in the limitless possibility of readings claimed by the deconstructionists.

Eco condemns what he calls such a 'suspicious interpretation' or more firmly dubs a 'paranoic interpretation' and which (to him) is an 'overinterpretation'. "In defence of overinterpretation" is precisely the title of a lecture given by Jonathan Culler, a leading figure in American literary theory, in reply to Eco. He makes the following remark from a semiotic and pragmatical perspective: "What Eco calls *overinterpretation* may in fact be a practice of asking precisely those questions which are *not* necessary for normal communication but which enable us to reflect on its functioning." (1992: 113-114) Are we not familiar with that strategy? We, too, teach our students never to start writing their translation on first inspiration, as an instinctive move, but to be suspicious of their idiosyncrasies and thus go to the deepest level of comprehension of the source text, analysing its contents and all its aspects, both formally and semantically. All the linguistics-oriented theories of translation (E. Nida, J.C. Catford, P. Newmark) call for a 'deconstruction' of the source text, bringing to light its basic structures. Culler gives an epistemological ground for such an interpretative strategy to which translation studies can easily relate.

Just as linguistics does not seek to interpret the sentences of a language but to reconstruct the system of rules that constitutes it and enables it to function, so a good deal of what may be mistakenly seen as overinterpretation or somewhat better, as overstanding, is an attempt to relate a text to the general mechanisms of narrative, of figuration, of ideology, and so on. (1992: 116)

Are there no limits to possible interpretations? The answer might help the translator save time in his interpretative work and will allow the translation teacher to give safer guidelines to the students. Eco agrees that human thinking functions by admitting principles of identity and similarity. But the problem is to distinguish between the significant and the insignificant similarities. Suspicious interpretation, not wrong in itself, becomes too extreme when it considers all textual elements at the same level of signification. To explain this, Eco cites an example and luckily enough the game between English and French versions of his text proves his point exactly. The French version (in *Les limites de l'interpretation*) reads: "À la limite on peut s'amuser à affirmer qu'il existe un rapport entre l'adverbe *alors* et le substantif *crocodile* parce que - comme minimum - tous deux sont occurents dans la phrase que vous êtes en train de lire."(1992b:66) And he states that the faulty, or paranoic, interpretation will draw a maximal conclusion from this minimal relationship, suspecting a secret meaning. Now the English version of this passage (in *Interpretation and Overinterpretation*) (unwittingly?) offers material for Eco's demonstration. It reads: "One may push this to its limits and state that there is a relationship between the adverb 'while' and the noun 'crocodile' because - at least - they both appeared in the sentence that I have just uttered." (1992a: 48) Should I have to translate this sentence into French, as a suspicious or paranoic interpreter, I could have noted that both terms rhyme (*while* and *crocodile*) and then proposed: "On peut s'amuser à affirmer qu'il existe un rapport entre l'adverbe *alors* et le substantif *alligator*..." In so doing, I would have acted in exact opposition to Eco's statement. Introducing such a contradiction in Eco's words would qualify as an overinterpretation. Now don't ask me if Eco was aware of the risk in the English version. It would be no surprise coming from the author of *Foucault's Pendulum*. Overinterpretation tends to isolate certain textual elements and link them in a brightly meaningful relationship but without any consideration of their connection with the general meaning of the text. To choose 'alors' and 'alligator' for 'while' and 'crocodile' proves my poetical talent but does this add anything to our comprehension of the source sentence? On the contrary, as we saw, it contradicts the general meaning.

"In theory", Eco comments, "one can always invent a system that renders otherwise unconnected clues plausible. But in the case of texts there is at least a proof
depending on the isolation of the relevant semantic isotopy." (1992a: 62) The
notion of isotopy comes from Greimas' semantic theory and designates a series
of semantic features which constitutes a whole allowing the reader to define the
topic dealt with in a text.

To produce a right interpretation, Eco states, the only way for the reader is "to
check it upon the text as a coherent whole" (1992a: 65). Such a coherence would
prevent the reader from sliding into his own idiosyncratic interpretative drives.
The strategy for the translator is thus not to deconstruct the text into minimal
semantic segments, the method often taught in translation classes, but to figure
out the global meaning structure of the text. "My idea of textual interpretation as
the discovery of a strategy intended to produce a model reader, conceived as the
ideal counterpart of a model author (which appears only as a textual strategy),
makes the notion of an empirical author's intention radically useless." (Eco,
1992a: 66) The distinction between the empirical author and the model author is
of great pedagogical interest since it helps us answer the traditional student ploy:
"If I could, I would have asked the author!" or: "How do you know? You're not
the author!" The text stands as the only valid witness between an absent empirical author and a too present reader.

Eco draws a distinction between semantic (or semiosic) interpretation and critical (or semiotic) interpretation. He explains:

> Semantic interpretation is the result of the process by which an addressee, facing a Linear Text
> Manifestation, fills it up with a given meaning. Every response-oriented approach deals first
> of all with this type of interpretation, which is a natural semiosic phenomenon. Critical
> interpretation is, on the contrary, a metalinguistic activity - a semiotic approach - which aims
> at describing and explaining for which formal reasons a given text produces a given response
> (and in this sense it can also assume the form of an aesthetic analysis). ... Ordinary sentences
> ... only expect a semantic response. On the contrary, aesthetic texts or the sentence *the cat is
> on the mat* uttered by a linguist as an example of possible semantic ambiguity also foresee a
> critical interpreter. (1990: 55)

I suppose I am allowed to articulate the notions of a semiosic translation and
a semiotic translation in the same way. "The cat is on the mat" to use Eco's example. A simple semiosic interpretation would translate: "Le chat est sur la
carpette" where an interpretation concerned with the semiotic dimension as well
would give: "Mistigris est sur le tapis" or: "La chatte est sur la natte".

Now the question is: could both my proposals be accepted? Following Eco's
arguments, I would say that the first one, "Mistigris est sur le tapis", could be
accepted because this translation plays on a common designation of any cat as
Mistigris and the synonimy of 'carpette' and 'tapis'. My second translation, "La
chatte est sur la natte", could be taken as an overinterpretation because it relies

on an unknown, unshared piece of information concerning the sex of the animal and on the too specific designation of a piece of fabric lying on the floor as 'natte'. So the second translation will be rejected because, following Eco's arguments, nothing in the text itself (here the sentence) allows me this interpretation. Any translation theory will agree on the principle put forward by Eco: "To decide how a text works means to decide which one of its various aspects is or can become relevant or pertinent for a coherent interpretation of it, and which ones remain marginal and unable to support a coherent reading." (1992a: 146)

Furthermore, to give such an overinterpretation or to propose my previous examples of overtranslation excludes me from the community of readers. Eco reminds us: "C.S. Peirce, who insisted on the conjectural element of interpretation, on the infinity of semiosis, and on the essential fallibilism of every interpretative conclusion, tried to establish a minimal paradigm of acceptability of an interpretation on the grounds of a consensus of the community (which is not so dissimilar from Gadamer's idea of an interpretative tradition)." (1992a: 144) The notion of community in translation theory is very important since for the translator the intentio auctoris does not exist in itself. The work is done for a community.

So to come back to our initial story and as a conclusion: perhaps the first villager was right, the second villager was right and the rabbi's wife was also right. But in his interpretation, the rabbi himself was wrong. For a rabbi, his wife and two villagers form a community and, given that social structure, the rabbi's interpretation would not gain the consensus of the community. He would be a bad translator.

Notes

1. He develops this reflection mainly in *The Limits of Interpretation* (1990) and *Interpretation and Overinterpretation* (1992a), the latter being a collection of lectures; both books are discussed in this article.

INTERPRETING AND CLASS

DRONNINGGAARD

INTERPRETING STUDIES AND THE HISTORY OF THE PROFESSION

Margareta Bowen, Georgetown University, USA

In recent years, the profession has shown a growing interest in the history of interpreting. The professional organizations - the International Association of Conference Interpreters and the American Translators Association - have included articles on the history of interpreting in their publications, as have a number of university schools for interpreters. In 1988, the AIIC General Assembly organized an exhibition of memorabilia, and in 1992 it showed a videotape on the history of the profession. The *History of Translation* project launched by the International Federation of Translators and slated for completion in Spring 1994, under the leadership of Jean Delisle, will include a chapter on the role of the interpreter through the ages.

Given this growing momentum, we may well ask ourselves the following questions: What can the history of interpreting contribute to teaching and learning how to interpret? Can such information be useful, directly or indirectly, to the teacher of interpreting and to the future interpreter? To what extent can the lessons of the past allow us to draw conclusions about professional ethics today? What are the sources available to us?

Sources

I shall first address the categories of sources, written and oral, their reliability, and the relative ease of access to them, since this will influence conclusions on the other questions. We should distinguish between information from interpreters themselves, comments from the users of interpreting services, and those from third parties who, for any number of reasons, may mention interpreting services. The last category is, understandably, open-ended: administrators, journalists, politicians, are only some who come to mind. Historians, it should be noted, have seldom gone into the details of specific interpreting situations and the possible effect of the interpreters' work on the outcome of a conference.

Interpreters and delegates have given interviews and written autobiographies, reminiscences, and diaries, which in turn were edited. Interpreters, if they are government officials or international civil servants, need the approval of their superiors to publish. Once retired, or as a free lance, the interpreter is free from this formal constraint. In the interest of confidentiality, however, extreme caution is nevertheless advisable. Christopher Thiéry, for many years the chief interpreter of the French Ministry of Foreign Affairs, has gone on record stating that interpreters must never write their memoirs.

Interpreters' memoirs have been written, however, and we should not neglect them. Most of those that exist in book form, as the title or the preface indicate, were written as a contribution to the historical record and to diplomatic history, not as case histories of interpreting as a profession. To a greater or lesser degree, A.H. Birse's *Memoirs of an Interpreter*, Charles E. Bohlen's *Witness to History 1929-1969*, Eugen Dollman's *Dolmetscher der Diktatoren*, Robert B. Ekvall's *Faithful Echo*, Paul Schmidt's *Statist auf diplomatischer Bühne*, and Vernon Walters' *Silent Missions* all concentrate more on events and personalities than on interpreting. Many of these authors did not consider interpreting their profession.

Other objections have been raised to autobiographies in general. Salvador de Madariaga, whose memoirs are among the sources about interpreting at the League of Nations, wrote in the preface:

> I remember having read somewhere that Freud thought all autobiographies to be but lies. If such is the fact, I mean that Freud did say so, it may count as yet another case of that overstatement of which the Viennese magician seems to have been fond; for autobiographies need not be lies. What they nearly always are is inaccurate. But an inaccuracy only becomes a lie when it is deliberate; while most of the inaccuracies in a life written by the man who has lived it come from other causes than the intent to deceive the reader." (Madariaga 1973: ix)

The grounds for inaccuracies listed by Madariaga are the nature of human memory and a certain lack of objectivity when writing about oneself, which may go as far as a desire for self-enhancement. This last motive one could easily attribute to Dollman and, to a lesser degree, to Bohlen and Schmidt. Dollman also seems to seek self-justification in his book. On both counts the interpreters, however, are no different from some of their principals. Sergei Witte, chief negotiator for Tsar Nicholas II with the Japanese at Portsmouth is outright self-congratulatory in his memoirs, at least in their abridged English version, and claims that his press relations signally contributed to the success of the Treaty of Portsmouth. Eugen Trani (1969: 178) notes that "One must be careful in using Witte's recollections." The diary of Witte's secretary, I. Korostovetz, gives a very detailed description of the negotiations, including the language arrangements:

> The use of many languages slowed the proceedings considerably, especially because of the Japanese insistence upon absolute precision. Witte spoke mostly in French, but his use of the language was far from skilled, and he often lapsed into Russian. Adachi [Adachi Mineichiro, who was first secretary of legation in Paris and knew French well] translated the French into Japanese. When Witte spoke in Russian, Nabokov translated into English. Komura [the leader of the Japanese delegation] spoke in Japanese, which Adachi translated into French. (Esthus 1988: 97, quoting from Korostovetz. *Pre-War Diplomacy*: 65)

Vernon Walters' autobiographical book gives a great many comments and examples on interpreting as such, including admissions of the odd mishap here and there, and is therefore of particular interest under the heading of "teaching."

These few examples show that verification, preferably by primary sources on interpreters, like personnel files, diplomatic dispatches, correspondence, etc., is necessary. Normally, such material only becomes accessible after a certain lapse of time, depending on the various countries' and organizations' rules and regulations. Searches for direct sources are time-consuming and often involve travel. Archives have had to become more protective of their materials and open shelves, the researcher's ideal, are becoming less prevalent in many places, including the United States.

These practical difficulties of access and verification would speak against the incorporation of the history of interpreting in a course of studies for future conference interpreters. But we should remember that some sources are always available. Depending on the location of the university in question, its programs for one or two semesters abroad, and the networking that may be possible, students could be directed to projects that are feasible and would acquaint them with approaches to research, which can only pay off in the future. At an international panel discussion organized at the university of Vienna in May 1993, it was mentioned that after a four-year course of studies, students often have not learned how to do systematic research. The investigation of past occurrences could provide hands-on research experience that is bound to be useful for future work because the candidate will have learned how to use different library resources, go through a mass of material, organize notes, etc. Also, considering that university faculty must engage in both teaching and research, schools for interpreters should not try to seek exceptions to the rule. This would only lower their standing in the system. For recruitment of faculty, a pool of practicing interpreters who have had research experience during their studies is necessary.

Contributions to teaching

From oral history, teachers of interpreting have been using some elements of professional lore in their courses. The caveat about students' engaging in historical research applies equally to teachers including the anecdotal in course work. Care must be taken that these enjoyable excursions do not take up too much time. Still, anecdotes have their place. They liven up class meetings and they help students remember what was said. From my own student days, I remember Colonel Dostert telling us about General Eisenhower getting too close to the front line for his entourage's comfort, and Louis Paulovsky acting out the travails of the interpreter who came unprepared to a session in consecutive. For years I would think of the late Paulovsky every time when, before going to a meeting in consecutive, I would make sure I had enough pencils or ball-point pens in my handbag, and I stopped to buy the right kind of note-block. The fact that the interpreter's work may include an element of danger is being forcefully brought home to us by the elaborate security measures at most conference sites.

Some anecdotes - true or false - have been spread by journalists or interpreters themselves and are taken seriously by outsiders. The exchange (delegate) "This is not what I said," and (interpreter) "But this is what you should have said," which has been attributed in turn to André and Georges Kaminker, has been quoted to me by any number of people who never knew either one. It will probably continue to be quoted. Both denied the story as long as they lived. Interpreter students should be prepared for this kind of question or comment and be able to respond, putting things in perspective. When including this kind of material in class, teachers must make a clear distinction between fiction, the anecdotal, and historic fact.

Motivation

"Studying the history of translation means, in a way, to go over the history of the world, the history of cultures, but through the study of translation." (My translation. Van Hoof 1986: 5, as quoted by Delisle 1991: 63). Many university programs for the training of interpreters include history courses, either as prerequisites, as we do in Georgetown University, or as background courses during the earlier part of a longer course of studies (the German and Austrian universities, the Moscow school, etc.). In either case, the history courses are designed for a general student population, often with the history major in mind. This frequently leaves interpreting candidates with a feeling of irrelevancy, and they tend to devote only scarce attention to the course. A reversal of Van Hoof's sequence, namely studying world history through the history of the profession, would certainly be more motivating for interpreter students and provide many insights into the consequences of interpreting performance, while providing a better knowledge of history.

The interpreter's role in peace-making is often given as a reason for wanting to become an interpreter, either as a volunteer or as a candidate to a professional course. Vernon Walters describes the first moves towards peace between the United States and Vietnam. The negotiations to end the Spanish-American War are an instructive example of the interpreter's delicate position when serving both delegations, reminiscent of the position of the court interpreter who is constantly being watched to prevent any favoring of one side over the other. A detailed study of these examples, and their list could be lengthened considerably, would make young people more aware of the working conditions of interpreters.

Ethics and working conditions
When discussing professional ethics with an interpreting class, examples are
needed. The motto "do no harm" in the abstract may be evanescent, but examples
like the one given by Ekvall (1960: 160) drive the point home. He describes the
dramatic incident during the 1954 Asia Conference, when during the closing
session a double misunderstanding was caused by a mishearing between Paul
Henri Spaak, the Belgian Prime Minister, and Chou-en-lai, Premier of the
People's Republic of China and led to bad feelings that could not be entirely
overcome. One interpreter had thought Spaak was saying "dans l'autre texte," [in
the other text] when actually he was saying "dans notre texte." [in our text]
During the exchange that followed, more confusion ensued and both statesmen
concluded that the other was trying to invalidate what had been so painstakingly
agreed upon. When the misunderstanding was finally straightened out, some delegates were left with the nagging doubt that something untoward might have
been attempted and all had been deprived of the sense of a job well done that a
smooth session would have provided. In a more recent article, Shlesinger (1989:
31) reports on a similar problem from a rogatory hearing in Israel. The interpreter
had misheard just one word in the question "Were there any officers *higher* than
[name of the accused]?" and rendered it as if the Defense Counsel had said
"Were there any officers *hired* by [name of the accused]?" Since two interpreters
were on duty, working in consecutive, one was monitoring the other and the error
was corrected immediately. The court either did not notice or decided to overlook
the exchange between the interpreters. Such examples show not only the dangers
of misunderstandings, but also the importance of working conditions (the number
of interpreters) and the need for teamwork.

Another example (Walters 1973: 494-95) tells about a dinner speech by General
Eisenhower in France:

... he was pausing from time to time for translation. In this speech, he came to a phrase that
said, 'There are those who say that General de Gaulle is a very stubborn man.' At this point
he paused for translation. This was awkward for me because the French word for "stubborn",
entêté or têtu, is not a kindly word and is more pejorative that the word "stubborn" in English.
Since I did not know what the next sentence would say, I was caught on the horns of a considerable dilemma. So, in translating it, I said in French "There are those who say that General
de Gaulle is a very tenacious man." General de Gaulle roared with laughter, as did most of the
people in the room who understood what had happened. President Eisenhower then went on,
'But when that stubbornness is in the service of his country and the cause of human freedom,
then it is a quality to be admired rather than reproved.' A French newspaper, describing what
had occurred, said, 'The colonel diplomat drew a delicate veil across the sensitive word.' Here,
once again, I had demonstrated to myself the danger of attempting to tamper with what is being
said by one of the principals for whom one is translating.

Walters (1973: 276) also discusses briefings, for instance when in 1953 he was sent to the summit meeting in Bermuda, between Eisenhower and Churchill. "I flew back to the United States and was briefed at the White House and the State Department on the various projects which the United States expected to present at this meeting and broadly the US view of the purposes of this meeting." Paul Schmidt's memoirs also show the value of interpreter briefing, an approach which unfortunately seems to be disappearing today.

The perception of interpreters
  Let us repeat the first question we raised: What can the history of interpreting contribute to teaching and learning how to interpret? The same question can, of course, be raised about the history of medicine, a subject taught at most Medical Schools, and the history of law, included in many Law Schools. I asked a lawyer and one-time translator whose answer was immediate: any profession needs a sense of perspective. If doubts persist on the place of interpreting studies in the university, let us remind ourselves that analytical history only came about as a result of 18th century enlightenment (Butterfield 1955: 4).
  A sense of perspective, I submit, is essential for the image of the interpreter. What journalists select for publication on interpreting are often the marginal aspects. It is true that the published biographies deal almost exclusively with the highest level of the job. The authors of these autobiographies had direct access to chiefs of state, generals, and cabinet members, but what applies to the famous and powerful often has general validity. The place in the hierarchy of an organiz- ation is important for a profession's image. In his article in this volume (p. ??? above) on the interpreting services at the European Commission, Christian Heynold makes the point that "Our service reports directly to President Delors." Edouard Roditi (1982:1) showed us another aspect of the profession, when he stated that interpreters often were from border regions, from minorities or mixed parentage. In a democratic society such considerations do not matter, qualifica- tions do. Again, Walters (1973: 173), is a valuable witness on the qualifications of interpreters. In July 1948, while travelling throughout the countries of the Marshall Plan, he had to interpret Harriman's discussions with political and labor leaders and with financial experts.

  Sometimes it was embarrassing because I would have to translate some rather complicated
  financial or currency convertibility matter which I did not fully understand and it is quite
  impossible to translate adequately into another language something you do not understand yourself. Many people believe that this type of translation is a purely mechanical process. It is quite
  impossible to convey in another language someone's meaning unless you have fully grasped
  and understood it in your own.

Conclusion

If we remind ourselves of the historian's warning: "The dead hand of vanished generations of historians, scribes, and chroniclers has determined beyond the possibility of appeal the pattern of the past." (Carr 1962: 13), and if we consider the importance of a profession's image, we can only conclude that we should not neglect the study of the history of the profession. We should not leave the collection of material to those who would select them from the outsider's point of view. In the interest of the efficient use of time in our programs, I do not advocate the institution of special courses, but would rather like to see some interdisciplinary work on the part of full-time faculty, some assignments for students built into existing courses, some theses written in our institutions.

We are about to witness and - it is to be hoped - participate in far-reaching changes in the language professions. The present-day translators and interpreters and their students need the sense of perspective that a knowledge of history can give. We should not have to re-invent the wheel every time we have to explain basic concepts of our profession.

Holmegård

TEACHING AND LEARNING STYLES

David Bowen, Georgetown University, USA

When young people contemplate studying at a school for interpreters, they tend to ask "Which is the best school?" I will try to show that the question cannot be answered in the abstract. Not only do the strengths and weaknesses of schools vary depending on the culture and the educational system in which the school is located, but the general approach and the personality of both student and teacher make for an optimal or suboptimal fit.

Working within the U.S. university system

The size of the institution, its rules and regulations, whether it is a private or a public university - and the degree of control the teachers have over admissions - are the first consideration. By an American universities' standards, my institution, Georgetown University, is small; it has a student population of about twelve thousand, including Law and Medicine. It is a private university and highly selective. Admission is not automatic upon presentation of a high school diploma or a Scholastic Aptitude Test score (whose validity is once more being questioned). Good test results are required in most cases, but they alone will not get you into any of the top twenty universities, of which Georgetown is one. The Division of Interpretation and Translation has an entrance examination (described in Bowen and Bowen 1989). Since the applicant pool is international, that is candidates offer a wide spectrum of previous experience and studies, we make every effort to be non discriminatory as to their cultural background, and to orient ourselves by the profession's requirements only.

Admission

Having control over who gets admitted to the course puts the responsibility on the Division's faculty who administer the entrance examination. They must decide whether or not a student is ready to begin interpreting studies - and at Georgetown, for a full time student in our Division, this means interpreting classes from the very start, not language enhancement or beginning a new language. Only those who lack prerequisite courses from the areas of philosophy, economics, history, government and English (or their native language) have a "preparatory" year in other departments or other universities. Some counselling takes place during the entrance examination, especially with borderline cases.

Someone recently asked me what the ideal profile of a student in interpreting and translation is. I couldn't really answer, because there isn't one. Various attempts to design a questionnaire for career counseling have not brought much light to the matter either, as shown by the most recent project of the Princeton Educational Testing Service, which is to include a set of questionnaires on translation and interpreting in its career kits. The basic tenet has always been the old cliche that translators are introverts and withdrawn, whereas interpreters are extroverts and expansive. This is simply not the case; I fail to see much difference between sitting in a booth all day, two floors up from the delegates' floor, or sitting in an office in front of a computer or a translator's workstation. Certainly, business sense and what personnel managers call "interpersonal skills" will also play a part in a beginning interpreter's chances of success, but this kind of prediction, regrettably, goes beyond the scope of an entrance examination. One can only mention the business factor and include it in the course on professional ethics offered by our Division under the heading *Interpretation and Translation as a Profession*.

Major factors for admission are age and language combinations. The law of the United States, as increasingly elsewhere, forbids discrimination for the *handicap of age*. For some European institutions this has meant doing away with the upper age limit. We never had one and did not fare badly with older students, and if there are doubts about an older candidate, advising has shown itself to be more effective than a strict "No, we don't want you." The "No, we don't want you" approach, regrettably, is sometimes necessary with the younger set. Usually it is accompanied with "At any rate, not now," which young people tend to see as the same thing.

In the present volume, Christian Heynold deals with the truly daunting number of languages that have become official conference languages as a result of the successive enlargements of the European Union. There is, clearly, also the problem for the interpreters of maintaining the required range of three, four or more passive languages. A serious investigation would be desirable on questions such as: How well can people know these languages, and at what age? What is the lead time for acquiring an extra language, of the same linguistic family as those already known as opposed to one of a totally different family? Some staunch souls have, to date, started modern Greek under the Commission's policy of educational leave; this may turn out a picnic compared to Finnish.

Our location in a city with the largest number of foreign embassies sometimes entails a different problem: Which, if any, is the candidate's 'A' language? Is it a real 'A' or an honoris causa 'A'? Did the candidate's family move from one foreign service post to another, from one school system to another? The school systems are different and consequently also affect the time needed for interpreter training. Here we also have the first one of several personality aspects: some people work best under pressure, others need time to work at their own pace. This does not necessarily imply that the second group is going to be too slow for simultaneous interpreting, but it may be a warning sign.

Student expectations

Student expectations may be completely wrong. They may think it is easy. "All you do is sit there and talk". Some people are misadvised by well-meaning language teachers. Fortunately, guidance counselors are less inclined today to tell female students they should opt for languages, even if truly talented for the sciences. Our environment, to a certain extent, also propagates the wrong ideas by separating foreign language departments, where there are any, from the English department (which every U.S. college and university has). As a result, English does not look like a language you study or perfect. You major in foreign languages. The mention "insufficient knowledge of the native language" which was listed many years ago by M. Bachrach as one of the three reasons why few candidates pass the European Parliament's recruitment test for translators, usually comes as a surprise to students. Yet, in U.S. colleges, English proficiency ranges from "honor student" in English to "remedial English."

Motivation, 'Operation Bootstrap' and 'Unrequited Love'

Regrettably, it is often the highly motivated students, those who were serious language majors and devoted great efforts to acquiring what language teachers call near-native fluency, who have to be told that they can not work into that language as conference interpreters. Not as simultaneous interpreters, anyway. One may have to explain patiently that all the sweet elderly gentlemen who had assured the candidate that her French was perfect, if attending a conference as delegates, would be the first to complain to the organizer that what was coming out of the French booth was pure nonsense. "But I love French!" is the usual reaction. The non-prescriptive approach to language teaching may be responsible for this kind of unrequited love, as well as some modern language teachers' fascination with near-native pronunciation. American candidates occasionally send us cassette recordings with a sample of their "perfect" accent, which can be quite deceptive if not accompanied by an in-depth knowledge of the unspoken but implied.

In most cases, motivation alone will not turn such situations around. What makes matters worse, is the lack of appropriate courses to improve a student's foreign language beyond a certain point and the uncertainty of the outcome. The easy way out taken by most teachers is to advise a prolonged stay in a country where the language is spoken. Sometimes this works. But we all know people who have lived in our country for ten or twenty years and still have not acquired the elusive "near-native" fluency which still would, at best, get them a B rating. We do know some success stories, fortunately, but we do not know enough about them to explain them. Often, what worked for one person, will not work for the next.

Learning styles

Beyond language acquisition, we have seen that, generally, there does not seem to be a Royal Road applicable to all. Therefore we looked at our successful candidates, those who worked well in class and did well once released upon society, and tried to compare their approaches to what experimental psychology has to say about learning styles. We soon came to the conclusion that learning styles, which are described differently by different authors, must meet matching teaching styles. The authors we found most helpful are Frederic Vester, Pierre Casse and Eric Berne. Both Vester and Casse distinguish four styles. Berne actually describes the patterns of interaction between people and the secret agenda they may have.

The sociologist Pierre Casse (whom we met at a seminar of the Society for Intercultural Education, Training and Research) gave us permission to use his self-assessment test on large groups of candidates to our entrance examination and made a video-recording of a lecture on his method for us. His four groups are: 'idea oriented', 'process oriented', 'people oriented' and 'action oriented.' These categories, which seldom are found as pure types, come close to Vester's groups of schoolchildren (Vester 1978: 40 and 205, illustrations) who may learn best by experience, or by a friendly talk with a classmate, or by detailed demonstration, or from listening to an abstract presentation. Obviously, a predominantly process oriented person will become frustrated when the teacher concentrates on criticizing results. Vester's questionnaires can be adapted for asking students to make suggestions in an interpreting class.

Teaching styles

In the present volume there are some outstanding examples of teaching styles to suit the process oriented student (Daniel Gile). Students appreciate a teacher who is genuinely interested in them, who changes the approach in accordance with the material studied and their needs. This dynamic approach to teaching means that one occasionally has to make concessions to a student's learning style, since we are bound to admit people who are different from one teacher or the other.

The role of the teacher is not to terrorize the undeserving, but to build confidence, which must be justified. A false sense of security is dangerous. When teaching translation and interpreting, teachers are all too often tempted to discuss only the mistakes. Of course, they must be taken up. Danica Seleskovitch recommends that in the beginning only the most serious ones be taken up, and as the students progress, more and more detail is to be insisted upon (Seleskovitch and Lederer 1989). We feel that at the same time students should be told when they have found a very good solution by themselves or shown specialized knowledge that can be shared with the rest of the group. Evaluation grids can help by showing different kinds of mistakes and awarding stars for unexpectedly felicitous solutions (Margareta Bowen 1989: 58, 59). Some mistakes must be corrected immediately, while the student is still working on a speech and is bound to repeat it. A post mortem of the performance is not sufficient to avoid the ingraining of certain mistakes. This need not be a long interruption; a disbelieving "WHAT?" from the teacher or a classmate will be enough to let the culprit know that a 'false friend', for instance, or a stylistically discordant colloquialism will not go unrebuked. One may add, for reinforcement, a pun or a brief anecdote, to help the students remember the correct formulation (see also Bowen p. 169, above). If, at a later time, the same mistake is repeated by the same person, one will know that the comment did not work as a memory prompt and should not be reused, and instead one may resort to a play-back of the recorded performance, preferably on the student's own time.

In addition to building confidence, the teacher must monitor listenability. Any particularly annoying speech mannerisms or patterns, for instance the "shrill suburban housewife" syndrome, or the "voice like a buzz-saw" must be corrected before training begins. A rising note of hysteria while under pressure and a "Christian Maiden Being Fed to the Lions in the Coliseum of Imperial Rome at its Most Decadent" delivery can be remedied by confidence building. Even the most dedicated teacher cannot teach constructive adrenalin flow.

Students in action

The recognition of the four basic types means that one can readily react to students. There may be the teacher-dependent student, who needs to be encouraged to be more assertive and make decisions independently. More common is the show-off, with a tremendous repertoire of trivia, which may or may not be of interest. There is also the discussant, who if left alone would take half a semester arguing over two paragraphs. There is the 'team-teacher' who helps you teach your course; she may get on your and other students' nerves and, worst of misinstruct gullible classmates. There are also those who must have a theory, system or rule. They are the ones who use card files, complain that the course is not well "organized", take to packets of texts, etc. An early warning of this student reaction is important, if the teacher is not personally given to card files or their modern equivalents. Schools that use the student-teacher evaluation system provide such feedback, but one may wish to get a reaction before the mainframe computer has spit out the results a few weeks after the end of the semester and ask all students to write an item for the suggestion box. This may well avoid the unpleasant surprise colleagues from one school had at a meeting, when a recent graduate had been invited as a panelist and this pride and joy of her school, like Oliver Twist in the orphan's home, politely said "Un peu plus [de pédagogie]!" ("A bit more pedagogy")[1]

One remedy to this longing for systematicity is special assignments to those students. Depending on the seriousness of the case, these could be more prescriptive material like resolutions, or appropriate readings on theory, the conclusions to be presented to the other students as an exercise for Public Speaking class, preferably recorded on videotape. The ensuing discussion can cover both content, presentation, and interpreting performance by classmates to give all their due.

The other extreme is the intuitive student who, if good, is excellent; if bad, is helpless and floundering around, never knowing what he did and why. In between, there is a continuum, on which most people fit. For those who want a system, it is usually in the attempt to beat it and to find shortcuts, for instance by looking for rules instead of reading background material, or trying to limit text preparation by studying word frequency lists. Unfortunately for this type of student, most speakers put their time to better use, and do not favor simple declarative sentences, similar to those of an earnest fifth grader. Those with extremely rule-bound 'A' languages, who are always asking "but, what is the rule?" need to learn how to work in a language operating on unwritten rules.

Once you have these people together, they begin to interact. If you are out of luck, they will fight. The show-off student, for example, is often resented by the others, and care must be taken not to let the most withdrawn one sit in a corner thinking abstract thoughts and going off on tangents. To have a workable class, one must watch over time management and still let students make the kind of creative contribution to the class that suits their personality.

Conclusion

Indeed, selecting students for interpreting studies is rather like choosing a doctor: you want one mature enough to have made any major mistakes elsewhere, but not old enough to retire or die on you. Once you have selected them, you must live with them.

Note
1. AIIC Schools symposium, Strasbourg, 1986.

Nylars Kirke

EXPERIMENTS IN THE APPLICATION OF DISCOURSE STUDIES TO INTERPRETER TRAINING

Robin Setton, GITIS, Fu Jen University, Taipei, Republic of China

Introduction

A review of the steadily growing literature shows the continued existence of several competing approaches to interpreter training, a specialisation within an already highly specialised field. A keen rivalry has developed between the exponents of a traditional, practice-based, intuitive approach, and researchers originating in 'harder' disciplines, who have proposed numerous teaching methods based on findings from cognitive psychology, communication science, and statistical studies.

The controversy over the most appropriate paradigm for research into conference interpreting is thus sadly reminiscent of an old-fashioned confrontation between the 'arts' and the 'sciences'. Interpreting being a social function, no test-tube type investigation can be expected to give a satisfactory account of it; any forced attempt to produce results in interpreting research, with its small samples and multiple factors, complying with 'scientific' imperatives such as reproducibility and predictability must run the risk of seriously distorting or over-exploiting the data. On the other hand, we lay ourselves open to the charge of technophobia, mystification or obscurantism if we wilfully ignore the latest methods and findings in those areas where parameters are quantifiable (scientific observation), as well as the latest extended conceptual apparatus in the humanities - notably, the burgeoning linguistics of *parole*. Recent writing suggests that developments in the study of natural language at new levels (pragmatics, discourse analysis, speech act theory) may offer a credible framework in which to formalise the 'naive-empiricist' training strategies pursued intuitively by trainers in the past.

In this article I shall describe some strategies used in the training of Chinese-English conference interpreters at the Graduate Institute of Translation and Interpretation (GITIS), Taiwan, focusing on devices to enhance the familiarity of trainees with discourse-level characteristics of public speech in the two 'working cultures'. This cross-cultural training experience has particularly highlighted the need for enhancement of pragmatic and rhetorical competence in both comprehension and production. In the discussion, a simple multi-level discourse model is proposed, both as a guide to identifying problems in performance, and as a component in a comprehensive description of interpreting, complementing other facets such as the very thorough catalogue of situational parameters (mode of presentation, speed, visual contact, preparation) explored by Franz Pöchhacker, and the wide-ranging analysis of interpreter strategies begun by Sylvia Kalina (both in this volume). The low assessment of Pöchhacker's recorded extract (below, p. 239), for instance, can be attributed to rhetorical failure: heartfelt thanks and welcome delivered in a hesitant, doubtful tone.

The exercises and training strategy described here were designed to address particular difficulties, some of which are local or culture-related, others task-related; these are described in more detail in a previous article (Setton 1993a). The influence of different historical conceptions of rhetoric and the role of the speech act in East and West, and other cultural contrasts, are also described elsewhere (Setton 1991 and 1993b).

Theoretical position

However, in view of some current controversies, I begin with a short statement of my pre-theoretical position on interpreting:

1. That insofar as the product (sometimes called the 'target text') of successful translation or interpreting is experienced as natural spontaneous language, the same criteria should apply in evaluating its effectiveness.

2. That spontaneous (not translated or interpreted) text is generated from a deep structure (to borrow modern terminology), and not from a prior and different surface structure; we assume that thought and the desire to communicate are pre-lexical, and hence that the success of *any* text as communication is proportional to (a) the extent that it is generated from deep structure, that is to the extent that it is assimilated at a pre-lexicalised level; and (b) its interactionality.

The question of *equivalence* presupposes agreement about some reliable definition of *units* of discourse and 'text'; and a reliable measurement of co-text and context *domains*. Since the latter demonstrably expand in the course of the text, and are constantly modified by the act of utterance itself, this direction of inquiry currently seems too open-ended (rather as generative semantics appeared by the 1970's).

However, translating or interpreting into a non-native language will require more frequent fallback on 'pragmatic' equivalence-based solutions.

3. That since there are at least two bipolar parameters (source text/target text, speaker/hearer), translation or interpreting are most usefully investigated by considering at least two components: comprehension and production. The assumption is that however fast the process, it is merely a blurring, or at most only partial

'pragmatic' short-circuiting, of two separate and overlapping activities: comprehension and formulation.

4. That it is more productive to focus on these activities in themselves independently before speculating on the whole process, thus dividing research and training into three distinct fields:

- Discourse *comprehension* at various levels: segmental/semantic/pragmatic, including any and all factors involved in drawing inferences and making interpretations.

- Discourse *production*: degrees of expressive proficiency: language performance and enhancement, memory and activation, lexical retrieval; higher expressive functions such as discourse ordering and presentation and rhetorical effects such as emphasis, foregrounding, abstraction, compression, ellipsis and cohesion.

- Discourse *handling*: technical skills and aids to the interpreting task (such as consecutive notes); and physical conditions favourable or unfavourable to one or both of the activities.

Chinese-English interpreter training
Local constraints
At this stage it is necessary to explain some of the special constraints on the Chinese-English and Chinese-Japanese training of interpreters in Taiwan - and probably on other non-European programmes - as compared to established programs in Western Europe.

Environment and culture-related problems
Training interpreters to work between two languages with very different social and cultural backdrops, such as Chinese and English, poses problems at levels not encountered in European programmes. The most obvious are:

(1) trainee recruitment, related to the status of the profession: it is difficult to find sufficient numbers of candidates highly qualified in both cultures and to attract them to what is still, outside Europe, a small, marginal and poorly paid profession (Setton 1993a).

(2) the culture gap (or the 'ethnosemantic' dimension): the traditional 'second language deficit' here extends into wide areas of culture and thought and the different conventions of communication, debate and the presentation of ideas.

Task-related challenges
The market requires interpreters to be fully 'bi-active', i.e. able to work accurately and produce acceptable grammar, vocabulary, register, etc. in two languages, both in consecutive and simultaneous. Also, since most multilingual con-

ferences require Chinese, English and Japanese, relay interpreting (in which inter-preters have to rely on a colleague's version from source languages they do not themselves understand) is the rule, not the exception, placing high demands on production of the acquired language, particularly in terms of clarity, compression and cohesion.

These constraints have prompted research at our institute into new strategies to improve students' familiarity with the pragmatic and cultural dimensions of dis-course. Fortunately, small class numbers (3 to 5 students per class) have made it possible to implement, refine or apply new experimental methods fairly rapidly.

Curriculum design

While some widely-accepted training principles, such as the progressivity of the interpreter training curriculum from consecutive to simultaneous interpreting, have been conserved (and extended, with 'B' to 'A' before 'A' to 'B', and in-tensive simultaneous-with-text in the final semester), the special constraints des-cribed above have prompted the following adjustments at various stages:

1. Entrance examination: one-language, context-related tests.
2. Introductory courses (2-3 months) in each of the working languages, con-sisting of various exercises to enhance *discourse familiarization*.
3. 'Reportage' sight translation.
4. Extensive training in simultaneous-with-text.
5. Relay training.

This article discusses my experiments using three exercises:

In comprehension: anticipation (introductory and again before beginning simul-taneous).

In production: speech construction (introductory and with consecutive note-taking).

In 'handling': 'smart shadowing' or same-language 'chunk' paraphrasing (trans-ition from consecutive to simultaneous, as explained below).

I now take a closer look at the context in which the exercises were introduced.

Entrance selection: combined cognitive and language testing

Since no-one may be admitted to postgraduate studies in Taiwan solely on the basis of an oral examination, the written part of the entrance exam must serve as a final test for translation students while also testing prospective interpreters, for whom it counts for 50% of the grade for admission. The written papers in the 'A' and 'B' languages must thus be designed to test active and passive language proficiency, but also whole-text comprehension, interpretive skills and general world knowledge. At the same time, in view of the scarcity of good candidates, it must allow potential interpreters such as overseas Chinese, non-Chinese etc, whose writing *skills* often cannot compete with locally-educated applicants, to have a chance at the orals.

This has led us to include tests such as paraphrase, summary, and the insertion of synonyms in context, as well as an evolved version of the *Cloze* test, which can be considered in its basic approach as a forerunner to some of the exercises in subsequent interpreter training.

'Discourse-level' Cloze

The standard Cloze test used in standard language proficiency testing consists of text with words omitted, usually randomly or at regular intervals, with a choice of only one 'correct' answer. The test is thus easy to grade (by an optical reading device), since it is context-independent; but as Sergio Viaggio has pointed out (1992b), this is precisely what disqualifies it as a test for trainee translators or interpreters, since it implies a one-to-one correspondence between sign and signification which not only flies in the face of linguistic science, but also enshrines the word as the only possible sign-unit, thus confining the test to one of 'isolated' morpho-syntactic proficiency.

The 'discourse-level' Cloze test given in our entrance examination is similar in principle to Viaggio's 'cognitive clozing', except for the progressive element (it is given as a one-time written test) and the length and choice of the omissions: candidates may be asked to supply a whole paragraph.

Completed versions are assessed to different standards ('A' or 'B' language) for grammatical and lexical, but also logical (semantic) acceptability, and for appropriateness on the basis of a minimum assumption of knowledge about the world. The use of this to test for admission shifts the emphasis to text comprehension, which is tested at several levels: the ability to construe meaning, to apprehend logical development and to recognise and adapt to the illocutionary force in the passage. Cognitive preparation (general knowledge of world affairs, etc.) can also be tested by an appropriate choice of text. Grammatical and lexical proficiency - 'language' proficiency in the restricted sense - are of course naturally tested both on the comprehension and production (performance) side.

The introductory courses
Goals

The three-month introductory module in our curriculum is designed to fulfil several functions:

a. *to enhance language comprehension and proficiency,*
b. *to train memory,* particularly each student's familiarity with his/her own

memory.

c. to create a *sensitivity to different types of discourse and register*, and to the relative significance of discourse parts in different contexts, while introducing the subject matters of international meetings.

d. *to draw attention to the pitfalls of interference.*

Contrary to expectation, the morphological and etymological distance between Chinese and English does not remove the problem of interference. Chinese has been heavily influenced by English in the last hundred years, both in terms of partial imitation of syntactic structures (Kubler 1985) and 'direct' translations of concepts which appear straightforward, but in fact have undergone the same subtle semantic and functional skewing as borrowings between all language pairs: the Chinese word *tupo(xing)*, for instance, conjures up the English word 'break-through', but it more often means 'groundbreaking', and can be used as adjective or verb, rarely as noun, while the English word is hard to use other than as a noun.

Introductory exercise

Exercises in this phase include:

1. Oral (consecutive) paraphrasing and memorisation.

These exercises begin along the lines of those described by Weber (1991: 404-9) as preparation for and introduction to consecutive, such as public speaking (reading aloud of speeches followed by same-language paraphrase) and memory exercises from simple narrative or descriptive extemporaneous speeches, but are then continued in the same language for a second and third month, with more difficult input from conference speeches, TV interviews, presentations on economic and political topics.

2. Language enhancement and 'agility' exercises such as at-sight paraphrase and gist extraction (Mackintosh 1991: 391). Register switching has proved difficult in the early stages, and is not recommended in the 'B' language before the second year, when students begin simultaneous into 'B'. Other exercises quoted by Mackintosh are recommended to students for enhancement of active proficiency in their own time: shadowing, reading out loud, active reading. Mock conferences are staged from the second semester, notably for training in relay interpreting.

3. Speech analysis and speech construction.

The majority of candidate trainee interpreters in Taiwan know little or nothing of public life, still less the world of international conferences; initiation to the vocabulary, procedures and structure of international organisations, treaties and conventions, budgets, voting etc., is begun in the introductory semester, then consolidated in the third semester.

Against this cognitive background, attention is drawn to differences in the patterns of discourse organisation and presentation in different language/cultures; comparative studies of speeches, and anticipation exercises (discussed below), raise awareness and familiarity on the receptive side. On the production side, confidence is increased by the speech construction exercise. Students also shadow real videotaped speeches on their own.

In a regular analysis of speechmaking, large numbers of speeches taken from actual conferences and public occasions (as far as possible in an international context) are analysed, and attention drawn to recurring patterns (a heuristic approximation is given in Figure 1 overleaf: p. 190). Articles and extracts from popular guides to speechmaking (such as Dale Carnegie's) are occasionally handed out as background reading.

Speech construction has been experimented with, both as active language proficiency and public speaking exercise and as a support to teaching consecutive interpreting (below).

In this exercise, the instructor constructed idealized consecutive notes from a speech. Conventional note-taking principles of verticalisation, indentation superposition and division were known to the student, as well as the use of arrows, horizontal lines and a number of commonly used symbols. After having other abbreviations and symbols explained, the student delivered a speech from the notes which are shown in Figure 2 (overleaf: p. 191).

The idealized notes are of course here merely a construct to illustrate this function/toolkit paradigm of consecutive with notes. The student's freedom of interpretation and representation (step 1) is not interfered with, since the exercise begins directly at the rendition stage.

Consecutive interpreting

The numerous analyses of the consecutive interpreting task in the literature are here interpreted (again borrowing from recent linguistics terminology in an attempt to relate the study of consecutive interpreting to mainstream discourse studies) in a simple two-step 'generative-functional' model:

1. *Audition*: Listening, comprehension, interpretation, representation in notes and memory.

Notwithstanding variations in the use of source language vs. target language abbreviations, symbols (individual or common) etc., by different interpreters, consecutive notes with their symbols, relations, layout and hierarchy can be described as an interlexical phase; they can be conceived of as representing one layer of a grid of functions, references, ties and rhetorical effects which is com-

Figure 1: Speech analysis

"[1]Guten Morgen, meine Damen und Herren. I am [2]honoured to be with you today, and I am [3]grateful to Minister Stoiber for the invitation. It is also a [4]pleasure for me to share the program with my [5]colleague and good friend, BKA President Hans Zachert.

I am [6]privileged to address this [6]illustrious group about [7]the United States experience in fighting the plague of organised crime. I accepted this invitation [8]in the hope that our experiences might help you as you engage in your [8]current crime-control debates. [9X]But I would like you to know that I have [9N]not come to speak in support of any political platform in the debate over organized crime legislation. I have [9N]not come to tell you how to solve your crime problems - [9Y]but rather I have come to share with you some facets of the FBI's experience in our [S]35-year war against crime.

Today, [10a]because organized crime and illegal drugs have become a global problem, they are of increasing concern to [10a]all nations. These problems are also of great personal concern to [10b]me. [11]I have lost two close friends and professional colleagues to violence perpetrated by organized crime [[12]names, dates].

[A]like an infectious disease,....to fight this disease, [13]all governments need to...

[14/1]Today, I would like to discuss with you how the FBI's techniques have evolved over the years. [14/2] then I'd like to share with you some of the techniques.... [14/3] Finally I'd like to share with you...work together....First,

FUNCTION		REFERENCE				
	d.e.	institution/person me you other	events	place	time	topic
greeting		1				
honour h pleasure p		2h		4p-*N* 5		
compliment c						
thanks		3*N* 6				7
introduction						
setting scene						**8timely - motive:** **x 9 N-Y**
description		11		12*N*		
reason/argument		10b 10a				
moral						
recommendation		13-13-13				**14/1-2-3**

Abbreviations:
RESOURCE: quotation, statistic S, news item NI, proverb, name *N*, analogy A
DEVICE: negation N/assertion Y, suspense (*), contrast (x), concession (/)
D.E. (displacement effect): humour, metalanguage
STRINGS: topic definition, analogic and discursive strings

*from: "Combatting Organized Crime", delivered by William Sessions, Director of the FBI, at a Symposium in Germany on Dec. 4th, 1992 and reprinted in *Vital Speeches of the Day,* Vol. LIX, no. 9, Feb. 15th, 1993, City News publishing Co., Mount Pleasant.

Figure 2: Speech construction

Context, situation (an international conference in Pyongyang, Korea), proper nouns and titles were given to the student in advance.

(1) **Constructed notes** (originally hand-drawn):

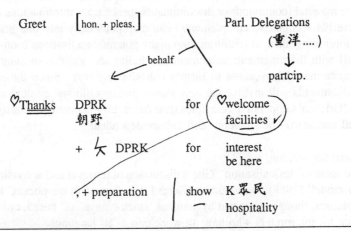

Guide to abbreviations:
Hon: honour; pleas.: pleasure
DPRK: Democratic People's Republic of North Korea
重洋 : beginning of a cliche meaning 'crossing seas and mountains'
朝野 : "court and populace" (also "government and opposition")
♡　　indicates cordiality, underlining indicates emphasis, tick　✓　indicates approval.

(2) **Reconstruction** (by a second-semester student with Chinese A, English B, after approximately 6-7 weeks of consecutive training. Pauses of one second, or of two or more seconds, are marked [ ] and [pause] respectively.

Distinguished Guests, Ladies and Gentlemen -

It is my great pleasure and honour to be here to extend my welcome to all delegates [pause]. We have come [pause] across the world to participate in this conference [pause] and on behalf of all the delegates here I'd like to express my wholehearted thanks to the peoples and the government of the [ ] Democratic People of [pause] Republic of Korea for their warm welcome [ ] and for the facilities provided to us. Especially I'd like thank the President of [ ] the Chairman of [ ] the Republic [ ] the democratic Peoples of the Republic of Korea [ ] for his interest of being here [ ] and, er [pause] the active participation of both the people and the government here showed that [ ] the [ ] Korean people's hospitality which we are very grateful for...

plemented by a second component in the interpreter's memory.

This terminology conveniently brackets the issue of whether discourse can exist in a 'deverbalised' state, leaving it to philosophy or a future breakthrough in cognitive science.

2. *Rendition*: Lexicalisation of the function-reference grid as a new 'surface structure' from the available language 'toolkit'.

Needless to say, the mapping processes are multiple and diverse: any form of utterance material (continuous or discontinuous speech acts, combinations of verbal/nonverbal + cognitive complements) can map potentially into one grid-item at audition/noting, then, at rendition, into many potential realisations (non-verbal included) with the pragmatic adjustments, including the addition or subtraction of utterance material, required to form a cohesive 'neotext'. Since these pragmatic adjustments will involve the new shared presuppositional context and the various 'Gricean' cooperative principles (relevance, informativeness, clarity, etc.) they will necessarily be situation- and culture-dependent.

The toolkit (or lexicon)

On the issue of 'lexicalisation', Gile's discussion of retrieval and activation (the 'gravity model' (1988)) is instructive. Gerard Ilg's "penny in the pocket" tips on useful phrases, though suspected by some as 'stock-equivalent' based, come into their own for interpreters who have to work into a 'B' language.

Frequent instructor's demonstrations, and attendance at conferences, have proved to be extremely effective at this stage.

Transition from consecutive to simultaneous

"Smart" shadowing, or real-time paraphrase

A review of the literature shows that there seems still to be some vagueness about the first steps in simultaneous interpreting. Among exercises proposed by cognitive psychologists, some, of the multitasking type (for example counting backwards while listening), have been accepted even by diehards among the 'empiricists'. Shadowing, on the other hand, is more than controversial. Some Japanese training schools fill the gap with 'booth sentence-by-sentence consecutive' in which trainees translate the previous sentence into the target language during pauses.

Our experience has been that in spite of everything, students at this stage still need every possible incitement to claim sovereignty over their own formulation and struggle free from the morphological straitjacket of the incoming language. Admittedly, one of the motivations for trying out these exercises was variety in classwork, since the traditional 'multitasking' exercises soon become monotonous.

"Smart" shadowing has been very well received by our students and appears so far to be the most effective way of guiding students into coherent simultaneous interpreting.

At first, 'processing units' are suggested by the instructor by pauses at possible sense-unit boundaries. Students can be encouraged to make complete syntactic units (even sentences) at each pause. Over a period of six to eight class hours, the various dimensions of the problem are introduced in steps:

- reader or speaker *pauses after incomplete sense units*: students' attention is drawn to various strategies: holding pattern; filler material (depending on length of pause or delay before next 'clue' is heard); 'open' grammar.

- *pauses are shortened*: trainees learn to keep listening while talking, finish their sentences etc.

- *the stop-go flow glides into normal speech.*

Time off is taken for suggestions as to opening structures, instructor demonstrations, and comments on lagging and leading.

Any of these steps can be done either from 'B' into 'A' or in the same language, providing practice in paraphrasing and verbal agility.

One spin-off of the technique has been an insight into 'segmentation'. Several authors have sought to measure lag, describing input discourse in terms of numbers of successive words or linear segments (Carey 1971; Moser 1978; Lambert 1988; Davidson 1992) but it appears that when real simultaneous begins to flow, it soon passes from the overlapping processing of a succession of segments (if it ever was that) to a series of sharpening approximations, in which semantic fragments (not words or clauses) are seized on to produce provisional non-committal output. Such fragments are suggested in bold in the following excerpt from same-language paraphrasing, where the pace of the original is slow and the interpreter cannot wait for too long:

*Source text: We have also **suffered** the consequences of the uncontrolled **international***
Interpreter: ...another **problem** we had is ... **all**
Source text: exports of hazardous nuclear waste
Interpreter: **over the world**...   ...dangerous nuclear waste is being sent to Thailand and...

Anticipation: a probe into the 'lead' dimension

In the anticipation exercises, speeches are read out, or tapes of speakers projected, after the trainees have been filled in on as much as they would be expected to know about the event, situation, players, place and so on. The tape or speaker stops occasionally and students try to continue the sentence. The exercise is reported here simply on the basis of student response, suggesting its value as a consciousness-raising exercise.

The role of anticipation in simultaneous interpreting is widely recognized in the literature, although - perhaps due to the greater difficulty of identifying and measuring it - it has not attracted the same interest as 'décalage' (lag).

Lederer (1978) posits two distinct types - anticipations based on sense expectation and those based on language prediction, as when the components of stock collocations like 'play...a role' or 'shoulder...responsibility' are separated by long stretches of intervening text. Wilss (1978), drawing largely on work by Mattern in German-English simultaneous interpreting, calls these moments *anticipation cues*, or *A cues*, classifying them as follows:

- 'co-textual' (intralingual);
- extralinguistic (situational); and
- context-independent cues, such as those based on a knowledge of standardised communication processes ("on behalf of my delegation I would like to...thank"), as well as cliches or "petrified, idiomatic phrases (collocations)".

Not surprisingly, interest in anticipation has been highest among those working with syntactically asymmetric language pairs requiring rearrangement at sentence level: typically, in simultaneous interpreting from German. Chinese and Japanese, being 'structurally problematic' source languages of this type, have seen similar studies (Davidson); strategies proposed by Zhuang (1991), for example, mainly address Wilss' third type of 'A-cue'.

Wilss claims that "the development of a subtle syntactic and semantic anticipatory ability is a useful goal in the linguistic and psychological teaching of [simultaneous interpreting]" (1978: 350). However, differences between Japanese or Chinese and English or French are not confined to the sentence level, suggesting the potential value of cultivating a 'wider angle' of anticipatory ability. Again, discourse analysis might contribute to building a knowledge base for such work.

Discussion

Personal experience of Chinese-English interpreter training, and a perusal of the literature on translation and interpreting between Japanese and Indo-European languages, indicate that problems 'above' the sentence level arise more frequently than in interpreting between European languages. At the same time, recent literature from Europe shows that 'macro' perceptions of interpreting are gaining ground generally, and a clear need is emerging for a more comprehensive account of the various components of the activity. In this volume (below, pp. 233-242), Franz Pöchhacker presents a good working overview of some objective situational factors affecting interpreter performance, and Sylvia Kalina has embarked on an extensive corpus-based study of interpreter strategies (below, pp.

225-232). As a third component, as it were 'upstream' of these dimensions, the theoretical and training project needs a framework capable of giving an 'extended-linguistic' account of tasks and difficulties in the comprehension, handling and production of discourse.

The 'handling' stage is now being explored, after a generation of plausible but unsubstantiated intuitive descriptions, by numerous process-oriented studies and contributions from the new cognitive sciences, while useful practical experimentation continues in the schools.

The last two decades have seen the emergence of an 'extended linguistics' offering new tools to describe macro-phenomena in language communication, raising hopes for a happy convergence of the arts and sciences in the overlapping fields of pragmatics and cognition. But in applying discourse analysis to conference interpreting we have to be very selective. It is doubtful at present whether the mainstream exponents of these disciplines are even aware of this application: the bulk of work still addresses written corpuses, while, even in the area of the spoken word, Grice's maxims were devised with reference to everyday conversation. There are also numerous studies of interviews with mental health patients, etc. This latter work will be of value to the community interpreter; but conference and media discourse, where the flow of communication is different from conversation, and speech is part spontaneous and part prepared, will require a different perspective, in which some traditional discourse analysis issues, such as turn-taking, or narrative structure, will be of marginal relevance:

CORPUS (TEXT TYPE):

WRITTEN	literary (narrative)	technical informative	graffiti recipes
ORAL	discursive conversation turn-taking		pathology (patient interviews)

Figure 3: Areas within current discourse analysis studies pertinent to conference interpreting (shaded)

Conclusion: theory and pedagogy

The big question remains of what can be taught. Traditionally, students were told to 'go away and learn the language', and later, to 'go beyond the words to the ideas'; but in some cultures - where speech is traditionally viewed as ritual, its content authoritative, and its forms canonical - this latter is not as obvious a contrast as it is to Europeans, and may have as little effect as the instruction to 'learn it all by heart' in a Western liberal arts college. Consequently - leaving aside the question of whether such 'exhortatory pedagogy' is ideal even in Europe - we are forced, in Asia, to find higher, credible explanation and illustration. Years abroad are indispensable, and at the skills level, instructor demonstration is very effective, but they are not always enough; we should not abandon the search for a structured pedagogy of conference interpreting articulated to the mainstream of communication studies.

At this stage, certain avenues in discourse analysis look more promising than others. Semantic and cognitive approaches still appear too abstract - and controversial - for use in pedagogy: Kintsch and van Dijk's proposition-based representation of discourse content (1978), for instance, is called into question by Chafe's suggestion that "knowledge is not stored propositionally ... the basic form of store may consist of individuated events and objects, each with an associated analogic content...until a need to verbalise them makes propositional decisions necessary" (1977: 54, as quoted in Brown and Yule 1983).

Some other approaches offer a less ambitious, but currently more solid basis for comparing input and output discourse; one example is the distinction between 'given' and 'new' items in a flow of discourse which provides a clear insight into the distribution of pragmatic features such as intonation and pitch, repetition, ellipsis and anaphoric pronominalization, and last but not least, the notorious use of the definite or indefinite forms a/the, all of which constitute an alien dimension to students with acquired English learned at undergraduate level.

The need for a formulation of discourse features at the macro-level becomes clear when we have to address certain higher, text-level expressive functions which are not generated automatically in trainees from outside the Aristotelian rhetorical tradition. Examples of pragmatic weakness, in particular, from Chinese-English student interpreter output show patterns which may not seem new, but are more frequent and striking than in European training.

A tentative 'extended-linguistic' model showing seven degrees of liberty - or error - in Chinese-English interpreting is given in Figure 4 on the opposite page. Features of the two languages as source (input) and tool (output) respectively can be seen either as resources or as hazards.

In offering this table I am fully aware of the jaundiced eye with which practicing interpreters and others may by now look on 'explanatory' systems and models. But this search for benchmarks to guide theory and training is prompted

Level	INPUT (Comprehension) RESOURCES	HAZARDS Chinese	HAZARDS English	OUTPUT (Production) RESOURCES	HAZARDS Chinese	HAZARDS English
1 phonetic/phonological	language knowledge	accents homophony	accents			
2 morphological	language knowledge	compact				inflected
3 syntactic	A cues	embedding		'sharpening approximation' holding patterns, 'open grammar', filler material		topic-pred SVO
4 semantic	A cues	topic-pred				
5 pragmatic	context, extralinguistic knowledge (general and topical - situation, players) reference, presupp., implicature	culture-specific	culture-diffuse	abridgement, anaphora, substitution	low	high
6 rhetorical	cues/transitions (familiarity with speech conventions)	'narrative' descriptive exemplary	'discursive' persuasive	cohesion/ties generalisation, abstraction	marked	discursive
professional (handling)	*selective listening, noting*	*real-time (linear)*		*'toolkit' lead/lag*	*voice/delivery*	
7 'displacement effects' (humour, irony, metalanguage)		!	!	*voice/deliv*		imagination

Figure 4: Linguistic/cultural resources and hazards in Chinese-English interpreting

by several considerations: firstly, to take advantage of the opening up of linguistics to areas more relevant to our craft and to attempt to articulate our concerns within an established field, in the hope of alleviating the difficulties translatology has had in establishing an academic footing; and secondly, to propose a conceptual vocabulary to formalise and vindicate the intuitions of a generation of practitioners.

In conclusion we might ponder the rueful words of the late celebrated translatologist and grammarian of spoken Chinese, Chao Yuan-ren, in his 1969 essay on the dimensions of fidelity in translation. After stressing that such dimensions - semantic vs. functional fidelity, frequency of occurrence, style - are necessarily non-measurable, dependent variables, Chao alludes to the then keen search for algorithms to express such variables with a view to the quantitative study of quality for application in machine translation (Carroll 1966):

> We are far from a workable definition of any of the dimensions, not to speak of formulating a mathematical function with a view to maximizing its value... the present state of affairs is still what in some of the formal disciplines is called the pre-systematic stage, which is another way of saying that the ideas are still half-baked, ... but so far as that is concerned, in what field is one not troubled with multidimensionality? (Chao 1976: 168)

Progress has nevertheless been achieved since the 1960's, if not towards the mechanisation of discourse, at least towards a fuller understanding of its components.

ON TEACHING NOTE-TAKING IN CONSECUTIVE INTERPRETING

Bistra Alexieva,
'St. Kliment Ohridski' University of Sofia, Bulgaria

Note-taking: the pros and cons

The growing need for Consecutive Interpreters as mediators in bilateral exchange of exact and specific information in the fields of economy, science and technology once again brings to the fore the much disputed issue about the role of Note-Taking in Consecutive Interpreting. On the one hand, experience provides evidence in support of Mahmoodzadeh's statement that "Even with the best of memory it is next to impossible for the interpreter to remember all that is said in lectures, negotiations or press conferences, particularly if names, dates and figures are involved" (Mahmoodzadeh 1992: 235). On the other, we have data from Gile's 1984 experiment in which the students asked to interpret without notes "had a better restitution for names" than those who did it with notes (Gile 1990a: 81). One explanation may be that the students - who are in the process of acquiring Note-Taking - put a greater effort into it, which diminishes their total processing capacity (Gile 1990a: 80), and more specifically, impairs the work their memory can do. In other words, their Note-Taking has not as yet become a sufficiently good tool as memory reinforcer, for it uses up more of their processing capacity and contributes less to the completion of the task.

A longitudinal study

This explanation seems to be corroborated by data from a longitudinal survey which I have conducted with four groups of students at three different stages of their training, namely:

1. The pre-Note-Taking stage in Consecutive Interpreting training (the first two weeks) characterised by lower performance parameters, in particular, by greater tension and faltering voices, which the students ascribe to their fear that they will not be able to remember the Source Language text in its entirety.

2. Pre-Instruction Stage. During the third week they are given permission to take notes of what they think could facilitate recall. This helps them not only subjectively but also objectively, for there is greater ease in their voices, and, in terms of content retrieval, their performance shows a slight improvement. Their self-confidence, however, wears out very quickly, for the 'left-to-right horizontal' note-taking they use soon proves inadequate for the purpose.

3. The Note-Taking Instruction Stage. The most marked improvement in student performance occurs at the very beginning of the Note-Taking instruction stage, with the introduction of Vertical Writing (the node- or step-patterns),

which seems the easiest to acquire and which immediately makes them aware of the importance of the lay-out of the notes for the reproduction of the semantic relationships in the source text. However, further instruction in Note-Taking, which introduces the currently used systems, brings about a trough in students' performance, which remains consistently low for a comparatively long period. It can be inferred that the period of Note-Taking acquisition is characterised by a weaker memory operational capacity, for most of the students' energy is spent on: (a) the trial-and-error strategy employed for deciding whether they should use the signs offered by their instructors or whether they should invent their own; (b) the effort to recall the signs and (c) decision-making about what information to note and what should be remembered.

It is essential that trainees do not get stuck in this 'trough'. "Despite individual variations due to personal aptitudes", as Gran suggests (1988: 1), there is "a common basic approach" in the modern note-taking systems developed by eminent scholars and practitioners, thanks to studies on memory processes, language comprehension and production and Text Linguistics (for instance Ilg 1980 and 1982; Allioni 1989).

Therefore, further optimization of Note-Taking and of Note-Taking Instruction in particular can be attained only if our strategies take care of both the general (systemic) and the specific (idiosyncratic) ways our memory operates in the comprehension and production of texts. This is why I shall address the following issues: (a) the priorities of note-taking and (b) the code in Note-Taking.

The source language text content

In order to discuss the part of the source text content that should be written down in order that the whole be recalled and reproduced, we must take into account: (a) the structure of the content, and (b) the procedures for retrieving it (Beaugrande and Dressler 1981: 87).

The text content structure is a coherent network of sequences of scenes, each consisting of configurations of predications (propositions = PN), in which there is a hierarchy consisting of:

- Participants (Entities), which play different semantic and pragmatic roles. They can be further subdivided into 'hyper', 'major' and 'secondary' depending on their importance and frequency;

- Relationships between Participants or, as Halliday has it: 'Processes', (1985: 101-157), which can be static or dynamic, and occur under specific Circumstances, in terms of Space, Time, Manner, Quantity, Intensity, etc.

Thus the basic building block of the content of a text is the predication (= PN): "Participant(s) involved in a Relationship/Process (static or dynamic) under specific Circumstances".

In the present context it is important that the Participants and the Predications play different roles in the continuity of meanings in terms of information load and control over the text. The different positions a PN can occupy in the hierarchically organised textual network of meaningful relationships, allow for a distinction as follows:

1. *Text-controlling (Hyper) PNs*, (such as "NGOs have a major role to play...") in this excerpt.

EXAMPLE 1
Non-government organisations (NGOs) have a major role to play in influencing Bulgaria's evolving environmental policies. ... We all recognize the crucial role of NGOs in carrying out education programmes and in influencing environmental policies, therefore better communication and coordination between the Ministry of Environment and the NGO community, as well as between NGOs themselves is essential, particularly in view of the limited resources available for such efforts.

2. *Major PNs*, containing at least one major Participant and representing ramifications of the hyper PNs in the recurrent structures ensuring the continuity of meanings, for instance "NGOs influence environmental policies" at the beginning of the second sentence; and

3. *Minor PNs*, which contain secondary Participants and Relationships (Processes) and supply additional information about major Participants, as in "...the limited resources available..." at the end of the second sentence in Example 1.

Procedures involved in the retrieval of the source text content

The recurrence of Predications and the role of familiarity in memory operations (Jacoby 1991: 513-38) make it possible to predict that:

1. Predications which recur no matter whether at the micro- or macro-text level leave deeper traces in our memory. Hence, their retention and recall will be much easier, for "familiarity as a basis for recognition memory judgments [is] - ... invariant across full versus divided attention" (Jacoby 1991: 513). We can also expect greater ease in retention and recall of such familiar PNs and the configurations of which they are part, because they represent big chunks of knowledge rather than individual items, thus ensuring greater economy of search (Beaugrande and Dressler 1981: 90), particularly when there is a good match between the textual world and the global cognitive patterns (frames, schemas, plans, scripts) with which the Consecutive Interpreter operates. We can therefore conclude that familiar PNs can be reproduced without note-taking.

2. The PNs introducing new Participants, Relationships and/or Circumstances, however, are more difficult to retain. In order to recall and reproduce them the Consecutive Interpreter will need memory reinforcers; therefore, they should be noted.

3. Notes, rendering the rhematic core of the source text content, can also act as memory reinforcers of the remaining portions, for they can activate a larger area of the semantic network and thus facilitate recall of what has not been written down.

Training Strategies
The pedagogical implications of these assumptions are:
1. The trainees' acquisition of the skill to analyze the source text's continuity of meanings as a hierarchical network of hyper, major and minor predications (Participants, Relationships and Circumstances) will help the students to identify recurrent PNs more easily and to distinguish between central and peripheral information. In my experience, exercises centering on this radically improve the students' analytic capacity to discover what Beaugrande and Dressler (1981: 95) term control centres in the text and to sort out its content into what can be easily retained and what must be noted.
2. It follows that trainees in consecutive interpreting can gradually acquire the skill to be selective, that is NOT TO TAKE NOTES OF EVERYTHING. This will improve their performance, since it will reduce the time when attention is divided between, on the one hand, listening and writing and on the other, writing and looking for visual signs (face expression, gestures, etc.) relevant to the speaker's intentions. The point is that writing is a strong distractor in face-to-face communication.

The importance of economy in note-taking is illustrated by a test conducted with four groups of Bulgarian students who had the following passage:
EXAMPLE 2
We must be global, we cannot wrap the environment up into neat national parcels, we cannot say this is mine, that is yours. What happens in Darlington or Detroit today may affect Accra or Djibouti tomorrow, and indeed vice versa.

Three of the groups were instructed to take notes only of what they thought was important, with a step-pattern layout, in which they were expected to leave empty slots, while one group (the control group) was left to its own devices. The control group scored only an average of 59 out of 100 points, whereas the three groups employing the "greater economy" strategy made a higher average score (73 points), with the following notes taken from the best performances:

```
                - wrap
                               env
                                               parc
        Darl & Detr
                  ╒═══╕
                  ╘═══╛
                                       Acr & Djib
```

It will be appreciated that these extremely economic notes carry the most important information and activate the whole network of relationships. The advantages of economic note-taking confront us with the need to develop exercises which can better the students' selectional and inferencing capacity. The latter can be improved by what I have labelled the 'Semantic Network Activation Exercise'. Its goal is to develop the students' skills in building chains of inferences from single key word(s) or phrase(s), supported by the minimum additional context. Such an exercise can be conducted along the following lines:

(a) The students are given a word or a phrase exponent of a major participant and/or the hyper or major PNs, as well as information about the communicative situation. For example: using the formula CO_2 and the additional information that it is from a discussion of environmental issues, the students are asked to build as many as possible semantic networks of which it might form a part of.

(b) The second version of the Activation Exercise consists of giving the students notes and information about the hyper PNs of the text (but not the text itself). The following notes were for instance proffered with the information that the text is about the ways in which pollution prevention can be made to pay and the corresponding measures taken in the steel industry in Germany.

EXAMPLE 3

recy(cle)

90% water

solid wastes

In spite of the variety of versions these notes generated, there is a great deal of similarity concerning the major PNs, for 90% of the students have made the necessary inferences and produced sentences like "The German Steel Industry has developed no-waste technologies. It recycles 90% of its industrial water and converts 90% of the solid wastes into useful materials."

Choice of code in note-taking

The discussion about which part of the content should be written down connects with the choice of code in Note-Taking. I shall address only the following two issues, namely, the choice: (a) between language and non-language codes, and (b) between the Source Language and the Target Language.

Language or non-language?

The guiding principles in the effort to find an answer to this question can, in my view, be formulated as follows:

1. The code chosen for Note-Taking should have the maximum economy in terms of: (a) the time used for writing it; (b) the effort of the hand, notably the

use of signs, which can be written down with one stroke of the pen, instead of
elaborate drawing and backwards movement; and (c) the mental effort to produce
the sign, for it takes much interpreter energy to make a complex combination of
squares, circles, arrows, crosses and language signs (usually abbreviations).

2. The second parameter is the amount of information the note sign can carry.
The greater its load, the greater its activation power. Answers from students cor-
roborate my view that a very general, and hence semantically poor, symbol such
as '"", or ':' for "say" is hardly worthwhile, for it can be easily inferred from the
remaining notes. Example 4 serves to illustrate this point.

EXAMPLE 4
The representative of the Vienna agency discussed the repair of the nuclear power station in
Kozlodoui in the nearest future.

_____   _____

rep.nuc.st.[

The note on the third step (the place for Argument Two of the PN), namely
"rep. nuc.st.", makes for easy retrieval of the first two empty steps, since the
Speaker is well-known to the interpreter and the Predicate of verbal expression
- 'Talk about' - can be easily inferred.

The requirement for a greater semantic load, however, should be combined with
the requirement for economy, particularly concerning the issues discussed above
under 1. (b) and 1. (c), for an elaborate time-, hand- and mental-effort-consuming
drawing can hardly be the best choice under the circumstances. It seems that the
natural language signs are best for carrying the greatest amount of information
in a comparatively small number of letters which can be written down easily and
quickly with the least effort and loss of time. The optimum code for Note-Taking
may therefore combine features from the following codes, each used for specific
portions of the source text semantic network, namely:

1. The Vertical lay-out (the step- and/or node-pattern) can be used for the relationships within predications and configurations of PNs, and thus ensure adequate recall of the semantic network of the source text;

2. Natural language words (written in full when short, or abbreviated when
long) are most suitable for semantically dense portions, as they can carry a large
amount of semantic information; and

3. Non-language signs and symbols which can act as general operators signalling: (a) the speaker's attitude, in terms of positive/negative evaluation and
different types of modality; (b) Relations between Participants in terms of identity, difference, similarity, comparison (along with the quality and quantity parameters); (c) Relations of causality, material implication (conditional) and
entailment, and (d) temporal and spatial coordinates.

Source language or target language notes?
The last issue I would like to address relates to the possibility of choosing between the Source Language or Target Language as the code of note-taking. In my view, this choice is not a mere surface structure issue. It goes much deeper, for it affects the nature of the process of Consecutive Interpreting, specifically its first phase. If the Target Language is chosen for Note Taking:

1. The first phase will not only consist of *Listening, Note-taking* and *Memory operations* (Gile 1990a: 80), but would also include *Transcoding*, that is an Interlingual Transformation, in order that the Consecutive Interpreter can take down notes in the Target Language he must first mentally transform the textual segment into it. It is not merely an increase in the number of functions that the Consecutive Interpreter has to perform. It is more complex, for it involves the workings of the interpreter's memory and the signs of the languages used in the process: if notes are taken in the Target Language, then Transcoding should precede both Note-Taking and Remembering.

2. The second reason for discouraging Note-Taking in the Target Language connects with the reliability of the transcoding operations in the absence of the context to follow, for the decisions taken may not be justified by what comes afterwards. This may lead to erroneous notes. Certainly, the Immediacy of Interpretation Hypothesis (Just and Carpenter 1980, 1987, as quoted by King and Just 1991) seems to hold good here too, for an interpreter will try to grasp the meaning of each word as soon as he encounters it (King and Just 1991: 582). But his strategy will attain optimum results if the "immediate" operation he performs on the incoming portion is something like a first "scanning" only, accompanied by flashes of transcoding, while the final decision about its meaning is postponed until the Production Phase, after the reception of the whole segment.

One can therefore conclude that postponing Transcoding for the Production Phase will: (a) make for less frustration in the memory operations relevant to the retention of the source text and the selection of what should be written down, and (b) permit the Consecutive Interpreter to employ the delayed commitment strategy (Connine, Blasco and Hall 1991: 246), which is in fact the most important advantage Consecutive Interpreting has over Simultaneous Interpreting.

In addition a strategy of Note-Taking in the Source Language creates a better balance between the Analysis and the Production phases, which is important for trainees, for in this way they can cope better with the first phase, a prerequisite for the realisation of the communicative act in Consecutive Interpreting.

Conclusions
We may therefore conclude that the optimization of Note-Taking, and more

specifically, the optimization of the process of its acquisition on the part of trainees, can be attained when the Consecutive Interpreters improve their skill and efficiency in:

1. Analysing the source text content in terms of the specific contributions its components have to the hierarchical network of continuity of meanings, which allows for an optimum decision-making for determining what can be remembered and what has to be written down for memory reinforcement, and

2. The selection of signs for their Note-Taking code, satisfying the major requirements for *economy of time, hand-and-mental-effort, high semantic load, activation power* and *avoidance of the Transcoding overload* of the first phase, thus creating a better balance between the Consecutive Interpreter's functions during the two phases and a more effective use of his processing capacity.

Notes

1. The survey was conducted during the academic years 1990/91 and 1991/92 with students from the Translation and Interpreting Specialisation, organised by the English Department of Sofia University.
2. Apart from the different intratextual values of a PN discussed above, it can also enter into a variety of intertextual and situational relationships, that is, it can partially or completely coincide with a PN or PNs (be they hyper, major or minor ones) from the preceding body of texts (the preceding macro-text, Alexieva 1985: 196) or feature Participants and Relationships that may be part of the communicative situation itself. The minor PN "The available resources are limited", which occurs in Example 1, is a major PN in the statement made by the previous Speaker.
3. The students' performance was assessed by the parameters: preservation of referential content; cohesion and coherence of the target text; fluency of delivery; and accent, prosody, rhythm.
4. The sentence in brackets was produced by one student only who said she knew that solid wastes could not be properly recycled the way that water can, but should rather be converted into a re-usable material. This stresses the importance of the Interpreter's knowledge of the subject matter, but this is not a question I am going to discuss here.
5. The use of language can also facilitate the acquisition of the skill of Note-Taking because the number of new signs the consecutive trainee has to learn will be smaller.
6. The frustration caused by the instruction to use the target language as a Note-Taking-code has been documented by a series of tests with four groups of consecutive trainees, for the performance of the fourth (control) group taking notes in the Target Language was markedly poorer than that of the others. The greater capacity of our memory to retain the source text in the absence of an effort to translate is also evidenced by the larger text segments reproduced as a Listening Task only, rather than as an Interpreting Task.

WHOSE LINE IS IT ANYWAY?
OR TEACHING IMPROVISATION IN INTERPRETING

Viera Makarová,
Comenius University, Slovakia, and University of Warwick, United Kingdom

Background

This article deals with the experience of interpreter training at the Comenius University in Bratislava, Slovakia. At our Department of English and American Studies, students who study English in combination with other languages can choose whether they want to become teachers or translators/interpreters. If they opt for the translator/interpreter specialisation, they have classes of consecutive and simultaneous interpreting for three years. They usually have different teachers each year and I have been teaching simultaneous interpreting. The vocabulary of most of my students has been excellent, because my colleagues have stressed the importance of that throughout their interpreting sessions.

Unlike most of my colleagues I do not teach new vocabulary, but I do teach improvisation. There are several reasons for this. First of all the students who come to my classes usually have a good vocabulary already. Then, the acquisition of new vocabulary can be done outside the class, by the students themselves. And, finally, they have other teachers who insist on mastery of words and expressions rather than on interpreting skills. In addition, it is my conviction that an interpreter will never, even at the age of Methuselah, come to possess all the relevant and potentially useful vocabulary relating to architecture, archaeology, astronomy, biology, chemistry, demography and the rest of the alphabet. I fully agree that interpreters have to specialize and should acquire as much knowledge about their area of specialization as possible, but in interpreting situations we can never avoid unpredictable vocabulary or unpredictable associations of the well-known vocabulary. There is also the specific situation of the Slovak market, where interpreters cannot specialize too narrowly, because there are not enough events taking place and most interpreters have to work in several areas. I have based my teaching method on a knowledge of this situation - having been interpreting in Slovakia for ten years, both consecutively and simultaneously. I see the ability to improvise as a form of extralinguistic preparation, which complements the basic, that is the linguistic preparation of an interpreter.

Teaching improvisation: components in the course

During the interpreting classes I give my students a *prima vista* text, usually a sample of spoken style, not a recording of a written article or written material, and I listen to their interpreting. During these sessions I accept renditions based on lack of knowledge of a word or an expression rather than precise equivalents. If, for example, *cystic fibrosis* is mentioned in the text, I accept the solution of students who say *this disease, the disease, the discussed disease.* In this way they provide the listener with at least partial information, rather than stopping in mid-sentence to try to find the most exact word or expression, and thus losing whole sentences and passages that follow. This is basically a question of setting one's priorities, among which I see the rendering of at least partial information in a particular textual unit much more important than belated full information which would entail the loss of a whole passage in between and all that connected the two passages in question.

This method of teaching requires a system of checks and balances, so that the students do not abuse it. However, in the one year I have been teaching improvisation, I have not noticed a single case of misuse. On the contrary, those students who have been encouraged to substitute a generic term for the exact technical (but unfamiliar) term, would either do this and continue interpreting without interruption, or would retrieve the exact word or expression more quickly, because their vocabulary would have contained it anyway. Certainly, in professional interpreting one has to insist on serious preparation before any commission, a careful preliminary study of vocabulary. However, in any real-life interpreting situation there are always at least two interpreters sitting in a booth, so one can always look the word up in the dictionary or the conference materials or even ask the delegates at the conference.

Improvisation cannot have a central place in real-life situations, it would be against the ethics of the profession to interpret without a sufficient knowledge of the area in question, but improvisation has to be known to the interpreter as one of the possible ways of crisis management. In this connection I never fail to point out to the students that it makes a world of a difference if the interpreter does not know the Slovak for *warted spindle tree* when it is mentioned by chance and only once or twice at that, whereas not to know the Slovak for *warted spindle tree* at an annual conference of the *Amateur Warted Spindle Tree Growers' Association* amounts to one of the seven deadly sins. In other words, the decision about whether one can or cannot improvise would depend on the centrality of the unknown word or expression in the text to be interpreted. The more central the particular technical term is in the given text, the more damage is done by resorting to improvisation.

After the initial interpreting in classes we always have a detailed discussion of the vocabulary. The students are also encouraged to take tapes home and listen to the recordings at their leisure so that they can pay due attention to every detail.

Students are deliberately not given a full list of new words and expressions before the lesson, since I try to ensure that they do not concentrate excessively on new words, becoming accordingly less attentive to other parts of the text.

In most real-life situations in Slovakia simultaneous interpreters do not receive any written conference materials beforehand. Sometimes they obtain certain materials immediately before the start of a conference. It must, therefore, be one of the skills of an interpreter to skim a text for technical terms. That is why we cover rapid underlining or highlighting in the class, in order to train students in this skill. I bring any conference materials I have, distribute them in the class and allow the students five minutes to underline whatever they find relevant. This exercise is geared towards real-life situations, where the technical terms have to be picked up as one goes along, because terminology lists and other relevant materials are not available.

Another exercise consists in guessing the missing words and expressions from newspaper and magazine articles that have been torn to pieces. Students realize the relatively high degree of predictability in their mother tongue: in most cases they can supply a close synonym for the missing word or expression. This training prepares them for situations when they do not *hear* something and have to substitute a plausible synonym. In simultaneous interpreting they will not be able to verify what was said and they will not be able to return to a passage they did not *hear* in the first place.

Coming back to checks and balances: one has to bear in mind that an interpreter enters the communication process at a stage, when the participants have already established certain patterns and have discussed the topic, so that if the interpreter says *the price will change*, because he or she has not heard properly whether it is going to *go up* or *down*, it is a much smaller mistake than it might seem. The participants will probably have already discussed it or at least mentioned it, so they would not be too surprised by its occurrence and, should the worst come to the worst, they can always ask for verification. My point is, that again at least partial information has been given.

My speciality in training covers nonsensical texts. These lack logical syntax, use incorrect gender of nouns and adjectives in Slovak, incorrect singulars and plurals, have incorrect relations between verbs and objects, make several starts and then stop without saying anything, use slang idioms, alternate rhythm from very fast to irritatingly hesitant and so on. The students are forced to work with such texts and dig out of them the 'pure nuggets of gold'. I have to use this type of text because the majority of authentic Slovak texts available for interpreting are stylistically poor, with incorrect cases of noun objects, bizarre collocations, sentences that start anywhere, or make a couple of repeated attempts at saying something, and fail completely. So exposure to the funniest distortions are nothing compared with real-life situations.

In order to prepare the students for all the unexpected situations in that wild world called interpreting, I expose them to a succession of texts with constant switching of languages. In the first few cases I record a couple of bars of music in between passages in different languages, to establish the Pavlovian reflex. Later I withdraw the music and still expect them to salivate at the right moments.

I make recordings where I lisp, stammer, speak with a heavy accent, cough, omit words, create noises that prevent the students from hearing and then, listening to their performance, jump with joy if they still manage to produce something by, for instance, adding neutral pieces of information where they heard or understood nothing.

No matter how much interpreters specialize, there will always be gaps in their knowledge and I am sure it is always better to provide the listeners with at least partial information, if the interpreter cannot provide complete information. In many cases it is a question of *something* or *nothing at all*.

My segment of our interpreter training programme is based on the 'forewarned-is-forearmed principle'. Let me nevertheless stress that I am the first believer in hunting for the meaning of words and expressions, in reading everything one can lay one's hands on; I am a staunch believer in constant language enhancement, I recognize the need for specialization, etc. etc., but in any interpreting I see space for flexibility and I would argue that this gap can be filled by clever, skilled improvising, and also that improvisation can be taught.

TRAINING FOR REFUGEE MENTAL HEALTH INTERPRETERS

Nancy Schweda Nicholson, University of Delaware, USA

Introduction

With increasing frequency, interpreter training courses meeting specialized needs are being developed in the United States. One such class for Southeast Asian refugee mental health interpreters was held at the University of Minnesota under the auspices of the Twin Cities Interpreter Project (= TCIP) during the summer of 1991. The languages involved were English, Hmong, Vietnamese, Cambodian (Khmer) and Lao.

As a principal instructor, I assisted in planning and implementing a specialized curriculum geared to the working requirements of this group.

This article (1) presents the background for the course and hence a framework for a discussion of the pedagogical techniques; and (2) examines successful teaching strategies when the instructor and the students share only one working language, in this case, English. The discussion concludes with my personal observations regarding the feasibility of 'generic' interpreter training.

The Twin Cities Interpreter Project: background

Formed in 1989, "the Twin Cities Interpreter Project (TCIP) is an informal, voluntary, interdisciplinary coalition of professionals in Minneapolis and St. Paul concerned with improving the quality of language interpreting services for refugees and others, especially in health care facilities and other social services" (Downing and Tillery 1992: 5). It continued and expanded on previous work and also drew on local experience regarding the provision of interpreting services in health care situations (or, perhaps better stated, the *lack* of such services!). Initially, I became a consultant to the project in the area of curriculum development and then was invited to teach during the intensive week of the Interpreting II course (discussed below).

The Twin Cities area is home to many Southeast Asian refugees, most of whom need access to social services. In the context of language and cultural barriers, making the initial contacts and securing the required assistance are often difficult and formidable tasks. There is a great need inasmuch as approximately one out of every twenty people in the Twin Cities (Minneapolis and St. Paul, total combined population of about 600,000) is a Southeast Asian refugee (Minnesota Department of Human Services 1988). The substantial refugee and immigrant population clearly warrants attention regarding cultural and linguistic issues.

The TCIP Community Interpreter Training Program

The Program offered two separate courses. Beginning in April of 1991, Interpreting I was open to interpreters employed at least half-time in medical and mental health settings. The course consisted of 40 hours of very *basic* interpreting training, and was characterized by large group lectures and small group practice.

An advanced course, Interpreting II, was offered in July and August of 1991 to participants who had completed Interpreting I. Both Interpreting I and Interpreting II were free of charge to residents of Minnesota, thanks to outside funding.[1] Interpreting II provided ninety additional hours of training for twenty-five individuals. The trainees' backgrounds varied significantly: some had college degrees and others did not; some had been interpreting for ten years while others had only six months' experience. Unlike Interpreting I, Interpreting II began with an intensive week of forty hours of instruction, during which I was a principal instructor. The class then continued meeting for ten hours per week (Friday afternoons and all day Saturday) for five more weeks. The goal of Interpreting II was to raise the participants to a professional level in medical and mental health interpreting by the end of the course. Included in the curriculum were (1) guidance on the development of a system for organizing and storing vocabulary; (2) instructor input on how to successfully internalize and implement strategies for self-assessment as well as for giving and receiving peer feedback (See Schweda Nicholson 1991 and 1993b for a detailed discussion); (3) extensive practice aimed at improving English fluency; and (4) scenarios which highlighted the interpreter's role and ethical responsibilities (See Schweda Nicholson 1994 for an examination of ethical issues in community interpreting).

The training team was composed of health care professionals, certified interpreters, English-language specialists, and bilingual tutors. Unlike conference interpreter trainees, many of the participants were not fully competent in English.[2] For this reason, trainers included English-language specialists as well as bilingual tutors. These experts worked with each language group to improve speaking skills, explain cultural differences, and assist with vocabulary building, both in a general sense and, more specifically, in the areas of medical and mental health terminology.

Most of the participants had preconceived notions about what the training would entail. They thought it would be a vocabulary-building course, not one in the techniques of interpreting. The students were obsessed with vocabulary and incorrectly believed that, once they increased their knowledge of technical terms, their job as interpreters would be trouble-free. In their minds, terminology expansion was the key to becoming a good interpreter.

Teaching strategies

My work with the Interpreting II students consisted of (1) sessions in English with the entire class, including all languages; (2) small group work when specific language combinations practiced consecutive interpreting during either self-generated or teacher-assigned scenarios; and (3) informal consultations with students between or after classes to offer one-on-one advice and address ethical questions which trainees might have been reluctant to raise in class.

Consisting of both lectures and interactive exercises, the large group sessions covered much material, such as: (1) the differences between oral and written language; (2) the fundamentals of consecutive interpreting; (3) the role of linguistic and extralinguistic factors in the interpreting process (Schweda Nicholson 1987); (4) the rationale for note-taking (Schweda Nicholson 1990a; 1993a); (5) the role of contextualized and non-contextualized information (Schweda Nicholson 1990a); and (6) note-taking techniques (Schweda Nicholson 1993a). The term 'lecture' is actually misleading, as students were constantly asking questions and relating their own experiences to the issues raised. Interruptions and discussion were heartily encouraged.

I provided more handouts for the students than I usually would because I had been informed that it was difficult for the trainees to take notes and listen in English at the same time.

Moreover, the intensive week also included a section on pre-interpreting exercises which I have developed, and these met with an enthusiastic reception (Schweda Nicholson 1990b).

The bilingual tutors were an integral part of the training and contributed in a number of ways. They would, for example, describe their own experiences, provide me with cultural elucidation, and explain difficult concepts and words to their group in its native language.

After the first day of preliminary lectures and discussion, much of the rest of the week was spent on consecutive interpreting practice in small groups. As the primary instructor, I roved from language group to language group, observing the scenarios and providing feedback in areas such as note-taking, public speaking skills, choice of English words, phrasing, and ethics. Although not a speaker of Hmong, Cambodian, Lao or Vietnamese, I could, in fact, comment on *extralinguistic* behaviour which was often directly related to a *linguistic* challenge. This situation can be illustrated by a typical example. During a small group session with the Vietnamese students, I noticed that the interpreter (obviously stymied) hesitated, crossed and uncrossed her legs, and looked away from the principals several times. I took note of the English subject matter and, after the scenario, questioned her about the problems. In each instance, the trainee explained that she was searching for a specific medical term. Inasmuch as the students knew that I did not speak their languages, they were often surprised that I could focus precisely on a point of difficulty. It goes without saying that, as I learned more about their culture, I was also able to identify more subtle manifestations of linguistic problems through their extralinguistic behaviour.

Taking notes along with the students was an effective strategy. At the end of an exercise, I showed my own notes to the trainees so that they could observe the techniques of an experienced note-taker. This was never done with the intention of *imposing* specific methods; the notes were simply offered for the students' examination. Inasmuch as note-taking is a highly personalized activity, the trainees made their own decisions regarding the adoption of particular symbols, abbreviations, and spacing.

It was also of great value that I, as the principal instructor, was a native speaker of the language which was *non-native* for all of the participants. While it is true that an instructor in this position cannot offer feedback and guidance to students regarding native language word choice and phrasing, she can provide much-needed input on use of the non-native language and native-speaker acceptability as well as cultural norms and appropriate extralinguistic behaviour. In my experience, this is the area where students generally require most assistance and direction.

Conclusion

When I first learned of 'generic' interpreter training courses in which the instructor and students share only one working language, I believed that such classes could not be successful. My own experience as a trainee and a trainer convinced me that it would be impossible to provide interpreting instruction without knowing both languages well.

I firmly believe that the situation in the TCIP training program was as close to ideal as possible for this type of class. If the instructors are native speakers of the students' acquired or weakest language(s), the trainees receive valuable input on linguistic and extralinguistic skill-building. Moreover, the presence of English-language specialists as well as bilingual tutors added much to the overall effectiveness of the course. Students were always provided with feedback and guidance in a variety of ways and in a variety of languages. The instructor-student feedback was strengthened by the student-student feedback, where the various group members offered comments to one another, both within their own language combination and outside of it. The learning environment provided an opportunity for much interaction.

Looking back, it would have been ideal if the trainees' English competence had been much stronger at the outset. However, we live in the *real* world, not an ideal one. As mentioned, the individuals selected for the training course were *already* part of the system - they were interpreters in hospitals and other health care facilities. It seemed logical to provide the skills and knowledge which would enable them to perform at a higher level. During the course, especially during the lecture/discussion sessions with the entire class, I consciously tried to adjust my vocabulary and also paraphrased and repeated myself when I noticed some puzzlement in the group. Additionally, more than the usual number of examples were provided to clearly illustrate all points.

From an instructor's perspective, my experience was extremely gratifying inasmuch as each and every one of the trainees was thoroughly interested and highly motivated. The students were hungry for training and were there to learn. They were excited about making videotapes and receiving critiques so as to continually better their performance.

My additional experiences offering courses in consecutive interpreting to Language Specialists for the Federal Bureau of Investigation (with up to eight languages in one class) and to members of the London-based Institute of Translation & Interpreting add weight to my strong endorsement of such programs.

To conclude, a skeptic has now been converted. There is no doubt in my mind that this type of course can meet with success, given the right mix of students and instructors. Training is in great demand, especially at the community level, which includes the courts, health care, and a diverse group of social services. As a result, one notes more and more specialized curricula springing up worldwide. From a practical perspective, the approach described allows interpreter trainers (who are a rare species and whose working languages are generally traditional conference languages) to reach out to far greater numbers of students. Classes like mine offer at least a partial solution to the paucity of interpreting courses available. If the bottom line is 'generic' training or no training at all, the former alternative is the most workable and practical option.

Notes

1. Funding was obtained from the Office of Refugee Resettlement through the Refugee and Immigrant Assistance Division of the Minnesota Department of Human Services.
2. Language ability are also discussed by Christian Heynold and Robin Setton in the present volume. Heynold refers to the necessity for interpreter trainees to speak both fluently and naturally in their mother tongue (above, p. 13-14). Setton stresses that, in Taiwan, he often has difficulty finding prospective students whose English skills are strong enough to undertake interpreter training in Chinese-English (above, p. 185).

INTERVENTION AS A PEDAGOGICAL PROBLEM IN COMMUNITY INTERPRETING

Leonor Zimman, King's College, University of London, United Kingdom

This article does not define good or bad interpreting but focuses on ethics in interpreting, notably on how to teach adequate and balanced intervention in community interpreting situations.

The methods and teaching materials discussed in this article were developed in connection with my courses for community interpreters.

Background: the controversy about intervention

Training courses for community interpreters are relatively new in Britain.

As in all other countries, teachers and students are immediately faced with the crucial controversy concerning the intervention of the community interpreter (who will henceforth be referred to by the neutral 'she').

Should she only transfer words and concepts from L_1 into L_2 and from L_2 into L_1? Or is it part of her role to intervene, to be an advocate and to act in some informative or advisory capacity? Is there any difference between a conference interpreter and a community interpreter?

Anderson (1976: 209-216) was clearly aware of the conflicting role of the interpreter:

> Understanding the role of the interpreter may also aid understanding of interaction between people of different statuses and backgrounds within a single-language community. For example, paraphrasing, which may be viewed as a special case of translation, commonly obtains in labour negotiation, doctor-patient interaction, parent-child interaction and resolution of disputes between dominant and minority groups...
>
> The interpreter commonly serves two clients at the same time. He is the 'man in the middle' with some obligations to both clients - and these obligations may not be entirely compatible...
> These [situations] illustrate the fact that the interpreter's role is always partially undefined - that is, the role prescriptions are objectively inadequate... (Anderson 1976: 209-216).

Conversationalists have interpreted dimensions of language use in conversation in different but complementary ways: they have been seen

(a) as a negotiation of mutual understanding when speaker and hearer have different perspectives (Stubbs 1983),

(b) as governed by rules which include negotiation of the speakers' rights and obligations during the speech event (Myers Scotton 1983),

(c) as governed by principles and maxims respected by speakers (Grice 1975),
(d) as knowledge of norms for language usage (Hymes 1977).

However, there is an overall agreement that social context affects the use of language. Therefore, the rules governing conversation are not only linguistic rules or linguistic 'maxims' but also partly socio-culturally determined.

When two monolingual people hold a conversation there is constant monitoring of the cultural and linguistic norms governing the speech situation; both of them know the 'maxims' of conversation, know their rights and obligations. They also 'know how' to flout the norms and share an understanding of this flouting.

When speakers do not share a common language and culture the interpreter acts as a mediator who can arguably be expected to 'interpret' not only words but also the conversational norms which include use of language according to role relationships. In other words, who is who in the speech situation, the respective status of the two parties, their role in the speech event and in the situational context. Hymes writes:

> Communities indeed often mingle what a linguist would distinguish as grammatically and as socially or culturally acceptable. Among the Cochiti of New Mexico J.R. Fox was unable to elicit the first person singular possessive form of "wings", on the grounds that the speaker, not being a bird, could not say "my wings".
> The nonidentity of the two kinds of rules (or norms) is more likely to be noticed when a shared variety is a second language for one or both parties. Sentences that translate each other grammatically may be mistakenly taken as having the same functions in speech, just as words that translate each other may be taken as having the same semantic function (Hymes 1977: 54).

Given its intercultural features there are then specific points that need to be borne in mind in a community interpreting speech event. There are cultural values, attitudes and beliefs that are not shared by the sender and the addressee between a non-English speaking client and an English speaking service provider in an English context.

In community interpreting situations, such a linguistic and cultural 'mismatch' of conversational maxims, rights and obligations in role relationships, exchanges and values may need to be matched by the community interpreter - most notably so when the mismatch concerns knowledge of the system of the service needed by the non-English speaking client.

A social worker I interviewed on the subject, Elena Pollard, said that the community interpreter may "explain to the client how the system works because it's very frightening for some clients to actually be interviewed by housing officers and social security officers without really knowing what it is about" (Zimman 1989c).

The same social worker pointed out that, conversely, "unqualified interpreters tend to get overinvolved, overidentified with the client, particularly if the client comes from the same culture" (Zimman 1989c). And a community interpreter,

Maite Bell, explained during an interview that she thought that the "limit [of the community interpreter] has been reached when it comes to making decisions for other people. They need the information but they don't need you to make up their minds for them" (Zimman, 1989b).

The *Guide to Good Practice* of the British Association of Community Interpreters (1989) lists four reasons why a community interpreter can intervene:

- to ask for clarification if she has not fully understood the concept she is being asked to interpret;
- to point out if a client has not understood the message although the rendition was correct;
- to alert a client to a possible missed inference. (An inference is information which has not been stated but the knowledge of which may have been assumed);
- to ask a client to modify their delivery to accommodate the interpreting process.

There is no controversy about the first and fourth cases; there is some controversy about the second; and the third one is heatedly debated: in order to decide between wrong or right inferences the community interpreter needs to be bicultural, have information and knowledge about both social systems, be familiar with the subject matter and be able to judge for herself 'on the spot'. Shackman has clearly stated the problem:

> A community interpreter has a very different role and responsibilities from a commercial or conference interpreter. She is responsible for enabling professional and client, with very different backgrounds and perceptions and in an unequal relationship of power and knowledge, to communicate to their mutual satisfaction (Shackman 1987: 18).

The controversy and trainees

It is important to define the role of community interpreters to interpreters, since they will at one extreme meet with the statement that they should be 'language machines' who translate from L_1 to L_2. At the other extreme it is said that a community interpreter can take over the interview and should have the power to do so. Between these two extremes there is a continuum of views on the role of the community interpreter. Perhaps the controversy reflects the fact that circumstances and role relationships that are crucial for defining the role of the community interpreter are not always taken into account. Instead of being a participant in a speech event and the person responsible for making sure that the linguistic or extra-linguistic manifestation of role relationships and culturallinguistic norms are transferred in the interpreting, she is merely considered a professional working in a vacuum.

Essentially, then, there is less controversy than one may think, but this is far from obvious to the uninitiated. To people uninvolved with community interpreting professionally, it seems tangible enough, but I believe that among clients (service providers and non-English speakers alike) it has led to their mistrusting interpreters.

The interviews

Accordingly I considered it appropriate that the prospective community interpreters (students/trainees) were confronted with the controversy in order to identify and clarify their professional role. So I carried out four interviews.

The four people interviewed were selected because they represented the whole spectrum of viewpoints mentioned above and because they were familiar with community interpreting either as users, organizers or interpreters.

Interviews were carried out with two aims: in addition to illustrating the controversy, I also wished to use the interviews as authentic material on the topic for the students' work.

I carried out the interviews by means of a questionnaire which served as a guideline and allowed for open answers. Each of these focused on the controversy but differed slightly according to the position of the person interviewed.

In order to illustrate the procedure, I reproduce here one of the questionnaires:

QUESTIONS FOR INTERVIEWS
(24th of July 1989)

INTERVIEW 1
Elena Pollard, you have worked as a Social Worker in London for a long time. I would like to ask you a few questions related to communication with clients who do not speak English.

1) When you work with an interpreter, do you expect anything more from her than translating words?
2) What else might she do beyond literal interpreting?
3) Would you be prepared to give some information to the interpreter before the interview?
4) Would you be prepared to agree for the interpreter to give some relevant information to the client?
5) In your opinion, could the interpreter act on behalf of the client as an advocate?
6) Can you summarise what you see as the role of the community interpreter?

The interviews as teaching material

The interviews have been incorporated in course work, and I shall present the teaching materials I wrote in the order they were used in the training courses I ran in 1989-1990 at Morley College, London (Zimman 1989a).

In the first exercise the trainees are given a worksheet. Then they listen to the recorded interviews in the language laboratory individually and work, in their respective languages, through the worksheet. There are four different worksheets, each tallied to one specific interview. This, for example, is that for the above series of questions:

INTERVIEW 1 - Elena Pollard
Elena Pollard is a bilingual social worker. She has worked extensively in her mother tongue (namely Spanish) as well as through interpreters in order to communicate with clients who do not speak Spanish or English.

1 - Decide whether the following statements are true or false in the opinion of the interviewee.

2 - Explain and elaborate your answer:
(a) I do not need anybody to tell me what my job is no matter whether my client speaks English or not
(b) A professional community interpreter needs to have a good knowledge of the agencies she is working for
(c) The professional community interpreter needs to organise what the client says and bring it to the level of the agency worker
(d) Any information given to the interpreter beforehand jeopardises the job of the agency worker
(e) It is a good idea for the interpreter to give some information to the client about how the system works before and after the interview
(f) The community interpreter must occasionally be allowed to take over the interview
(g) The interpreter should never act as an advocate
(h) Agency workers do not use interpreters because they do not know that they are available

3 - List the qualities and/or comment on the role of a good community interpreter according to the interviewee.

In the next exercise the students form four groups, one for each interview, they exchange the results of their exercise and advance their own view on the subject. The main objective is to make them aware of the controversy about the role of the community interpreter and at the same time to help them to identify their future roles as community interpreters.

The third step is to confront trainees with real life cases so that they can use the preceding discussion and decide the most adequate course of action in each situation.

For this purpose the trainees are presented with five cases which they discuss in pairs. After this discussion they have to give reasons for agreeing or disagreeing with the course of action taken by the interpreter in each case. The following are examples of cases the trainees are presented with at this stage.

CASE A
This is an extract from an interview between the headteacher of a primary school and a Chilean whose eight year old son was repeatedly bullied in the school's playground by a classmate. The father expresses his anger at what happened and the headteacher explains that the child responsible for the bullying has been suspended for two weeks:

SPANISH SPEAKING FATHER: (angry) But, what have you done about it? Tell me what you've done about this barbaric behaviour.
BILINGUAL INTERPRETER: (neutral tone) What have you done about this intolerable behaviour?
HEADTEACHER: We had a chat with the child and his parents, and later on he was suspended for two weeks.
BILINGUAL INTERPRETER: We had a chat with the child and his parents, and now he cannot attend school for two weeks.
SPANISH SPEAKING FATHER: (tells the interpreter in confidence and in a sarcastic tone) So she is telling me that the child who insulted and beat my kid has been sent on holidays for two weeks; in bloody England a child who is a bully gets a prize; what a cheek! (still angry) Can you tell me what sort of regulations you apply for discipline?
BILINGUAL INTERPRETER: (neutral tone) Can you tell me the regulations you apply for discipline?

CASE B
A community interpreter is asked to go to a police station to interpret for an elderly Chinese man (who speaks no English) who has been mugged. This is part of the interview:

POLICE OFFICER: Can you describe the clothes the mugger was wearing?
BILINGUAL INTERPRETER: Can you describe the clothes the mugger was wearing?
CHINESE ELDERLY MAN: Well, he was wearing a blue.... No, I think it was black, no, no.... It was definitely grey, a grey coat, it was too big for him.
BILINGUAL INTERPRETER: Well, he was wearing a grey coat which was too big for him.
POLICE OFFICER: Can you tell us the colour of his eyes, his hair and other features you remember?
BILINGUAL INTERPRETER: Can you tell us the colour of his eyes, his hair and other features you remember?
CHINESE ELDERLY MAN: I don't think I saw his eyes very well. Everything happened so quickly, but as he was blond his eyes must have been blue, yes, that's right. I think he had blue eyes.
BILINGUAL INTERPRETER: He was blond and I think he had blue eyes.

CASE C
You are an interpreter and a Turkish female client (who speaks no English) phones you at 9 p.m. (you interpreted for this person once in the past, that is why she has your phone number). She tells you: 'My son has just fallen down the stairs. My husband isn't home yet. He won't stop crying and his arm is swollen. Please help me. What shall I do? Where should I go?'
You, the community interpreter, tell the client: 'I'm sorry, I can't really do anything. I'm only an interpreter. If you still need an interpreter tomorrow, contact the Borough's Interpreting Services in the morning, they will make the necessary arrangements'.
(adapted from Shackman 1987)[2]

It is immediately understood that, ideally, the trainees should be able to come up with good and reasoned explanations of the course of action they would take in each case, bearing in mind role relationships, intercultural differences, linguistic and cultural norms, knowledge or lack of knowledge of the system, variations in interpreting needs for different settings. The list is far from exhaustive, but it suffices for the bottom line: it is all right to summarise in some cases but in other circumstances a summary may send an innocent person to jail.

As a fourth step the trainees are asked now to role-play an interpreting scenario. In groups of four, three of them can role-play the scenario and one can observe their performance for later comment. One group is asked to perform the interpreting assignment strictly in accordance to the briefs. In the other groups, the trainees who are 'the interpreters' are allowed to modify the brief according to their own informed judgement of the situation. The scenario all groups must enact is as follows:

ROLE-PLAY
PATIENT'S BRIEF: You are a young Moroccan woman. You have had a lot of bowel trouble and constipation. You saw the doctor a week ago and he gave you a laxative. The laxative worked and you want some more because you are constipated again. You respect your doctor and agree with all his advice. You say 'yes' and 'thank you' to everything he says and leave the surgery without being sure of what cereal you should eat (you have never eaten cereal for breakfast before), what 'bran' is and where to buy it.
INTERPRETER'S BRIEF: Neither the doctor nor the patient have briefed you. You have not met this patient before. The doctor has asked you to interpret for her. You do not know what is wrong with the patient. You interpret everything that is being said. At some point you have the impression that the patient is saying 'yes' without actually understanding what the doctor's advice is. At the end of the appointment you say goodbye to both parties and leave. You wait for the patient outside and ask her if there is anything she did not understand. You then explain to the patient a few things about high fibre diets without informing the doctor you have done so.
DOCTOR'S BRIEF: Patient with bowel trouble. You saw her a week ago and prescribed some laxative. You want her to re-establish natural patterns, so you do not want to give regular laxatives. You ask her about regularity, pain, flatulence, and the patient's normal diet. You give your normal advice, which is to eat bran with the morning cereal. (Adapted from Shackman 1987)[2]

The trainee groups enact the scenarios for the whole group. Accordingly everybody can see the problems and judge on suitability of the trainee's intervention.

As a fifth and final exercise after all the groups performances it would be interesting to have comments from the observers.

Given all the material in classwork it should be possible for the trainees to make some conclusions about the role of the community interpreter and the type of intervention she ought to make. The main points to surface in these conclusions would be:
a) Types of intervention
b) Circumstances that determine the intervention or non-intervention
c) Consequences of underintervention
d) Consequences of overintervention

Conclusion

In practical work the result of both non-intervention and intervention in community interpreting may be disastrous unless all the circumstances are borne in mind by the mediator. Although the perfect and well defined roles do not exist for the community interpreters, it is of immense importance that this fact is brought home to would-be interpreters at a very early stage of their career. In so doing, the teacher can, however also make each trainee fully aware of the fact that each community interpreter has to develop a clear and justifiable role for herself with the capacity to adjust to particular circumstances, concepts and situations which will depend on such factors as the service (police, social services, health, etc.), the clients (both service provider and non-English speaking client), the cultural differences and the immediate circumstances.

Notes

1. There are minor changes in the questionnaires and assignments cited in the main text to make it easier to read for outsiders/persons with no first-hand knowledge of the people or topics involved.
2. Reproduced with the kind permission of the copyright-holder, National Extension College, 18 Brooklands Avenue, Cambridge CB2 21 IN, United Kingdom; telephone + 44-223-316644.

ANALYZING INTERPRETERS' PERFORMANCE: METHODS AND PROBLEMS

Sylvia Kalina, Heidelberg University, Germany

History of the corpus

This article is about empirical research in interpreting, without which any discussion of theoretical models will remain in the abstract. Such empirical research is also, I think, a prerequisite for developing adequate methods of teaching interpreting, and it should therefore be of help both to the researcher and the teacher.

In a previous article (Kalina 1992), I set out to suggest a model of discourse processing which I then applied to interpreting, emphasizing that there are a number of specific strategies characteristic of this type of processing and especially of simultaneous interpreting.

As empirical studies of simultaneous interpreting are much rarer than theoretical contributions, I felt it would be advisable to look for authentic empirical evidence for my hypotheses. Until then, I had based my assumptions on experiments carried out in a more or less artificial setting, often with material collected from student interpreting performances, and I felt I needed some real life interpreting by professionals to see whether the strategies I had identified could be found there as well.

Unfortunately, it is not easy to get hold of professional interpreting recordings. It may be that the conference organizers and contributors wish to keep their discussions confidential or want to publish their papers themselves, or that the interpreters claim that the conference in question is not at all typical, or that they cannot work easily and spontaneously when they know they are being recorded by a colleague, etc.

However, in 1992, I had the unexpected chance of working at a three-language (German, English, French), three-booth simultaneous conference where all the booths were being taped.

The organizers and my interpreter colleagues working at the conference agreed to let me use the recorded material to analyze interpreting strategies, and I am most indebted to them for their consent. It is all the more valuable as they agreed unanimously that the conference was very difficult, conditions were far from perfect, and there was insufficient time for preparation, so that interpreters were unable to perform to their normal standards.

As the recordings of the original conference were made by the company that supplied the technical equipment, we obtained only single track recordings of the original speakers and the three booths respectively, and whenever tapes were full and needed to be changed, a few sentences were lost. Sound quality was another problem, with people not waiting until they had a microphone, etc. - all the well-known irritations of simultaneous interpreting work.

Despite these problems, when I returned from the conference with more than 20 tapes of 90 minutes each, I felt as if I had stumbled on a goldmine and could set about immediately to exploit my riches.

Recordings and transcripts of good interpreting performance are understandably more readily accessible and have formed the basis for most research hitherto. Some authors tend to neglect difficult circumstances, and some even claim that they will not work under such conditions. However, such situations are, in fact, part of interpreters' daily lives and must therefore be coped with. So how do interpreters cope with them? And can this be taught?

As stated above, we had already collected some material based on experiments in artificial settings, with students as interpreters, in order to study certain well-defined research questions, such as consecutive interpreting and note-taking, error analysis, results of think-aloud protocols, user attitudes and expectations (Kalina 1991). We had even called in audiences with as little knowledge of English as possible to make our setting similar to real-life conditions. Nevertheless, we always felt after such events that one important feature had been missing, namely the user's complete dependence on the interpreter's rendition; and that another feature namely the presence of other student interpreters and, even more crucial, of teachers, might affect the results.

Moreover, we wondered whether perhaps professionals make use of strategies in ways other than those chosen by trainees. So one hypothesis to be tested was that professionals' strategic processing differs from that of trainees. This leads to the question: what are those differences? In order to obtain more information about these questions, we organized a 'mock conference', where we tried to have the same conditions as at the 'real' conference: It therefore took place during the same hours on the same days of the week and the same documents were made available at the same time as at the original conference, etc. There were inevitably serious deficiencies and differences which could not be overcome: we had only audio recordings (which, in fact, resembled the real-life conference, as the view of the

Sylvia Kalina, Germany

speakers had been very poor), and furthermore there were no legal experts or high-ranking officials among the audience.

Methodological problems

In studying real-life conditions and professional interpeting, one problem is that one will rarely find several interpreted versions of the same text, a fact which makes direct comparison impossible. Even a large volume of authentic material will thus yield only limited information. Furthermore, there is a high degree of individuality in interpreting, and this makes it even more difficult to draw valid conclusions. Accordingly, large numbers of studies need to be carrried out to validate any given hypothesis.

There are certainly strategies that vary depending on the languages, processing direction ('A' language into 'B' or vice versa) and cultural differences, but for the purpose of this study we tried to identify those strategies that interpreters seem to use when working with English and German (and French) and likely to be found in more than one language combination. One major difficulty was the fact that at the original conference all booths were staffed by native speakers, whereas in the mock conference we had only German mother-tongue students, who were expected to work from English (or French) into German and vice versa - and were, in fact, eager to do so.

Recordings and transcription

Transcription turned out to be much more of a problem than I had expected, especially in terms of the procedures to be used for it.

Real problems began to crop up. Even a superficial transcription of the German and English versions alone would be a full-time job even for someone familiar with the subject, let alone a student. It became clear that this time-consuming effort had to be made by more than one person.

Yet, when different people set out to transcribe even the same recording and along identical principles, there will still be considerable deviations. Indeed, the same person will do the job quite differently when repeating it at other times (Shlesinger 1992b).

After careful consideration of various transcription methods and criteria described by different authors (Brown and Yule 1983; Chafe 1987; Halliday 1967), we decided that, rather than trying to develop one single method to be applied to all transcribing, we would opt for different methods that were to be a function of the research goal defined. A catalogue of rather general guidelines was drawn up; these were to be followed by everybody, but within this broad framework specific methods were adapted to individual research questions. For instance, if the objective was to analyze intonational phenomena, types of presentation were used other than those used where compression or other macro-strategies were at issue. After all, it should be borne in mind that the material to be studied is not the transcript but the recording.

Definition of potential research questions

I wanted to identify strategies, but this may in itself represent quite a problem. This, for instance, goes for anticipation as a strategy in the interpreting process. Firstly, the use of this strategy is only to be traced in cases where the interpreter utters an anticipated hypothesis before the speaker has produced it, or in cases where the anticipated hypothesis proves to be wrong, which may trigger off other strategies such as relativation, outright correction, or may lead to an error. Secondly, anticipation can only be analyzed when dual track recordings and sophisticated technical equipment for transcription are available, so that one can gain a precise picture of the degree of simultaneity between utterances of the source text producer and the interpreter.

Interdependence of individual strategies is even more difficult to trace. In the booth, one can hardly distinguish between comprehension strategies and production strategies, as there is a considerable degree of interaction between them, and the success or failure of one strategic operation will affect other strategic choices to be made.

Other strategies worth analyzing, as findings may be relevant for teaching simultaneous interpreting, include preparation strategies (expert knowledge vs. interpreters' knowledge, manuscript marking etc.), text compression in cases where source text is produced at an extremely fast rate, approximation strategies, and situationally and culturally induced elaborations or deletions; each of these strategies, however, has its own analytical problems which must first be solved. And it is only after careful studies of an interpreter's strategic choices to solve a given problem that it will be possible to prove the high degree of interdependence between individual strategies.

There is another methodological problem in connection with a large corpus such as the one described above. Should the recording of one person be analyzed longitudinally as it evolves, perhaps from a turbulent start to a phase of smoother processing, when a certain degree of ease and reassurance is reached, and eventually to processing under fatigue, in order to find out something about differences in processing strategies under these conditions?

Sylvia Kalina, Germany

Or should the rendering of the same part of text by different interpreters be compared - which is only possible, or course, when using experimental material, in this particular case our 'mock conference'?

Preliminary results

Some of the very preliminary results have led us to establish the following hypotheses:

Professionals vs. students

There turned out to be a major difference between a superficial impression of 'listenability' and detailed investigation. The professional English booth was underrated when one merely listened to its performance, owing to severe deficiencies in delivery. When it had been analyzed for errors, completeness, relevancy, etc., and compared with the performance of student booths, we found that the professional performance was semantically much more reliable. One conclusion that may be drawn from this finding is that the reception of semantically reliable information produced by the interpreter is adversely affected by the inadequacy of performance-geared strategies. This underlines the importance of professional self-control and efforts to brush up (e.g. by recording one's own performance from time to time, etc.). This can also be stressed to student interpreters with a view to their future careers when they will not be supervised by others but must rely on themselves. Moreover, it suggests that students should already be made aware of the continued need for refinement of their performance throughout their professional careers.

Strategic approaches

As mentioned above, a hypothesis resulting from our analyses was that professionals tend to use strategies in ways differing from those used by students. We found that the strategies of professionals seem to be at a higher level. As regards monitoring, for example (a term which refers not only to output control and repair operations but also to planning and aspects of semantic equivalence, namely all components of an interpreting process), professionals face fewer interference problems, have a lower correction rate for minor errors and a higher correction rate for significant errors. They are also more user-oriented, as can be observed in increased cohesion or connectivity. The professionals' attitude towards their own deficiencies seems to be different, too, with problems not successfully solved having fewer far-reaching effects on other parts of the text than is the case in student performances. Professionals seem to manage their capacity more efficiently (to borrow a term from Gile 1991a) and sometimes even build in a higher degree of connectivity, whereas students seem to try to break down their task into smaller units.

Sentence splitting is a case in point. Contrary to our expectations, we found that the professionals made less use of this strategy than the students, and that professionals even tended to interconnect more utterances than source text producers did. This finding certainly needs further investigation, but, if it can be verified, the conclusion might be drawn that professionals' total capacity is not as quickly exhausted by interpreting long interconnected utterances as that of students.

Moreover, if the situation allows them to do so, professionals seem to be able to facilitate the user's comprehension task by making a text more connective and stating things more explicitly than the source text producer did.

This could lead to the hypothesis that sentence splitting is a strategy which is useful for beginners but which interpreters tend to use less and less as they become more experienced.

Intonational strategies

Shlesinger described the strange character of simultaneous interpreting intonation (1992b). In our corpus, we found a significantly higher number of nucleus (stressed) syllables even where intonation was not awkward. This strategy seems to serve to give different segments of an utterance more weight, facilitating the interpreters' own structuring of their output and facilitating listeners' comprehension. But interpreters may also stress more syllables with the aim of clarifying and memorizing the semantic content and information structure of a message for themselves, or they may simply have to make up for deficient knowledge by increasing communicative content of those utterances that they have clearly understood.

Monitoring strategies operate during the whole process, probably at all levels. However, when capacity is exhausted, the monitoring strategy is the one which tends to break down first.

As has been shown in a number of other studies, there are various types of monitoring: (a) anticipatory monitoring which cannot be traced in the utterances of the interpreter, (b) simultaneous monitoring, where corrections may be made as or just after a word has been pronounced, and (c) retrospective monitoring, which may or may not entail repair operations of a higher order (Kohn 1990; Hilverkus 1991). These include interference, where it is as yet unclear whether one can speak of an outright 'interference avoidance strategy' (Riedmüller 1989; Hack 1992), as well as self correction. Again, professionals tend to use such repair strategies only when grave errors or planning faults are identified, and they tolerate quite a high rate of minor semantic or grammatical imprecisions. Students, on the other hand, seem to be over-concerned about even the slightest inadequacy, resulting in an extremely high rate of repair operations, often not even successfully completed nor even an improvement on the first version, and leading to an excessive amount of attention being given to this process, so that inevitably other components are neglected.

Open questions and implications for teaching

As the above discussion is far from conclusive, I cannot offer any 'conclusions' nor an accurate description of processes or valid statistical evaluation, nor, indeed, a model for teaching. I have rather tried to describe some problems encountered in empirical studies of interpreting processes and strategies at work. I am aware that the experience gained in collecting and analyzing data is very personal, but I think that many of the problems I have mentioned are of a more general nature and will be faced by any researcher conducting empirical research in simultaneous interpreting. Among those points which are of general interest and need further investigation, I would emphasize the following:

(a) the representativity of corpora consisting of individual conferences, interpreters, or experimental sessions;

(b) the accessibility of material for comparative studies;

(c) problems of transcription from recorded tapes, with the constraints entailed by a typed and readable transcript;

(d) the persons expected to carry out such research work: students, professional interpreters, linguists, psychologists may all have useful contributions to make.

Despite these open questions there are, I think, some useful lessons outlined above for the teaching of simultaneous interpreting:

1. Adequate teaching of simultaneous interpreting must be based on a theory of the processes involved, and for developing such a theory, empirical research is necessary.

2. Professional standards can be defined on the basis of such research, and teaching will have to be geared to making students fully aware of what is required from them and enabling them to achieve such standards.

3. The strategies that beginners learn will have to be continuously refined and adjusted if their performance is to become truly professional.

4. Students must be motivated to continue checking the quality of their performance even when they have finished their training and have achieved a professional level.

5. Teaching must therefore not concentrate on ideal conditions and artificial settings alone, but must prepare students to cope with all the problems and difficulties of professional interpreting.

QUALITY ASSURANCE IN SIMULTANEOUS INTERPRETING

Franz Pöchhacker, University of Vienna, Austria

Aims - Insights - Visions

The *quality* of the services rendered by professional interpreters has been among the prime concerns of the international conference interpreting community. Defining and measuring such quality, however, particularly in simultaneous interpreting, has apparently been a lesser preoccupation. The *Practical Guide for Professional Interpreters* published by the International Association of Conference Interpreters AIIC (1982) refers to "quality" as "that elusive something which everyone recognises but no one can successfully define" (AIIC 1982: 1). In terms of the subtitle of this volume, it is the "aim" of this article to pin down "that elusive something", to try to get a grip on the notion of quality in simultaneous interpreting.

I will review some of the "insights" gained by fellow researchers and hope to add to these by reporting on my own research. While the approach to be outlined here has been developed for the analysis of professional interpreting in an authentic conference setting, it is equally relevant for the *teaching* of simultaneous interpreting. Since the level of performance to be attained by graduates must be in line with professional standards, it is essential to establish the quality criteria by which candidates will be assessed in their final examinations.

In this attempt to establish criteria of quality in simultaneous interpreting I will emphasize a much neglected component of quality assurance - the inspection of the actual product. I am aware that inspection and analysis of interpreters' output is only part of an overall scheme for quality assurance in simultaneous interpreting. But it is a necessary, indeed an indispensable step towards a "vision" of quality assurance both in the relationship between interpreters and clients in professional conference assignments and in the joint efforts of trainers and students to improve performance in the interpreting classroom.

Views concerning quality

Over the past decade the issue of quality has clearly gained prominence in the literature on simultaneous interpreting. In 1983, Cartellieri's reflections "On Quality in Interpreting" essentially came down to the statement: "Much still remains to be done to overcome the present unsatisfactory state of affairs in the sphere of reliable quality parameters." (Cartellieri 1983: 213) Gile (1983) also deplored the lack of an objective and precise definition of quality and outlined a methodological approach in which the interpreter's output ("presentation") was to be judged by delegates with the help of questionnaires, while "informational fidelity" was to be investigated by a comparative analysis of source and target text recordings. This method was not applied to on-site quality assessment among delegates until seven years later (Gile 1990c), but several empirical studies were carried out to establish the relative weight of factors considered relevant to quality judgments in simultaneous interpreting (Bühler 1986; Kurz 1989; Meak 1990). It is significant that the relative importance accorded to quality criteria like native accent, pleasant voice, fluency of delivery, logical cohesion of utterance, sense consistency with original message, completeness of interpretation, correct grammatical usage and use of correct terminology (Bühler 1986: 234) was found to vary not only between conference participants and representatives of the interpreting profession (Kurz 1989) but also among different groups of users (Kurz 1992). This variability of user expectations, which is also reflected in the results of Gile's (1990c) direct quality assessment study, has recently been confirmed and elaborated by Kopczyński (1994).

There is thus a growing body of empirical evidence for (a) the principal factors and criteria underlying judgments of quality in simultaneous interpreting and (b) the relative variability of expectations among different groups of users. Yet these data on various 'views on quality', on the inevitably subjective perception of quality in simultaneous interpreting, do not address the issue of how to describe and analyze the 'objective' reality on which such judgements are based. (Objective in the sense that the interpreter's recorded product is open to replicable analysis and assessment.) Even though Gile's (1990c) study is concerned with delegates' subjective perception of quality rather than the comparison between that perception and some clearly defined objective reality, it does hint at the potential discrepancy between delegates' judgements and the actual features of the interpreter's recorded output. Elsewhere Gile (1991b) explicitly states that "in some cases, the correlation between 'satisfactory quality' as perceived by a given communication actor and the quality of fidelity, linguistic acceptability, clarity and/or terminological accuracy of the Translator's output is weak, to say the least." (Gile 1991b: 193) The question then arises as to how we should best go about defining and analyzing the text produced by the interpreter as an 'objective', that is, physical reality. What are the textualized parameters and variables underlying judgements of quality in simultaneous interpreting, and how can they be measured and quantified in a corpus of texts?

The process-orientation of most previous research on simultaneous interpreting may explain why there are few answers to these questions in the literature concerning interpreting. The statement by Stenzl (1983: 47) that there are "practically no systematic observations and descriptions of interpretation in practice" has lost little of its validity over the past ten years. On the other hand, the criteria used in the ranking studies by Bühler (1986) and Kurz (1989; 1992), as well as in the above quotation from Gile (1991b), indicate that there is a general consensus within the interpreting community on the quality standards for professional interpretation. We seem to know what *the* product *should be* like, but we are less sure about a method for establishing what *a* particular product *is* like in a given situation. Quite obviously, researchers, teachers and trainees need a method for looking at the product.

Product-oriented research

A term like 'product inspection' may seem like a blatant misnomer in the field of simultaneous interpreting, since, as a rule, the target text in interpreting is nowhere to be seen. It is precisely this evanescence of the text (*'verba volant'*) that makes product-oriented research in simultaneous interpreting an improbable undertaking. It should have become clear from the above, though, that such an undertaking must be of prime concern to any researcher interested in knowing not only what sort of quality users expect but also what sort of quality they actually get. Such research would in turn provide the analytical tools and criteria for intersubjective quality assessment in the training of simultaneous interpreters.

Methodological problems

The methodological problems confronting the product-oriented researcher are nothing short of daunting throughout all stages of research design and procedure - from the recording and the methods of transcription and documentation to the issues of analysis and evaluation. Four major questions might be asked to identify some of the main problem areas: (1) How does one gain access to a text (corpus)? (2) What should be done with the recordings? (3) What should one look for in a textual corpus? and (4) How can parameters for quantitative description be turned into values for qualitative analysis?

Question number (3) is crucial as it hinges on the underlying theoretical conception and the hypothesis to be tested against the data. In any case, the search for parameters in a corpus of spoken texts is likely to be hampered by "a lack of analytical methods and techniques" (Stenzl 1983: 42). Thus, it should not be too embarrassing here to suggest a list of textual features which *may* be relevant to the description and analysis of an authentic textual corpus. The fact that the analytical scheme described below was developed on the basis of an authentic conference corpus indicates that the difficulties referred to in question number (1), such as professional secrecy and interpreters' unwillingness to submit their work to analytic scrutiny, are not altogether insurmountable. The answers to question number (2) are largely interlinked with question number (3): the way a textual corpus is transcribed and documented will constrain the depth and scope of analysis, while the parameters to be considered in turn constrain the 'transdescription'.

For the time being, I shall leave aside question number (4), which concerns the link between quantitative parameters and qualitative evaluation, and will turn from problems to solutions by outlining a model for descriptive text analysis in simultaneous interpreting.

A multi-parameter model for description and analysis

Although my focus here is clearly, if not exclusively, on the text, my overall approach must not be misconstrued as a narrowly linguistic one. I have previously stressed that texts in simultaneous interpreting must be placed within the wider multi-level context of assignment type and situation (Pöchhacker 1992a). I have argued that it is only within a holistic conception of the conference as a "hypertext" and the "situation" as a socio-psychological constellation of interacting parties that one can safely narrow one's focus to the parameters of the product or text as such.

In simultaneous interpreting the "text as such" is again a multi-parametric semiotic whole, which, in its full complexity, often defies description. In Pöchhacker (1994) I have suggested a text model with constituents in both the auditive and the visual channel, on a "verbal-paraverbal-kinesic continuum" (Poyatos 1987). From this constituent model of the "audio-visual text" in simultaneous interpreting one can derive a number of textual features or parameters, such as slips and structure shifts in verbal production, voiced hesitation markers, peculiarities of voice quality and articulation, the use of (pictorial or verbal) visual information (such as slides), as well as prosodic and/or paraverbal features. To these textual constituents must be added temporal phenomena like speed, pausing, and rhythmical pattern, which are often dominant in shaping the overall impression of a spoken text. Finally, the modalities of text presentation (such as extemporaneous speech, use of a manuscript, notes or slides) merit particular attention in the documentation of (source and target) text corpora in simultaneous interpreting.

Thorough description and analysis of recordings from conferences with simultaneous interpreting thus require a combination of detailed transcription (including false starts, slips in production, extended pauses, hesitation markers, and paralinguistic elements like clearing one's throat, laughing, etc., as well as indications of the delivery modality and temporal characteristics) and some sort of intersub-

jective assessment of prosodic/paralinguistic features. A number of these delivery
parameters can be projected onto a parametric grid as suggested in Figure 1:

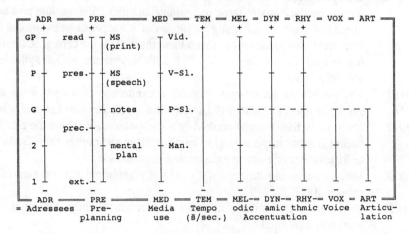

Figure 1: Text delivery profile (parametric grid)

It lies outside the scope of the present article to justify and explain, in sufficient and convincing detail, why specific parameters were chosen for incorporation in the text delivery profile. The entire analytical scheme was developed on
the basis of a thorough theoretical and conceptual discussion laid down in
Pöchhacker (1992b).

It is possible to assign numerical values (mostly between 1 and 5, from bottom
to top on the scale) to all parameters in Figure 1 and use the text delivery
profiles for a quantitative analysis of an entire conference corpus. The parameters
cover the following information:

ADR: The *addressees* of the text can be *1* or *2* persons, a *Group* of listeners,
        the *Plenary* (everybody present) and/or, when the media are being
        addressed, the *General Public*.

PRE: The degree of *pre-planning* of a text can range from *extemporaneous* to
        read, with *presented* and *preconceived* texts as intermediate stages. One
        can *read* or *present* a publishable manuscript (*MS print*) or a speech
        written specifically for oral delivery (*MS speech*). A *preconceived* text
        is one produced on the basis of - but without reading - a written text or
        by drawing on written *notes* or merely a *mental plan*.

MED: *Media use* includes *manual* aids such as boards or flipcharts, *pictorial*
        or *verbal* (overhead or photographic) *slides* and even *video* films (for

instance when surgical techniques are shown and commented on by a
speaker at a medical conference).

TEM: The presentation rate (*tempo*) of a speech assessed in syllables per
          minute on the basis of three one-minute samples (first, middle and last
          minute of a speech, adjusting for pauses of 1.5 seconds or more) can be
          converted into syllables per second and marked on the central scale. (In
          my corpus the average was 219.5 syllables/minute = 3.6 syllables/
          second.)

MEL-   The *melodic, dynamic* and *rhythmic accentuation* of a speech (as as-
DY-   *sessed by four bilingual professional voice specialists who listened to the*
RHY: audio-recordings) can be marked on a five-point scale, where the middle
          point (3) refers to the normal or baseline value and ratings below indica-
          te insufficient and above exaggerated accentuation.

VOX: *Voice quality* can be normal (3), slightly abnormal (2), or markedly
          abnormal (1).

ART: *Articulation* is similarly assessed as normal, slightly abnormal, or
          markedly abnormal.

This description of the analytical tools, however sketchy, should suffice to indicate the variety and complexity of the parameters that may be considered in a
product-oriented analysis of the texts in simultaneous interpreting. To illustrate
what 'a look at the product' actually looks like, Figure 2 (overleaf, page 239)
shows a sample of text 'trans-description' and analysis.

I am not really concerned here with the specifics of particular transcription conventions or sets of parameters. Rather, I want to emphasize the fundamental principle that product-oriented research in simultaneous interpreting means, to me at
least, a study of the target text as a complex and multi-faceted whole within a
communicative situation. This prospective, intratextual view of the target text is
a logical outgrowth of the functionalist principles of the General Theory of
Translation and Interpreting on which my specific conceptualizations and models
are based (Pöchhacker 1992a). Emphasis is shifted to the interpreter's product as
a whole rather than the temporal and semantic correlations and correspondences
between source and target texts. The latter are central, for instance, to Lederer's
(1981) transcription method for the study of mental processes and have played
a dominant role in a number of diploma theses on error analysis in simultaneous
interpreting. The target-text oriented approach is a direct reflection of a functionalist theory of text transfer which rejects the chronically ill-defined notion of
equivalence (Snell-Hornby 1988) on the level of words, phrases, sentences or
larger linguistic units in favour of the functional adequacy and coherence of the
(target) text-in-situation.

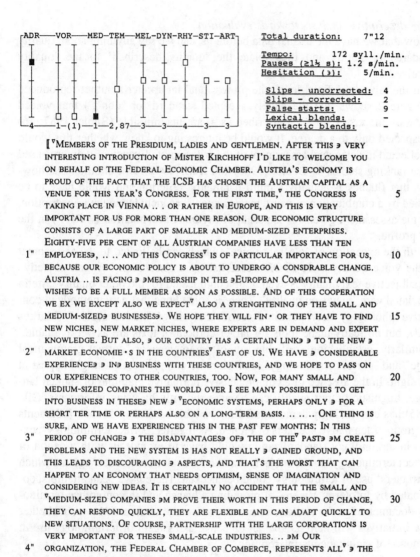

Total duration: 7"12

Tempo: 172 syll./min.
Pauses (≥1½ s):   1.2 s/min.
Hesitation (ə):   5/min.

Slips – uncorrected: 4
Slips – corrected: 2
False starts: 9
Lexical blends: –
Syntactic blends: –

⟦ᵛMEMBERS OF THE PRESIDIUM, LADIES AND GENTLEMEN. AFTER THIS ə VERY
INTERESTING INTRODUCTION OF MISTER KIRCHHOFF I'D LIKE TO WELCOME YOU
ON BEHALF OF THE FEDERAL ECONOMIC CHAMBER. AUSTRIA'S ECONOMY IS
PROUD OF THE FACT THAT THE ICSB HAS CHOSEN THE AUSTRIAN CAPITAL AS A
VENUE FOR THIS YEAR'S CONGRESS. FOR THE FIRST TIME,ᵛ THE CONGRESS IS   5
TAKING PLACE IN VIENNA ... OR RATHER IN EUROPE, AND THIS IS VERY
IMPORTANT FOR US FOR MORE THAN ONE REASON. OUR ECONOMIC STRUCTURE
CONSISTS OF A LARGE PART OF SMALLER AND MEDIUM-SIZED ENTERPRISES.
EIGHTY-FIVE PER CENT OF ALL AUSTRIAN COMPANIES HAVE LESS THAN TEN
1"   EMPLOYEESə, ... AND THIS CONGRESSᵛ IS OF PARTICULAR IMPORTANCE FOR US,   10
BECAUSE OUR ECONOMIC POLICY IS ABOUT TO UNDERGO A CONSDRABLE CHANGE.
AUSTRIA .. IS FACING ə əMEMBERSHIP IN THE əEUROPEAN COMMUNITY AND
WISHES TO BE A FULL MEMBER AS SOON AS POSSIBLE. AND OF THIS COOPERATION
WE EX WE EXCEPT ALSO WE EXPECTᵛ ALSO A STRENGHTENING OF THE SMALL AND
MEDIUM-SIZEDə BUSINESSESə. WE HOPE THEY WILL FIN · OR THEY HAVE TO FIND   15
NEW NICHES, NEW MARKET NICHES, WHERE EXPERTS ARE IN DEMAND AND EXPERT
KNOWLEDGE. BUT ALSO, ə OUR COUNTRY HAS A CERTAIN LINKə ə TO THE NEW ə
2"   MARKET ECONOMIE · S IN THE COUNTRIESᵛ EAST OF US. WE HAVE ə CONSIDERABLE
EXPERIENCEə ə INə BUSINESS WITH THESE COUNTRIES, AND WE HOPE TO PASS ON
OUR EXPERIENCES TO OTHER COUNTRIES, TOO. NOW, FOR MANY SMALL AND   20
MEDIUM-SIZED COMPANIES THE WORLD OVER I SEE MANY POSSIBILITIES TO GET
INTO BUSINESS IN THESEə NEW ə ᵛECONOMIC SYSTEMS, PERHAPS ONLY ə FOR A
SHORT TER TIME OR PERHAPS ALSO ON A LONG-TERM BASIS. .. .. .. ONE THING IS
SURE, AND WE HAVE EXPERIENCED THIS IN THE PAST FEW MONTHS: IN THIS
3"   PERIOD OF CHANGEə ə THE DISADVANTAGESə OFə THE OF THEᵛ PASTə əM CREATE   25
PROBLEMS AND THE NEW SYSTEM IS HAS NOT REALLY ə GAINED GROUND, AND
THIS LEADS TO DISCOURAGING ə ASPECTS, AND THAT'S THE WORST THAT CAN
HAPPEN TO AN ECONOMY THAT NEEDS OPTIMISM, SENSE OF IMAGINATION AND
CONSIDERING NEW IDEAS. IT IS CERTAINLY NO ACCIDENT THAT THE SMALL AND
ᵛMEDIUM-SIZED COMPANIES əM PROVE THEIR WORTH IN THIS PERIOD OF CHANGE,   30
THEY CAN RESPOND QUICKLY, THEY ARE FLEXIBLE AND CAN ADAPT QUICKLY TO
NEW SITUATIONS. OF COURSE, PARTNERSHIP WITH THE LARGE CORPORATIONS IS
VERY IMPORTANT FOR THESEə SMALL-SCALE INDUSTRIES. .. əM OUR
4"   ORGANIZATION, THE FEDERAL CHAMBER OF COMBERCE, REPRESENTS ALLᵛ ə THE

Fig. 2: *Sample "trans-description"* (from day 1 of ICSB Congress
(June 24-26, 1991, Vienna), German -> English.

Legend: Text profile: ■ = same as original; □ = value in target-text profile.
Transcript: ⟦ = mike on; ᵛ = time marker every 30 seconds), full minutes in left
margin; ə = voiced hesitation ("uh"); · = hesitation; .. = pause (one dot = 0.5
seconds).

From descriptive analysis towards evaluation

Now that we have the textual data before us, can we say anything about quality standards or norms and thus relate the 'quality described' to the 'quality perceived'?

On the most superficial level, the professional interpreter's output reproduced in Figure 2 shows that the widely accepted standard (or "don't") that voiced hesitation markers ("uh's"; transcribed as ɜ) are inadmissible (Bühler 1987: 16) is respected only to a degree. It would be interesting to know whether this would be reflected in delegates' assessment of the criterion of "fluency of delivery" used in the ranking studies by Bühler (1986) and Kurz (1992). One should note, however, that fluency is actually a multi-parametric criterion and would have to be studied by a combination of pause measurements, as included in the transcription, and the assessment given for the scale of rhythmic accentuation (= RHY) in the text profile.

With the exception of "pleasant voice", which can be linked to the assessment on the voice quality scale (VOX), establishing a correlation between objective and subjective text quality is even more complicated for the other quality criteria associated with 'views on quality'. There is some hope that new methods in contrastive phonology may permit a sound analysis of "native accent" (Markus 1993), but no ready-made tools for larger corpora of texts are as yet available.

Similarly, establishing verifiable sets of parameters for "correct grammatical usage" and "correct terminology" is much more complex than it might appear at first sight. In the absence of a comprehensive normative grammar of spoken language, linguistic output quality can be assessed only by using informants. Gile (1985) has convincingly demonstrated the variable reliability of such judgments in a group of ten native speakers of French. As regards "correct terminology", experts in terminology standardization would have to provide us with a canon of "correct terminology" in the subject area of a particular conference, against which interpreters' use of terminology could be checked. There have been attempts, coordinated by Infoterm, Vienna, at providing advance and in-conference terminology documentation for conference interpreters, and it remains to be seen whether these initiatives will help us give an objective assessment of terminology use in a product of simultaneous interpreting.

A truly fundamental problem arises for the criteria "sense consistency" and "completeness". If we reject linguistic/semantic equivalence relations between elements of the source and target texts as our analytical yardstick, the notions of sense (cognitive content) and completeness (which is linked to variables like explicitness vs. implicitness and redundancy) become extremely cognitive. Since the information to be transmitted by means of a text is constructed in the minds of the listeners as a function of their general, specialized, personal and contextual knowledge and competence as well as their expectations and communicative intentions, it is beyond *my* analytical grasp to establish whether and to what extent specific renditions "make sense" (Pöchhacker 1993).

To end this section on a more optimistic note, it seems plausible that the criterion of "logical cohesion" is somewhat more amenable to analysis. It must be borne in mind, however, that, in essence, the 'logic' of the rendition studied stems from the producer of the source text. Verifying logical consistency will therefore necessitate intertextual rather than intratextual product analysis.

As a result of the conceptual and methodological issues raised above, the analytical scheme actually applied to my conference corpus is admittedly 'superficial', limited, that is, to features of the 'text surface', and covers only the most obvious cases of logical contradiction and lack of coherence. The method outlined is therefore only a modest first step towards product inspection in simultaneous interpreting. Nevertheless, it is in accordance with Cartellieri's suggestion for resolving the question of quality: "The answer may be found in trying to describe a number of features whose quantity may very well develop into quality criteria." (Cartellieri 1983: 213)

Conclusion

The methodological approach described in this paper is undeniably fraught with limitations. My scheme for text trans-description and analysis takes into account some but by no means all conceivable parameters in the recorded text. In particular, it neglects the analysis of linguistic and paralinguistic variables which call for the application of (text)linguistic methods and procedures. Clearly, my suggestions for describing and analyzing the product in simultaneous interpreting can only be a first step towards a method for detailed and rigorous product inspection. And even if such a method were achieved, our analytical study of the products would have to be complemented and correlated with delegates' (subjective) assessment of the texts under study. The methodological difficulties of such onsite evaluation are immense, since listening for errors of grammar and terminology and listening for the substance of a given topic are altogether different things. Direct delegate response is indispensable, however, if we want to establish the thresholds at which a particular constellation and quantity of quality-related features in the material text reaches 'critical mass' and leads to 'bad marks' for the interpreting services.

Once empirical work on both delegates' in-conference quality assessment and the analysis of the material text yields a broad enough body of findings, we will have to take yet another series of steps and relate the 'objective' and subjective quality of a text to the conditions under which it was produced. It is a well-known fact that speakers' non-native articulation, speed of delivery, or use of written documents not available to the interpreters, among regrettably many other things, often leads to inevitable deficiencies in professional interpreters' output. The text delivery profile presented in this article includes some of the relevant parameters. Ultimately, then, documenting not only the text(s) but also the circumstances of meeting organization and text delivery will enable us to evaluate not only 'quality' but 'quality under the circumstances'. This would be my vision for comprehensive quality assurance in simultaneous interpreting - in support of the interpreting community's endeavour to assure clients of the professional quality of interpreters' services and as a basic prerequisite for putting the training and assessment of future interpreters on a sound conceptual and methodological footing. Admittedly, it will take some time and plenty of effort on the part of researchers in the field of simultaneous interpreting to turn that vision into reality.

Højerup Kirke

SCREEN TRANSLATION

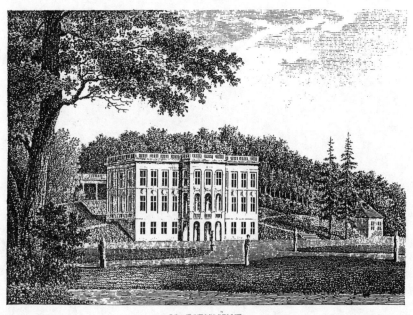

MARIENLYST
ved
HELSINGØER

RELEVANCE AS A FACTOR IN SUBTITLING REDUCTIONS

Irena Kovačič, University of Ljubljana, Ljubljana, Slovenia

Introduction

Special courses for subtitlers are still rare, a fact partly due to the widespread belief that the special skills needed for a good subtitler can only be developed through experience. The reasoning behind this attitude is that adaptations necessary in subtitles are made intuitively and there is no global principle underlying them.

In the present article I would like to argue against this view, using one particular type of subtitling adaptation, reductions, to demonstrate how apparently random, intuitive and very different adaptations all have the same general 'raison d'être'. It is such general principles and the particular subtitling strategies which result that should be part of subtitlers' training.

Reductions are a typical feature of subtitling. They are dictated by the extralinguistic requirements of the media: reduction depends not only on the speed of the dialogue, but above all on the systemic similarities and differences between source and target language. Subtitling into a language with similar syntactic patterns and a similar average word length as those of the source language may call for little reduction, but when the target language does not allow for condensing patterns abundantly used in the source language, the importance of performing reductions in the optimal way comes to the fore. Consequently, the principles underlying reduction deserve a prominent place in the training of subtitlers working with such pairs of languages.

Subtitling English texts in Slovene is a typical example. The Slovene language does not accept premodification of nouns by other nouns, it is very restrictive in the use of non-finite, especially participial clauses, etc. According to some counts, this makes Slovene translations of English texts 10 to 30 percent longer than the originals. Consequently, subtitlers frequently have either to leave out the structure in question or, if it is indispensable for the understanding of the story, to sacrifice other parts of the text.

This leads to the fundamental question: what criteria (if any) does the subtitler use in deciding what and how to reduce? A discussion of this point is pertinent not only to practising subtitlers, but also to teachers and students of translation, who should be conscious of problems in their chosen trade and ways of coping with them.

In a previous attempt to analyse the processes underlying subtitling reductions, I began by using a model of language functions and traditional structural categories of linguistic analyses (Kovačič 1992). As the work progressed, I found myself increasingly expanding the model by introducing more general cognitive notions. By the time the analysis was completed, I realised that many of the reductions which appeared random if analysed by traditional linguistic analytic categories, fell into consistent patterns when viewed within a general relevance-theoretic framework. In the following discussion, I therefore also implicitly argue that relevance theory can be used as part of the teaching of subtitling, both as an explanatory procedure and as a set of notions providing subtitlers with some guidelines in their work. The approach I have chosen here is a discussion of brief examples which can also be used in class work.

Relevance theory

Relevance theory (Sperber and Wilson 1986) builds on the cognitive approach to language as a mental activity operating within certain cognitive schemata, claiming that we can communicate because we are capable of drawing inferences from one another's behaviour. Inferences we make as hearers in a communication arise from the tacit expectation that the speaker follows the principle of relevance: "Every act of ostensive communication communicates the presumption of its own optimal relevance." (Sperber and Wilson 1986: 158)

Relevance is always related to a given context (and context is not defined in the usual linguistic terms, but rather as a psychological construct, as "a subset of the hearer's assumptions about the world"; and the context of an utterance is "the set of premises used in interpreting it" (Sperber and Wilson 1986: 15)). "An assumption is relevant in a context if and only if it has some contextual effect in that context." (122)

The degree of relevance is determined by the *extent conditions*: "Extent condition 1: an assumption is relevant in a context to the extent that its contextual effects in this context are large. Extent condition 2: an assumption is relevant in a context to the extent that the effort required to process it in this context is small." (125)

There are three types of *contextual effects*: (a) addition of contextual implications, (b) strengthening of old assumptions, and (c) elimination of false contextual assumptions (108-16).

In lay terms we could say that the two extent conditions define relevance as a cost-benefit notion: we want to achieve maximum benefit (the maximum contextual effect) at minimum cost (the hearer's minimum effort in processing a communicated assumption).

Relevance theory and translation

Gutt (1991) presents relevance theory as THE translation theory, claiming that it offers theoretical foundations for "accounting for translation in terms of the communicative competence assumed to be part of our minds" as "its domain is... mental faculties rather than texts or processes of text production" (Gutt 1991: 20).

Gutt's starting point is the notion of interpretive resemblance, which Sperber and Wilson defined as follows:

Two propositional forms P and Q (and by extension, two thoughts or utterances with P and Q as their propositional forms) interpretively resemble one another in a context C to the extent that they share their analytic and contextual implications in the context C." (Wilson and Sperber 1988: 138)

The translator's objective is - to put it simply - to make a translation interpretively resemble the original text as much as possible, that is to provide similar - if not identical - contextual effects. In order to understand the nature of translation it must be kept in mind that the notion of relevance is context-dependent; in the same way, the translator's choice of a term or structure is dependent on the contextual effects of an utterance in a given context (of a given person, culture etc.). "The success or failure of translations, like that of other instances of ostensive-inferential communication, depends causally on consistency with the principle of relevance. (Gutt 1991: 189)

Relevance and subtitling reductions

Reductions in subtitling are either partial ('condensations') or total ('deletions'). Total reductions are at least relatively easy to identify, if not always to analyse, even within more traditional linguistic frameworks, as the basic feature is the absence of a corresponding carrier of a meaning component in the surface structure. Conversely, partial reductions are - at the current state of the available inventory for semantic decomposition of language items - virtually unanalysable.

Partial reduction in English-Slovene subtitles

Relevance theory provides useful insights into the strategies and factors behind partial reduction. The change in example 1 can be explained by a deduction string leading to an interpretive resemblance:

EXAMPLE 1
English source: *I woke up THREE MINUTES AGO.*
Slovene translation: PRAVKAR sem se zbudila. [I JUST woke.]

Students can be made aware of the deduction string "three minutes ago = short time ago = just", through which the subtitler arrived at an interpretive resemblance that justifies the condensed translation. The point to note is that subtitlers frequently use such deduction strings without being aware of the cognitive nature of this procedure. However, there is a significant difference between applying it intuitively as opposed to being aware of it, knowing when to use it and what this use entails.

Similarly, it can be shown that such an analysis may apply even to language elements with no underlying propositional form, for instance personal and interpersonal elements or textual connectives:

EXAMPLE 2
> *I SWEAR I'm not lying.*
> RES, ne la`em. [Indeed, I'm not lying.]

EXAMPLE 3
> *LET ME REPEAT THE QUESTION,*
> *what are we going to do?*
> TOREJ, kaj bova storila?
> [= SO, what are we going to do?]

In examples 2 and 3 the condensed translations may not be regarded as interpretively resembling the original utterances in a semantic sense, but they do preserve a functional resemblance: (2) in the sense of interpersonal emphasis, persuasiveness; (3) in the sense of textual cohesion.

In relevance-theoretic terms, linguistic elements with no propositional equivalents can be tackled by constructing an appropriate description, which then makes manifest further assumptions. These assumptions then allow for an extended interpretive-resemblance analysis without a propositional form. Such resemblances are context-dependent: two utterances (or parts of utterances) may resemble each other interpretively in one context, but not in another. (Gutt 1991: 39-44) In example 3, "so" may be described as implying "I am going to refer to something already mentioned or implied", and also with a rising intonation "and I want to get your response". In other words, in all the above examples the original texts contained explicatures (= explicitly communicated assumptions (Sperber and Wilson 1986: 182)) while the Slovene translations contained implicatures (= assumptions that are communicated, but not explicitly so (Sperber and Wilson 1986: 182)).

Total reductions in English-Slovene subtitles

In cases of total reductions ('deletions'), the overall statistics in Kovačič (1992) show a significant difference between personal/interpersonal and textual elements on the one hand and ideational (representative) ones on the other. But any further subcategorisation of the three functional groups requires at least partial use of cognitive (relevance-theoretic) notions. This may be illustrated by Example 4, an excerpt from a Sherlock Holmes film, where relevance can account for the different treatment of vocatives, appellatives and similar linguistic elements.

EXAMPLE 4

[Holmes-bookseller:]	(I have) just the books you need to fill up your bookcase, DOCTOR (a). It looks untidy, does it not? ...
[Holmes-Holmes:]	WATSON (b), do you mind if I smoke a cigarette in your consulting room? A thousand apologies, MY DEAR WATSON (c), I had no idea you would be so affected.
[Watson:]	HOLMES (d). Is it really you?

The two vocatives functioning as simple terms of address (a, c) are left out; similarly (d), which is used only to express surprise and therefore performs the same function as the following "Is it really you?". The only vocative preserved in translation is (b), which is highly relevant in the given situation: by using it and by switching from the polite "doctor" to the familiar "Watson", Holmes reveals his identity.

If we look only at the syntactic pattern, grammatical categorisation and macrofunctional categorisation (Halliday 1985), they do not furnish us with a criterion for differentiating (b) from a, c, and d. Relevance theory can help: (b) has significant contextual effects, it changes Watson's assumptions about the other man's identity and is for that reason indispensable.

As an example (d) is not as clear, but it can still be accounted for in terms of relevance theory. "Holmes" and "Is it really you?" perform the same function: they express the speaker's surprise. Such double constructions are very common in speech, as they intensify the emotive effect. Consequently, it can be argued that (if some reduction is necessary) the subtitler is faced with an open choice. "Holmes" could have been retained and the other part of Watson's response deleted. It is the second condition determining the various degrees of relevance that is decisive in this particular case. In terms of extent condition 1, both utterances are equally relevant as they have comparable contextual effects. However, "Is it really you?" is more transparent and requires less effort to be processed in the intended meaning than "Holmes", which relies more heavily on the intonational clues.

In structural descriptive terms, deleted elements range from individual words to whole sentences and suprasentential elements (turns or adjacency pairs).

EXAMPLE 5

She stabbed him NINE TIMES.

EXAMPLE 6

I may come around tomorrow morning AROUND 10.

EXAMPLE 7

It was the destroyers WITH THE CONVOY
shooting at the submarine.

EXAMPLE 8

I managed to obtain his courteous permission
to write the note WHICH YOU AFTERWARDS RECEIVED.

The above examples show, respectively, deletion of circumstantials (Examples 5, 6) and of modifiers (7, 8). Decisions about deletions are context-dependent and hinge on the translator's judgment about whether the viewer can have access to the intended interpretation without them. In (5) and (6) the circumstantial details given in large letters were left out because the modifications they entail are unimportant in the story: what matters in (5) is that the woman stabbed somebody to death, while the number of stabs only contributes to the dramatic effect. The relevant piece of information in (6) is the promise to come around, not the exact time, as this is not dealt with further.

It can be argued that these elements are deleted as their absence relieves the viewers of some processing effort, without making the processing of the rest of the utterance (and of the preceding and following utterances) more difficult. Considerations of the processing effort involved in the interpretation of such reduced utterances are very tricky. Although a considerable part of our speech is redundant, that is of lesser relevance, it is indispensable to facilitate the processing. When the subtitler leaves out a (partly) redundant element which is present in the original text to facilitate the identification (proper interpretation) of another part of the utterance, one must assess what this means for the necessary processing effort. On the one hand, the target audience is spared the effort of processing the missing part, but, on the other hand, they may find it more difficult to process the remaining part. It is up to the subtitler to decide which of the two prevails. Examples (5) and (6) are cases of deletions entailing less effort. With the modification omitted, (7) and (8) probably demand more effort to access the assumptions necessary for interpreting the headword nouns. The subtitlers obviously counted on the viewers' ability to retrieve the necessary information from the previously created cognitive context: Example 7 is from a letter written by a boy about the first days of war. The convoy is mentioned previously in the letter, and it is part of general knowledge that a convoy is a group of (war) ships or vehicles; therefore the 'destroyers' can be assumed to belong to the convoy. Consequently, the deletion of the modifying phrase does not significantly increase the effort necessary to process "the destroyers", but it eliminates the effort needed to process "with the convoy". A similar line of reasoning applies to (8), except that here the deleted modification is based on the speaker's and the hearer's shared private cognitive context rather than on a common cognitive context.

Whole utterances are deleted, especially when their relationship to a preceding one is basically that of expansion or explication. The following English originals (which have not been subtitled (yet)) will serve for illustration:

EXAMPLE 9
THE AIR BITES SHREWDLY; it is very cold.
EXAMPLE 10
- How's John?
- Better. HE THREW UP LAST NIGHT, BUT HIS FEVER BROKE TODAY.

In such cases it is important for the (future) subtitler to be able to perform an efficient analysis of the passage. In terms of relevance theory, examples 9 and 10 can be viewed as instances of deletions of those sections that would demand more effort to interpret. In (9) the everyday version is preserved and the metaphorical picture is omitted; in (10) the explanatory part is longer and has no immediate importance for the story. Analysis of such examples (not in isolation, as present here, but in context) should sensitize students to the factors underlying such decisions.

Conclusion

I have presented a few examples of how the domain of subtitling reductions can be provided with a satisfactory explanatory framework that will account for cases as different as (1) and (10). It should be pointed out to students (and to practitioners) of subtitling that awareness of the relevance principles in itself will not make a perfect, infallible subtitler. As Gutt points out, the translator "does not have direct access to the cognitive environment of his audience... - all he can have is some assumptions or beliefs about it" (Gutt 1991: 112). Added to this, the subtitler's own context may be insufficient or inadequate for him to make the right decision. Nevertheless, the theoretical framework of relevance theory does provide a valuable explanatory tool. It is also general enough to form part of training programmes for subtitlers (and translators in general). If nothing else, it will help them to avoid the unpleasant feeling of not knowing what they are really doing and what they are expected to be doing, and will thus heighten their awareness of their trade.

TRANSCULTURAL LANGUAGE TRANSFER: SUBTITLING FROM A MINORITY LANGUAGE

Ian Roffe and David Thorne, University of Wales, United Kingdom

Background

In November 1982 the Independent Broadcasting Authority launched a new broadcast television channel in Wales. This new television channel, called Sianel Pedwar Cymru (S4C), was established in response to social and political concerns in Wales regarding the future use of the Welsh language. The channel was charged with broadcasting a full and comprehensive Welsh language service including a considerable part of its programmes at peak hours. However, within the reception area of these transmissions, only a minority of the population was able to speak the language and S4C was required to provide a service for the total Welsh audience, not for Welsh speakers alone.

Interlinguistic subtitling appeared to be a means of bridging this linguistic and cultural divide and led to the introduction of an in-house Welsh-English subtitling service on a trial basis in 1986. This initial experiment in language transfer proved successful and served to convince groups in the Welsh learners' community of the value of the service. Nonetheless the scarcity of translation resources imposed a practical limit to the expansion of the number of broadcast subtitling hours.

Two events stimulated subtitling output. Firstly, in 1990, a new strategic direction was formulated for S4C which re-focused much of its programme output towards the principal centres of population rather than on the rural heartland. This reorientation meant that the broadcasting channel was now targeting market segments where the Welsh language abilities of people were not as strong; there were also accompanying cultural differences in this group. A second stimulus came from the passing into law of the 1990 Broadcasting Act, which stated that the percentage of subtitled television programmes broadcast must reach a minimum of 50% by the end of 1998 with further growth in subtitling to continue after this date. In response to the Act, S4C pledged to increase its subtitled output to 75% by 1998.

Along with these legislative and broadcasting changes there have been technical developments and changes in the distribution pattern of types of television receivers in Wales. Ten years ago the percentage of households which were equipped with a television receiver for Teletext transmissions, by which subtitles are superimposed over ordinary programmes in the United Kingdom, was negligible, whereas today over 40% of homes in Wales have such television receivers. These factors led S4C to a new approach to subtitling in order to preserve high-standard subtitling and increase interlinguistic subtitling on television. It was envisaged that it would be necessary to widen the pool of subtitlers so that independent television companies and translation agencies could provide economic and competitive services for broadcast television.

With this in mind S4C approached our College. We already had activities in common resulting from research and educational interests in translation and from undergraduate course options in media studies. Our interests converged in the challenge of teaching subtitling.

Initially, we surveyed British and American databases for previous research on interlinguistic subtitling but, at first, nothing was discovered. Until recently, most significant information for the providers of subtitling services originated from studies of subtitling for the hard of hearing. A research group from Southampton University (Baker et al 1984) had studied the most effective techniques for the production and presentation of subtitles. This early work set the standards for current subtitling in the United Kingdom and provided detailed guidance on the production of multi-line subtitles and the editing of text to permit logical display in the subtitles.

Kyle (1992), who investigated preferences for style, formats, accuracy and speed, has examined the attitudes of deaf people to subtitles. He reports (p.10) that the "evolution of subtitling seems to have created a *de facto* standard which would be difficult to change even if more effective means of providing programme information were found". This standard represented a first step in the quality control of subtitles for broadcast programmes.

Programme development
In the course design stage following the survey we identified the following four key practical difficulties.
(i)   Financing the initiative.
(ii)   The introduction of practical subtitling expertise into the University.
(iii)   The entry requirements demanded from participants.
(iv)   Establishing an acceptable standard for subtitling in translation.
The cost of equipment is a significant barrier to the start of subtitling training. Since access to subtitling equipment is a pre-requisite for practically based training, this barrier had to be overcome. S4C hired and loaned to us subtitling equipment to operate two work stations. Our University in turn provided technical support as well as a dedicated suite in a new and purpose built Media Centre.

Subtitling expertise was designed for staff in order to develop in-house experience. This initial instructor-training was organised by S4C and provided by themselves in association with a translation agency. This led to the creation of a cadre of internal College staff who could design and deliver an accredited training programme.

The entry qualification demanded was bilingualism. There was already a small pool of promising translators, and the central task of an intensive programme would be teaching them new skills associated with subtitling. This helped to focus the strategy of the course as a bridging programme for experienced translators to commercial broadcast standards of subtitling. This conscious decision meant that the course assessment would be based solely on subtitling ability to broadcast standard.

Our knowledge of the potential employment market made it clear that the training initiative would be most successful if the programme was flexible. The first programme commenced in October 1990 with eight graduates in Welsh Language and Literature as trainees; none of them had experience of the media industry and they were all newcomers to subtitling. The trainees' background meant that familiarisation and the development of confidence in using the technology were prime concerns. The programme had five distinctive stages.

1. Translation of script.
2. Preparation of a script.
3. Entry of subtitle text and display parameters.
4. Synchronisation to the programme videotape.
5. Review and editing.

The ability to work accurately at speed and under pressure of time was considered to be essential in a professional subtitler, so the coursework materials prepared provided increasing challenges for the trainee.

The pilot programme involved all aspects of subtitling. Practical tuition was organised on a 1:2 staff/student ratio in a workshop format. Each student worked on exercise tapes with weekly attainment targets which were closely monitored for technical competence, translation and cultural interpretation. Every trainee prepared a professional workbook to record the development of learning on the course.

The trainees' work was assessed by an external examiner who viewed two 15 minute compilation tapes consisting of clips from a variety of programme genres. These were presented after completing one third and two-thirds of the course respectively. Final assessment was based on a compilation tape which included both linguistic and cultural dilemmas in addition to a variety of programme excerpts. This tape had to be completed within a three hour period which meant that the examiner was also judging the standard of delivery under pressure and consequently under conditions simulating commercial practice. Trainees who passed the standard were then awarded a Certificate in Subtitling, an academic certificate approved by our University and S4C.

Commentary on evaluation

The original course was organised in three-hour sessions and delivered weekly over a six month period which met the needs of trainees for part-time study. Subsequent courses have been provided in a more intensive format of 10 week parttime and 3 week full-time immersion courses. The latter programme was devised for experienced translators operating in organisations within the United Kingdom and internationally, who find a longer term commitment impossible.

The central issue in the training programme was whether the objectives would be entirely practical or composed of a combination of practical and theoretical training. In the event the latter option was chosen as this allowed a stronger focus on translation and helped the scheduling of practical sessions. The course programme has been adjusted according to our experiences. It was evident that student familiarisation with the subtitling equipment was more time-consuming than we had anticipated. This was mainly due to the fact that a part of the course was taught in a group format: *students* had relatively few opportunities to receive individual guidance and the *tutor* had little indication of progress made by individual students during the initial stage of the course. This led to difficulties as students struggled to meet deadlines.

There has, therefore, been a shift in teaching methods away from the group format in order to concentrate more on individual tuition. Immersion weekends give students an accelerated introduction to the machines and to the technical aspects of subtitling. During the 1992-1993 subtitling course the students received tutoring on a one-to-one basis and were then expected to work for a minimum of five hours per week on structured exercises that were to be presented for assessment. These amendments have proved effective; all the students following the 30 week course were technically competent within the first four weeks, a fact which allowed them to concentrate on effective synchronisation and on the linguistic and cultural content of captions.

The programme is a considerable investment in time and effort for all participants. All the students have acquired more confidence from applying their linguistic skills in a new context and the experience of working in a technological environment has also been of value, since students have usually only been exposed to an academic environment. The need to respond to commercial pressures has been more deeply appreciated by the course. And finally, the requirements

of live subtitling is an excellent way of introducing team work.
The programme has fulfilled the original objectives. A resource centre with facilities and a core training team has been founded at our University. It has provided services which have been well received by organisations in the media industry in Wales and beyond. The standard of successful participants is at broadcast level as assessed by professional commercial subtitlers.

As a course team we often ponder whether we have found the correct match for the expectations of the trainee group and/or of their potential employers and of the programme content. Addressing the trainees' aspirations for employment in media companies, we have in recent courses introduced a study tour for young graduates including visits overseas to observe and digest the work of particular companies and facilities houses. This is meant to broaden the students' perspective of the industry. Meeting colleagues who have successfully made the transition into commercial employment has also heightened understanding of this career path. Moreover it has served to establish personal contacts between trainees and potential employers in an industry which relies heavily on such links.

Transfer problems

Another feature of the work intimately associated with linguistic and cultural transfer problems and encountered by trainees and professional subtitlers alike is interpreting the divide between Welsh and English and anticipating audience reaction to broadcast captions. We will recount some of our practical experiences in order to illustrate these difficulties.

(i). As a rule, song lyrics are not subtitled, but students following the course are asked to subtitle a song, from a popular satirical programme, lampooning recent events in a soap opera. This lyric was broadcast with subtitles when it was screened originally, since the rendition would be meaningless to non-Welsh speakers without captions. The target audience was, of course, familiar both with the characters portrayed and the events described in the song, and the subtitler was constrained by the content of the original Welsh version. The task was made even more difficult because the words of the Welsh version were set to a well known English melody, and therefore the subtitled version had to follow the pre-set rhyming and rhythmic patterns as well as conveying the lyrical content of the original version in order to satisfy the audience.

(ii). One of the most difficult tasks for the trainees is to appreciate the perspectives and expectations of the target audience. For example a fashion programme included references to the imperial monetary system which was replaced by the decimal system in 1971. The programme was aimed at youngsters who consequently would not know this system and who would therefore not understand the references made to the steep rise in the cost of living during the last fifty years. In this case, the original subtitler decided to convert prices from old money into decimal pounds and pence in order to ensure that the target audience understood the content of the programme.

(iii). On occasion subtitling is made very difficult by the inclusion of English words in Welsh programmes. The audience will expect the subtitles to include these English words. The following situation was presented in our current subtitling course. The Welsh lexical item to express the English spider is '*pryf copyn*', a similar form means literally 'chief cop', and this was then punned as 'chief constable' in the programme. It is very difficult for a subtitler to interpret this nuance. Most students abandoned the set script completely in their effort to include a natural reference to 'chief constable' in their captions.

(iv). Forms which are uncharacteristic or inappropriate must never be attributed to subjects. In this respect the subtitler faces difficulties when subtitling a programme which contains taboo forms. Students were set the task of subtitling a documentary in which the pig farmer used extremely earthy language! Whilst it is important that the audience appreciates the thrust of informal register, written crudeness is always more offensive than actual oral usage. In this latter case, the would be subtitler must aim to strike a difficult balance between familiarising the target audience with the undoubted colour of a crude character, and offending it by excessive reproduction of dirty talk.

Visions

In Wales we continue to be confronted by a shortfall of competent interlinguistic subtitlers. The difficulty is compounded by the problem of recruiting and retaining high calibre specialist staff. This arises from the highly competitive nature of television contract work tendered for by independent television producers and the consequential uncertainty of employment. Such opportunities compete unfavourably with more traditional and stable career routes, in the field of education for example, which appeal to the small number of single honours graduates in Welsh who qualify from the University of Wales each year. (A total of 63 in 1992). So we intend to continue our interlinguistic courses for the foreseeable future to meet commercial needs.

The subtitling machines have proved valuable tools in giving learning assistance in order to gain another perspective on a language. Currently we are applying the techniques to Swedish and to German in our in-house undergraduate programmes and we have received very positive feedback from our students. The machines are providing a form of Computer Assisted Language Learning and we consider that there is considerable scope for extending the applications to perhaps include a machine interactive form of learning.

Finally, the factors which make subtitling an attractive means of language transfer between Welsh and English are present in other language combinations. For speakers of European languages such as Irish, Catalan, Basque and Welsh, who form a minority linguistic set within their native countries and who have language capability in the predominant national language, there has historically been relatively little language transfer. We have provided a programme for minority language subtitlers. So far, subtitlers from Ireland, Scotland, Brittany, the Basque country, Catalonia, Galicia, Portugal, Sweden and Germany have participated in our courses of intensive three week instructor-training programmes, so that the know-how can be cascaded through their organisations by way of further programmes in the home country.

It is our experience that the development of interlinguistic subtitling expertise must be seen as a continuous process which has the full support and confidence of regional broadcasting organisations - and not merely viewed as a one-off course attendance activity. In this respect the set of conditions which existed at the start of the project in the United Kingdom, namely: stable pre-course links between TV broadcasting organisations and academia, and the close specification of a solution which makes economic and financial sense to both partners, is pivotal in the successful extension of our programme as well as in others that are similarly structured.

Nyborg Slot

SUBTITLING: PEOPLE TRANSLATING PEOPLE

Henrik Gottlieb, University of Copenhagen, Denmark

For decades, subtitling has been the prevalent mode of screen translation in the minor Western speech communities on the shores of the Atlantic: from Portugal via Wales to Iceland, and from Belgium and the Netherlands to the Nordic countries.

The dominant European nations, as well as the minor countries in Central Europe, have maintained their habit of dubbing,[1] in both cinema and television. According to the European Broadcasting Union, this pattern will change in the near future:[2] the increasing exchange of films and television across the European language barriers, will - coupled with a growing appetite for linguistic authenticity amongst the European TV audience - lead to a notable increase in the need for a shared European subtitling strategy, and for competent subtitlers.

To cater for this situation, the Copenhagen University Center for Translation Studies is now planning a series of international courses in subtitling, to be held at the new European Film College in Ebeltoft, Denmark.

The Ebeltoft courses

The Ebeltoft courses will be based on the *Copenhagen University Postgraduate Course in Audiovisual Translation,* taught since 1991.[3] This two-module course, focusing on TV subtitling, is aimed at Open University students at BA level.

Module 1 includes two exams:

A) an oral examination in translation theory and critique relevant to audiovisual translation, and

B) a practical 3-hour "prima vista" subtitling of a 5-minute sequence, produced on a professional subtitling workstation.

Module 2 includes:

C) a 20-page paper on a specific topic within audiovisual translation, illustrated by

D) a ready-for-broadcast subtitling of a 25-minute TV program or film sequence of the candidate's own choice.

At Ebeltoft, we offer three different courses:

1) *General course.* For media critics as well as filmmakers and TV producers. This course aims at providing an understanding of the role of subtitling in the increasingly multilingual media world of today, emphasizing the function of sub-

titling as an integral part of international film and TV production.

2) *Special course*. For interpreters and translators, translation teachers, and - last but not least - dubbers and other screen translators from countries hitherto unfamiliar with subtitling. Here, the emphasis is put on the visual nature of subtitling, seen as a mode of language transfer that combines elements of drama translation, interpreting and literary translation. The aim is set at obtaining, or improving, skills in interlingual subtitling, focusing on practical, esthetic, linguistic and journalistic aspects alike.

3) *Advanced course*. For experienced translation scholars and subtitlers interested in the technical and the theoretical state of the art. On the practical side, we will exploit all editing and time-cueing facilities of the newest equipment on the market. On the scholarly side, we will discuss recent international research in the field of subtitling, covering the disciplines of translation studies, media studies and psychology. The aims are:

a) Perfecting skills in interlingual subtitling, focusing on the optimal correspondence between genre-specific features, viewers, and subtitles.

b) Providing a theoretical framework for discussing subtitling at a general level, and developing critical judgment of existing subtitling practices.

The general and the special subtitling courses (courses 1 and 2), both lasting 5 days, will follow the same schedule, with a series of plenary sessions (in English), interspersed with practical 4-hour workshop sessions. In all these sessions, participants work individually, learning the nuts and bolts of subtitling. In the plenary sesssions, however, the emphasis differs: whereas course 1 focuses on the *presence* of subtitles as sound-synchronous visual elements, course 2 concentrates on the linguistic *content* of subtitles. Accordingly, course 1 participants - who are not translators, anyway - are trained in subtitling from and into their own language (*intralingual* subtitling), while course 2 participants work *interlingually*, from a foreign language into their own language. The advanced subtitling course (course 3) covers two more days, and one additional exam: a "ready-for-broadcast" interlingual subtitling. Thus, course 1 includes exam B1: *intralingual prima vista subtitling* - converting, for example, French dialog into French subtitles. Course 2 includes exam B2, *interlingual prima vista subtitling from English* - into, for example, German. Course 3 includes exams B3 and D, *interlingual prima vista subtitling* - from, say, Spanish into Swedish - and *interlingual ready-for-broadcast subtitling* - from, for example, Finnish into English.

In all courses, each participant works on his or her personal subtitling workstation. Consequently, applicants ought to have some word-processing knowledge, a fact I took for granted when we launched our Copenhagen course in subtitling in 1991. However, a number of our middle-aged[4] Open University students found it difficult to cope with the dedicated keyboards on our subtitling workstations. It turned out that a few of these students did not even feel comfortable with a normal typewriter. Even some of the more keyboard-familiar students surprised me: until the beginning of the course, I never realized that you could insert a good old-fashioned 5 ¼ inch diskette into the disk drive in 8 different ways! Of course, only one of these will work, and the right one soon became obvious to everyone in class. But, apart from a modicum of computer-literacy, no special technical qualifications are needed to sign up for the Ebeltoft general and special courses in subtitling. The necessary knack for language I take for granted in everyone interested in the discipline of subtitling.

Subtitling: constraints and virtues

In the rapidly expanding literature on subtitling,[5] many authors - be they practitioners or theorists - refrain from defining subtitling as a type of translation. A typical example is found in one of the few books on screen translation published so far, titled *Overcoming language barriers in television* (Luyken et al. 1991). Throughout this work, the term *Language Transfer* is used, instead of simply *translation*.

A decade ago, a *Danmarks Radio* subtitler bluntly stated:

We don't translate. We subtitle. To subtitle from a foreign language is to Danicize, with due respect to the typographical constraints, the reading speed of the viewers, the composition of the screen image, the cutting, and the speech tempo in the foreign original.

Now, if subtitling is not translation, then what is? The standard answer will be: "A literary translation, of course." And indeed, this type of paper-to-paper translation has been known for at least two thousand years, yielding hundreds of running meters of theoretical works on the subject.

But the concept of translation is now widening. In their recent work, *Discourse and the translator*, Hatim and Mason (1990: 2) state that "the way is open to a view of translating which is not restricted to a particular field ... but which can include such diverse activities as film subtitling and dubbing, simultaneous interpreting, cartoon translating, abstracting and summarising, etc."

As even translation scholars grow used to the electronic media, subtitling and other types of audiovisual translation are gaining access to theoretical works on translation. With the exception of a few non-English works on translation (Cary 1956; Söderlund 1965; Mounin 1965, 1967; and Dollerup 1978), the pre-1980 concept of translation limited its scope to 'premeditated writing': translation of dialog was accepted only when this was not genuine, and not heard. Only filtered through an author could spoken discourse claim any interest.

But had the audiovisual media been the original means of mass communication, antedating printed sources, the endeavor to translate abstract representations of human communication, such as books, would have been inconceivable. The audiovisual establishment might then, with some justice, have said the following about the prospects of translating novels, for instance: "Trying to re-create such fictitious, printed descriptions of alien cultures, with events often taking place in the past and the text supported by neither visuals nor sound - a foolhardy enterprise - hardly deserves being called translating."

All text types present the translator with constraints: unillustrated fiction (also known as literature) as well as comic books, feature films as well as TV serials. Printed literature just happens to have a long history in our culture, so we have become used to interpreting the signals that the author tries to communicate via the one, fragile channel at his disposal: the printed word.

Compared to certain types of literature, audiovisual media provide a relatively safe ground for translations, *because of* the constraints involved in those media. In an earlier article (Gottlieb 1992) I have described the time and space constraints specific to screen translation, a set of constraints easily identified by scholarly observers, such as Titford 1982, Fawcett 1983, and Mayoral et al. 1988. However, a number of admittedly trivial factors are at least as important in determining the quality and nature of the end product, as are the more spectacular media-specific constraints. As one of the above-mentioned authors aptly puts it:

> Written translation suffers like dubbing and subtitling from physical constraints, including the economic. The most important are: poor wages ...; absurd deadlines ...; poor originals ...; and finally, poor training of translators. (Fawcett 1983: 189, column 2)[7]

This does not mean that the demands put on literary translation and on subtitling need to be the same: the best book translator is not necessarily the best subtitler, but the best translation is reached only by acknowledging the premises of the media in question. Knowing these premises, the quality of a translation is defined by the talent of the translator, not by the constraints of the specific media.

Equivalence: ideal for technical translation

A translation can never be a clone of the original. Structural differences alone preclude a fully equivalent transfer of verbal content and intentions between human languages:

> Perfect translation is in the best of circumstances a virtual impossibility. Languages are not ossified nomenclatures, parallel lexical lists from which one need merely choose matching items on the basis of a one-to-one correspondence. (Shochat and Stam 1985: 42)

All human languages express nothing but their own culture: different languages have different semantic fields and different usage-governed rules for collocation and cohesion between elements. And not only do languages differ in terms of what *can* be said; they also differ in terms of what is *likely* to be said in specific situations.

To modify the initial statement of the previous paragraph, certain written text types which are culture-neutral, explicit and impersonal may indeed be translated "equivalently". In *technical texts*, as for instance instruction manuals, neither people, nor language, nor culture, is in focus. Such texts are purely informative, and to a large extent predictable, which allows them to be translated *mechanically*, either by computers, or by people, with or without computer assistance. The aim is, generally, consistency in terminology and denotative precision. But when we talk about text types dealing with human beings, their thoughts, their behavior, and their interpersonal relations - their nature and culture - mechanical transfer of the discourse involved is impossible.

Authenticity: the obligation of subtitling

As the realm of film and television is people and their world, TV programs and films will have to be translated *organically*: by an interpreting person, in this case a subtitler. Mechanical translation in the audiovisual media is - even without considering media-specific obstacles - quite unfeasable. Hence, the notion of equivalent translation is an illusory ideal for film and TV dialog.

In trying to get the message through to the target audience, across language and culture barriers, a more realistic ideal would be achieving the same effect on the audience as the one the original audience experienced; the same text they cannot get.[8] But perhaps the ultimate result a (screen) translator can opt for is simply giving the target audience the experience they would have had if they already knew the foreign language in question.[9]

Any translated text must function in the communicative situation around it. In the case of *monosemiotic* texts, such as (unillustrated) books, the translator is in control of the entire expression. In *polysemiotic* texts, the translator is constrained by, and in some situations supported by, other communicative channels present. Film and TV, being of a polysemiotic nature, force the translator to consider four such simultaneous channels:

1) The verbal audio channel: dialog, background voices; sometimes lyrics
2) The non-verbal audio channel: music and sound effects
3) The verbal visual channel: captions and written signs in the image
4) The non-verbal visual channel: picture composition and flow

In dubbing, where foreign-language dialog is replaced by domestic-language dialog, the balance of the individual film or TV program is maintained: The four semiotic channels each hold the same semantic load as in the original version.

In subtitling, however, the balance is shifted from channel (1) to channel (3), the latter normally the one with the lowest semantic content in original-language films and TV. Although subtitling retains the original dialog, with the target audience thus enjoying the voice quality and intonation of the original, the authenticity gained this way is partly lost when it comes to reconstructing the polysemantic puzzle. The reception work going on in the minds of the audience differs considerably from the way in which the original was perceived, and this brings us back to discussing the "equivalence of effect" notion.

How can a film that is partly *read* convey the same impression as the "same" film listened to, with hardly any visual verbal signs? In trying to answer such questions we clearly leave translation studies proper and enter the realm of psychology. And in fact, psychologists have considered this issue. For nearly a decade, the Department of Experimental Psychology at the Catholic University of Leuven, in Flemish-speaking Belgium, has conducted studies in viewer reception of subtitles, interlingual as well as intralingual (see for instance d'Ydewalle et al. 1987 and 1989). However, most studies so far deal with the more *behaviorist* side of the issue, notably subjects' eye movements when reading subtitles on the screen. Genuinely *cognitive*, linguistically founded research is still very rare, indeeed. With often conflicting results in the field of subtitle reception, establishing a "scientific" ideal for polysemiotic texts, let alone testing this, is a risky enterprise. One might simply conclude that "it is hardly fair to ask more of a translation than we demand from monolingual communication, i.e. functional adequacy." (Pedersen 1988: 15)

Ideals and facts of subtitling: the foundations of teaching

Unlike traditional literary translation critique, modern translatology does not play the game of "spotting errors" in a particular translation. Although it is evident that not all possible renderings of a word, a phrase, or a text, are equally suited, in non-technical texts, there is always more than one acceptable solution. Discarding translatological fundamentalism, based on a black-and-white, *absolute* attitude to language, a *relative* approach makes it possible to deal with the intricate pragmatics of polysemiotic translation. The subject of study is what translators *do*, rather than what they *should* do. But this analytic, descriptive approach on behalf of the translation scholar is not irreconcilable with a more prescriptive, pedagogical stance. In teaching translation, the scholar-as-teacher may use the 'George Orwell principle': "Some renderings are more equal than others!"[10]

I believe that to fully understand the relativity of human communication, in this case translation, one must know all the rules and roles of the game:

1) How to translate;
2) How to analyze and evaluate the translations of yourself and others;
3) Teaching others (1) and (2).

In this way, creative, descriptive, and prescriptive activities go hand in hand.

In evaluating our students' achievements in practical subtitling, as tested in exams B and D (see this article: p. 261), we look at the subtitles as they present themselves on the screen. On the Copenhagen course, we apply professional criteria, as we will in the Ebeltoft courses to come. Accordingly, every assignment is evaluated in terms of

A) *Understanding* the spoken dialog in its audiovisual context: What has the student heard and seen in the sequence subtitled?

B) *Interpretation* of extra-textual, genre-specific and historical qualities of the program: What are the central themes, and what is the point of view behind the dialog?

C) Authenticity and correctness in the *rendering* of the dialog: Is this what this kind of person might have said in the source language - with due respect to the standards of written language - and is the spelling all right?

D) *Segmentation and layout* of the subtitles: How filmically adequate is the continuing dialog 'cut up' into subtitle blocks, and how reader-friendly are these blocks being structured?

E) Subtitle *cueing*: How elegantly are the individual subtitles presented on the screen, and how well are the expected viewers able to perceive them? Do they get enough reading time for each subtitle?

The teaching of screen translation thus involves the basic concerns of written translation, and of good usage in general, but adds several dimensions, as expressed here under (D) and (E), and - to a certain extent - (A), since on our courses we rarely use manuscripts. The students, like simultaneous interpreters, must rely on their eyes and ears in order to receive the message correctly. In practice, this has proven not to be all that difficult, whereas segmentation, layout, and cueing - work procedures that demand a well-developed sense of timing, and some flair for film esthetics - seem to be insurmountable obstacles to some.

The quest for authenticity, treated under (C), is something subtitling has in common with other 'people-oriented' translations, as opposed to translations of technical texts. However, as a consequence of a relative outlook on translation, it must be admitted that sometimes even a 'human' translator may have good reasons for choosing very source-text flavored solutions. These may be cases of what Nida called *formal equivalence*, with the intention of transferring certain lexical elements of the original, rather than merely the semantic and stylistic content.[11] When found in subtitles, the strategy of formal correspondence may be consciously used, to emphasize culture-specific elements in the dialog, etc. But quite often, the subtitler is simply lured by the original phrasing, especially when working from a language related to the target language. Even more often, form-

ally correspondent renderings in subtitles are triggered by expected audience reactions: cinemagoers or TV and video viewers do not always *want* the "same"
impression as the original audience. The feedback-effect from the original -
whether that consist of recognizable words, prosodic features, gestures, or background visuals - may be so strong that a more idiomatic, 'functional' rendering
will be counterproductive. In many cases, people want a direct translation of what
is being said, not a complete reconstruction of the dialog in their own language.
This means that a consistently target-language oriented, 'idiomatic' translation
may backfire. This happens when the distance between the effect of the subtitle
and the total effect of the multi-channel original text - in the poly-semiotic sense
described above - becomes too great. In such cases the friction between original
and subtitle causes noise, and the illusion of the translation as the *alter ego* of
the original is broken.

An example of this, taken from the TV genre *political satire*, will illustrate the
problems encountered when trying to domesticize the objects of ridicule:

> When we subtitled the [British] series 'Not the Nine O'Clock News' we had this brilliant idea
> of giving Danish names to the people commented on, for instance Jan Bonde Nielsen, in the
> case of a big-time entrepeneur - or Allan Simonsen [a well-known Danish footballer in the
> 1980s]. They were used in the same context, and then we realized that the threshold of
> credibility had been crossed. Well, we were not as brilliant as we thought. ("Der er altid nogen
> der ved bedre", press release by Danmarks Radio 1989: 4. My translation)

Even in printed translations, a too markedly target-language oriented translation
may backfire: In his polemic against the present doctrine of idiomatic translation
aimed at rendering the meaning behind the words, Brian Mossop mentions the
problem of rendering people - not their names, this time, but their statements -
in other languages than the one they speak themselves. In his critique of a possible, idiomatically correct, translation of the resignation speech of a premier of
the French-speaking Quebec province, Mossop suggests a more 'rough', source-
language oriented translation, for this reason:

> ... most English Canadians would have heard the former Quebec premier being interviewed on
> television and radio, and [the communicative] translation just does not sound like him. Unlike
> former prime minister Pierre Trudeau, he was not known as someone who spoke English in the
> same way as a native speaker, and even though this is writing, not speech, readers might
> wonder whether the 'voice' they are 'hearing' is that of the same person they have heard on
> TV. (Mossop 1989: 13)

Both examples show the problems that may occur when two or more semiotic
channels collide. In the Danish example, the references in the TV subtitles clash
with what can be seen on the screen, and what is heard, even by non-English
speaking Danes. In the Canadian example, the readers' knowledge of how the
original spoken discourse might sound runs contrary to the 'correct' written translation. Translating in a bilingual society may easily cause problems of authenticity. Even though the target audience is not bilingual, strictly speaking, and thus

in need of a translation, everybody in a speech community like Quebec knows the peculiarities, especially the spoken features, of 'the other language'. A translation devoid of elements pointing to that language may present itself as sterile, losing its credibility. The parallel to the English-Danish subtitling of TV satire is evident. In any audiovisual translation from English in a country to a large extent (passively) bilingual, the same problem of authenticity enters the picture, literally speaking. In such cases, because of situational factors, the translation is forced to retain some of the linguistic features or culture-specific references that an ideal communicative rendering would have modified.

Subtitling as cross-cultural communication
Any translation is an adaptation of the original message to a culture outside the original speech community:

According to the Sapir-Whorf hypothesis, language is culture, and those who 'inhabit' different languages might be said to inhabit different worlds. (Shochat and Stam 1985: 36)

Neither film nor language can be transferred in total from one culture to another. Attitudes and ideas, as well as tangible items of daily life, may be specific to the original speech community. In some cases, the constraints of subtitling make things even more complicated:

A drama or a film deriving from another culture will be in part based on assumptions and concepts which may not exist in that form outside that culture, and which cannot be adequately summed up in a four second subtitle. (Manzoufas 1982: 18)

Culture-specific elements in a film or TV dialog need not be extra-lingual, as exemplified above. Intra-lingual features peculiar to the source language may be just as difficult to tackle for the subtitler. For any translator, a crucial question will always be: "Should I bring the source culture to my audience, or vice versa?" In answering this, intra- and extra-linguistic features may have to treated differently:

Only references to the surrounding culture should have local colour. Linguistic formulations should preferably be exclusively target language wordings, no matter what they refer to. (Nedergaard-Larsen 1993: 235)

Types of screen translation: the time factor as distinctive feature
Earlier in this paper, I classified subtitling, or rather, the subtitled film or TV program, as a *polysemiotic* text type. In the following, I will list a number of such multi-channel types juxtaposed by some central *monosemiotic* text types.

Within polysemiotic translation, the relevant distinctive feature is *time*. This term covers two phenomena: time of text *production*, and time of text *presentation* to the target-language audience. In this context, 'time' is seen as a point in the continuum from the past to the present. For the notion of continuous time (time as a line rather than a point) I will reserve the term *duration*.

Any translation type is defined by two factors: (*A*) time and (*B*) semiotic composition.
A) Three points in time will suffice:
T1, the time for production of the original verbal element
T2, the time for presentation of the original verbal element
T3, the time for presentation of the translated verbal element
If T1 precedes T2, and T3 is simultaneous with T2, the translation is *synchronous*. If T1 precedes T2, and the original verbal channel is not perceived by the target audience, the translation is *non-synchronous*. Finally, if T1 is simultaneous with T2, and T2 precedes T3, the translation is *delayed*.

In other words, whereas at a word-to-word level non-synchronous translation is not concerned with synchrony between original and translation - as in the case of book translations - delayed types of translation, such as the so-called 'simultaneous' interpreting, can be seen as less lucky varieties of synchronous translation. Here, as with the synchronous types, simultaneity is relevant.

As opposed to non-synchronous translations, where the receptor - reading a book, for instance - controls both time and duration for reception, synchronous and delayed translations are both *immediate*. Here, the translated product - say, a TV film - defines the time and duration available to the receptor.
B) The basic distinctions of semiotic composition are:
1)   *Monosemiotic* text types, with only one channel of communication, versus *polysemiotic* types, with two or more channels.
2)   *Isosemiotic* text types, where the translation communicates via the same channel - or set of channels - as the original, versus
3)   *diasemiotic* text types, with different channel(s) used.
Coupling the tripartite time-defined distinction with the two-times-two distinction referring to semiotic composition, a total taxonomy of translation types can be established. In the table on the opposite page, I have included the intralingual *simultaneous subtitling*, used in news broadcasts for the deaf and hard of hearing, and non-electronic polysemiotic types as (translated) comic books.

As is clearly seen, subtitling differs from other types of verbal transmission by virtue of its *additive* nature. In adding written text to speech, subtitling earns its diasemiotic status. Unlike subtitling, the three isosemiotic types of screen translation listed above all work with *voice replacement*, or - to use a more common term - *revoicing*.[12] In a TV program with *voice-over*, the original dialog is still partly audible, 'drowned' by the target-language speak. In Russia, this is still the common way to transmit foreign TV films, whereas lip-synchronous dubbing is dominant in the German, French, Italian, and Spanish speech communities. The method of *commentary* deletes the original speak and replaces this off-screen narration with target-language narration.

TYPOLOGY OF TRANSLATION

Semiotic composition	*Time-defined categorization*		
	Synchronous	**Delayed**	**Non-synchronous**
Mono- & isosemiotic			
Speech	----------	Radio interpreting	---------------
Writing	----------	------------	Written translation
Mono- & diasemiotic			
Speech	----------	------------	Book translation on audiotape
Writing	----------	Interpreting for the deaf	Minutes (from a meeting)
Poly- & isosemiotic			
Writing + Image	----------	------------	Translation of comic books and advertisements
Speech + Image	----------	Simultaneous interpreting	---------------
Speech + Image + Music & Effects	Dubbing	TV voice-over	TV commentary; Performance of translated drama
Poly- & diasemiotic			
Speech + Image + Music & Effects + Writing	Subtitling	Simultaneous subtitling	---------------

Interlingual translation: a comparison of types

In the following table, interlingual subtitling and four other major types of interlingual communication are juxtaposed, and compared with reference to ten communicative parameters. The types are placed in the table according to degree of 'naturalness', ranging from the abstract monosemiotic *printed translation* in the far left column, to the more simple polysemiotic *consecutive interpreting*.

CHARACTERISTICS OF SELECTED TYPES OF TRANSMISSION

Media:	BOOK	PLAY	FILM & TV		ENCOUNTER
Type:	Printed transl.	Acted drama	Sub-titling	Dub-bing	Consecutive interpreting
Parameters:					
Polysemiotic	No	Yes	Yes	Yes	Yes
Isosemiotic	Yes	Yes	No	Yes	Yes
Impromptu	No	No	No	No	Yes
Immediate	No	Yes	Yes	Yes	Yes
Spoken original	No	Yes	Yes	Yes	Yes
Spoken translation	No	Yes	No	Yes	Yes
Condensed translation	No	No	Yes	No	Yes
Acting translator	Yes	No	Yes	No	Yes
Known receptor	No	No	No	No	Yes
Open for two-way communication	No	(No)	No	No	Yes

All ten qualities are typical features of *natural communication*,[13] while the counterparts of these represent what could be called *symbolic communication*. Following from this, the 'naturalness' of the different types of transmission can be expressed on a scale from 10 to 1, depending on the number of 'yes'answers:

Interpreting	10 "points"
Dubbing	5 - - - -
Subtitling	5 - - - -
Drama translation	5 - - - -
Printed translation	2 - - - -

Reduction: the evil spirit of subtitling?

Throughout the history of subtitling, the necessity of dialog condensation has always been stressed. Many scholars and critics lament this seemingly inescapable fact,[14] as does this editor of a Canadian film journal:

... scripts must be heartlessly abridged to be accommodated on a screen.
(Moskowitz 1979: column 1)

But the late *directeur fondateur* of UNESCO's International Journal of Translation, *Babel*, saw the demand for reduction in subtitling as a gift:

En condensant des phrases on s'aperçoit qu'on peut presque tout dire en si peu de mots que l'exercise du langage paraît une fonction humaine pour ainsi dire superflue. (Caillé 1960: 109)

An experienced subtitler expresses a more matter-of-fact attitude:

The shortening of the text for subtitling purposes is nothing more than deciding what is padding and what is vital information. (Reid 1987: 28, column 3)

Not only does the immediate nature of subtitling - controlled by speech tempo and cutting - press for brevity. Two other, less obvious, factors are at work:

1) Intersemiotic redundancy, which enables the viewer to supplement the semiotic content of the subtitles with information from other audiovisual channels - notably the image, and prosodic features in the dialog

2) Intrasemiotic redundancy in the dialog. Especially with *spontaneous speech*, not only the informative content, but also the verbal style and characterization of the speaker are better served with some reduction in the subtitles.[15] However, even *deliberate speech*, including script-based narration, often contains so much redundancy that a slight condensation may enhance the effectiveness of the intended message. Take this excellent statement by Rafael Nir (1984: 85):

It seems indisputable that the translation of dialogue in films belongs to the category of translations which can be defined as highly contextualized. [148 characters]

No great harm is done by trimming this heavyweight into the following 'subtitle':

The translation of dialogue in films
is highly contextualized. [61 characters]

Many scholars would do their readers, lay and learned alike, a favor by 'subtitling' themselves. Or, to condense myself: "Scholars in the world, be brief!"

Notes

1. In dubbing, the original dialog is replaced by postsynchronized target-language dialog.
2. By the late eighties, the *EBU Review* Editor-in-Chief was already admitting that "if we absolutely must discern a trend, let us say that subtitling is gaining ground". (Derasse 1987: 10).

Or, citing a more recent source: "As educational standards have, and are likely to continue to rise over time in Europe, subtitled audiovisual versions of foreign language productions might therefore become increasingly more acceptable to wider parts of the peoples in Europe." (Luyken et al. 1991: 187)

3. As of August 1993, this course has produced 21 candidates. A more detailed description of the course, as well as a theoretical presentation of the concept of subtitling, is found in Gottlieb 1992.

4. Looking at the achievements of my first two subtitling classes, containing a total of 58 students, the only statistically significant factor guiding good results in subtitling is 'age'. Younger Open University students, aged 25-39, fare better than their would-be colleagues in their forties or fifties. In traditional practical translation, age is often considered a plus, but in the case of subtitling neither previous (literary) translating experience nor academic title(s) are safe indicators of success.

5. By the end of 1993, I had 544 titles on interlingual subtitling - most of them dating less than five years back - listed in my bibliography (see Gottlieb, forthcoming). A large number of these items were unpublished university papers, in-house material produced by TV subtitling companies, etc.

6. My translation of a statement by Danish TV subtitler Jesper Kjær in a letter to the editor (*Politiken*, April 1984), answering a critique by a TV reviewer of the "translation" of the American comedy series *M.A.S.H.*

7. In Scandinavia, interpreters and technical translators are far better paid than literary translators, with subtitlers occupying a middle position. In terms of deadlines and workload, subtitlers - with their efficient dedicated equipment - often fare better than literary translators.

8. This ideal, sometimes called *equivalence of effect*, is in keeping with Nida's concept of *functional equivalence* (see Nida and de Waard 1986).

9. This no-nonsense attitude, in spite of its irrefutable logic, is rarely encountered in scholarly literature. However, it was expressed in a recent Danish undergraduate paper (see Lind and Sestoft 1992).

10. In the article *Subtitling: Diagonal Translation*, (Gottlieb 1994) I suggest nine 'pedagogical pillars' to consider when creating and evaluating subtitles. Partly prescriptive, partly descriptive, this article complements the present paper.

11. See Nida 1964: 159. This strategy is often used involuntarily: in his article *The traps of formal correspondence*, Sándor Albert (1993) illustrates how any translation not considering the text as a whole runs the risk of pragmatic defectiveness.

12. To my knowledge, the invention of these collective terms is rather recent: the term 'revoicing' was introduced by the European Institute for the Media (see Luyken et al. 1991), whereas 'voice replacement' is found in *Watching your language: Foreign version issues* in *Screen Digest*, July 1992.

13. 'Natural' in the sense 'phylogenetically and ontogenetically original': Before human beings began expressing themselves through written signs, people mastered spoken discourse, and before children are taught how to read, they are able to talk.

14. Recent experiments at Leuven University, Belgium, (d'Ydewalle et al. 1989) showed that young and old subjects spent "an average of 55.4% of the presentation time on the normal two-line subtitles". That is to say that people seem to have almost half of their television viewing time left for watching the action on the screen. If this is generally true, it raises the possibility of speeding up normal subtitling, abandoning the present European standard of 6 seconds per two-liner. This would eventually lead to a fuller rendering of up-tempo dialog (see Gottlieb 1992: 164-165).

15. The transition from spoken dialog to written subtitles is treated in Gottlieb 1994, where a number of redundant features of spoken discourse are listed.

AUDIO-VISUAL COMMUNICATION: TYPOLOGICAL DETOUR

Yves Gambier, University of Turku, Finland

In this article, I shall focus mainly on subtitling. Subtitling is a force to be reckoned with in subtitling countries, like Portugal, Greece, Wales, the Netherlands, the Nordic Countries. For instance, in Finland some 3,000 foreign TV programmes are shown per year, up to seven per evening. This would correspond to reading approximately 200 novels of 300 pages each, a total of 60,000 pages or a complete novel every other day. We are not only *watching* but also *reading* TV! There is, however, more to it than that.

In the modern world there is a multiplicity of audiovisual messages: documentary films, short-length films, cinema films, TV broadcasts, children's programmes, radio interviews, business videos and home videos. Cinema, video and TV do not call for precisely the same type of subtitling, for reasons which fall under two headings.

There are technical and economical reasons:
* they are imported by different firms
* they require different working conditions
* the speed of the picture is different
* the definition of the screen is different

There are linguistic reasons: in Finland, for instance, bilingual subtitling (into Swedish and Finnish) is used in the cinema and monolingual subtitling into Finnish alone on TV.

Up till now, research has mainly been concerned with the subtitling and dubbing of fiction films. In view of the enormous variety of audiovisual communication, this may seem somewhat surprising; but it reflects the prevailing orientation in translation theory, which is still strongly dominated by literary translation.

In this article, I shall discuss three points: the types of multilingual transfer in audiovisual communication, two effects of subtitling, and finally some challenges to translator training.

Types of multilingual transfer in audiovisual communication

We are not concerned here with intralingual subtitling (such as that provided for deaf or hard-of-hearing people). The tentative typology which follows is a first stage going beyond the current prescriptive standpoint.

There are various means of conveying the linguistic meaning of a foreign-language message to a target audience:

1. *subtitling*: of films, commercials, TV series and programmes
2. subtitling in real time or *simultaneous subtitling*, for instance live performance interviews
3. *dubbing* (lip-synchronisation)
4. *interpreting*, in four possible modes:
   - consecutive, often shortened interpreted renditions, on the radio (interview with a singer or politician, telephone calls), on TV (cultural debates such as 'Apostrophes' in France);
   - *prerecorded* consecutive interpreting, close to voice-over;
   - consecutive interpreting *in duplex*, long-distance communication, for instance during teleconferences
5. *voice-over*: simultaneous interpreting, characterised by the faithful translation of original speech and approximately synchronous delivery. This means was extensively used during the Gulf War (1990-1991): it allows scoops and news flashes in different languages, mixing orality, audibility and a more or less high degree of information.

In cases (4) and (5), the original voice/sound is either heard, fading away slowly, retained at a low level or reduced entirely.

6. *Narration.* The difference between (5) and (6) is linguistic. With narration, the original speech is prepared, translated and possibly condensed in advance and is then read by a journalist or an actor, while voice-over is applied mainly to spontaneous speeches. In both cases, delivery remains synchronous, especially if the narrator appears on the screen. The verbal sense/content works together with the visual information being presented.

7. *Commentary* is a way of adapting a programme to a new target audience - not literally duplicating the original speech but adding new information, like creating a new work, with the identity of the commentator (actor) distinct from that of any of the programme's participants. The synchronisation is with on-screen images rather than with the original voices.

(6) and (7) are used with children's programmes, documentary films, business videos, slide shows, industrial short-length films; they fall in between translation and interpreting, because of the condensation, the reshaping of the original, and the oral output. Modes (3) to (7) constitute different types of *revoicing, spanning from quite free expression to renditions involving extremely tight technical and linguistic constraints to quite free expression.*

8. *Revoicing or multilingual broadcasting*: the receiver selects a sound track with an appropriate language.

9. *'Surtitles' or 'supratitles'*: for instance in opera houses or theatres. These are

normally presented on a line-screen using digital print.

10. *Simultaneous translation* is a type of sight translation from a script or a subtitle in a foreign language taken from a written source text; thus the term 'simultaneous translation'. It is used during film festivals and in film libraries (cinamathèques). If no script is given in advance, the work becomes genuine simultaneous interpreting (or voice-over).

The ten modes confuse and obscure the usual borders between translation and interpreting on the one hand, and between written and oral codes on the other. Subtitling, for instance, is a kind of written simultaneous interpreting; voice-over is close to drama translation and resembles 'oral subtitling'; dubbing resembles interpreting because of the oral synchronisation with the original. Subtitling (from the oral to the written form) seems to be the converse of drama translation (written cues to be acted out) but both work within a split communication between the original, actors and an audience. Could there be analogies between sight translation (written/oral) and subtitling (oral/written), especially in the neurolinguistic schemata or processes?

In short, the audio-visual translation in the media is *a new genre*, still largely unexplored in the field of translation studies.

Even subtitling is not an homogeneous activity; one may work with or without a script, with or without a planned schedule, with or without the pictures. The working conditions are quite different. Subtitling with the script entails different translating strategies than working without the script.

What are the factors determining the choice of a method of audio-visual language transfer made ? Even though it is easy to see that specific methods are preferred according to the type of programme (drama, cartoon, educational or entertainment programme, children's film, science or art programme) and target audience, it is more difficult to determine how TV broadcasting companies and film importers have made decisions in favour of one or the other method in the past, and the role which linguistic norms and conventions have played in these decisions.

What are the effects of subtitling?
Oral vs. written discourse
The traditional approach to translation and interpreting has often relied on the following conceptions:
- the original product is uttered by a single 'speaker'
- the *output* is seen as a homogeneous, stable, and finished product
- the translation aims at an interlinguistically *'equivalent'* transfer of the 'original'.
In the case of media (TV, cinema) using different semiotic systems, it is better

to speak of an 'adjustment', resulting from both the complexity of the media (text and image), and from the immediate conditions of reception and interpretation of the message.

With a film, in fact, we must take into account at least four phases, each producing a meaning in collaboration between interlocutors:

- there is a transformation of a linear text (fiction or non-fiction) into a *scenario* (or the reverse, which is less common)

- there is a switching/transformation/conversion from a scenario or a script to a *dialogue* articulated by the actors (semiotic translation, which also involves interlingual translation if the language of the script and that of the actors is not the same)

- *iconic and linguistic features* are related to one another (another kind of semiotic translation)

- finally, there is an interlingual transfer of dialogue in *subtitles*, a process which can be regarded as semiotic and interlingual since it involves a) a change of code - the oral code is converted into a written code - and b) a change of language.

It should be stressed in this context that this double mutation is not confined to the cinema and TV alone. To mention just a few examples: at numerous international conferences the debates are transcribed and stenographed and then reformulated in another language, while operas may be 'surtitled'.

In the case of subtitling, the original message is delivered by various enunciators with different voices and different personalities. But what is more, in passing from the script writer to the director and the actors, the message has undergone changes and transformations. Before reaching the spectator's eye, the message has thus in fact already been changed and adjusted several times. These changes are determined by different factors.

This being the case, it is too limited to view subtitling as a mere 'condensation' of a so-called 'original'. To regard subtitling as reducing the number of words is not applicable as a method of comparative analysis of intercultural communication. Of course, it is naturally easy to perceive and count the number of omissions, deletions and substitutions (for instance, of phrases of politeness, exclamations and interjections). But to do so is also to be under the spell of a quantitative, mathematical theory of information (information entropy) which considers cross-linguistic communication in terms of losses or additions and sees translation as a process of mimetically copying a literary work, a duty to repeat. In subtitling, it is important to study what is *transformed* and why. Reduction may be one of its components; it is not, however, a property of subtitling alone. It is also characteristic, for example, of interpreting and cartoons. What is unique in subtitling as a form of selective translation is the fact that it operates at two levels simultaneously: (1) the change in code from the temporally organized oral code to the linear written code and (2) the switch from one language to another.

In writing, there is normally at least some delay between production and reception, and thus no immediate feedback. Furthermore, no prosodic or pragmatic means are available. In the cinema, the recoverability of the written code is weakened. Under normal conditions, the spectator does not have the opportunity of going back in order to reinterpret the subtitling, and in this respect it is close to the oral code. But whereas the multiform, co-produced oral message is intimately intertwined with the image, the interpretation of the written message (subtitling) creates a certain delay and distances the moment of interpretation and that of the appearance of the original complete message. The oral message is fused with various semiotic systems and thus activates the visual and auditive sensitivity of the spectator. In writing, the utterance is detached from other sense-making systems which are separated from one another, since the spectator's attention is now caught mainly monosensorially (the eye) and in one direction (from left to right). In addition, the written code is valued differently from the oral code in our culture. The anthropology of writing has shown the extent to which power is based on writing, and the amount of power the written word possesses. In fact, when a written discourse is processed, it fascinates readers. This also goes for readers of subtitling, even if they understand the original language behind the subtitles.

In processing subtitles, the spectator is caught by the various spontaneous meanings involved in visual, aural and paralinguistic signs. He becomes himself an enunciating subject of the utterance, thus adding his interpretations to those of the actors and the translator. He reads and interprets a text which itself is a double interpretation, from oral to written and from one language to another.

Seeing, hearing and reading are three different skills and their social and symbolic values are also different. If we 'interpret' a speech or 'translate' a text, what do we do with subtitling? Is subtitling 'translation' merely because the end product is a written 'text', even though it deals both with a transcript and with the audible dialogue which the translator also interprets, and which the spectator can hear even if he does not understand it?

Norms

The difference between oral and written codes is not clearcut but forms a continuum. We have, for example, literary written discourse, educated written discourse, written discourse imitating the oral, cultivated oral discourse, and spontaneous oral discourse; the last of these has its own registers, such as ordinary, familiar and vulgar, which are in fact not easily defined. The stress on oral or written discourse varies also in literary texts (dialogue, interior monologue, sociolect markers). The two codes are integrated in different ways in different literary genres and also vary from epoch to epoch, according to the status of written and spoken language during a given period and the prevailing stylistic norms.

This has a bearing on the relationship between subtitling and literary translation. What is said on the screen (the dialogue) has its origin in a written scenario. However, this does not mean that the actors merely recite the scenario. They also add to the written lines their own interpretation and their presence on the scene. Naturally they are guided by the director, but even he cannot control, for example, the actors' voice quality. Consequently, we have spoken about oral discourse in a communication situation which is partly limited by the script writer and the writer. This is in contrast with the procedure employed by an author of fiction in which the output can be developed and polished endlessly and the message be delivered by a single person, the author.

The translator is thus not in the same position as the author; the relationship between oral and written discourse is not the same in these cases, nor are the norms. An author elaborates a written code and rhetorical conventions, in order to perpetuate, modify and/or go beyond them. The reception of his work and the underlying expectations are purely literary. A subtitler does not have the same rights. He must render in writing what has been formulated orally, but at the same time respect both technical exigencies and a certain sanctity attached to written discourse in our culture. While one of the writer's tasks might be said to be to transgress certain taboos (thematic, stylistic or discoursal), the translator must respect (1) norms of good usage (avoiding elements considered extremely vulgar or offensive if they appear in written discourse), (2) readability (textual coherence being dependent on phenomena such as word order, repetition, a certain amount of redundancy, discourse markers and pragmatic connectors that are very frequent in oral discourse (e.g.in French 'bon', 'ben', 'alors', 'à propos', 'tu sais'). This is one of the reasons why strong sociolinguistic variation or particular linguistic features typically characterizing the protagonists are often neutralized, making them unrecognisable and unmarked.

At this point it is worth posing the question: what kinds of norms, if any, are followed in subtitling? It seems that broadcasting companies and film distributors give translators no explicit norms. On the other hand, it is apparent that some of the countries where subtitling is used (for instance Austria and Flemish-speaking Belgium) have adopted standardised linguistic norms which have in fact been defined elsewhere, for example in Germany and in the Netherlands. Does their relative linguistic insecurity contribute to their desire to stick more closely to certain traditions of written discourse? And how about the situation in countries like Sweden and Norway or in bilingual Finland? So far there have been no studies investigating possible similarities between the conventions of subtitling in Sweden and those of Swedish subtitling in Finland. Does the concept of bilingualism include other factors than those discussed here or do we simply have to look at these factors in a different way?

Having described the perspective from which I see subtitling, I wish once more to emphasise my conviction that it is useless to reflect on the process as a mere difference in lexical quantity (amount of words). Such a reductionist standpoint means ignoring the functional differences between oral and written discourse, between psycho-auditive, if not audiovisual, perception (comprehension-interpretation) and linear perception (comprehension-readability), and the culture-bound differences involved in both oral and written discourse.

An interesting analogy arises at this point between subtitling and simultaneous interpreting. In simultaneous interpreting, a discourse which is too colloquial, or which follows the conventions of written discourse too strictly, tends to be transformed into 'cultivated' oral discourse, that is, to be neutralized by either 'de-oralising' or 'oralising' the speech. As in subtitling, there is a tension between the codes, but interpreters have a certain margin within which they can operate, thus striking a balance between the heaviness of the formal, controlled discourse and the more or less normative expectations of the audience.

Training in audiovisual language transfer

Subtitling comprises:
- language conversion from longer units to shorter ones,
- transfer from spoken language to written text,
- transfer from one language to another, and
- interpretation of verbal speech combined with numerous other cultural and socio-symbolic signs or with other types of semiotic systems.

Subtitling is, however, only one of many new types of multilingual mediation in the audiovisual media. So we are facing an educational challenge. Most studies dealing with interlinguistic aspects of audiovisual communication have come to fairly negative conclusions. As has been stressed several times in this article, it is easy to enumerate omissions, condensations, résumé translations, etc. This is a one-dimensional approach which reinforces the illusion that visual communication is unproblematic and that iconic and aural means most readily overcome semiotic and cultural barriers.

In the discussion, the importance and nature of multilingual audiovisual communication is too often underestimated. It is considered either as one aspect of literary translation (or similar to it) or as a technical problem, more or less irrelevant to training courses.

I believe that a degree course in language transfer within the media needs to be developed. Such courses have been organised in Finland, Denmark (Copenhagen), France (Lille, Strasbourg), Wales (Lampeter), and Ireland (Dublin). These courses have usually focused on a single method (subtitling or dubbing). But the need for collaboration - between schools of translation studies and departments of mass communication, and journalism studies, between professional translators and television, between translators and script writers or producers, between translators, interpreters and representatives of the film industry and of TV companies (decision-makers, importers), between translators of dominant languages and translators of minor or minority languages - still needs to be discussed. And what can we expect from computers and machine translation? Do they or will they have any implications for self-learning?

In Turku (Finland), our university training programme in television subtitling is offered in cooperation with the national TV broadcasting company. It is based on the use of a floppy disk and a software called 'scantitling'. With such a tool, it is relatively easy to generate the timing of insertion and removal of the subtitles, the duration of the two-line texts on the screen (exposure time) and the display and format of the subtitles (font type and size, box-framing of the lines, position on the screen, sentence division and/or any combination of sentences). The intensive course (14 hours, with 12 students) includes exercises in transcription, practice in condensation, elaboration of subtitles on a diskette with and without pictures, and a comparison between the student's product and the actual TV output. Among problems still to be solved, are the need for 'progression' in learning in order to avoid repetitive work, the types of film and programme to work with, the criteria of assessment in order to improve critical knowledge and quality, and the possibilities of learning in small groups.

In conclusion, I want to stress three main characteristics of subtitling and two potential lines of research:

1) As with other forms of translation, the subtitler has to choose certain strategies so that the message conveyed fulfils certain social, moral, didactic, aesthetic and linguistic functions, which go beyond the subtitler himself acting as an individual.

2) Subtitling is permanently and simultaneously constrained by two factors: first by the demands of coherence (to make comprehensible a content which is intertwined with the visual side), and, secondly, by the need to appeal to and captivate the spectator's senses, that is the ability to hear and to read and to stimulate the spectator's interest.

3) Subtitles are constantly juxtaposed with the original - the oral discourse. This is rare with other forms of translation, except for interpreting and bilingual publication. This co-presence of two codes and two languages will hopefully make us

more tolerant towards multilingualism, if not multiculturalism.

4) Technological developments mean not only satellites, cables, high definition TV, etc. but also digital pictures, virtual imaging, overcoming the differences between reality and reflection, resemblance and questioning the concept of probability. What will be the function of language in these contexts?

5) Language acquisition through viewing subtitled foreign programmes and films has not yet been closely studied. In a multilingual Europe in search of an identity, it might be worth looking at the media as a stimulating way of learning not only the languages but also the cultures of our neighbours.

Vor Frue Kirke, domkirken i Haderslev

Vallø Slot

TOOLS

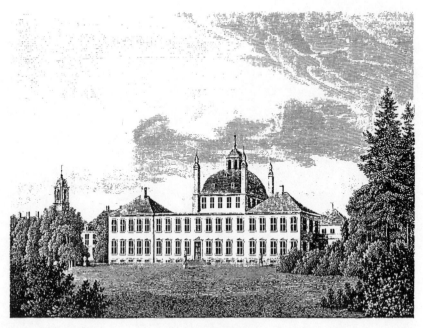

SOESTDIJK

TEACHING LINGUISTS TRANSLATION

M.K.C. Uwajeh, University of Benin, Nigeria

Rationale

Translation studies, although somewhat recent in linguistics, are actually recognised as part of linguistic inquiry by many linguists. Since Eugene Nida's pioneering study in the 1940s, linguists have increasingly appreciated the importance of translation as a fitting subject for linguistics. Works by other linguists, such as Catford (1965), Mounin (1976), Kittredge (1983), Kittredge and Grishman ((eds) 1986), etc., amply attest to the ever-increasing interest of linguists in the nature of translation. Nowadays, translation is generally recognised as an important part of Applied Linguistics - whether this is interpreted restrictively as "the application of linguistics to the domain of language teaching only/essentially" (Corder 1973: Preface), or defined broadly to subsume "the application of linguistics to any domain whatsoever of human endeavour where it is applicable." (Perren and Trim 1971)

All the same there remains in certain academic circles, especially among translation experts themselves, a persistent mistrust of the relevance of linguistics to translation theory and practice. The general thrust of the underlying argument - as deducible from, for example, Le Feal (1992:23: 26) or Lederer (1992: 29) - goes more or less like this: linguistics can be used in translation, but its role there is quite limited because translation, by its nature, goes well beyond Saussure's *langue* or 'language as such' (which is understood to be the one and only preoccupation of linguistics) and also deals with the particularities of Saussure's *parole* or 'language use' (which some linguists erroneously believe lies outside the subject matter of modern linguistics). By and large, however, non-linguists have increasingly appreciated the contribution of linguistics to translation theory and practice since the Second World War. It takes the linguist's grammar, for instance, to demonstrate the limitations of machine translation - discussed in Coughlin (1988) - and the linguist's grammar is surely needed to develop those 'super-intelligent' language using machines of the post-1990 era, the fifth-generation computers discussed in Doi et al. (1987).

If the importance of linguistics for translation is obvious nowadays to linguists and non-linguists alike, it is generally not appreciated by linguists that linguistics itself could benefit immensely from the findings of translatology. Many linguists would in fact not hesitate to assert that expertise in translation is not essential to the practice of their science; yet, since in his characterisation of language (the central preoccupation of modern linguistics) the linguist now and then has to deal with the structural features of foreign languages, he must know how to translate *properly* in order for his grammatical pronouncements to be valid. Therefore, the rationale for a translation course designed specifically for linguists is that ideally linguists should also be trained translators.

Contents of the course

I propose that a translation course for linguists should include all aspects of translation - its definition, history, application(s), etc. - and that, in particular, its central structure should be based on the tenets of 'Uwajeh's Four-Level Model of Translation' (1992).

The notion of 'level' in my model needs clarification, since it is crucial to understanding its tenets, and differs radically from that associated with, for example, Catford's (1965) classical model of translation. The fundamental problem of translation theory being that of *equivalence*, a 'level of translation' in my model constitutes a particular degree of 'finesse' within an ascending order of target language equivalents for specific source language texts, so that the first and 'lowest' translation level presents the crudest, while the fourth and 'highest' translation level conveys the finest possible rendition. The 'level of translation' in my model is similar to Catford's (1965: 24-26) classical model 'rank of translation' (and *not* to his own 'level of translation'). The *four* levels of translation in my model (instead of the traditionally recognised three ranks), are presented with their respective orthographic conventions, explained, and illustrated as follows:

'Lexical Translation' = Lex. Tr., refers to lexical item-by-lexical item translation: it aims at an approximate *conceptual equivalence* of the source language text, through the use of appropriate target language symbols (that is, form units).

'Literal Translation' = Lit. Tr. , refers to a rough-rendition translation: at this level, the overall *propositional equivalence* of the source language text, as suggested by the conceptual units of the corresponding lexical-level translation, is now conveyed with some judicious concatenation of the target language symbols.

'Free Translation' = Fr. Tr., is a smooth-flowing translation: at this level both the semantic and symbolic aspects of the chosen target language seek the *thematic equivalence* of the source language text.

'Figurative Translation' = Fig. Tr., where applicable, and if feasible, refers to a special-effects translation: here, the translator makes every effort to choose that target language text which, over and above expressing directly the information conveyed with the source language text, also captures the *contextual equivalence* of the source language text by manifesting as far as posssible the peculiar, culture-specific and contextual factors which are only communicated indirectly.

It is necessary to expatiate on the above presentation: the first and 'lowest' (lexical) level of translation is 'crudest' in the sense that it is farthest removed from an acceptable target language-specific rendition of the source language communication (and therefore closest to source language-specific texture features), while the fourth and 'highest' level of translation, the figurative one, is 'finest' in the sense that it constitutes the closest target language-specific textual rendition feasible (and therefore also farthest removed from source language-specific structural particularities). It follows from the above not only that 'equivalence' does *not* refer to exactly the same notion at the different translation levels (that is, each level deals with a *different* type of intrinsic equivalence) but also that the different equivalences characteristic of the different levels of translation collectively make an ascending order of refinement in target language equivalents for the given source language texts - ranging, then, from the lowest equivalence at the first, lexical, level, to the highest equivalence at the fourth, figurative, level of translation.

Furthermore, the four levels of translation are abstractions from the repertoire of the translator's linguistic judgements. It should be noted that all four levels are *not* needed for every translation exercise, but depend on the text and the goal of the translation. In some cases the fourth level may thus be inapplicable and therefore unnecessary; the first and second levels, or the second and third, may sometimes be so similar to one another that it is unreasonable to differentiate between them in a given context; and, occasionally, just one level may suffice for the translator's implicit or explicit objective(s). However, it is obvious from the nature and function of each of the levels that these clarifications do not detract from the theoretical and practical validity of each of the translation levels' separate identity.

Below are three sample presentations, together with appropriate conventions of orthography stipulated for the different levels, for three different sentence examples of English, Igbo, and Nigerian Pidgin English respectively - with French as the target language for the English sentence example and English for the Igbo and Nigerian Pidgin sentence examples.

EXAMPLE 1
>   *It's raining cats and dogs*
> Lex. Tr.:   Il-est   pleut-ant chat-s et chiens.
> Lit. Tr.:   Il est pleuvant des chats et des chiens.

Fr. Tr.: Il pleut des chats et des chiens.
Fig. Tr.: Il pleut à verse.
EXAMPLE 2
    Àwo àsé íbewe "wókòm".
Lex. Tr.: Frogs are-tell peers-they "wokom".
Lit. Tr.: Frogs are telling their peers "wokom".
Fr. Tr.: Frogs mock their peers for saying "wokom".
Fig. Tr.: The pot is calling the kettle black.
EXAMPLE 3
    Trouble dey sleep, nyanga go wake am.
Lex. Tr.: Trouble is sleep, pride go wake him.
Lit. Tr.: Trouble is sleeping, pride goes to wake him.
Fr. Tr.: Trouble is asleep, but pride would wake him.
Fig. Tr.: Let sleeping dogs lie.

Of the four levels of my model, the first two - those of lexical and literal translations - are of special interest to linguists taking a course in translation, since these levels are source language-oriented, in the sense that they emphasise source language text structural peculiarities. As such, these are the levels whereby the linguist draws attention to source language grammatical peculiarities by means of the target language. Correspondingly, the third and fourth levels of the model - those of free and figurative translations - are target language-oriented in the sense that they emphasise target language-specific features. These higher levels of translation are obviously complementary for a linguist communicating source language grammar: they help a target language user compare and contrast the source language with his target language by making reasonable sense of what the source language community members are expressing directly and/or indirectly with their different textual structures. This is done by confronting him with a rendition using his own target language-specific particularities at the lexical and literal translation levels.

Method

From the above discussion, it is fairly evident that the objective of the course in translation for linguists which I envisage is to teach linguists to *translate* properly. In other words, the course has a practical bias. This does not mean, of course, that theory should be excised from the course - the central structure of its content, as outlined above in 'Contents of the course', is theory-laden - but that such theory should be geared towards the pragmatic function of making good translators of linguists. Theory is no doubt also indispensable in the following non-trivial respect: since translation theory is part of general linguistic theory, every linguist should be interested in whatever insights the nature of translation gives us about the nature of language, but that is *not* the concern of the present article.

Some other possible pedagogical issues of the course, besides the question of bias or focus, are those of *who* is to teach linguists translation, and *when* this should be done. It is here recommended that, as far as possible, teachers of translation to linguists should be translation experts who are professional translators themselves and have had sufficient training in linguistics to understand intimately the need of linguists for a practical translation course. The best period to teach linguists translation is, I think, in the early formative years - say, by the second semester of their first year or the first semester of their second year of undergraduate studies, before they have been initiated into deep grammatical analyses; in Nigeria, these students would be about twenty years of age. Professional linguists could get their dose of translation practice in specially designed crash-programme translation workshops or seminars.

In teaching linguists translation, special attention should be paid to pitfalls in translation which are (most) likely to invalidate the linguist's scientific results. There are several such (possible) pitfalls; but here I shall examine only two - one at the lexical level, and one at the literal level of translation.

At the lexical level of translation, a fairly common source of error for the unwary linguist is due to a target language/source langue 'categorial interference'. In these cases the linguist's translation reveals that he has ascribed to the source language a lexical category which it does not have in that context, but which the target language normally does have in free usage. This is illustrated in the following examples.

EXAMPLE 4
      Pòlínà èjí Njí.
Fr. Tr.:   Paulina is black.
EXAMPLE 5
      Ákpáná jò Njó.
Fr. Tr.:   Akpana is ugly.
EXAMPLE 6
      Óbyé-Nkwuzí lì úlá.
Fr. Tr.:   The teacher is asleep.
EXAMPLE 7
      Wà jì áká-ódo tigbú ónnyé-óshi.
Fr. Tr.:   They beat the thief to death with a pestle.
EXAMPLE 8
      Úkàdíke sì Kádùná jé Jòsì.
Fr. Tr.:   Ukadike went from Kaduna to Jos.

Although 'black' is the English Free Translation equivalent of the Igbo 'Njí' of sentence 4 above, for example, the English lexical item here is an adjective while the corresponding Igbo element is a noun. An inappropriate approach to translation leads to the grammatical mistake that 'Njí' is also an adjective merely because 'black', an adjective in English, can be translated freely. 'Njó' and 'úlá' (in 5 and 6), which can similarly be substituted with the English adjectives 'ugly' and 'asleep', respectively, in Free Translation, are both, again, nouns in Igbo. Also the Igbo elements 'Jì' and 'sì' (in 7 and 8), which appear to be freely translatable with the English 'with' and 'from' respectively are not prepositions in Igbo but verbs. Appropriate lexical-level translations avoid possible grammatical blunders by underscoring any source language/target language categorial differences in these examples:

EXAMPLE 4

> *Pòlínà èjí Njí.*

Lex. Tr.: Paulina is-'black' blackness.
Lit. Tr.:   Paulina 'is blacking' blackness.
Fr. Tr.:   Paulina is black.

EXAMPLE 5

> *Ákpáná jò Njó.*

Lex. Tr.: Akpana 'ugly' ugliness.
Lit. Tr.:   Akpana 'uglies' ugliness.
Lit. Tr.:   Akpana is ugly.

EXAMPLE 6

> *Óbyé-Nkwuzí lì úlá.*

Lex. Tr.: One-teaching is sleep.
Lit. Tr.:   Teaching-person is sleep.
Fr. Tr.:   The teacher is asleep.

EXAMPLE 7

> *Wà jì áká-ódo tigbú ónnyé-óshi.*

Lex. Tr.: They held hand-mortar beat-kill one-theft.
Lit. Tr.:   They used hand-mortar to beat-kill theft person.
Fr. Tr.:   They beat the thief to death with a pestle.

EXAMPLE 8

> *Úkàdíke sì Kádùná jé Jòsì.*

Lex. Tr.: Ukadike went-from Kaduna go Jos.
Lit. Tr.:   Ukadike went from Kaduna go to Jos.
Fr. Tr.:   Ukadine went from Kaduna to Jos.

For its part a good literal translation draws attention to certain facts and mysteries about a source language which would otherwise elude the linguist in a careless translation. In the constructions which follow below, the relationship between the verb and indirect object may be quite unclear in Igbo (of the Onicha-Ugbo dialect). It is not clear, indeed it is a mystery, what exactly the Igbos in question are reporting with the verb-indirect object construct in the sentences.

EXAMPLE 9

> *ícho mádù ókwú*

Lit. Tr.   to seek a person word
Fr. Tr.   to seek a confrontation with someone,

Here the question is: is one seeking the 'word' *off* someone or *of* him?

EXAMPLE 10

> *ijì mádù úgwo*

Lit. Tr.   to hold a person debt.

Fr. Tr.   to be indebted to someone.

It is not clear as to whether one is 'holding the debt' *from* someone or *to* him? And in EXAMPLE 11,

> *ísó mádù ámú*

Lit. Tr.   to 'sweet' a person laughter

Fr. Tr.   to amuse someone,

it is not obvious whether the thing is 'sweeting' someone *with* or *by* laughter, or is the thing 'sweeting' laughter *to* someone.

It could well be that the questions I have asked in the above paragraph are the *wrong* (kinds of) questions for the Igbo source language - a reflection of present ignorance of the facts involved, and only the result of feeble attempts to capture the subtlety of the Igbo world picture through a radically different mode of apprehension peculiar to the English language community. One cannot be sure what is what until linguists have conducted the necessary semantic investigations satisfactorily. One thing that linguists should certainly not do - as I have seen done too often in modern linguistics - is to pretend that no mysteries really exist in the examples of my illustration above and innumerable other similar ones, by simply imposing target language semantic structures on the source language with bad literal translations, and thereby wiping out summarily any source language/target language inherent differences.

Conclusion

I have examined the modalities for teaching translation to language scientists in linguistics like myself, who need help from translatologists. I have tried to explain the rationale for such a course of study, to determine what its content should be, and how it could be conducted so as to be effective.

The proposals made in this study are meant to be tentative in the short term, but in the long run they should provoke reactions which will lead to the establishment of a comprehensive programme for the novel field of translation pedagogy with which I am concerned in this article.

Engelsholm

TECHNICAL TRANSLATION:
PUTTING THE RIGHT TERMS IN THE RIGHT CONTEXT

Peter Baumgartner, Flensburg Polytechnic, Germany

In its translation studies program, the Flensburg Polytechnic specializes in the training of technical translators, therefore the strategies and insights discussed in this article refer exclusively to such training.

Teaching components in the technical translation program

At the Flensburg Polytechnic the teaching of translation centers on English and German. It takes place in three units. The first unit - teaching of the subject matter - in the case of Flensburg mechanical engineering, electrical engineering and computer science - lays the foundation and provides the knowledge base for the other two units, which are translation classes. Unit two covers the translation classes conducted by engineers and/or natural scientists, and focuses on why an engineer or scientist would express the technical facts contained in a source text in only one specific way and no other way in the target language. Unit three covers translation classes which investigate and concentrate on the language used to express these technical facts. The first two units deal mainly with the "what" and "why" and are technical and subject-oriented, whereas the third unit is predominantly concerned with the "how" and is language-oriented.

Typical difficulties encountered in technical translation

This article concentrates on the third unit. My former experience in translation services in industrial companies and my present experience at the polytechnic show that the major problems technical translators have to grapple with lie in the following areas: (a) translators may have difficulty in understanding the technical information in the source text, and (b) they may have difficulty in formulating the technical facts in the target language by appropriate linguistic means so that specialist readers will not realize that they are reading a translated text. In extreme cases the translators understand the technical information in the source text perfectly and even know the proper technical terms in the target language, but still cannot render this information in the target language, simply because they do not know "how to say things" in a certain field of knowledge, no matter whether the language involved is the mother tongue or a foreign language.

Stages in the technical translation process

Technical translators have to understand the technical information as far as possible, extract this information from the text and dress it in the appropriate words of the target language. On the language side, this means that they have to know and master not only the special terms forming a network throughout the texts dealing with the subject area in question, but also the typical contexts in which these terms occur. That is, the technical translator must convert the source text into abstract knowledge and subsequently this abstract knowledge must be materialized again by converting it into a text in the target language. In order to be able to do this the translator must understand the text and at the same time must have at his or her fingertips the linguistic means required for text building in the target language. When building the new text, he or she first needs the terms representing the technical concepts. This one may regard as the more technical knowledge-oriented aspect, because in order to decide which term represents which concept, the translator must draw on his or her technical knowledge base. Once the correct term has been found, it must be incorporated in a syntagma of some sort. Finally, the syntagmas have to be incorporated into larger units to constitute a text (Baumgartner 1990: 7). Finding the appropriate syntagmas, that is packaging the terms properly, is one major problem area of our students. This problem exists irrespective of whether they translate into their mother tongue or into a foreign language, in the case of our polytechnic, exclusively English.

Translation students vs. engineering students

In this light, it is interesting to compare our translation students with the engineering students. In principle, the engineering students have the same problem. They, too, have to learn a new language, namely a sub-language of their mother tongue. The difference between the translation students and the engineering students, however, is that the latter acquire the means for depicting technical subject matter in language (in their mother tongue) while dealing with the subject matter proper. This is both to their advantage and disadvantage. It is to their advantage that on the one hand they use the language tool to acquire knowledge of the subject matter and in so doing they unconsciously learn the sub-language of their field. They pick up the subject matter and in the process the language. It is to their disadvantage, however, that this process takes place unconsciously, instinctively and automatically and, therefore, to a certain degree, arbitrarily and in an uncontrolled way, which means that to a large extent the level of competency in their technical sub-languages is left to chance. Using it merely as a tool, most of them are not aware of the language they use and see no need to reflect on it. Whereas the engineering students learn the typical technical terms and syntagmas of the sub-languages of their mother tongue while learning the technical subject, the students in the technical translation program have to learn the terms and their usage in syntagmas consciously and by a separate and systematic effort.

Theoretical assumptions for teaching work in the third unit

Work in the third unit is based on the assumption that a translator working in a particular field has to deal with a finite number of technical facts which come up again and again and which are translated into language in a finite number of ways and thus constitute a major part of the source texts encountered in actual practice (Baumgartner and Kraus 1992: 57). In translation the standard technical facts expressed in the source text can be translated into the target language again only in a finite number of ways. Therefore, one could consider them as the static portion of technical texts. The dynamic portion of the texts would be determined by the text category, the purpose of the writer, etc. The standard facts representing the static portion of technical texts are, so to speak, fixed modules of thought which can be transformed into a limited number of modules of language both in the source and the target language. These modules are integrated into larger units so as to form a text. This means that students have to learn the modules of thought and the various ways of converting them into the sub-language of the subject areas of specialization. It also means that when our students graduate as technical translators from the polytechnic they must master a certain number of these modules of thought and language which will serve as a basis for their future translation work.

Ideally, translators must master the technical subject matter of the field in which they do translation work, but on the other hand they must also master the linguistic means used to describe these facts.

Some approaches tested in the teaching of technical translation

As mentioned before, it is a common experience in our translation classes that students have problems in doing technical translations not only in their foreign language but also in their mother tongue due to a lack of familiarity with the technical texts of a special field. Very often they are insecure, for example, about what verbs, adjectives and prepositions can be used as partners of a given term (Arntz and Picht 1991: 34) and do not know the building blocks required for the construction of the strictly technical parts of their texts.

To remedy these deficiencies, I have been and still am looking for ways which help overcome these difficulties. One approach has been to start translation exercises in a particular technical field by analyzing technical texts within the same field in the target language before actually starting any translation work. Hohnhold (1990: 24) calls these texts 'Gegentexte' (similar texts in the target language). Ideal for this purpose are texts in which the typical technical facts of the area in question are linguistically described. In the process of such an analysis, the terms representing typical concepts are isolated and their textual environment is investigated, that is, a closer look is taken at the collocational partners of the terms. Not only the terms, but also the larger modules in which the terms occur must be studied (Warner 1966: 9). In this phase, I also use 'cloze' texts in the target language to demonstrate to students that knowing the partners of the terms is not a matter of course and cannot be left to the creative imagination of the translator. It also makes them aware of the special difficulties in finding the valid word combinations in a particular field and that only a limited number of them is available.

In another step, I use overheads on which the texts to be translated are reduced to sets of terms and text fragments, each set representing one item of information. From these sets of terms and text fragments in the source language, the students have to build a text in the target language. In this way they no longer have syntactic patterns in the source text which may serve as a crutch and are often misleading. They have to identify the concepts behind the terms, think of possible relationships between these concepts and find ways of representing this information linguistically. In order to be able to do this they have to resort to their technical knowledge base which means that their translation approach is no longer language-, but subject-oriented. In a first run, for example, we move from term to term, and the students have to be able to make minimal true statements using these terms. To facilitate the task I usually give directions of some sort. I may, for instance, ask them to use the broader or narrower generic term in a statement, cite special qualities of a technical object, describe typical movements, functions and so on. Technical texts are, among other things, characterized by the fact that special typical relationships exist between the terms occurring in the texts (Sager 1990: 29-37). Therefore, when we start relating the terms and text fragments to one another to arrive at more complex statements, I may ask my students to establish a generic, partitive or causative, etc. relationship between two terms, to express certain facts nominally or verbally, etc. Thus we move from one set of information to the next, each set being linguistically depicted by one or more sentences. In this way we obtain a number of true statements about all kinds of technical facts within a given field of knowledge. In itself, this accumulation of sentences, however, does not constitute a text. While in the first run we look at the terms and text fragments and find out what their relationships are, in a second run, we look at the statements produced and look for possibilities of whether or how they can be related to each other. In order to obtain coherence and cohesion, we may have to switch sentences around, split single sentences up into two or more, combine simple sentences into more complex ones, supplement with logical connectors to make things clearer, or even add new sentences. These are the finishing touches applied in the second run, resulting, hopefully, in a text in the target language which is a true picture of the source text.

One might argue that exercises of the type described above apply more to the domain of technical writing. But then it could also be said that good technical translation is nothing but "technical rewriting" of the source text in the target language.

Viborg Domkirke

Bregentved Slot

COMPUTER-ASSISTED TRANSLATION:
THE STATE OF THE ART

Robert Clark, Praetorius Limited, United Kingdom

I am not an information scientist, not a computational linguist, and I am definitely not a salesman. I am not writing this to sell anything to anybody, but as Software Editor of *Language International* I am constantly reviewing and evaluating translation-related software products as they appear on the market. As a result, I am in a position to recognise the crucial role that technology plays in the translation process.

On this background, I shall:
- give you a brief overview of the state of the art of commercially available Machine Translation systems and computer-based translation tools. I stress the term *commercially available*, because people can claim what they like when systems are still at the developmental stage, but it does not mean much to us until we can actually go out and purchase them.
- discuss prevailing attitudes of translators to computer-based translation, especially Machine Translation.
- and, finally, discuss the impact that language technology is having on the translation industry as a whole and the implications this *should* have on translator training.

The career of a new translator entering a university today will take place mainly in the 21st century. We have to concern ourselves with what sort of knowledge this translator needs to meet the challenges and survive the competition of that century. Advances in language technology are already starting to produce changes in translation practice, but the major impact is yet to come. The importance of language engineering is illustrated by the fact that the European Commission is planning a 667-million ECU programme to promote language technology in the period 1994-98. This programme signals the shift away from a situation where a handful of isolated developers was working producing systems. It is hoped that this initiative, and others like it, will result in greater development cooperation and the sharing of information on natural language processing research.

In this discussion we must take into account the fact that translators often have their reservations about using computers in the translation process and are less than totally accepting of the idea of computer-based translation.

The reservations volunteered from an informal survey produced the following list:

1. We might be out of a job.
2. Computers do not have enough knowledge to produce good translation.
3. We are put off by extravagant claims.
4. Machine Translation has no soul.
5. A computer has no idea of sense/meaning.
6. A computer cannot produce nuances of meaning.
7. Computers are difficult to master.

The list can serve as a point of departure for discussion.

In his *Introduction to Machine Translation*, John Hutchins defines it as "a computerised system which produces translations from one natural language to another, with or without human assistance" (Hutchins and Somers 1992:3). By qualifying his definition with "human assistance" he is implying that fully automatic, high quality translation actually exists. That was certainly the dream over forty-five years ago, but even today the output of the best systems is still unpolished. As early as 1951 Yehoshua Bar-Hillel insisted that translation of a standard comparable to that produced by human translators was not only an unrealistic aim for research but also impossible in principle. He was not implying that Machine Translation should be scrapped, but that efforts should be redirected to more realistic aims. In his opinion, translation involved certain human abilities, such as real-world knowledge, which no computer could ever assimilate. Recent advances in Artificial Intelligence indicate that real-world knowledge can, in fact, be incorporated into Machine Translation systems. But it has not happened yet. So the best we can expect is human assisted machine translation (= HAMT). In other words, currently, no fully automatic systems can translate to the same high standard one would expect from a human translator. There must be human assistance at some stage or some kind of restriction on the source text, so the human translator is still very much in the frame. Although Machine Translation is less than perfect, it is here to stay. Given these premises, we can freely discuss its role in the translation industry.

Machine translation is discussed in-depth at many conferences. At a conference of the American Translators Association in November 1992, L. Chris Miller presented the results of a survey that she had done of commercially available Machine Translation systems in North America and Europe, but, unfortunately, not in Japan and the rest of the world.

The mainframe/workstation systems were, for instance, SYSTRAN, LOGOS, METAL and TOVNA. The personal computer translation systems were PC TRANSLATOR and GLOBALINK. A few of these systems have been around for quite a while. Although they have not reached perfection, they have been

MT User Sample

USER	SYSTEM	DOC TYPE	STAFF	YEARLY OUTPUT
US Air Force	SYSTRAN	Scientific/ Technical Articles & Documents	13 Full-Time Post-Editors 1 Half-Time Post-Editor 2 Half-Time Terminologists	50,000 pp
XEROX Corporation	SYSTRAN, ALPS	Service & Customer Documentation	50 Full-Time Translators	36,000 pp
Pan American Health Organisation	SPANAM, ENGSPAN	Texts on Public Health, Agriculture, Management, etc	3 Full-Time Post-Editors, 23 Part-Time Post-Editors, 1 Contract Terminologist	10,000 pp
Siemens Stromberg-Carlson	METAL	In-House Technical Documentation	2 Full-Time Post-Editors, 1 Full-Time Terminologist	10,000 pp
Lexi-Tech	LOGOS	Technical Manuals	45 Post-Editors, 1 Terminologist	100,000 pp
Hartmann International	SYSTRAN	Technical Manuals	1 Full-Time Post Editor, 1 Full-Time Terminologist, 43 Part-Time Post-Editors	12,000 pp

steadily fine-tuned and more and more language pairs are being offered. Four of the mainframe systems are also available on desktop models. This 'down-sizing', to use the current jargon, is probably the most significant development in Machine Translation. Systran is now available on an IBM PS2 desktop computer using an AST 3270 emulation card. The PC system does exactly the same job as the mainframe - only quicker! SYSTRAN are currently porting their code to the C programming language which should allow the system to operate on an ordinary 486 PC. They also hope to offer a scaled-down version which would enter the marketplace at about the same price as Globalink GTS or PC Translator.

One can get an impression of annual translation volume that is machine processed from the sample shown on the opposite page. It lists a few major users of Machine Translation in the US and Canada, and it was compiled by Joann Ryan of the Systran Corporation.

It may be that the figures are not impressive in, say, a European context, but it allows for making a few general points.

Except from the SPANAM and ENGSPAN systems, all others employ the old 'workhorse' systems, SYSTRAN, LOGOS and METAL. It is also evident that technical documents with very limited domains are the type of text best suited for processing by Machine Translation. As mentioned, people are sceptical about Machine Translation because it has "no soul". But there is little "soul" in most technical translation work. To describe it as boring would be charitable. If a computer can eliminate that kind of drudgery, then roll-on Machine Translation! It will also be noted that there is a high number of post-editors. Post-editing is rapidly becoming a profession in its own right. In the US, SYSTRAN started to sell finished machine-processed translation directly to the consumer in 1990. In the first year of the experiment, they processed 7,000 pages. In 1992 they processed 17,000 pages. Their post-editing work is subcontracted to translation companies. So, machine translation, instead of depriving human translators of work, is creating new jobs.

To summarise, Machine Translation developers have not broken the linguistic equivalent of the sound barrier - Fully Automatic High Quality Translation. However, significant progress has been made. Development has reached a third generation of systems. The increase of performance coupled with the enormous decrease in the price of personal computers is putting Machine Translation within the reach of everyone.

Of course, the most important spin off from Machine Translation development is the ever-growing supply of tools that are being produced to assist the translation process. Not long ago you could count the number of translation tools commercially available on one hand. Today there are so many that it is becoming

a full-time job just to keep informed of what is being released. At present the list comprises:
Word Processors
Spell, Grammar & Style Checkers
Electronic Dictionaries
Terminological Databases
Text Retrieval Packages
Modems
BBS Services
Workbench-style Integrated Packages
Word processing packages have become very powerful. The new version of WordPerfect includes a spreadsheet feature and will soon incorporate a grammar and style checker. On-line electronic dictionaries are now commonplace and powerful terminological database programs such as MutliTerm and Termex are an essential part of a translator's reference material. Sophisticated searches of previously translated documents are now possible with text retrieval packages such as WordCruncher. Terminology exchange regularly takes place using modems with Compuserve or the worldwide dedicated translator bulletin board services that are being created. The most ambitious of these tools are the translation memory-based integrated packages. At *Language International* we have gained hands-on experience with three systems which have come on the market during the past year, namely:

- **IBM's Translation Manager/2**, which we reviewed when it was still being tested internally at IBM European Language Services, Birkerød, Denmark.
- **TRANSIT**, developed by STAR AG, a software company based in Stein am Rhein, Switzerland.
- **Translator's Workbench II**, developed by Trados, a Stuttgart-based company.

I shall not discuss the differences between these systems, such as language and file format support, hardware requirements, etc., but concentrate on what they have in common.

- **Terminology management**
The key to consistency of terminology use in any large-scale translation project is the ability to identify terms beforehand and ensure their consistent use by the translator. As projects become larger and deadlines become shorter, it is not unusual for more than one translator to work on the same project. Therefore, it is essential that a common terminology database is used for each project and maintained throughout the process.

- **Word processing**

An efficient, user-friendly word processor with powerful editing features is the core of any translation project.

- **Automatic dictionary look-up**

There is little point in going to the trouble of ensuring that terminology is agreed beforehand and stored in a database if translators choose not to look up the term. The choice is, therefore, taken out of their hands by having terms automatically checked against the database.

- **Tag protection**

It is time-consuming to reformat texts when formatting tags have been lost as a result of exporting and importing files. It is, therefore, vital that all formatting tags remain intact and are protected from accidental deletion during the translation process. This is done by the three systems.

- **Translation memory**

This is probably the most revolutionary feature of the programs we are discussing. A database stores previously translated material in such a way that each segment of source text is linked to a corresponding segment of target text, thereby producing a synchronised bilingual text file. Each segment is usually a sentence. During the translation process each segment of the source text is matched against the translation memory database. If a match is found, the previous translation is made available for use in the current translation. After each segment of the source text is translated, it, in turn, is stored on the database and becomes part of the translation memory.

- **Automatic translation**

During the analysis stage, that is when the source text is being processed and checked against the terminology database and the translation memory database, an option is available to have all exact matches against the translation memory automatically translated.

Until now, all translations had to go through the program in order to become part of the translation memory database, but IBM now supply an algorithm with their product that allows you to create a translation memory using source and target texts that have not been processed within Translation Manager/2. This implies that *any* previously translated text in electronic form is potentially translation memory material.

The other thing these products have in common is that they are not cheap. Prices range from three to five thousand dollars, so most of us would have to be convinced that, by purchasing one of these packages, our output and quality would improve. It is obvious that the translation-memory approach is best employed for medium to large-scale projects that involve a fair amount of repetition.

Under these circumstances, once the translator has become familiar with the new environment, our experience indicates that speed and consistency are definitely improved.

Impact on translation work

Translation buyers have always had to consider delivery time, cost and quality. They *always* want the translation yesterday. It seems that translation is always the last thing considered in the production of documentation. The salesman has promised the product on a certain date and that is when the product *will* be delivered. Quite often the translation is not even commissioned until the product is sold to the customer. Obviously, if two translation suppliers are competing for the same contract and one is equipped with tools that allow for faster production of the translation, the job will be awarded to that company, for, the translation buyer does not care about "soul"! Next in priority to delivery time is cost. Translation is *always* too expensive. Ideally, the translation buyer would like the translation to be free! Time is money, so it follows that if the translation supplier can produce a translation faster than the competition, there is a good chance that production is also cheaper. If the translation buyer requires quality in the traditional sense, the advantage of ensuring consistency of terminology is obviously attractive. If one of the ways that you plan to guarantee quick turnaround is to use a team on a translation project, the translation buyer is certainly going to like the idea of all translators using the same terminological database containing pre-agreed terminology. On the other end of scale there is translation for information purposes: The translation buyer does not always require a perfect translation. He might have a stack of documents that fill a room that would never get translated in the first place if traditional translation was the only option. Unfortunately, the translator is not only reluctant to produce a less than perfect translation, it would probably not be possible for him or her to do so. A human translator is either "off" or "on". This is where Machine Translation comes in. If a translation is only required for information purposes, it does not really matter how many howlers are produced.

Conclusion

I have discussed the impact that language technology is having on the translation industry out in the real world. The question is, how prepared is the average language graduate for survival in this real world? Dieter Wälterman's article on the programme for translation students at Carnegie Mellon discusses what is happening at one end of the scale (below, pp. 307-317). Many other institutions, the University of the Saar at Saarbrücken to name one, are offering advanced courses in language technology to their translation students. At the other end of the scale, there are people graduating from universities around the world, without ever having even touched a word processor. I am not saying that every language graduate should be able to leave university with enough knowledge to enable him or her to build their own translation system, but they should be acquainted with the basics. You may also feel that all this technology has no relevance to literary translation. If you can earn a living translating James Joyce, then maybe there is no problem. However, the bulk of commercial translation work is technical. It is the responsibility of educators to arm students with the skills that will be expected by potential employers.

It is not fair to send them out into the real world without these skills.

MACHINE TRANSLATION SYSTEMS
IN A TRANSLATION CURRICULUM

Dieter Wältermann, Carnegie Mellon University, USA

Background

The need and demands for translations have in recent years increased considerably, primarily due to an ever-growing internationalization and globalization of existing markets. This need and demand for translation has also outpaced the production capability of human translators. While it is true that more and more translators rely heavily on a wide variety of basic computational means to speed up their translation tasks in order to meet the increased demands for translation services, their computational means tend to be limited to basic word processing equipment, dictionary packages and, possibly, higher-end computer systems. But this use of more or less basic computational means must not be confused with machine translation (= MT) as it is used in the context of the following discussion.

The constantly growing demand for translations has also led to a tremendous increase in activities centering on various forms of machine translation systems. The European Union, with its nine working languages, is one of the major parties interested in expanding MT technology; others include the US government and major international companies, such as IBM and Siemens. Depending on the type of MT system, researchers differentiate between:

- Machine-Aided Human Translation (= MAHT),
- Human-Aided Machine Translation (= HAMT), and
- Fully Automatic Machine Translation (= FAMT).

In the past, accuracy of translations produced solely by MT systems has frequently proved to be a problem. Integrating human translators into the machine translation process has, therefore, been viewed by some as the necessary step to augment the existing chain in order to produce fast and accurate translations.

Today's FAMT systems are neither a suitable pedagogical environment nor suited for training new translation students. Yet, machine-aided human translation and human-aided machine translation (henceforth referred to as Machine-Aided Translation [= MAT]) can serve the purpose of educating students in the use of such systems as well as training the students in the fields of scientific-technical translations. However, the process of integrating human translators into the MT environment has not received the pedagogical attention it deserves.

Future translators must be brought up to a level of sophistication where they are routinely able to use state-of-the-art computational environments. Institutions training translators must, therefore, develop symbiotically the pool of highly trained human translators and the technological base for machine-aided translation. Today's state-of-the-art MT systems can be successfully deployed only if a human translator is present in the translation loop. This presence depends, in essence, on the different types of approaches to MT, the type of system in use, and the quality of the system. The human translator must, therefore, take on the role of a pre-editor, an interactive editor, or a post-editor. One reason why MT systems have not been accepted in actual translation environments is due to a severe shortage of formally trained specialists who can perform these tasks. This situation persists even though, from the purely economic standpoint, the use of MT already makes sense today, as evidenced by several commercially available MT systems, such as InterLingua, LOGOS, and Metal. However, training in the application and maintenance of such MT systems is still rudimentary. This situation can be remedied by training translation students in the fields applicable to MAT.

In 1992, the Department of Modern Languages at Carnegie Mellon University realized the shortcomings outlined above and initiated first steps to establish an innovative translation program by collaborating with the institution's Center for Machine Translation which has long been recognized as one of the leading MT research centers. The new program is technology-based and concentrates on teaching translation skills using MT tools. The unique aspect of the program is best witnessed in the fact that no other translation program in the United States is currently utilizing MT technology in its teachings leading to a degree or certificate in translation.

In addition to high levels of proficiency, the education of a modern-day translator must centrally involve a technological angle, including the knowledge of up-to-date computer-based word processing equipment, document processing, and desktop publishing software, among others. Specialized translators' work stations will enhance the productivity of any translator. Yet, it is essential to train translators in the use of such workstations from the very beginning.

This training must, however, do more than merely expose students to machine-based translation tools and present them with introductions to MT systems. In an attempt to classify the current needs of translators and to establish a comparative database, an extensive survey of translation degree and certificate programs available in the United States was conducted during the fall 1991 and spring 1992 semesters (Wältermann 1992b). Based on this survey, it was decided to provide technology training using a translation-based curriculum in the Department of

Modern Languages. This means that the students work with high-end UNIX-workstations to perform translation task - they are not merely being taught the use of computational facilities. Such a technology-oriented translation program is also extremely beneficial from a research and development perspective. The program integrates, and relies on, expertise of researchers at CMU's CMT and experienced translators in the Department of Modern Languages. It also integrates existing and future translation tool research and development projects in the curriculum.

Parallel investigations into the possible group of students interested in the translation courses revealed a variety of undergraduate and graduate students at CMU and the University of Pittsburgh: students who are double majors in a language and a scientific field (computer science, engineering, chemistry, physics, graphics design, and others), and language-proficient students who are enrolled in science courses. All students are computer-literate since they had to take required introductory computer workshop classes lasting several weeks during their first semester (if they had no computer skills), so that there is no need to allot any course time for teaching computer skills.

Students interact and react with available MAT systems. This interaction greatly benefits the students by giving them an opportunity to work in a state-of-the-art computational translation environment and by acquainting them with MT testing and evaluation procedures. Another benefit is the valuable feedback from the students to developers of MAT technology, which will guide improvements to the existing technology. The importance of this program is evident in the fact that it addresses the existing lag between technological advances and pedagogical environments with sound, high-quality computational translation teaching program-environments, and in the fact that it teaches actual translation skills in a classroom setting using an MAT system, the Translator's WorkStation (= TWS).[1]

The TWS consists of a number of application modules integrated through the central user interface. Each application uses the facilities of the user interface for display and input, each module uses a standard window to interact with the user, and each window has standard menus which allow the user to invoke any other module. Each module also has special menus. Text editing can take place in any window, and text may be moved between windows with the help of the global kill-ring facility (for a detailed view, see Cohen et al. 1993; and Wältermann 1992a).

The TWS in the translation curriculum

The translation program survey identified several gaps in existing translation curricula (see also Benton 1989; Vasconcellos 1990), uncovering the following needs:

- post-editing machine output,
- training, coordinating, and supervising teams of translators using MT systems, and
- learning the skills to augment the lexicons and other rule bases of MT systems.

Training students in these translation-related skills plays a central role in our translation courses. Besides giving the students the linguistic and cultural skills required of translators, they are being trained in maintaining and updating MT systems. This skill will be increasingly in demand as an ever-growing number of MT systems is deployed. The development of a curriculum to train such specialists is predicated on the use of advanced computerized translator's tools. A curriculum concerned with these issues must rest on a firm technological structure. Technology will not only allow the students in such a program to reach new skill levels. It will also lead to an intensification of the basic translation curriculum itself. As the first step, we established a two-course sequence at the undergraduate level teaching scientific and technical translation skills (fourth and fifth-year studies).

The first course serves as an introduction to scientific and technical translations and to the MT system with which the students will be working throughout the first and second course. The second course presents students with an actual translation project to be performed using MAT tools. Both courses are served by the technology available at CMU. Existing networking capabilities allow instructor and students alike to share their translations for immediate comparison and editing. TWS allows students to see their own translations next to the translation of one (or more) of their peers or the instructor. Students are encouraged to act as peer editors which will help them learn to improve their writing and translating abilities. The first course provided not only a testing ground for the new curriculum, but also for the technological structure. Recommendations and improvements resulting from the classroom evaluation of TWS were then applied in further developing the system for use in the second course.

Since TWS supports multiple editing windows, students may view and edit several translations simultaneously. In order for students to translate using the TWS as well as to perform editing and consolidating tasks, it will be necessary to incorporate appropriate scientific and technical texts and to prepare this material for translation purposes, in addition to augmenting dictionaries and termbanks to accommodate the new technology presented in the text materials. Part of this work is done by the translation students as outside assignments. The students generally work in small groups according to their background and their area of studies (major or minor) in order to take advantage of their terminology skills.

Contents of the courses
   The contents of the courses are as follows:

SCIENTIFIC-TECHNICAL TRANSLATIONS: COURSE 1

A. Historic and Linguistic Background to Technical and Machine Translation
a. Introduction to Scientific-Technical Translation and Machine Translation
*   History of (scientific and technical) translation; Survey of machine translation; Influence of linguistics and computer science on machine translation
b. Language Knowledge in Scientific-Technical and Machine Translation
*   Text types: analysis, role of pre-editing and post-editing; Characteristics and limitations of scientific-technical texts; Linguistic analysis of scientific-technical texts (word, sentence, text level); Basic concepts and system characteristics of machine translation systems; Importance of terminology

B. Introduction to the Translator's WorkStation
c. The Translator's WorkStation
*   Underlying rationale (Machine-Aided Translation vs. Machine Translation); Basic functionalities and special features
d. TWS Practicum
*   Role of text features and variance; Role of linguistic aspects
e. Evaluation and Discussion of TWS: Language Coverage & Ergonomic Issues

SCIENTIFIC-TECHNICAL TRANSLATIONS: COURSE 2

A. Setting up the translation project
*   Previewing translation project: Introduction to translation management; Establishing terminology needs; Creating terminology and dictionary databases; Coordination and management of translator's tasks; Introduction to the Pedagogical TWS (= PTWS)
B. Performing the translation project: Pre-Translation Stage
*   Time management; Resource management; Task hierarchy management; Group assignments and group/task coordination; Training in the use of PTWS (continued); Preparation of project-wide terminology bank
C. Document production: Translation Stage
*   Translation of document; Desktop Publishing skills applicable to translation task; On-going terminology and translation archive management using the PTWS
D. Post-Editing of Translation Document
*   Assessing editing needs; Coordination and management of post-editing tasks; Post-editing using PTWS of both human and machine output
E. Maintenance of MT Systems
*   Introduction to LAI; Updating English lexicons; Updating German lexicons
F. Discussion and Evaluation
*   Set-up stage, Pre-translation stage; Document production; Post-editing stage; Overall course and courseware

Development of the Pedagogical TWS (PTWS)

   The previous section identified three major areas in which translation instruction must be modernized. The current TWS supports most of the activities connected with these tasks. For instance, TWS is used to simulate post-editing by manually presenting the original in the left-hand-side window of the TWS editor and a translation (not necessarily generated by a computer) in the right-hand-side window. In order to implement TWS in the translation curriculum and to provide adequate technical support for teaching the above skills, the following three developments are presently underway to transform the TWS into the PTWS:

- a translation-by-example facility to help in teaching post-editing,
- a translation archive database to support the translation team management task, and
- a lexicon acquisition interface for training in maintaing and updating MT systems.

Figure 1: The different components of the
Pedagogical Translators Work-Station

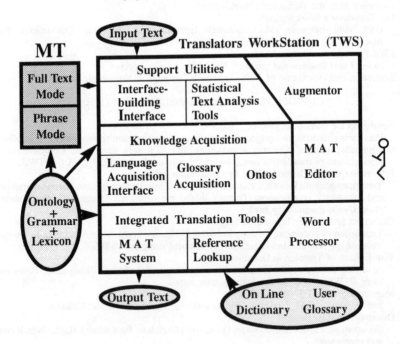

At present, most work related to system maintenance and MAT carried out by translation students centers on the following system components: statistical text analysis tools, augmentor, lexicon acquisition interface, glossary acquisition,

Ontos, and user glossaries. The system environments with which students perform most of the system-related work concentrate on the three developments outlined above.

The translation-by-example environment increases the efficiency of translators and translation editors by providing candidate translations based on identity or similarity of current text material to previously translated text material. This module also relies on the availability of a large multilingual corpus of texts in which passages in the source and target language are aligned. Such an environment is important because in many practical translation tasks, documents (e.g., manuals and handbooks) which have to be translated into a number of languages undergo regular changes such as revisions and updates.

The translation archive is but one instrument that is used both for Translation-By-Example (= TBE) and for instruction in translation management. This facility is constantly updated with new translations, a task which is carried out primarily by the translation students since their translation assignments are added to the translation archive. An alignment algorithm for translation passages in each text is currently under development at the Center to increase the efficiency of the TBE and the Translation Archive (= TA). The TWS interface is used in both instances, so that very little interface-related work is involved. To train translators in the maintenance and update of MT systems, it is necessary to teach them the skills needed for updating the static knowledge sources of an MT system - such as the system-oriented lexicon, grammars and (for knowledge-based machine translation) domain models. In the framework of the CMU program, researchers offer translation students training in lexicon building. The technological structure for this task is provided by the Lexicon Acquisition Interface (= LAI), consisting of a set of questionnaires organized in decision trees and presented to the user by means of TWS dialog boxes and an entry browser window. The questionnaires guide the user through the list of morphological, syntactic, semantic and other properties required for a particular lexicon entry format. The system records information entered by the user in a specified formalism and displays the appropriate lexicon entry in a browser window. Although a version of LAI exists in the current TWS, it supports the acquisition of lexicons only for English and is supposed to be used exclusively by expert computational lexicographers. CMT intends to develop a version devoted to German and a version of the interface intended for non-expert users. The statistical text analysis tools provide students with a concordance facility which can be used to look up the translation of any given expression while specifying the depth or narrowness of the context (up to 7 words before and after the term in question). The search results are displayed in a special window, and the students can view each occurrence found in the database in its full context in a separate window, thereby examining the different or identical translation decisions for any given word or multi-word expression.

Most text material used in both translation courses comes from state-of-the-art documentation in scientific and technical fields. Some of the texts may present material which is not only innovative but also challenging linguistically so that students may encounter new terms which are not yet present in the MT diction-aries and customized user glossaries, and which may not be found in any general dictionary or termbank. Whenever students encounter such terms or expressions during the translation task, they can be added to a user glossary by applying the menu option 'ADD-A-TERM'. The glossary acquisition tool invokes the appro-priate user glossary (e.g. engineering or electronics glossary) and automatically places the user at the correct point within the glossary for the term in question. Thus, students can build task-specific or domain-specific glossaries in consulta-tion with on-line reference materials, fellow students, and the instructor.

The Pedagogical Translator's WorkStation in the translation instruction curriculum

The PTWS provides the framework for the second course in the new translation program. This course centers on a real-life translation task which will be spon-sored by two translation agencies, one in Pittsburgh, Pennsylvania, and the other in Austin, Texas. By providing an interaction with an industrial partner students will become directly involved with the needs and difficulties provided by actual translation tasks. The translation survey showed that several of the major trans-lation programs offer translation projects in which students interact with an advi-sor, either a faculty member or a translator affiliated with the individual institution.

Our translation project differs from previous ones by allowing students to per-form actual translation work in collaboration with a translation agency and to use MAT tools throughout the translation and editing stages of the translation pro-cess. In addition, this project differs with respect to the overall translation task: instead of offering individual translation projects, the CMU course involves all students in all the various tasks associated with the production of a single large translation project, thereby giving all students a chance to learn firsthand about each stage of a real-life translation project. The students will not only benefit from translating a larger document, but also learn the various aspects involved in coordinating several translators working on a single project. During the whole project, the PTWS is the common denominator to all tasks and to all partici-pants.[2]

Notes

1. TWS is implemented on a UNIX-based workstation using the X-11 window system, the C-based X-11 toolkit called MOTIF (OSF/MOTIF 1991) and its CommonLisp interface called CLM (Babatz et al. 1991). MOTIF provides a high-level interface to X-11 by defining various types of widgets, e.g., windows, scroll bars, menus, and buttons, and it also allows multitasking. Finally, CLM uses a control-flow discipline known as callbacks which help to enforce good system modularity. Before deciding to use the above environment, other substrates had been taken into consideration, such as GARNET (Myers et al. 1990) and SERPENT (Bass et al. 1990).

2. I would like to acknowledge the help and support of my colleague, G. Richard Tucker, whose comments on earlier versions of this paper have been extremely valuable. I would also like to thank the participants of the *Second 'Language International' Conference* - their comments and suggestions in response to the presentation of a shorter version of this paper have been very helpful. Finally, I owe a great debt of gratitude to my friend, Esther Sydow, for her suggestions, her time and her endless patience.

Jens Bangs Stenhus i Ålborg

WORKS CITED

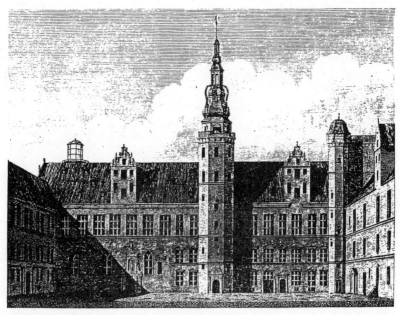

CRONBORG
Slotsgaard

WORKS CITED

Editors' notes

The present list is compiled from individual contributions to the volume. The 'Works Cited' largely follows the MLA style sheet. Italics are used for titles of journals, magazines and books. Authors are listed alphabetically by surnames. Collective books (e.g. *Proceedings*) are marked with 'In:' before the title and listed immediately after the article, if there is only one reference in the present book. In case there are references to two contributions or more, the collective book is listed alphabetically by its editor(s). 'ü', 'ä', 'ö' are listed as Danish 'y', 'æ' and 'ø' at the end of the alphabet.

AIIC. 1982. *Practical Guide for Professional Interpreters*. Geneva: Association Internationale des Interprètes de Conférence.

ALBERT, SÁNDOR. 1993. The traps of formal correspondence. *Perspectives: Studies in Translatology* 1, 11-21.

ALEXIEVA, BISTRA. 1985. Semantic Analysis of the Text in Simultaneous Interpreting. In: BÜHLER, HILDEGUND (ed). 1985. *Proceedings of the Xth World Congress of FIT*. Vienna: Braumüller. 195-198.

ALLIONI, SERGIO. 1989. Towards a Grammar of Consecutive Interpretation. In: *The Theoretical and Practical Aspects of Teaching Conference Interpretation*. Udine (Italy): Campanotto. 191-197.

ANDERSEN, ERIK SKØTT & CLAUS DETLEF & JENS RAAHAUGE. 1991. *Sæt ord på din verden*. Copenhagen: Dansklærerforeningen.

ANDERSON, R.B.W. 1976. Perspectives on the role of interpreter. In: BRISLIN, RICHARD W. (ed). 1976.

ARNTZ, REINER & HERIBERT PICHT. 1991. *Einführung in die Terminologie-arbeit*. Hildesheim & Zurich & New York: Georg Olms Verlag.

BABATZ, R. & A. BACKER & C. BEILKEU & T. BERLAGE & M. SPEN-KE. 1991. *CLM: A Language Binding for Common Lisp and OSF/Motif User Guide and Reference Manual Version 2.0*. Technical report. German National Research Center for Computer Science.

BAKER, R.G. & A. D. LAMBOURNE & G. ROWSTON. 1984. *Handbook for Television Subtitlers*. IBA/Oracle Ltd, Southampton University.

BARADUC, JEAN. 1972. La dénotation dans les annonces publicitaires. *Communications et langages* 14, 105-115.

BARTLETT, FREDERICK C. 1932. *Remembering. A Study in Experimental and Social Psychology*. Cambridge: Cambridge University Press.

BASS, L. & B. CLAPPER & E. HARDY & R. KAZMAN & R. SEACORD. 1990. Serpent: A User Interface Management System. *Proceedings of the Winter 1990 USENIX Conference*.

BASSNETT-McGUIRE, SUSAN. 1980. *Translation Studies*. London: Methuen.

322   *Teaching Translation and Interpreting 2*

BASSNETT-McGUIRE, SUSAN. 1988 & 1991. [Revised Edition]. *Translation Studies*. London & New York: Routledge.
BAUMGARTNER, PETER. 1990. Sprachmittel zum Ausdruck des Zwecks in der englischen Fachsprache der Elektrotechnik. In: REKTORAT der Fachhochschule Flensburg (eds). 1990. *Fachhochschule Flensburg - Forschung und Technologietransfer*. 7-16.
BAUMGARTNER, PETER & ROLAND KRAUS. 1992. Der Sachverhalt "Aufwand" und seine sprachliche Realisierung in deutschen und englischen technischen Fachtexten. *Lebende Sprachen* 38, # 2, 57-60.
BEAUGRANDE, ROBERT de. 1978. *Factors in a Theory of Poetic Translating*. Assen: Van Gorcam.
BEAUGRANDE, ROBERT de. 1980. *Text, Discourse and Process. Toward a Multidisciplinary Science of Texts*. Norwood, New Jersey: Ablex.
BEAUGRANDE, ROBERT de & WOLFGANG DRESSLER. 1981. *Introduction to Text Linguistics*. London: Longman.
BEAUGRANDE, ROBERT de. 1984. *Text Production. Toward a Science of Composition*. Norwood, New Jersey: Ablex.
BELL, ROGER T. 1991. *Translation and Translating. Theory and Practice*. London: Longman.
BENJAMIN, WALTER. 1977 [1968]. The Task of the Translator. In: ARENDT, HANNAH (ed). 1977. *Illuminations*. Translated by Harry Zon. New York: Schocken Books. 69-82.
BENTON, P. M. 1989. A practical test of machine assisted translation systems and agencies. In: HAMMOND, DEANNE L. (ed). 1989. 443-448.
BERGER, PETER L. & THOMAS LUCKMANN. 1989 [orig. 1967]. *The Social Construction of Reality. A Treatise in the Sociology of Knowledge*. Garden City: Doubleday.
BERNE, ERIC. 1964. *Games People Play*. New York: Ballantine Books.
BOHLEN, CHARLES E. 1973. *Witness to History 1929-1969*. New York: W.W. Norton.
BOWEN, DAVID AND MARGARETA. 1989. Aptitude for Interpreting. In: GRAN, LAURA & JOHN DODDS (eds). 1989. 109-125.
BOWEN, DAVID AND MARGARETA (eds). 1990. *Interpreting - Yesterday, Today and Tomorrow (= American Translators Association Series on Translation and Interpretation IV)*. Binghamton: State University of New York.
BOWEN, MARGARETA. 1989. Language Learning Before Translator/Interpreter Training. In: KRAWUTSCHKE, PETER W. (ed). 1989. 51-64.
BRISLIN, RICHARD W. (ed). 1976. *Translation: Applications and Research*. New York: Gardner Press.
BRITISH ASSOCIATION OF COMMUNITY INTERPRETERS. 1989. *Guide to Good Practice*. Cambridge.
BROWN G. & G. YULE 1983. *Discourse Analysis*. Cambridge: Cambridge University Press.
BRUNDAGE, D.H. & D. MACKERACHER. 1980. *Adult Learning Principles and Their Application to Programme Planning*. Ontario: Ontario Institute for

Studies in Education. 21-31.

BUTTERFIELD, HERBERT. 1955. *Man on his Past.* Cambridge: Cambridge University Press.

BÜHLER, HILDEGUND. 1986. Linguistic (semantic) and extra-linguistic (pragmatic) criteria for the evaluation of conference interpretation and interpreters. *Multilingua* 5, 231-235.

BÜHLER, HANNS HERMANN. 1987. Die Diktatur des Dolmetschers? Bemerkungen zu den "Grundregeln für das Dolmetschen". *Mitteilungsblatt des Österreichischen Übersetzer- und Dolmetscherverbandes 'Universitas'*, # 2, 15-18.

CAILLÉ, P.F. 1960. Cinéma et traduction. *Babel* 6, 103-109

CARR, EDWARD HALLET. 1962. *What is History?* New York: Alfred A. Knopf.

CARTELLIERI, CLAUS. 1983. The inescapable dilemma. Quality and/or quantity in interpreting. *Babel* 29, 209-213.

CARY, EDMOND. 1956. *La traduction dans le monde moderne.* Geneva: Librairie de l'Université.

CASSE, PIERRE. 1981 [2nd ed]. *Training for the Cross-Cultural Mind: A Handbook for Cross-Cultural Trainers and Consultants.* Washington, DC: Sietar.

CATFORD, J.C. 1965. *A Linguistic Theory of Translation.* Oxford: Oxford University Press.

CHAFE, WALLACE. 1977. Creativity in verbalisation and its implication for the nature of stored knowledge. In: FREEDLE. L. O. (ed). 1977.

CHAFE, WALLACE. 1987. Cognitive Constraints on Information Flow. In: TOMLIN, R.S. (ed). 1987. 21-51.

CHAO Y. R. 1976. Dimensions of Fidelity in Translation, with special reference to Chinese. In: *Aspects of Chinese Sociolinguistics. Essays by Yuan Ren Chao.* Selected and introduced by Anwar S. Dil. Stanford University Press. 148-169.

CHESTERMAN, ANDREW (ed). 1989. *Readings in translation theory.* Helsinki.

CHESTERMAN, ANDREW. 1993. Theory in Translation Theory. *The New Courant* (Department of English, University of Helsinki) 1, 69-79.

CHOMSKY, NOAM. 1965. *Aspects of the Theory of Syntax.* Cambridge, Massachusetts: M.I.T. Press.

CHUKOVSKY, K. 1984. *A High Art. The Art of Translation.* Translated by L. G. Leighton. Knoxville: University of Tennessee Press.

COHEN, A. & P. COUSSEAU & D. GRANNES & C. McNEILLY & S. NIRENBURG & P. SHELL & D. WÄLTERMANN. 1993. *Translators WorkStation: User's Manual.* Pittsburg: Carnegie Mellon University. School of Computer Science.

COLLINI, STEFAN (ed). 1992. *Interpretation and Overinterpretation.* Cambridge: Cambridge: Cambridge University Press.

CONNINE, CYNTHIA M. & DAWN G. BLASCO & MICHAEL HALL. 1991.Effect of Subsequent Sentence Context in Auditory Word Recognition:

Temporal and Linguistic Constraints. *Journal of Memory and Language* 30, 234-250.

CORBETT, EDWARD P. J. 1971 [2nd ed]. *Classical Rhetoric for the Modern Student.* New York: Oxford University Press.

CORDER, S.P. 1973. *Introducing Applied Linguistics.* Penguin Books.

COUGHLIN, J.M. 1988. Artificial Intelligence and Machine Translation: Present Developments and Future Prospects. *Babel* 34, # 1.

CULLER, JONATHAN. 1992. In Defence of Overinterpretation. In: COLLINI, STEFAN (ed). 1992. 109-123.

CUNNINGHAM, JAMES W. 1987. Toward a Pedagogy of Inferential Comprehension and Creative Response. In: TIERNEY, ROBERT J. & al. (eds). 1987. 229-253.

DAMIDA, A. 1977. *L'Éducation en Afrique á la lumiére de la conférence de Lagos.* Paris: UNESCO.

DAVIDSON, P.M. 1992a. Segmentation of Japanese Source Language Discourse in Simultaneous Interpretation. *The Interpreter's Newsletter.* Special Issue 1, 2-11.

DAVIDSON, P.M. 1992b. Simultaneous Interpreting Research, Past, Present and Future. *Interpreting Research* (Journal of the Interpreting Research Association of Japan) 3, # 2, 23-44.

DELISLE, JEAN. 1980. *L'analyse du discours comme méthode de traduction.* Ottawa: Presses de l'université d'Ottawa.

DELISLE, JEAN. 1981. De la théorie à la pédagogie: réflexions méthodologiques. In: DELISLE, JEAN (ed) 1981. 135-152.

DELISLE, JEAN (ed). 1981. *L'enseignement de la traduction et de l'interprétation.* Ottawa: Éditions de l'université d'Ottawa.

DELISLE, JEAN. 1991. Projet d'Histoire Thématique de la Traduction. In: JOVANOVIĆ, M. (ed). 1991. *Proceedings of the 12th World Congress of FIT.* Belgrade: Prevodilac. 63-68.

DERASSE, BERNARD. 1987. Dubbers and subtitlers have a prime role in the international distribution of television programmes. *EBU Review* 38, # 6, 8-13

DETWEILER, RICHARD A. 1980. Intercultural Interaction and the Categorization Process: A Conceptual Analysis and Behavioral Outcome. *International Journal of Intercultural Relations* 4, 275-293.

DOI, N. & K. FURUKUWA & K. FUCHI. 1987. Fifth-generation Computer Systems and Their Impact on Society. Impact of Science on Society. No. 146. UNESCO/Taylor & Francis.

DOLLERUP, CAY. 1978. *Omkring sproglig transmission (= Anglica et Americana 3).* Copenhagen: Department of English, University of Copenhagen.

DOLLERUP, CAY. 1982. An analysis of some mechanisms and strategies in the translation process based on a study of translations between Danish and English. *The [Incorporated] Linguist* 21, 162-169.

DOLLERUP, CAY & ANNE LODDEGAARD (eds). 1992. *Teaching Translation and Interpreting. Training, Talent and Experience.* Amsterdam & Phila-

delphia: John Benjamins.
DOLLERUP, CAY.1993. Interlingual transfers and issues in translatology. *Perspectives: Studies in Translatology* 1, 137-154.
DOLLERUP, CAY & IVEN REVENTLOW & CARSTEN ROSENBERG HANSEN. 1993. Identity in Practical Translation: Conducting Cross-cultural Studies. *Le Langage et l'homme* (Brussels) 28, 11-25.
DOLLMANN, EUGEN. 1967. *The Interpreter. Memoirs of Dr. Eugen Dollmann.* Translated from the German by J. Maxwell Brownjohn. London: Hutchinson.
DOWNING, BRUCE T. & KATE HELMS TILLERY. 1992. *Professional Training for Community Interpreters.* Minneapolis: Center for Urban and Regional Affairs.
DUMBLETON, C.W. 1982. *Language Services in West Africa.* Geneva: UNCTAD/ECDC/l40.

ECO, UMBERTO. 1990. *The limits of interpretation.* Bloomington and Indianapolis: Indiana University Press.
ECO, UMBERTO. 1992a. Interpretation and Overinterpretation. In: COLLINI, STEFAN (ed). 1992.
ECO, UMBERTO. 1992b. *Les limites de l'interprétation.* Paris: Grasset.
EKVALL, ROBERT B. 1960. *Faithful Echo.* New York: Twayne Publishers.
ERVIN, S. & C. OSGOOD. 1954. Second language learning and bilingualism. *Journal of Abnormal Social Psychology* 49, 139-146.

FAWCETT, PETER. 1983. Translation modes and constraints. *The Incorporated Linguist* 22, 186-190
FURNHAM, ADRIAN & STEPHEN BOCHNER 1986. *Culture Shock. Psychological Reactions to Unfamiliar Environments.* London & New York.

GÉMAR, JEAN-CLAUDE. 1983. De la pratique à la théorie, l'apport des praticiens à la théorie générale de la traduction. *Meta* 28, 323-333.
GENTILE, ADOLFO. 1991. The Application of Theoretical Constructs from a Number of Disciplines for the Development of a Methodology of Teaching in Interpreting and Translating. *Meta* 36, 344-351.
GERVER, D. & W. H. SINAIKO (eds). 1978. *Language Interpretation and Communication.* New York: Plenum Press.
GILE, DANIEL. 1983. Aspects méthodologiques de l'évaluation de la qualité du travail en interprétation simultanée. *Meta* 28, 236-243.
GILE, DANIEL. 1985. La sensibilité aux écarts de langue et la sélection d'informateurs dans l'analyse d'erreurs. *The Incorporated Linguist* 24, 29-32.
GILE, DANIEL. 1990a. *Basic Concepts and Models for Conference Interpretation Training.* Paris: INALCO & CEEI (ISIT).
GILE, D. 1990b. Scientific Research vs. Personal Theories in the Investigation of Interpretation. Paper given at the Scuola Superiore di Lingue Moderne per Interpreti e Traduttori, Università degli Studi, Trieste.

GILE, DANIEL. 1990c. L'évaluation de la qualité de l'interprétation par les délégués: une étude de cas. *The Interpreters' Newsletter* 3, 66-71.

GILE, DANIEL. 1991a. The processing capacity issue in conference interpretation. *Babel* 37, 15-27.

GILE, DANIEL. 1991b. A Communication-Oriented Analysis of Quality in Nonliterary Translation and Interpretation. In: LARSON, MILDRED L. (ed). 1991. 188-200.

GILE, DANIEL. 1992a. Les fautes de traduction: une analyse pédagogique. *Meta* 37, 251-262.

GILE, DANIEL. 1992b. Basic theoretical components in interpreter and translation training. In: DOLLERUP, CAY & ANNE LODDEGAARD (eds). 1992. 185-193.

GOMES DE MATOS, FRANCISCO. 1991. Human Rights Applied to Translations. In: LARSON, MILDRED L. (ed). 1991. 254-259.

GOTTLIEB, HENRIK. 1992. Subtitling - A new university discipline. In: DOLLERUP, CAY & ANNE LODDEGAARD (eds). 1992. 161-170.

GOTTLIEB, Henrik. 1994. Diagonal Translation. *Perspectives: Studies in Translatology* 2, 101-123.

GOTTLIEB, HENRIK. Forthcoming. *Literature on interlingual subtitling since 1932 (= Copenhagen Studies in Translation 4).*

GRAHAM, JOSEPH F. 1985. *Difference in Translation.* Ithaca: Cornell University Press.

GRAN, LAURA. 1988. Interaction between Memory and Note-Taking in Consecutive Interpretation. In: *Übersetzungswissenschaft und Sprachmittlerausbildung, Proceedings.* Berlin: Humboldt Universität.

GRAN, LAURA & JOHN DODDS (eds). 1989. *The Theoretical and Practical Aspects of Teaching Conference Interpreting.* Udine (Italy): Campanotto.

GRICE, H.P. 1975. Logic and conversation. In: COLE, PETER & JERRY MORGAN (eds). 1975. *Syntax and Semantics, Speech Acts.* New York: Academic Press. 41-58.

GROSMAN, META. Forthcoming. Huckleberry Finn for Non-American Readers. *Proceedings of the Conference "American Literature for Non-American Readers".* Bellagio, June 1-5 1992.

GUMPERZ, JOHN J. 1982. *Discourse Strategies (= Studies in Interactional Sociolinguistics 1).* Cambridge: Cambridge University Press.

GUTT, ERNST-AUGUST. 1990. A Theoretical Account of Translation - Without a Translation Theory, *Target* 2, 135-164.

GUTT, ERNST-AUGUST. 1991. *Translation and Relevance: Cognition and Context.* Oxford: Basil Blackwell.

GÖHRING, HEINZ. 1978. Interkulturelle Kommunikation: Die Überwindung der Trennung von Fremdsprachen- und Landeskundeunterricht durch einen integrierten Fremdverhaltensunterricht. In: *Kongressberichte der 8. Jahrestagung der GAL.* Stuttgart. 4.9-14.

GÖHRING, HEINZ. 1980. Deutsch als Fremdsprache und interkulturelle Kommunikation. In: WIERLACHER, ALOIS (ed). *Fremdsprache Deutsch. Grund-*

lagen und Verfahrender Germanistik als Fremdsprachenphilologie I. Munich: Wilhelm Fink. 70-90.

HACK, ANNE-CAROLINE. 1992. *Interferenzen beim Simultandolmetschen*. Heidelberg: Institut für Übersetzen und Dolmetschen der Universität Heidelberg. Unpublished diploma thesis.

HALÁSZ, LÁSZLÓ. 1991. Understanding Short Stories: An American-Hungarian Cross-Cultural Study. *Empirical Studies of the Arts 9*, 143-163.

HALL, DONALD. 1982. The Weather for Poetry. Michigan: University of Michigan Press.

HALLIDAY, MICHAEL A.K. 1967. Notes on Transitivity and Theme in English. *Journal of Linguistics* 3 (Part 2), 199-244.

HALLIDAY, MICHAEL A.K. & RUQAIYA HASAN. 1976. *Cohesion in English*. London: Longman.

HALLIDAY, MICHAEL A.K. 1985. *An Introduction to Functional Grammar*. London: Edward Arnold.

HAMMOND, DEANNE L. (ed). 1989. *Coming of Age. Proceedings of the 30th Annual Conference of the American Translators Association*. Medford, N.J.: Learned Information.

HARRIS, RICHARD JACKSON & LAWRENCE M. SCHOEN & DEANA L. HENSLEY. 1992. A Cross-cultural Study of Story Memory. *Journal of Cross-cultural Psychology* 23, 133-147.

HATIM, BASIL & IAN MASON. 1990. *Discourse and the Translator*. London: Longman.

HEWSON, LANCE & JACKY MARTIN. 1991. *Redefining Translation. The Variational Approach*. London & New York: Routledge.

HILLOCKS, Jr., GEORGE. 1986. *Research on Written Composition*. Urbana, Illinois: NCTE/ERIC.

HILVERKUS, BARBARA. 1991. *Monitoringstrategien beim Simultandolmetschen*. Heidelberg: Institut für Übersetzen und Dolmetschen der Universität Heidelberg. Unpublished diploma thesis.

HOFSTADTER, DOUGLAS R. 1980. *Gödel, Escher, Bach: An Eternal Golden Braid. A Metaphysical Fugue on Minds and Machine in the Spirit of Lewis Carroll*. Middlesex: Penguin.

HOHNHOLD, INGO. 1990. *Übersetzungsorientierte Terminologiearbeit*. Stuttgart: InTra.

HOLMES, JAMES S. 1988. *Translated! Papers on Literary Translation and Translation Studies*. Amsterdam: Rodopi.

HOLZ-MÄNTTÄRI, JUSTA. 1984. *Translatorisches Handeln. Theorie und Methode (= Annales Academiae Scientiarum Fennicae B 226)*. Helsinki: Suomalainen Tiedeakatemia.

HOLZ-MÄNTTÄRI, JUSTA. 1986. Translatorisches Handeln - theoretisch fundierte Berufsprofile. In: SNELL-HORNBY, MARY (ed). *Übersetzungswissenschaft - eine Neuorientierung. Zur Integrierung von Theorie und Praxis*. Tübingen: Francke (= *Uni-Taschenbücher* 1415).

HOLZ-MÄNTTÄRI, JUSTA & CHRISTIANE NORD (eds). 1993. *Traducere navem. Festschrift für Katharina Reiss zum 70 Geburtstag.* Tampere: Tampere University Press. Distributed by University of Tampere, Sales Office, P.O. Box 617, SF-33101 Tampere/Finland, Fax: +358 31 157 150.

van HOOF, HENRI. 1986. *Petite histoire de la traduction en Occident.* Louvain-la-Neuve: Cabay.

HUTCHINS, W. JOHN & HAROLD L. SOMERS. 1992. *An Introduction to Machine Translation.* London: Academic Press.

HYMES, D. 1977. Models of Interaction of Language and Social Life. In: GUMPERZ, JOHN & DELL HYMES (eds). 1977. *Directions in Sociolinguistics: the ethnography of communication.* New York: Holt, Rinehart and Winston, 35-71.

HÖNIG, HANS G. 1992. Von der erzwungenen Selbstentfremdung des Übersetzers - Ein offener Brief an Justa Holz-Mänttäri. *TEXTconTEXT* 7, 1-14.

IBRAHIM, HASNAH. 1992. *OH BABEL! Problems of translating Malay verse into English.* Unpublished PhD dissertation.

IBRAHIM, HASNAH. 1991. Translation Spectrum: Problem in Description. In: NOOR, NOOREIN MOHD & ATIAH HJ. SALLEH (eds). *Pragmatik Penterjemahan. Prinsip, amalan dan penilaian menuju ke abad 21 [The Pragmatics of Translation: Principles, Practice and Evaluation. Moving towards the 21st Century].* Kuala Lumpur.

IHENACHO, A. 1991. Planning translation studies in Nigeria. In: ANYAEHIE, E. & A. IHENACHO (eds). *Language studies and relevance.* Uturu: LC Publications.

ILG, GERARD. 1980. L'interprétation consecutive. *Parallèles* (Geneva) 3, 109-136.

ILG, GERARD. 1982. L'interprétation consecutive. La pratique. *Parallèles* (Geneva) 5, 91-109.

INHELDER, B. & J. PIAGET. 1966. *La psychologie de l'enfant.* Paris: Presses Universitaires de France.

IVIR, VLADIMIR. 1989. Procedures and Strategies for the Translation of Culture. In: TOURY, GIDEON (ed). 1989. 35-46.

JACKENDOFF, RAY. 1985. *Semantics and Cognition.* Cambridge, Massachusetts: M.I.T. Press.

JACOBSEN, HENRIK GALBERG & PEDER SKYUM-NIELSEN. 1988 [2nd edition]. *Erhvervsdansk.* Copenhagen: Schønberg.

JAKOBSEN, ARNT LYKKE. 1993. Translation as textual (re)production. *Perspectives: Studies in Translatology* 1, 155-166.

JAKOBSON, ROMAN. 1959. On Linguistic Aspects of Translation. In: BROWER, R. A. (ed). *On Translation.* New York: Harvard University Press. 232-239.

JACOBY, LARRY L.A. 1991. Process Dissociation Framework: Separating Automatic from Intentional Uses of Memory. *Journal of Memory and Language* 30,

513-541.
JIASHUI, WU S. 1991. Task-Oriented and Comprehensive Training of Translators and Interpreters. In: *Proceedings, Asia-Pacific Conference on Translation and Interpreting: Bridging East and West.*
JUMPELT, R. W. 1961. *Die Übersetzung naturwissenschaftlicher und technischer Literatur.* Berlin-Schöneberg: Langenscheidt.

KADE, OTTO. 1968. *Zufall und Gesetzmäßigkeit in der Übersetzung. (= Beihefte zur Zeitschrift Fremdsprachen I).* Leipzig: VEB Verlag Enzyklopädie.
KALINA, SYLVIA. 1991. Zur Rolle der Theorie in der Dolmetscherausbildung. *TEXTconTEXT* 6, # 2/3, 101-113.
KALINA, SYLVIA. 1992. Discourse processing and interpreting strategies - an approach to the teaching of interpreting. In: DOLLERUP, CAY & ANNE LODDEGAARD (eds). 1992. 251-257.
KANG, HEE-WON, 1992. Cultural Inference in Second Language Reading. *International Journal of Applied Linguistics* 2, 95-119.
KARKER, ALLAN. 1993. *Dansk i EF - en situationsberetning om sproget (= Nordisk Språksekretariats Skrifter 16).* Copenhagen & Oslo: Gad.
KEMPSON, RUTH (ed). 1988. *Mental Representations: the Interface between Language and Reality.* Cambridge: Cambridge University Press.
KENDON, ADAM (ed). 1981. *Nonverbal Communication, Interaction, and Gesture. Selections from Semiotica (= Approaches to Semiotics 41).* The Hague: Mouton.
KENDON, ADAM. 1982. The organization of behavior in face-to-face interaction: observations on the development of a methodology. In: SCHERER, KLAUS R. & PAUL EKMAN (eds). 1982. *Handbook of Methods in Nonverbal Behavior Research (= Studies in Emotion and Social Interaction).* Cambridge: Cambridge University Press. 440-505.
KING, JONATHAN & MARCEL ADAM JUST. 1991. Individual Differences in Syntactic Processing: The Role of Working Memory. *Journal of Memory and Language* 30, 580-602.
KINTSCH, WALTER & EDITH GREEN. 1978. The Role of Culture-Specific Schemata in the Comprehension and Recall of Stories. *Discourse Processes* 1, 1-13.
KITTREDGE, R. 1983. Sublanguage - Specific Computer Aids to Translation - a survey of the most promising areas. Université de Montréal & Bureau des Traductions.
KITTREDGE, R. & R. GRISHMAN (eds). 1986. Analysing Language in Restricted Domains: Sublanguage Descriptions and Processing. Hillsdale, N.J.: Lawrence Erlbaum.
KOCK, CHRISTIAN & BIRTHE TANDRUP. 1989. *Skriv kreativt.* Copenhagen: Gyldendal.
KOHN, KURT. 1990. *Dimensionen lernersprachlicher Performanz. Theoretische und empirische Untersuchungen zum Zweitsprachenerwerb.* Tübingen: Gunter Narr.

KOLLER, WERNER. 1979. *Einführung in die Übersetzungswissenschaft.* Heidelberg: Quelle & Meyer (= *Uni-Taschenbücher* 819)
KOLLER, WERNER. 1993. Zum Begriff der 'eigentlichen' Übersetzung. In: HOLZ-MÄNTTÄRI, JUSTA & NORD, CHRISTIANE (eds). 1993. 49-63.
KOMISSAROV, VILEN. 1985. The practical value of translation theory. *Babel* 31, 208-212.
KOPCZYŃSKI, ANDRZEJ. 1994. Quality in conference interpreting: Some pragmatic problems. In: SNELL-HORNBY, MARY & FRANZ PÖCHHACKER & KLAUS KAINDL (ed). 1994. 189-198.
KOVAČIČ, IRENA. 1992. *Jezikoslovni pogled na podnaslovno prevajanje televizijskih oddaj.* [A linguistic approach to subtitling television programs]. Ljubljana: University of Ljubljana. PhD dissertation.
KRAWUTSCHKE, PETER W. (ed). 1989. *Translator and Interpreter Training and Foreign Language Pedagogy (= American Translator Association Series III).* Binghamton: State University of New York.
KRISHNAMOORTHY, K. 1985. Dhvani or Suggestion: A Study in Perspective. *Indian Literature.* July-August, 113-122 .
KRUSCHE, DIETRICH. 1990. Vermittlungsrelevanten Eigenschaften literarischer Texte (1985). In: KRUSCHE, DIETRICH & ALOIS WIERLACHER (eds). 1990. *Hermeneutik der Fremde.* Munich: Iudicum. 103-126.
KUBLER, C. 1985. *A Study of Europeanized Grammar in Modern Written Chinese.* Taipei: Student Book Co.
KURZ, INGRID. 1989. Conference Interpreting: User Expectations. In: HAMMOND, DEANNE L. (ed). 1989. 143-148.
KURZ, INGRID. 1992. *Simultandolmetschen als Gegenstand der interdisziplinären Forschung.* Vienna: University of Vienna. Unpublished Habilitationsschrift.
KYLE, K. 1992. *Switched On: Deaf people's views on television subtitling.* A report for the ITC and BBC by the Centre for Deaf Studies, University of Bristol.

LADMIRAL, J.-R. 1990. La traduction proligère? - Sur le statut des textes qu'on traduit. *Meta* 35, # 1.
LAKOFF, GEORGE. 1987. *Women, Fire, and Dangerous Things. What Categories Reveal about the Mind.* Chicago: University of Chicago Press.
LAMBERT S. 1988. Information Processing among Conference Interpreters: A Test of the Depth-of-Processing Hypothesis. *Meta* 33, 377-387.
LAMBERT, W. E. & J. HAVELKA. 1958. The Influence of language acquisition contexts on bilingualism. *Journal of Abnormal Social Psychology* 56, 239-244.
LAROSE, ROBERT. 1992. La théorie de la traduction: à quoi ça sert? *Meta* 37, 405-407.
LARSON, MILDRED L. 1984. *Meaning-based Translation: A Guide to Cross-Language Equivalence.* Lanham: University Press of America.
LARSON, MILDRED L. (ed). 1991. *Translation: Theory and Practice. Tension and Interdependence (= American Translators Association Series V).*

Binghamton, New York: State University of New York.

LÁSZLÓ, JANOS & STEEN FOLKE LARSEN. 1991. Cultural and Text Variables in Processing Personal Experiences While Reading Literature. *Empirical Studies of the Arts* 9, 23-34.

LE FEAL, K.D. 1992. Linguistique et traduction. *TURJUMAN* 1, # 1.

LEDERER, MARIANNE. 1976. Synecdoque et traduction. *Études de Linguistique Appliquée* 24.

LEDERER, MARIANNE. 1978. Simultaneous Interpretation: Units of Meaning and Other Features. In: GERVER, D. & W. H. SINAIKO (eds). 1978. 323-332.

LEDERER, MARIANNE. 1981. *La traduction simultanée - expérience et théorie*. Paris: Minard-Lettres Modernes.

LEDERER, MARIANNE. 1992. Principes et méthodes de l'enseignement de l'interprétation. *TURJUMAN* 1, # 1.

LEECH, GEOFFREY. 1983. *Principles of Pragmatics*. London: Longman.

LEFEVERE, ANDRÉ. 1977. *Translating Literature: The German Tradition*. Assen: Van Gorcum.

LENNEBERG, E. H. 1967. *Biological foundations of language*. New York: Wiley & Sons.

LIND, JENS NØRMARK & MORTEN SESTOFT. 1992. *Tv-tekstning af "El Quijote"*. Term paper, Department for Romance Languages, University of Copenhagen.

LIU, C.C. (ed). 1991. *Fanyi xin lun ji*. Hong Kong: Commercial Press.

LOSA, EDITH F. (ed). 1993. *New Frontiers. Proceedings of the 33rd Annual Conference of the American Translators Association*. Medford, New Jersey: Learned Information.

LOTMAN, JURI & B.A. USPENSKY. 1978. On the Semiotic Mechanism of Culture. *New Literary History* 11, 211-232.

LUYKEN, G.-M. & THOMAS HERBST & JO LANGHAM-BROWN & HELENE REID & HERMAN SPINHOF. 1991. *Overcoming language barriers in television*. Düsseldorf: The European Institute for the Media.

LVOVSKAJA, Z. D. 1985. *Teoreticheskie problemy perevoda*. Moscow: Vyshaja Shkola.

MACKINTOSH J. 1991. Language Enhancement for Interpreters. In: LIU, C. C. (ed). 1991. 389-402.

MADARIAGA, SALVADOR DE. 1974. *Morning Without Noon. Memoirs*. Westmead, Farnborough, Hampshire: Saxon House, D.C. Heath Ltd.

MAHMOODZADEH, KAMBIZ. 1992. Consecutive interpreting: its principles and techniques. In: DOLLERUP, CAY & ANNE LODDEGAARD (eds). 1992. 231-236.

MALONE, JOSEPH L. 1986. Trajectional Analysis: Five Cases in Point. *Babel* 13.

MANZOUFAS, MARENA. 1982. The art of the subtitle: The subtitling unit at Channel 0/28. *Media Information Australia* # 25, 17-18; 25.

MARKUS, MANFRED. 1992. Rhythm, stress and intonation in English and

German seen contrastively. In: MAIR, CHRISTIAN & MANFRED MARKUS (eds). *New Departures in Contrastive Linguistics.* Innsbruck: Universität Innsbruck. I, 21-36.

MARTINS, MARCIA DO AMARAL PEIXOTO. 1992. For a Process-oriented Methodology in Translation Teaching. Paper given at the Translation Studies Congress: "Translation Studies - An Interdiscipline", 9-12 September 1992, Vienna, Austria.

MAYORAL, ROBERTO & DOROTHY KELLY & NATIVIDAD GALLARDO. 1988. Concept of constrained translation. Non-linguistic perspectives of translation. *Meta* 33, 356-367.

McDAVID, JOHN & HERBERT HARARI. 1967. *Social Psychology.* New York: Harper & Row.

MEAK, LIDIA. 1990. Interprétation simultanée et congrès médical: attentes et commentaires. *The Interpreters' Newsletter* 3, 8-13.

MINNESOTA DEPARTMENT OF HUMAN SERVICES, OFFICE OF REFU GEE MENTAL HEALTH SERVICES. 1988. *Assessment of Refugee Mental Health Needs, Part 2: Survey of Mental Health Service Providers.* St. Paul: Department of Human Services.

MOSER, B. 1978. Simultaneous Interpretation: A Hypothetical Model and its Practical Application. In: GERVER, D. & W. H. SINAIKO (eds). 1978. 353-368.

MOSER, B. 1991. Paradigms Gained, or the Art of Productive Disagreement. *Bulletin* XIX-2 (Association Internationale des Interprètes de Conférence, Geneva).

MOSKOWITZ, KEN. 1979. Subtitles vs. dubbing: Debate goes on. *Take One* (Toronto) 7, # 5. 58.

MOSSOP, BRIAN. 1989. "Write idiomatically and translate ideas not words". Three defects of the prevailing doctrine of translation. In: SÉGUINOT, CANDACE (ed). *The translation process.* H.G. Publications, School of Translation, York University, Canada. 1-20.

MOUNIN, GEORGES. 1965. *Teoria e Storia della Traduzione.* Torino: Einaudi.

MOUNIN, GEORGES. 1967. *Die Übersetzung. Geschichte, Theorie, Anwendung.* Munich: Nymphenburger Verlag.

MOUNIN, GEORGES. 1976. *Linguistique et traduction.* Brussels.

MYERS SCOTTON, C. 1983. The negotiation of identities in conversation: a theory of markedness and code choice. *International Journal of the Sociology of Language* 44, 115-136.

MYERS, B. & D. GIUSE & R. DANNENBERG & B. ZANDEN & D. KOSBIE & E. PERVIN & A. MICKISH & P. MARCHAL. 1990. Garnet: Comprehensive Support for Graphical, Highly-Interactive User Interfaces. *IEEE Computer* 23, # 11.

MÜLLER, BERND-DIETRICH. 1980. Zur Logik interkultureller Verstehensprobleme. *Jahrbuch Deutsch als Fremdsprache* 6, 102-119.

MÜLLER, BERND-DIETRICH. 1986. Interkulturelle Verstehensstrategien - Vergleich und Empathie. In: NEUNER, GERHARD (ed). 1986. *Kulturkontraste im DaF-Unterricht* (= *Studium Deutsch als Fremdsprache - Sprachdidaktik 5*). 33-84.

NEDERGAARD-LARSEN, BIRGIT. 1993. Cultural factors in subtitling. *Perspectives: Studies in Translatology* 1, 207-241.
NEUBERT, A. 1985. *Text and Translation*. Leipzig: VEB Verlag Enzyklopädie.
NEWMARK, PETER. 1981. *Approaches to Translation*. Oxford: Pergamon.
NEWMARK, PETER. 1988. *A Textbook of Translation*. Cambridge & New York: Prentice Hall.
NEWMARK, PETER. 1991. *About Translation*. London: Multilingual Matters.
NIDA, EUGENE A. 1945. Linguistics and Ethnology in Translation Problems. *Word* 1, 194-208.
NIDA, EUGENE A. 1964. *Toward a Science of Translating*. Leiden: E. J. Brill.
NIDA, EUGENE A. & C.R. TABER. 1982. *The Theory and Practice of Translation*. Leiden: E. J. Brill.
NIDA, EUGENE & J. de WAARD. 1986. *From one language to another*. Nashville: Thomas Nelson Publishers.
NIDA, EUGENE A. 1990. The role of rhetoric in verbal communications. *Babel* 36, 143-154.
NINTAI, MOSES. 1993. African Literature in European Languages: Major Features and Implications for Translation. In: *Proceedings of the 13th FIT World Congress*. London: ITI. I, 564-572.
NIR, RAFAEL. 1984. Linguistic and sociolinguistic problems in the translation of imported TV films in Israel. *International Journal of the Sociology of Language* 48, 81-97.
NORD, CHRISTIANE. 1988. *Textanalyse und Übersetzen. Theoretische Grundlagen, Methode und didaktische Anwendung einer übersetzungsrelevanten Textanalyse*. Heidelberg: Groos.
NORD, CHRISTIANE. 1991. *Text Analysis in Translation: Theory, Methodology, and Didactic Application of a Model for Translation-Oriented Text Analysis. (= Amsterdamer Publikationen zur Sprache und Literatur 94)*. Translated by C. Nord and P. Sparrow. Amsterdam & Atlanta: Rodopi. Translation of Nord 1988.
NORD, CHRISTIANE. 1992. Text Analysis in Translator Training. In: DOLLERUP, CAY & ANNE LODDEGAARD (eds). 1992. 39-48.
NORD, CHRISTIANE. 1993. *Einführung in das funktionale Übersetzen: Am Beispiel von Titeln und Überschriften*. Tübingen: Francke (= *Uni-Taschenbücher* 1734).
NUNAN, DAVID. 1984. *The learner-centred curriculum, a study in second language teaching*. Cambridge: Cambridge University Press.

OITTINEN, RIITTA. 1992. Teaching Translation of Fiction - A Dialogic Point of view. In: DOLLERUP, CAY & ANNE LODDEGAARD (eds). 1992. 75-80.
OJO, ADE. 1986. The Role of the Translator of African Written Literature in Inter-cultural Consciousness and Relationships. *Meta* 31, 291-299.

OSF/Motif Programmer's Guide, Revision 1.1. 1991. Open Software Foundation Engelwood Cliffs, N.J.: Prentice Hall.

PATTANAYAK, D.P. 1981. Multi-Lingualism and Mother Tongue Education Delhi: Oxford University Press.
PEDERSEN, VIGGO HJØRNAGER 1988. *Essays on Translation.* Copenhagen: Nyt Nordisk Forlag Arnold Busck.
PERREN, G.E. & J. L. M. TRIM (eds). 1971. *Applications of Linguistics.* Cambridge: Cambridge University Press.
POPPER, KARL R. 1972. *Objective Knowledge. An Evolutionary Approach.* Oxford: Clarendon Press.
POYATOS, FERNANDO. 1983. *New Perspectives in Nonverbal Communication. Studies in Cultural Anthropology, Social Psychology, Linguistics, Literature, and Semiotics (= Language and Communication Library 5).* Oxford: Pergamon.
POYATOS, FERNANDO. 1987. Nonverbal communication in simultaneous and consecutive interpretation: A theoretical model and new perspectives. *TEXTconTEXT* 2, 73-108.
POYATOS, FERNANDO (ed). 1988. *Cross-Cultural Perspectives in Nonverbal Communication.* Toronto & Göttingen: C.J. Hogrefe.
POYATOS, FERNANDO (ed). 1992. *Advances in Nonverbal Communication. Sociocultural, Clinical, Esthetic and Literary Perspectives.* Amsterdam & Philadelphia: John Benjamins.
PYM, ANTHONY. 1992a. *Translation and Text Transfer.* Frankfurt-am-Main: Peter Lang.
PYM, ANTHONY. 1992b. The Relations Between Translation and Material Text Transfer. *Target* 4, 171-189.
PÖCHHACKER, FRANZ. 1992a. The role of theory in simultaneous interpreting. In: DOLLERUP, CAY & ANNE LODDEGAARD (eds). 1992. 211-220.
PÖCHHACKER, FRANZ. 1992b. *Simultandolmetschen als komplexes Handeln. Ein Theorie- und Beschreibungsrahmen, dargestellt an einer Fachkonferenz.* Vienna: University of Vienna. Unpublished PhD dissertation.
PÖCHHACKER, FRANZ. 1993. From knowledge to text: Coherence in simultaneous interpreting. In: GAMBIER, YVES & JORMA TOMMOLA (eds). 1993. *Translation and Knowledge.* Turku: University of Turku. 87-100.
PÖCHHACKER, FRANZ. 1994. Simultaneous interpretation: "Cultural transfer" or "Voice-over text"? In: SNELL-HORNBY, MARY & FRANZ PÖCHHACKER & KLAUS KAINDL (eds). 1994. 169-178.

RADICE, WILLIAM. 1986. The Rules of Translating Tagore. *Indian Literature,* May-June 1986, 33-40.
von RAFFLER-ENGEL, WALBURGA, 1988. The Impact of Covert Factors in Cross-Cultural Communication. In: POYATOS, FERNANDO (ed). 1988.
RATH, RAMAKANT. 1985. *Sri Radha.* Cuttack: Agradut.
REGE, M.P. 1990. Editorial. *New Quest,* March-April 1990, 65-67.
REID, HELENE. 1987. The Semiotics of Subtitling, or Why don't you translate

what it says? *EBU Review* # 6, 28-30.
REISS, KATHARINA. 1983. *Texttyp und Übersetzungsmethode.* Heidelberg: Groos.
REISS, KATHARINA & HANS J. VERMEER. 1984. *Grundlegung einer allgemeinen Translationstheorie (= Linguistische Arbeiten 147).* Tübingen: Max Niemeyer.
REUTER, E. & H. SCHRÖDER & L. TIITTULA. 1989. Deutsch-Finnische Kulturunterschiede in der Wirtschaftskommunikation. Fragestellungen, Methoden und Ergebnisse eines Forschungsprojekts. *Jahrbuch Deutsch als Fremdsprache* 15, 237-269.
RIEDMÜLLER, THOMAS. 1989. *Strategien beim Simultandolmetschen.* Heidelberg: Institut für Übersetzen und Dolmetschen der Universität Heidelberg. Unpublished diploma thesis.
ROBERTS, RODA P. 1992. The Concept of Function of Translation and Its Application to Literary Texts. *Target* 4, 1-16.
ROBINSON, DOUGLAS. 1991. *The Translator's Turn.* Baltimore & London: Johns Hopkins University Press.
RODITI, EDOUARD. 1982. *History in a Nutshell.* Washington, DC: National Resource Center for Translation and Interpretation, Georgetown University.
ROSE, MARILYN GADDIS (ed). 1981. *Translation Spectrum.* Albany: State University of New York.
ROY, DEBI. 1992. Maa. *Desh* (India). 17 October 1992.
RSMB Television Research Limited. 1993. *Language, Community and Leisure: a study of the understanding and use of Welsh in Wales.* Prepared for SAC, Cardiff.
RØNN-POULSEN, ANNI & FINN BRANDT-PEDERSEN. 1986. *Skriveværkstedet.* Copenhagen: Nøgleforlaget.

SAGER, JUAN. 1990. *A practical course in terminology processing.* Amsterdam & Philadelphia: John Benjamins.
SAGER, JUAN. 1992. The translator as terminologist. In: DOLLERUP, CAY & ANNE LODDEGAARD (eds). 1992. 107-122.
SAINZ, MARÍA JULIA. 1992. Developing Translation Skills. In: DOLLERUP, CAY & ANNE LODDEGAARD (eds). 1992. 69-73.
SAVORY, THEODORE. 1957. *The Art of Translation.* London: Jonathan Cape.
SCHMIDT, PAUL. 1954. *Statist auf diplomatischer Bühne.* Bonn: Athenäum.
SCHWEDA NICHOLSON, NANCY. 1987. Linguistic and Extralinguistic Aspects of Simultaneous Interpretation. *Applied Linguistics* 8, 194-205.
SCHWEDA NICHOLSON, NANCY. 1990a. Consecutive Note-Taking for Community Interpretation. In: BOWEN, D. & M. (eds). 1990. 136-145.
SCHWEDA NICHOLSON, NANCY. 1990b. A New Look at the Cognitive Flexibility Factor in Interpreter Training. In: WILLSON, A. L. (ed.). 1990. 107-117.
SCHWEDA NICHOLSON, NANCY. 1991. Self-Monitoring Strategies in Simultaneous Interpretation. In: PICKEN, C. (ed). 1991. *Proceedings of the Institute of Translation and Interpreting Conference 5.* London: The Association for In-

formation Management (Aslib). 46-51.

SCHWEDA NICHOLSON, NANCY. 1993a. An Introduction to Basic Note-Taking Skills for Consecutive Interpretation. In: LOSA, E. (ed). 1993. 197-204.

SCHWEDA NICHOLSON, NANCY. 1993b [In press]. The Constructive Criticism Model for Post-Interpretation Analysis. *The Interpreters' Newsletter.*

SCHWEDA NICHOLSON, NANCY. 1994 [Forthcoming]. Professional Ethics for Court and Community Interpreters. In: HAMMOND, DEANNE L. (ed). *Professional Issues in Translation and Interpretation (= American Translators Association Series on Translation and Interpretation VII).* Binghamton: State University of New York.

SCHWEITZER, A. D. 1973. *Perevod i lingvistika.* Moscow: Vojenizdat.

SCHWEITZER, A. D. 1988. *Teorija perevoda: Status, problemy, aspekty.* Moscow: Nauka.

SELESKOVITCH, DANICA. 1981. *L'enseignement de l'interprétation et de la traduction: de la théorie á la pédagogie.* Ottawa: University of Ottawa Press.

SELESKOVITCH, DANICA. 1989. *Teaching Conference Interpreting (= American Translators Association Scholarly Monograph Series III).* Binghamton: State University of New York.

SELESKOVITCH, DANICA & MARIANNE LEDERER. 1984. *Interpréter pour traduire.* Paris: Didier.

SELESKOVITCH, DANICA & MARIANNE LEDERER. 1989. *Pédagogie raisonnée de l'interprétation (= Collection "Traductologie" 4).* Paris: Didier.

SETTON, ROBIN. 1991. Training Conference Interpreters with Chinese: Cultural Factors. Paper given at the Third International Conference on Cross-Cultural Communication: East and West. National Chengkong University, Tainan, Republic of China.

SETTON, ROBIN. 1993a. Is non-intra-IE interpretation different? European models and Chinese-English realities, *Meta* 38, 2.

SETTON, ROBIN. 1993b. Speech in Europe and Asia: Discourse Processes in the Training of Cross-Cultural Conference Interpreters. *Interpreting Research* (Journal of the Interpreting Research Association of Japan) 3, # 2, 2-11.

SHACKMAN, J. 1987. *The Right to be Understood.* Cambridge: National Extension College.

SHLESINGER, MIRIAM. 1989. Monitoring the Courtroom Interpreter. *Parallèles* (Geneva) 11, 29-34.

SHLESINGER, MIRIAM. 1992a. Lexicalization in translation: an empirical study of students' progress. In: DOLLERUP, CAY & ANNE LODDEGAARD (eds). 1992. 123-128.

SHLESINGER, MIRIAM. 1992b. Intonation in the Production and Perception of Simultaneous Interpretation. Paper given at the Translation Studies Congress: "Translation Studies - An Interdiscipline", 9-12 September 1992, Vienna, Austria.

SHOCHAT, ELLA & ROBERT STAM. 1985. The Cinema after Babel: Language, Difference, Power. *Screen* 26, # 3-4, 35-58.

van SLYPE, G. & J.F. GUINET, F. SEITZ, E. BENEJAM. 1983. *Better*

Translation for Better Communication. Oxford: Pergamon.
SNELL-HORNBY, MARY. 1988. *Translation Studies - An Integrated Approach.* Amsterdam & Philadelphia: John Benjamins.
SNELL-HORNBY, MARY, & FRANZ PÖCHHACKER & KLAUS KAINDL (eds). 1994. *Translation Studies - An Interdiscipline.* Amsterdam & Philadelphia: John Benjamins.
SPERBER, DAN & DEIRDRE WILSON. 1986. *Relevance: Communication and Cognition.* Oxford: Basil Blackwell.
STACKELBERG, JÜRGEN & BURKHART KROEBER. 1986. Alter Mönch - strenger Greis [eine Kontroverse]. *Der Übersetzer* 22, # 3, 1-4.
STEINER, GEORGE. 1975. *After Babel.* London: Oxford University Press.
STENZL, CATHERINE. 1983. *Simultaneous interpretation: Groundwork towards a comprehensive model.* London. Unpublished M.A. thesis.
STUBBS, M. 1983. *Discourse Analysis.* Oxford: Blackwell.
SVANHOLM, FLEMMING. 1992. The Happy Triad - The Human, the MAT, and the MT. In: *Translating and the Computer 14, Quality Standards and the Implementation of Technology in Translation.* London: Aslib. 15-20.
SÖDERLUND, BÖRJE. 1965. *Att översätta.* Stockholm: Bonniers Uggleböcker.

TIERNY, ROBERT J. & AL. (eds). 1987. *Understanding Readers' Understanding.* Hillsdale, N. J.: Lawrence Erlbaum.
TIRKKONEN-CONDIT, S. 1992. A Theoretical Account of Translation Without Translation Theory? *Target* 4, 237-245.
TITFORD, CHRISTOPHER. 1982. Sub-titling - Constrained Translation. *Lebende Sprachen* 27, # 3, 113-116.
TOMLIN, R.S. (ed). 1987. *Coherence and Grounding in Discourse.* Amsterdam & Philadelphia: John Benjamins.
TOURY, GIDEON. 1979. Interlanguage and its manifestations in translation. *Meta* 24, 223-231.
TOURY, GIDEON. 1989. Integrating the Cultural Dimension into Translation Studies: An Introduction. In: TOURY, GIDEON (ed). 1989. 1-8.
TOURY, GIDEON (ed). 1989. *Translation across Cultures.* Delhi: Bahri Publications. Book edition of special issue of *Indian Journal of Applied Linguistics* (1987)
TRANI, EUGENE P. 1969. *The Treaty of Portsmouth. An Adventure in American Diplomacy.* Lexington: University of Kentucky Press.
TYTLER, ALEXANDER FRASER. 1978 [original: 1791]. *Essay on the Principles of Translation.* Amsterdam & Philadelphia: John Benjamin.

UNESCO. 1962. *Conférence des ministres de l'éducation des pays africans participant á l'exécution du plan d'Addis-Abeba: rapport final, 26-30 mars, 1962.* Paris: UNESCO.
UWAJEH, M. K. C. 1992. Uwajeh's 'Four-Level Theory of Translation' and the Study of African Languages. Paper prepared for the 23rd Annual Confer-

ence of African Linguistics, USA.

VARGO, EDWARD. Forthcoming. (Non)American Readers "Writing" (Un)American Literature. *Proceedings of the Conference "American Literature for Non-American Readers"*. Bellagio, June 1-5 1992.

VASCONCELLOS, MURIEL. 1990. Practical and linguistic strategies for post-editing machine translation. In: WILLSON, A. L. (ed). 1990. 339-351.

VERMEER, HANS J. 1978. ein rahmen für eine allgemeine translationstheorie. In: VERMEER, HANS. 1983. *Aufsätze zur Translationstheorie*. Heidelberg: Julius Groos.

VERMEER, HANS J. 1989. Skopos and commission in translational action. In: CHESTERMAN, ANDREW (ed). 1989. 173-187.

VERMEER, HANS J. 1989. What does it mean to Translate? In: TOURY, GIDEON (ed). 1989. 25-33.

VERMEER, HANS J. & HEIDRUN WITTE. 1990. *Mögen Sie Zistrosen? Scenes & frames & channels im translatorischen Handeln (= TEXTcon-TEXT, Beiheft 3)*. Heidelberg.

VERMEER, HANS J. 1990. *The CERA Lectures 1990*. Unpublished manuscript for the CERA Chair for Translation, Communication and Cultures, Katholieke Universiteit Leuven, Belgium, 25 June-19 July 1990.

VERMEER, HANS J. 1992 [orig. 1989]. *Skopos und Translationsauftrag - Aufsätze*. Heidelberg.

VERMEER, HANS J. 1992a. Describing Nonverbal Behaviour in the Odyssey: Scenes and Verbal Frames as Translation Problems. In: POYATOS, FERNANDO (ed). 1992. 285-299.

VESTER, FREDERIC. 1980. *Neuland des Denkens*. Stuttgart: Deutsche Verlags-Anstalt.

VESTER, FREDERIC. 1978. *Denken, Lernen und Vergessen*. Munich: Deutscher Taschenbuchverlag.

VIAGGIO, S. 1992a. Translators and Interpreters: Professionals or Shoemakers? In: DOLLERUP, CAY & ANNE LODDEGAARD (eds). 1992. 307-312.

VIAGGIO, S. 1992b. Cognitive Clozing to Teach Them to Think. *The Interpreters' Newsletter* 4, 40-44.

VIAGGIO, SERGIO. 1992c. Few Ad Libs on Communicative and Semantic Translation, Interpretation and Their Schools. *Meta* 37, 278-288.

VINAY, J.-P. & J. DARBELNET. 1958. *Stylistique comparée du français et de l'anglais. Méthode de traduction*. Paris: Didier.

VINAY, J.-P. & DARBELNET, J. 1977 [orig. 1957]. *Stylistique comparée du français et de l'anglais. Méthode de Traduction*. Quebec: Beauchemin.

WALTERS, VERNON. 1978. *Silent Missions*. Garden City, N.Y.: Doubleday.

WARNER, ALFRED. 1966. *Internationale Angleichung fachsprachlicher Wendungen der Elektrotechnik. Versuch einer Aufstellung phraseologischer Grundsätze für die Technik. Beihefte der ETZ # 4.*

WEBER, W. 1991. Improved Ways of Teaching Consecutive Interpretation. In:

LIU, C.C. (ed). 1991. 403-412.
WILLSON, A. L. (ed). 1990. *Looking Ahead. Proceedings of the 31st Annual ATA-Conference.* Medford, N. J.: Learned Information.
WILSON, DEIRDRE & DAN SPERBER. 1988. Representation and Relevance. In: KEMPSON, RUTH (ed). 1988. 133-53.
WILSS, WOLFRAM. 1977. *Übersetzungswissenschaft - Probleme und Methoden.* Stuttgart: Klett.
WILSS, WOLFRAM. 1978. Syntactic Anticipation in German-English Simultaneous Interpreting. In: GERVER, D. & W. H. SINAIKO (eds). 1978. 323-332.
WILSS, WOLFRAM. 1992. *Übersetzungsfertigkeit. Annäherung an einen komplexen übersetzungspraktischen Begriff.* Tübingen: Gunter Narr.
WITTE, HEIDRUN. 1987. Die Kulturkompetenz des Translators - Theoretischabstrakter Begriff oder realisierbares Konzept? *TEXTconTEXT* 2, 109-136.
WITTE, HEIDRUN. 1992a. Zur gesellschaftlichen Verantwortung des Translators - Anmerkungen. *TEXTconTEXT* 7, 119-129.
WITTE, HEIDRUN. 1992b. El traductor como mediador cultural. Fundamentos teóricos para la enseñanza de la Lengua y Cultura en los estudios de Traducción. In: *Actas del II Congreso Internacional de la Sociedad de Didáctica de la Lengua y la Literatura, Las Palmas de Gran Canaria, Diciembre 2-3-4, 1992 (= El Guiniguada 3).* 407-414.
WITTE, Sergei. 1921. *The Memoirs of Count Witte,* translated and edited by Abraham Yarmolinsky. Garden City, N.Y.: Doubleday.
WÄLTERMANN, D. 1992a. Integrating Machine Translation in a Translation Curriculum. In: LOSA, EDITH F. (ed). 1992. 167-177.
WÄLTERMANN, D. 1992b. *A Survey Report on Translation Programs in the United States.* Pittsburg: Carnegie Mellon University. Modern Languages Program. Unpublished report.

d'YDEWALLE, GÉRY & JOHAN VAN RENSBERGEN & JORIS POLLET. 1987. Reading a message when the same message is available auditorily in another language. The case of subtitling. In: REGAN, J. O. & A. LÉVY-SCHOEN (eds). 1987. *Eye Movements: from Physiology to Cognition.* Amsterdam: Elsevier Science Publishers. 313-321.
d'YDEWALLE, GÉRY & LUK WARLOP & JOHAN VAN RENSBERGEN. 1989. Television and Attention. Differences between young and older adults in the division of attention over different sources of TV information. *Medienpsychologie: Zeitschrift für Individual- und Massenkommunikation* 1, 42-59

ZHUANG, M.L. 1991. Han-ying tongsheng chuanyi de jiqiao [Skills in Simultaneous Interpretation from Chinese into English]. *Zhongguo fanyi* (Chinese Translators Journal), # 2, 24-26.
ZIMMAN, L. 1989a. Interview with Elena Pollard. London. Mimeo.
ZIMMAN, L. 1989b. Interview with Maite Bell. London. Mimeo.

ZIMMAN, L. 1989c. *Teaching materials for community interpreters' training.* London. Mimeo.

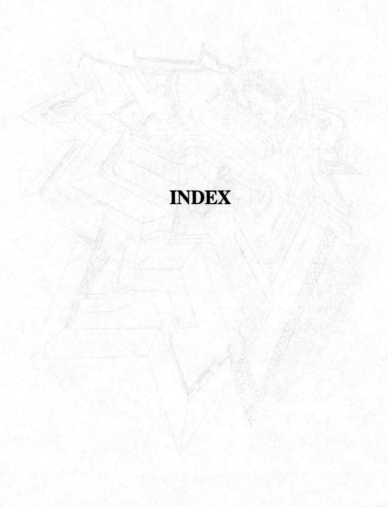

INDEX

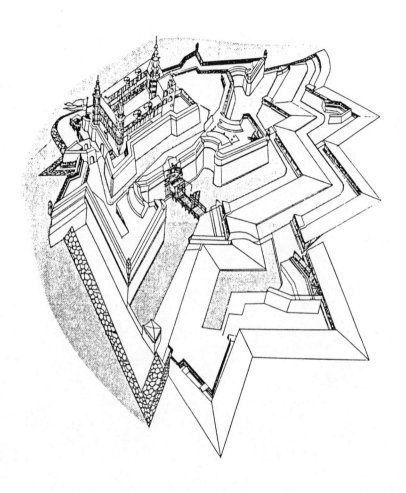

INDEX

The present index is not exhaustive. In order to increase the usefulness of the index, indexing terms may deviate from the wording in the text. Authors quoted are indexed, whereas references are not. Clarity has overridden consistency on minor points.

Abbreviations used: 'Also:' refers to related terms; 'cons.' = consecutive (interpreting); 'def.' = definition/description given in article; 'int.' = interpreting; 'sim.' = simultaneous (interpreting); 'tr.' = translation, translator.

Entry words are normally abbreviated to one letter.

121, 125, 131, 138
Interactant, 70, 217, 236. Also: 'Student-teacher relation'
Interaction of texts, 184, social, 71-75, student, 180, student and machine, 311
Interference, 229, 231, (English and Chinese) 188, categorial, 291-292
Interlanguage, 121, 124, 130, i. errors, 122-132
Interlingual translation, types of, 272
International organisations, 4-5, 11, 20, 41, 188-189
Interplay between teacher and students. See 'Student-teacher relation'
Interpretation, 157, 185, 267, indefinitiveness of i., 160, limits to, 161; culture-bound i., 52-53
Interpretation and Overinterpretation, 161
Interpreter training, and history, 169-170, 172-173; int. training in the Republic of China, 183-198; int. training, use of research in, 184-196, 229-232, 233, 242; and note-taking, 199-206; in working conditions/improvisation, 208-211; with non-native instructor, 213-215
Interpreter as advocate, 217-224
Interpreters on int., 167-169
Interpreter, types of students, 178, 179-180
Interpreters, candidates for, 14-15, 185, lack of qualified candidates, 14, 186-187
Interpreters' working conditions, 170-172
Interpreters' information on, 167-169
Interpreting, directionality of, 21, nature of, 184-185, price of 13, strategies, 225, 228; int., asymmetric, 12, partial, 210, poor, 13; modes of i., 276
Interpreting services at the European Commission, 11-18
Intertextuality, 61-62
Intervention in community int., 217-224
Intonation, 230, 249, 265
Intra-African English-French bilingualism, 20
Intuition/Intuitive, 93, 183, 195, 198, 245, 248
'Invention', 145, 149
Ireland, 11, 258, 283
Irish, 258
Isotopy, 162
Italian, 11, 55, 270
Italy, 16

Jacoby, L., 201

Japan, 192
Jerome, 158

King Report, the, 12
Knowledge, culture-specific background, 52-53, 54-57
Knowledge, background k. of tr., 42
Knowledge of African literature, 42, of audience, 92, of cultures, 36; audience k., 241; real-world k. 302, nature of k., 90, scientific k., 89, 93, collective translatorial knowledge, 98,99; background knowledge of clients, 72, for int., 207-208, of tr., 42, 72, 108-110, tr.'s economic k., 115, 118, tr.'s technical k., 295-299
Knowledge storage, 196,
Koller, W., 60-61
Korostovetz, I., 168
Krishnamoorthy, K., 32
Kyle, K., 254

L$_1$, L$_2$, L$_3$, L$_4$, 19, 27-28, 217. Also: 'A', 'B', 'C', 'D'-language
'Langage', 159
'Langue', 159
Language professionals, 4-5, 141
Language of published literature, 41
Language acquisition, 19, first vs. second, 21, l. a. by means of audiovisual mass media, 283
Language combinations, 17, 258, at course in Minneapolis, 213, for interpreters, 176
Language learning and int., 187, learning and int. training, 212-213, 215, l. teaching vs. int., 175, teaching and tr. teaching, 97, 121
Language norms, 157, l. professionals, status of, 4-5, 20, 24 (Also: 'Professionals'), l. rights, 24
Language as culture, 25
Language use in conversation, 217, used in note-taking, 203-205
Language technology, 308. Also: 'Machine tr.'
Language, functions of, 95
Language International, 305
Languages at the EC, 11-12, 17-18, l. of colonisation, 41
Languages, regional and English, 26-28
'Langue', 287
Lao, 211
Larson, M., 152
Latin, 18

Laye, Camara, 43
Layout, 77, of subtitles, 267
League of Nations, 168
Learning styles, 179
Length of tr. works, 245
Level, textual, 313
Levels, 65-66, in communication, 70, in tr.
as communication, 122-123, of solutions,
90-91, of tr., 288-290, of understanding,
101; l., linguistic and semantic, 113
Lexical, 289, errors, 117-120
Lexical Translation, (Uwajeh) 288-293
Lexicon, 192, 312, 314, 315. Also: 'Vocab-
ulary'
Limitations in audiovisual media, 264. Also:
'Constraints'
Limitlessness of interpretation, 158
Limits to acceptability in subtitling, 266, l.
to interpretation, 161, 163, to tr., 157
Linguistic acceptability, 110, 234
Linguistics Association of Nigeria, 20
Links, conceptual, 113-120
Lip-synchrony, 271, 276
Listenability, 176, 229
Listening ability, 15
Literal rendition in int., 220
Literal translations, 47-48, 62, 63, 103, 122,
125, 152, 154, (Uwajeh) 288-293
Literary texts, 124
Literary translation, 41-46, 47-50, 51-57, 59-
66, ex. 73, 98, 280, 308
Localisation of concept, 22
Lodge, David, 55
Logic, 108, 241
Longitudinal study, ex. 199-200
Loss in subtitling, 278, in tr., 53-54, 56; l.
of teacher control, 148; quality of l., 208
Lotman, Juri, 25
Loyalty, 61, 63, 66, 122-123, 124, 152, 155,
198, 234
Luther, Martin, ex., 81-82
Luxembourg, 13

Machine interactive form of learning, 258
Machine translation, 42, 90, 130, 155, 198,
287, 301-308, 309-317; number of m. t.
documents, 305
Machine translation systems in curriculum,
309-317, types of m. tr. systems, 309
Macro-evaluation, 134
Man-woman relationship in India, 29-30
Manual, 97, ex. 101-105, 143, 265, 315.
Also: 'Instruction'

Manzoufas, M., 269
Marshall Plan, 172
Materialism, 31, 49
McDavid, J., 78
Meaning, 158, 161-162, and context, 162;
uncertainty of m., 157
Media, 254, 255, m. discourse, 195, use,
238. Also: 'Audiovisual', 'Subtitling'
Member states of the EU, 11, 12, of the
UN, 12
Memorisation, 188
Memory, 15, 147, 179, 185, 187-188, 189,
192, 199, 200, 205; in machine tr., 306
Methodological problems in int. research,
227, 235
Methods, teaching, for technical translation,
297-298
Micro-evaluation, 134
Minimal segment vs. global meaning, 162
Minimisation of effort of processing, 246,
250, of errors, 94-95
Minor(ity) languages, 258, 261
Mishearing, in int., 171 ex.
Misperception. See 'Errors'
Mistakes. See 'Errors'
Mistranslation. See 'Errors'
Misunderstanding, 95, 171
Mock conference, 188, (def.) 226, 227, 229
Model tr., ex. 127, 129
Modules, 296
Monitoring, 139-140, in int., types of, 230-
231
Monolingual(ism), 21, 22-23, 35, 143, 275
Monosemiotic channels, 265
Moscow Linguistic University, 170
Mossop, Brian, 268
Mother tongue, 26, m. t. education, 19,
incomplete command of, 21
Motivation, 66, 112, 121, 146, 147, 148,
170, 215, 232
Multi-level context, 236
Multiculturalism, 283
Multilingual culture and translation studies,
20
Multilingual(ism), 1, 19, 21, 22-23, 35, 185-
186, 283
Multilingual media world, 261
Multilingual transfer, types of, 277-279
Music and sound effects, 265

Naive intercultural communication, 70-71
Narration (in audiovisual media), 271, 276
National language, (Hindi) 26

This is the book from

The Second *Language International* Conference
"Teaching Translation and Interpreting: Insights, Aims, Visions"

Together with the previous volume

Teaching Translation and Interpreting: Training, Talent and Experience
(Edited by Cay Dollerup and Anne Loddegaard.
Published by John Benjamins B.V. Amsterdam, 1992)

it prepares the common ground for:

The Third *Language International* Conference:
"Teaching Translation and Interpreting: New Horizons"
The conference takes place 12:00 noon, Friday 9 June to 14:00, Sunday 11 June, 1995
at the LO-Conference Centre, Elsinore, Denmark

Attn. Cay Dollerup
Center for Translation Studies and Lexicography
University of Copenhagen
DK-2300 Copenhagen S
Denmark

In the BENJAMINS TRANSLATION LIBRARY the following titles have been published thus far or are scheduled to appear in the course of 1994:

1. SAGER, Juan C: *Language Engineering and Translation: Consequences of automation*, 1994.
2. SNELL-HORNBY, Mary, Franz POCHHACKER and Klaus KAINDL (eds): *Translation Studies: An interdiscipline*. Selected papers from the Translation Congress, Vienna, 9-12 September 1992. 1994.
3. LAMBERT, Sylvie and Barbara MOSER-MERCER (eds): *Bridging the Gap: Empirical research in simultaneous interpretation*. 1994.
4. TOURY, Gideon: *Descriptive Translation Studies — and beyond*. 1994.
5. DOLLERUP, Cay and Annette LINDEGAARD (eds): *Teaching Translation and Interpreting 2: Insights, aims, visions*. Selected papers from the Second *Language International* Conference, Elsinore, 4-6 June 1993. 1994.